ASCENT TO GLORY

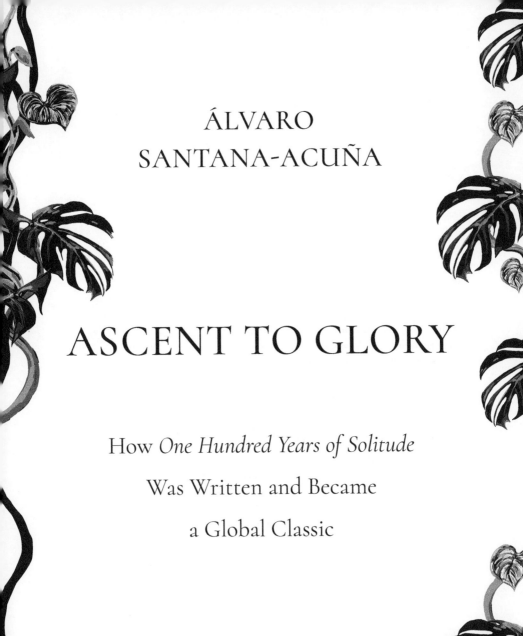

ÁLVARO
SANTANA-ACUÑA

ASCENT TO GLORY

How *One Hundred Years of Solitude*

Was Written and Became

a Global Classic

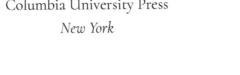

Columbia University Press
New York

Columbia University Press
Publishers Since 1893
New York   Chichester, West Sussex
cup.columbia.edu

Library of Congress Cataloging-in-Publication Data
Names: Santana-Acuña, Álvaro, author.
Title: Ascent to glory : how One hundred years of solitude was written and became a
    global classic / Álvaro Santana-Acuña.
Description: New York : Columbia University Press, 2020. |
    Includes bibliographical references and index.
Identifiers: LCCN 2019056923 (print) | LCCN 2019056924 (ebook) |
    ISBN 9780231184328 (hardback) | ISBN 9780231184335 (trade paperback) |
    ISBN 9780231545433 (ebook)
Subjects: LCSH: García Márquez, Gabriel, 1927-2014. Cien años de soledad.
Classification: LCC PQ8180.17.A73 C5377 2020 (print) |
    LCC PQ8180.17.A73 (ebook) | DDC 863/.64—dc23
LC record available at https://lccn.loc.gov/2019056923
LC ebook record available at https://lccn.loc.gov/2019056924

Cover design: Lisa Hamm
Canary shape: detail from "Gabriel García Márquez" by Wolf Gang, CC BY-SA 2.0.
House shape: detail from first page of typescript of *One Hundred Years of
    Solitude* (1966), Harry Ransom Center.
Tree shape: detail from Vicente Rojo's cover for *One Hundred Years of
    Solitude* (1967).
Butterfly shape: detail from cover of first edition of *Leaf Storm* (1955).

To Félix Álvaro Acuña Dorta

&

María Teresa Bennasar González

CONTENTS

ASCENT TO GLORY

INTRODUCTION

In the summer of 1965, an unknown writer was driving from Mexico City to Acapulco for a vacation with his wife and two children when, suddenly, a cow crossed the road in front of his car. He stopped abruptly. What happened next was a Newtonian moment, a miracle of the imagination. Right there on the road, in a stroke of brilliant insight, the writer came up with the first sentence of a novel that would change world literature: "Many years later, as he faced the firing squad, Colonel Aureliano Buendía was to remember that distant afternoon when his father took him to discover ice." Knowing there was not a second to lose, he turned his car around and rushed back home to Mexico City. He quit his job and locked himself up in his studio until he finished the novel. Debts skyrocketed as he spent months writing. He fell behind on rent payments, lived on the generosity of his friends and neighbors, and ended up pawning his car, his wife's dowry jewels, and even his typewriter. Nothing could stop him. Eighteen months later, he emerged from his studio with a completed manuscript. When he went to the post office to mail it to a possible publisher in Argentina, the bankrupt writer realized that he did not have enough money to send the whole manuscript. He had to divide it into two parts and mailed only one part. When he arrived home, he looked at the pages in his hands and discovered his mistake: he had just mailed the second part of the manuscript, not the first as he had intended. What a terrible way, he might have thought, of pitching the novel that took him so much effort to write! Luckily, the pages that he sent astonished the publisher, who knew that the novel would be a great success and hurried to offer the writer a publishing contract. The writer was Gabriel García Márquez and the novel was *One Hundred Years of Solitude* (*Cien años de soledad*).[1]

This story about how this Colombian author created *One Hundred Years of Solitude* is in reality a fascinating legend, now passed on from generation to generation. Parts of this legend are true and other parts are not, like Isaac Newton's story about discovering the theory of gravity after an apple fell on his head. What is remarkable about these cases is how legends often find in the pages of famous books and in the minds of people the most fertile soil to take root and grow. Shared and reinvented again and again, legends eventually become myths. One such myth refers to the artist who, after a stroke of inspiration, has to struggle financially in order to create a work of art. Poverty loomed over Mozart while composing works that revolutionized music, over Edgar Allan Poe while writing short stories that transformed modern literature, over Picasso while striving to sell his first cubist paintings, and over García Márquez while writing *One Hundred Years of Solitude*. Yet this myth of the creative genius cornered by economic hardship is more than a familiar story: it is a social pattern that ends up magnifying the difficulties that artists faced while creating their work. And as myths of this kind grow over time, they also obscure important details about how a work of art was really conceived and hence make it more challenging to explain how it turned into a classic.

The story of how *One Hundred Years of Solitude* actually came into being is even more fascinating than the legends and myths that surround this novel. When it was released in 1967, neither the publisher nor the author expected much of it. They knew, as publishing giant Alfred A. Knopf once said, "many a novel is dead the day it is published."[2] Yet something unexpected happened. This novel did not die the day of its publication. Instead, it started to live what would prove to be a long life. The story of how this novel about a remote Caribbean town has become the most famous work of Latin American literature and a global classic is spellbinding. *Ascent to Glory* seeks to tell this story, using especially numerous new sources, including the ones kept in García Márquez's personal archives.

At the heart of *One Hundred Years of Solitude* is the tale of the Buendía family and their town of Macondo, which was the scene of natural catastrophes, civil wars, and magical incidents. In the end, as prophesized by a manuscript that generations of Buendías tried to decipher, a biblical hurricane destroyed Macondo after the last Buendía was born with a pig's tail. To readers familiar with the global success of the novel since its publication in 1967, choosing it as the subject of this book comes as no surprise. *One Hundred Years of Solitude* is the work of Latin American literature par excellence. It is also the most read literary work in Spanish after *Don Quixote*. It has been translated into forty-nine languages, has sold over fifty million copies, and is listed among the top thirty best-selling literary works of all time. A 2009 survey among international writers published in the British newspaper the *Guardian* ranked it as the novel that has most influenced world literature over the past three decades. This influence still continues and is largely due to the novel's association with magical realism, a style that mixes stories of ordinary life with magical events. This style has now expanded into a global genre with its own art market.

Magical realism is present in award-winning works and international best sellers such as *The House of the Spirits* by the Chilean writer Isabel Allende; *Pig Tales* by the French author Marie Darrieussecq; *Big Breasts and Wide Hips* by the Chinese author and Nobel laureate Mo Yan; *Midnight's Children* by the Indian Salman Rushdie; *Illywhacker* by the Australian Peter Carey; *The Wind-Up Bird Chronicle* by the Japanese Haruki Murakami; and *Beloved* by the American author and Nobel laureate Toni Morrison. The influence of magical realism has grown so vast in literature that scholars and common readers use the term to talk about literary works written in different countries and decades before the birth of *One Hundred Years of Solitude*, books such as *The Master and Margarita* by the Russian writer Mikhail Bulgakov; *Their Eyes Were Watching God* by the American Zora Neale Hurston; or *Ficciones* by the Argentine Jorge Luis Borges. The reach of magical realism extends beyond literature. In cinema, this style is present in Hollywood productions, international blockbusters, Oscar winners, and indie movies such as *Life of Pi*, *Amen*, *Birdman*, *The Shape of Water*, *Amélie*, *The Purple Rose of Cairo*, and *Beasts of the Southern Wild*. In these and other works of art, *One Hundred Years of Solitude* is customarily (and incorrectly) credited as the founding work of magical realism, an attribution that helps to maintain the global visibility of this novel generation after generation.

The global impact of *One Hundred Years of Solitude* now extends beyond its magical realist style. One finds the presence of this novel in paintings, operas, ballets, plays, cartoons, video games, social media, web pages, newspaper articles, blogs, scholarly publications, songs, drinks, household objects, public parks, restaurants, peoples' names, and even distant celestial bodies. The 2020s started with the announcement that Macondo is the name of the star HD 93083, located about ninety-one light years away from the Earth. Orbiting this star is the extrasolar planet HD 93083 b, also known as Melquíades, a character in the novel.

Not coincidentally, one of the most familiar characteristics of the classic is its unstoppable power to be a part of our lives, often without our permission and often in formats that are different from the one set by its creator. *One Hundred Years of Solitude* is linked to one of the worst environmental accidents in history: the oil spill in the Gulf of Mexico in 2010 took place in a prospect called Macondo. If a classic is a social institution that shapes the taste and actions of artists, art industry gatekeepers, influencers, and consumers across generations, nations, and cultures, then *One Hundred Years of Solitude* has become one. Its total number of readers forms a community that, if it were a country, would be among the thirty most populous in the world.

THIS BOOK AT A GLANCE

I wrote *Ascent to Glory* for two kinds of readers: first, fans of *One Hundred Years of Solitude* and García Márquez in general and, second, sociologists, historians, and literary scholars. To both audiences, this book offers a study of the novel's conception, best-selling success, and consecration as a classic. Fans will find detailed answers to many of their questions about how the novel was written and how it became so famous globally. Sociologists, historians, and literary scholars will find that this book throws new light on key issues in their disciplines, such as value and cultural brokerage, genius and the universal, and power and world literature. (For more details on these and other issues, see the appendix.)

Chapters 1 through 4 cover the years 1920 through 1967. Using rare and new evidence from the García Márquez archives and libraries in five countries, these chapters examine the four decades prior to the novel's publication. They study the ideas, conventions, styles, objects, people, and organizations that made *One Hundred Years of Solitude* imaginable as a work of art in the first place. When García Márquez was born, the artistic principles of Latin Americanism and cosmopolitanism were spreading in Latin America, and years later they compelled him and his contemporaries to imagine and write their works as region-spanning Latin American literature. These principles were central to imagine his novel but not enough to produce it. The fate of *One Hundred Years of Solitude* could have been completely different without the rapid modernization of the Spanish-language book industry in the 1960s. Due to this booming industry, the novel was part of an avalanche of literary works that began in 1962. Their success created a space of imagination, production, and reception; thanks to this space (or niche), *One Hundred Years of Solitude* easily entered the publishing market five years later as a best seller. But how did García Márquez actually write the novel? While struggling to put it on paper for seventeen years, he learned many professional skills and conventions over two decades of traveling in more than ten countries and after joining several groups of artists. Collaborators in Mexico, Peru, Venezuela, Colombia, Chile, Argentina, the United States, the United Kingdom, France, and Spain assisted him as he was writing it. When the novel was published, it became an instant hit. It was the new product of the modernizing Spanish-language book industry and of the successful trend known as the New Latin American Novel. And it was written by a skillful and well-connected Latin American author.

Yet being a best seller guarantees nothing long-term. A work of art, no matter how successful was at first, is not born a classic but rather becomes one. Chapters 5 through 7 show what happened to *One Hundred Years of Solitude* over the next six decades, from 1967 to 2020. These chapters analyze data from more than ninety countries and forty-five languages to explain its ascent to glory. For this ascent to happen, scores of cultural brokers had to intervene. They facilitate the circulation of the work of art from one culture, country, and generation to another. These brokers are more than the usual suspects, critics and scholars. They are a broader constellation of people, groups, objects, and organizations quite often unrelated to one another. Yet their individual actions yield a collective result: the consecration as a classic work of art. Thousands of brokers have done so for *One Hundred Years of Solitude*.

These cultural brokers are, for example, the Chinese reader that despises this novel as a story about "a bunch of lunatics"; a private company that named one of its cargo ships after Macondo, a vessel that now sails under the flag of Panama; the Japanese company that manufactures a US\$130 alcoholic drink called "One Hundred Years of Solitude"; or an African American father who recommends this novel to his daughter and just happens to be the president of the United States.

To further understand how a literary work becomes a classic, chapter 8 studies five literary works that met the conditions to become global classics but did not do so. Their trajectories show us that the making of a classic work of art is never simply a Newtonian moment but a social story. In the case of *One Hundred Years of Solitude*, this story spans over a century and includes millions of readers and thousands of cultural brokers on seven continents, including Antarctica, where a British explorer read the novel during the first circumpolar navigation of the Earth. More generally, the making of a classic is a social story that can help us understand why it is so difficult to imagine social life without classics. To preserve classics, we bury them deep down within the Earth and we even launch them into outer space. Digitized copies of Dante's *Divine Comedy* and Edvard Munch's *The Scream* are protected in the Doomsday Vault, constructed in the event of an apocalypse on our planet. In this vault, these and other classics are stored within the permafrost of an abandoned coal mine in Norway's Arctic archipelago of Svalbard. And musical selections from classics such as Mozart's *The Magic Flute* and Beethoven's *Fifth Symphony* can be played from a golden record attached to the outside of the *Voyager 1* and *Voyager 2* spacecrafts, launched into the depths of space where no human has ever been.

PART I

FROM THE IDEA
TO THE BOOK

M any years before García Márquez sat down to write *One Hundred Years of Solitude*, he first had to learn how to transform the memories of his childhood and family history into literary characters and stories. In 1950, the writer, who was then twenty-two, visited his hometown of Aracataca, a village in Colombia's Caribbean region. This visit prompted vivid memories of his childhood, when he lived in his maternal grandparents' house and spent time with his relatives and extended family. The same year, he published "The Buendía House: Notes for a Novel," the first known version of what eventually became *One Hundred Years of Solitude*. For the next two years, he kept publishing fragments of a manuscript in progress called "The House." These fragments described the everyday life of a rural village as seen by a child. In these, certain characters in *One Hundred Years of Solitude* appeared for the first time, Úrsula and Colonel Aureliano Buendía among them. Central themes in the future novel appeared, too: solitude and nostalgia. García Márquez returned to Aracataca in 1952 and expected to finish the novel in two years. To do so, he worked as an itinerant book salesman and spent several months touring the region, conducting literary fieldwork, and listening to people and their stories. Old memories and new experiences started making their way into his imagination. At the same time, he had to figure out how to connect life to literature, that is, how to turn people's lives and stories into literary fiction.

THE MAKING OF *ONE HUNDRED YEARS OF SOLITUDE*

1927	García Márquez born in Aracataca, Colombia.
1927–1936	Spends childhood in his maternal grandparents' house in Aracataca, source of inspiration for his novel.
1944	Starts reading writers who shape his literary imagination.
1948	Joins art groups in Cartagena and Barranquilla that train him professionally.
1950	Visits Aracataca and comes up with the first ideas for the novel that becomes *One Hundred Years of Solitude*.
1950	Publishes the story "The Buendía House: Notes for a Novel."
1950–1951	Publishes fragments from a manuscript called "The House."
1952	Visits Aracataca and announces that "The House" will be ready in two years.
1953	Travels in the Colombian departments of Cesar, Magdalena, and La Guajira, where the novel is partly set.
1956	Resumes work on "The House" in Paris but ends up writing *No One Writes to the Colonel*.
1957–1961	Publishes numerous pieces of literary journalism in which he develops the style in *One Hundred Years of Solitude*.
1961	Joins, in Mexico City, the art group called the Mafia, which soon leads the way for the New Latin American Novel.
1962	Tries to resume work on an old project, a book of fantastic stories, but instead stops writing fiction and moves to scriptwriting.
1963	A defeated García Márquez gives up on writing the biography of Colonel Aureliano Buendía, the central character in *One Hundred Years of Solitude*.
1964	International success of the New Latin American Novel, of which García Márquez was well informed and more involved.
1965	Signs a contract with Balcells Agency to represent him in all languages.
1965	Starts writing *One Hundred Years of Solitude* and initiates conversations with publishers Sudamericana, Seix Barral, and Harper & Row.

1965-1966	Friends, writers, and critics in eleven countries on three continents do research for the novel or read fragments as García Márquez writes it.
1966	The writer and his peers start promoting the novel in over twenty countries three months before finishing it and one year before its publication.
1967	Sudamericana publishes *One Hundred Years of Solitude* in Buenos Aires.

To connect life to literature, García Márquez needed to learn skills and conventions used by professional writers, such as telling a story with a given style and developing credible characters. This professional training came through groups of artists that he joined in several countries in Latin America and Europe over the next decade. Yet these groups did not teach García Márquez skills and conventions for literary writing in a naked way. They taught him skills and conventions that were dressed, so to speak, with the clothing of certain ideas. And some of these ideas were present in exemplar texts that the young García Márquez imitated in his early works. These texts were written by modernist authors such as William Faulkner, Franz Kafka, and Virginia Woolf, Colombian writers such as poets of the movement *Piedra y cielo*, Latin American authors such as Pablo Neruda and Jorge Luis Borges, and Spanish writers such as Federico García Lorca and Ramón Gómez de la Serna. Other ideas were shared with him in person by influential peers.

Seeking to work as a full-time writer, García Márquez moved from one country to another, joining other art groups. In each location, he practiced new skills, and new ideas entered his literary imagination. Rather than being unique, his imagination in reality was becoming more and more similar to that of three generations of writers, critics, and publishers that had started to believe that Latin American literature existed and that its moment had finally arrived. What followed the collaboration across these generations was the rise of the New Latin American Novel in the 1960s, also known as the Latin American Boom. García Márquez saw this boom unfold firsthand and soon was one of the writers at the center of this international literary movement. By then, he knew that works of the New Latin American Novel were instant best sellers and award-winning books in Latin America, the United States, and Europe. Like several of his peers, he realized that his moment had come. Between 1965 and 1967, he committed all his time and energy to writing a story that he had struggled to finish for more than a decade. The result was *One Hundred Years of Solitude*.

García Márquez wrote a book about solitude in the company of many collaborators. They lived in eleven countries on three continents. From their locations, they helped him to imagine the novel and gave him feedback on his writing from beginning to end. Even when he felt alone writing, he could say so to his collaborators in person, over the phone, and by mail, and they listened and sought to relieve him. Never before had the solitary writer been so accompanied as a creator. Some of his collaborators even worked as his research assistants, gathering information that he added to the manuscript. His collaborators also played an active role in the novel's production and early reception. Several of them published reviews of the novel when García Márquez was still months away from finishing the manuscript and over a year away from its publication. This networked creativity, which moved the novel from an idea to a book, from imagination to production, was the true genius behind the making of *One Hundred Years of Solitude*.

1

IMAGINING A WORK OF ART

The Great Novel of America.

Main line on cover of *Primera Plana* magazine on *One Hundred Years of Solitude*, 1967[1]

I n 1927, the year Gabriel García Márquez was born, *Revista de Occidente*, a popular Spanish journal among artists and intellectuals, published the article "After Expressionism: Magical Realism," written by German art critic Franz Roh. His piece had nothing to do with literature. It was about the present and future of European painting. Roh ended it with a vague but prophetic statement, "Someday man too will be able to recreate himself in the perfection of this concept."[2] Little could he suspect that magical realism, the concept he just coined, would become synonymous with the literature of Latin America and, especially, with the novel *One Hundred Years of Solitude*. For this to happen, magical realism had to migrate from Europe to Latin America and then to the rest of world.

The newborn García Márquez, of course, did not know that magical realism would influence his literary imagination so much. It took four decades and the participation of dozens of people for this influence to take form in *One Hundred Years of Solitude*. One of these people was Arturo Uslar Pietri, a Venezuelan writer living in Paris in the late 1920s. There, he read the article by Roh and mentioned it on the terrace of a Parisian café to two fellow writers, Guatemalan Miguel Ángel Asturias and Cuban Alejo Carpentier. The three were then under the spell of French surrealism. Two decades of writing had to pass before they realized that magical realism could work in literature. In 1948, Uslar Pietri was the first to use this term to make sense of literary works. The same year, Carpentier wrote that the mixture of reality and the marvelous was "the heritage of all of

America." And he concluded that the writer's job was to turn this mixture into a literary style.[3]

Fourteen years later, in 1962, Carpentier published the novel *Explosion in a Cathedral*. García Márquez read it and confessed in a letter to a friend, "It is a masterpiece of universal literature." Admiration turned into influence and influence shaped the imagination of a book. In *Explosion in a Cathedral*, García Márquez found numerous ideas and techniques to write *One Hundred Years of Solitude*, a novel he had struggled to imagine for more than a decade. Along the way, he even gave up on it. Tormented, he said in an interview in 1963, "The biography of Colonel Aureliano Buendía [the novel's main character] will never be written." But the following year García Márquez saw Carpentier several times, who advised him on style, language, use of time in fiction, and how to write as a Latin American author. Carpentier's help proved decisive. Three years later, in 1967, *One Hundred Years of Solitude* took the world by storm. The same year, the third member of the Parisian group, Asturias, became the first Latin American novelist to win the Nobel Prize in Literature. The award consecrated his literary portrayal of the magical legends and traditions of the peoples of Latin America. The next Latin American novelist to win this award was García Márquez in 1982. He received it for a similar reason: "for his novels and short stories, in which the fantastic and the realistic are combined in a richly composed world of imagination, reflecting a continent's life and conflicts." By then, many readers and critics called him the creator of magical realism and praised *One Hundred Years of Solitude* as the novel that put Latin America on the map of world literature. But none of these statements are correct.[4]

The origins of magical realism and its transformation into a literary style was, in reality, part of a larger transformation in aesthetic ideas, intellectual principles, professional values, and social expectations that shaped the imagination of García Márquez and many other writers in the region. This transformation started in earnest in the 1920s. In Peru, writer José Carlos Mariátegui launched his literary journal *Amauta*, in which he aimed to combine ideas from Marxism, European avant-garde art, and the indigenous cultures of Peru. This publishing venture was not unique. Asturias published the literary journal *Nuevos Tiempos* and, in collaboration with Carpentier, *Imán*. The pages of these short-lived journals, along with those of *Proa* and *Repertorio Americano*, tell the story of a major intellectual change underway during the 1920s: the invention of a region-spanning literary tradition, *literatura latinoamericana* (Latin American literature). Its invention is key to understanding how, four decades later, *One Hundred Years of Solitude* became imaginable as a work of art.[5]

Imagination is the first and often overlooked stage that an artist goes through in order for the work of art to move to the stage of production. In the arts, imagination hardly runs free and unstrained. The so-called muses that inspire artists are, at a closer look, ideas, principles, rules, values, and expectations that guide what artists can imagine. These "social" muses enable or restrict an artist's choices during the creative process. Imagination is, simply put, the first gatekeeper. This is why the study of cultural production is incomplete without explaining what goes on in the stage of imagination— that is, during the coming into being of the work of art when it is just an impulse, intuition, or idea that is worth pursuing. And what occurs during this stage, of course, goes beyond understanding what happens in the artist's head. One of the obstacles that García Márquez had to face in order to imagine *One Hundred Years of Solitude* was the absence of a region-spanning Latin American literature. He was not the only one in the region aware of this obstacle. *Primera Plana*, a popular magazine of current affairs, reminded its quarter of a million readers in August 1966, exactly when García Márquez was about to finish writing his novel, that things were changing. Now there was a "sense of a constituted, autonomous literature, at a level of achievement comparable to that of other literatures of the world."[6]

How did imagination take the form of concrete aesthetics, conventions, creators, organizations, objects, and audiences that shaped García Márquez's creativity for four decades before he finished *One Hundred Years of Solitude*? This novel exemplifies the power that imagination has over creators' choices. Having taken the form of ideas, people, and works, this imagination that molds creators' artistic choices can often develop decades before they start creating art. Ever since its publication, *One Hundred Years of Solitude* has been considered among the greatest works of Latin American literature. Yet when García Márquez was born, most writers, critics, and readers believed that this region's literature was no more than the sum of its national literatures: Peruvian, Venezuelan, Cuban, and so on. But from the 1920s onward, in the pages of journals such as the ones mentioned above, writers and critics started to imagine the region's literature as different from the sum of national traditions. This collective enterprise paid off. By the 1960s, Latin American literature was an entity of its own and no longer occupied a peripheral position in the international market. Rather, as highbrow journals and mass media agreed, "the literature now coming out of Latin America is of the first importance."[7]

TOWARD A REGIONAL LITERATURE

Geographic labels that designate peoples, territories, and continents are not neutral terms but deeply political ones. So are aesthetic labels. In April 1927, a few days after García Márquez's birth, Spanish critic Guillermo de Torre—who two decades later rejected for publication the writer's first novella—wrote "Madrid, Intellectual Meridian of Spanish America." His essay caused an intellectual tsunami in the region. It attacked the name Latin America for being "false and unjustified" and despised the word "Latin Americanism." For him, the right name for the region could only be "Spanish America." Since he knew that Paris was also attracting a growing number of artists and students from the region, de Torre defended Madrid "as the most authentic line of intersection between America and Spain." And he concluded, "The American intellectual area [is] an extension of the Spanish area." In the following months, over thirty writers from six countries in the region united in their rejection of de Torre's arguments. Carpentier summarized the disapproval of many of his colleagues in stating, "The only aspiration of America is America itself." De Torre, though, was right about something; the now popular name of Latin America was invented in Paris. In the 1850s, expat writers Chilean Francisco Bilbao and Colombian José María Torres Caicedo first used it. The latter also coined the label *literatura latinoamericana* in 1879 to argue that the region "does not have a literature of its own" and that it lacked originality because "our literature imitates all others."[8]

The situation described by Torres Caicedo changed in the first decades of the twentieth century. Then, a region-spanning intellectual class started to emerge, including full-time writers such as José Enrique Rodó, Rubén Darío, José Martí, and Eugenio María de Hostos and literary critics and scholars such as Pedro Henríquez Ureña, Alfonso Reyes, Arturo Torres-Rioseco, and Alberto Zum Felde. Although they set the foundations of what was to come, the label *literatura latinoamericana* "had little usage in our own America during the first half of the century." As figures 1.1 and 1.2 show, growth in its usage was part of a process of nationalism in the region that gained acceptance during and after World War II, accelerated with the decolonization of Third World countries, and flourished in the 1960s after the Cuban Revolution in 1959.[9]

By the 1960s, most writers, critics, and literary scholars could easily embrace the idea of a Latin American literature. They did precisely that during the decade of *One Hundred Years of Solitude*'s publication. By then, the ideas of Latin America and Latin American literature were inseparable components of the imagination that made this novel conceivable as a work of art.

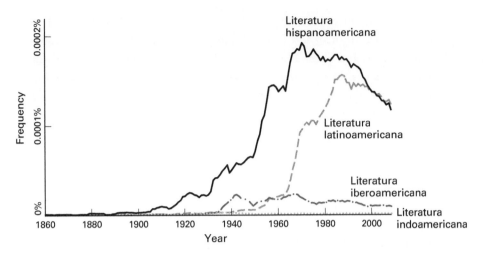

1.1 Frequency of labels in Spanish used to name the region's literature (1860–2008).

Source: Google Ngram Viewer.

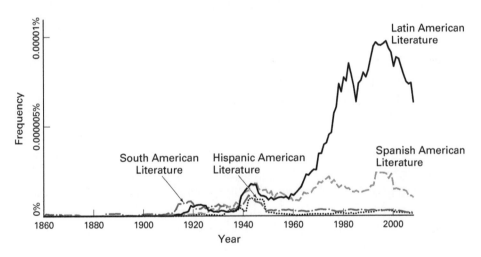

1.2 Frequency of labels in English used to name the region's literature (1860–2008).

Source: Google Ngram Viewer.

LATIN AMERICANISM AND COSMOPOLITANISM

At the time of García Márquez's birth, when critics and readers referred to *literatura latinoamericana*, they had in mind a fragmented territory of over sixty languages, twenty nations, and their corresponding national literatures. Writers more readily pledged allegiance to a nation or a literary style rather than to the idea of Latin America. For this reason, there were Argentine and Uruguayan realists, Mexican and Peruvian indigenists, Colombian and Ecuadorian regionalists, and so on. But there were no writers regarded as, say, Latin American realists. In fact, most writers were not committed to imagining works that transcended the boundaries of their national literature. So how did the region's literature become more than the sum of its different national literatures? Writers and critics started to develop uniforming principles in the 1880s. But it took four decades before they spread beyond national borders. Two principles in particular, despite variations of each, came to dominate the idea of a region-spanning Latin American literary tradition: Latin Americanism and cosmopolitanism.

Latin Americanism aimed at rethinking the region's common indigenous roots and its shared history as a whole, rather than emphasizing the singular trajectory of each country in the region. Contrary to the provincial styles of *regionalismo* and *indigenismo*, followers of Latin Americanism had to imagine in their writing that a common history and culture united all countries of Latin America. And they had to believe that this common legacy made the region unique in literary terms when compared to the rest of the world. As Uruguayan literary critic Ángel Rama put it, "Latin Americanism facilitates the mediation between regionalism and external modernity." If practitioners of Latin Americanism imagined the region as a whole, their literary works would connect with the experiences of most of its peoples, regardless of their nationality. If written this way, readers would read their works as truly *Latin American*. This transformation of the collective imagination did not occur suddenly. In the 1940s and 1950s, Latin Americanism was still a conversation among a small group of "isolated creators," among whom was Carpentier. Only in the 1960s, when creators like García Márquez and Carpentier had more opportunities to meet and talk about their works regularly, did Latin Americanism become a widely shared regional conversation and literary agenda.[10]

The second principle, cosmopolitanism, sought to connect Latin America with foreign cultural traditions and to understand the region as part of the world. The cosmopolitan view consisted of inserting the region's literature within the larger cultural tradition of the West. For writers, this insertion meant that they should imagine their works as if they were written for readers in Latin America, Europe, and the United States. Cosmopolitanism did not seek to simply imitate the West but to create a friendly dialogue with works of Western literature. The diffusion of this cosmopolitan viewpoint changed writers' imaginations. A telling case, given the author's influence on the region's literature, was that of Argentine Jorge Luis Borges. In the 1930s, he went from being a local poet inspired by the beauty of Buenos Aires to a fiction writer interested in "universal" themes such as identity, time, and memory. Not all writers welcomed his cosmopolitanism. Argentine nationalists attacked Borges, accusing him of being "foreignizing or Europeanist." But over the years, he found ample support in the region for his cosmopolitan agenda, which he continued to develop. In 1951, in his famous lecture "The Argentine Writer and Tradition," he said, "I believe that our tradition is the whole of Western culture, and I also believe that we have a right to this tradition, a greater right than that which the inhabitants of one Western nation or another may have." By 1966, in *Into the Mainstream*, a best-selling volume of interviews with Latin American writers, Borges went a step further in defending the region's right to "discove[r] the universality of our tradition," and he added "we no longer have to deny any one part of it."[11]

In the 1920s, when writers like Borges started their writing careers, other fellow writers and critics saw Latin Americanism and cosmopolitanism as incompatible. But in many works published from this decade onward, there was a growing desire to abandon these "Manichaean attitudes," as Peruvian writer Mario Vargas Llosa put it. His colleague Mexican writer Carlos Fuentes defended that these two principles complemented more than excluded each other. For him, the strength of the region's literature resided in the complementarity of these principles. A general agreement that it was possible to reconcile them peaked during the decade when *One Hundred Years of Solitude* was imagined, written, and published.[12]

How did the intellectual principles of Latin Americanism and cosmopolitanism take concrete form in literary writing? Along with the belief in a Latin American race and history, aspiring works of *literatura latinoamericana* had to highlight the region's nature and language as distinctive ingredients of a region-spanning literature. Nature is the first ingredient that plays a large role within the literary imagination of cosmopolitan Latin Americanism. Nature is everywhere in Latin America and fosters an unpredictable relationship with the surrounding civilization. "The man besieged by nature," to use the words of Fuentes, at first natural nature and then urban nature, was a theme present across national literatures. And its presence permitted the uniformization of literature in the region along this theme. Therefore, the struggles of pioneers in Argentina's wild nature in the Pampa described in Domingo Faustino Sarmiento's *Facundo* (1845) were similar to the fights of characters in *Cumandá* (1879), a novel about indigenous peoples in the Amazon forest by Ecuadorian Juan León Mera. It was also the same conflict with nature that appeared in the uncivilized backcountry in Euclides da Cunha's *Rebellion in the*

Backlands (Brazil, 1902), in Horacio Quiroga's short stories such as "The Feather Pillow" and "Anaconda" (Uruguay, 1917 and 1921), in José Eustasio Rivera's novel *The Vortex* (Colombia, 1924), whose characters ended up "devoured" by the jungle, in the clash between civilization and barbarism in Rómulo Gallegos's *Doña Bárbara* (Venezuela, 1929), and in the crudeness of the countryside in the communities of José de la Cuadra's *Los Sangurimas* (Ecuador, 1934), Ciro Alegría's *Broad and Alien Is the World* (Peru, 1941), and Juan Rulfo's *Pedro Páramo* (Mexico, 1955). And of course, the theme of the conflict between man and nature found its way into the formidable jungle in Carpentier's *Explosion in a Cathedral* (Cuba, 1962), which hindered the diffusion of the French Revolution in Latin America, and in García Márquez's abandoned Spanish galleon in *One Hundred Years of Solitude*, which locals found in the jungle near the town of Macondo.[13]

Along with nature, language was the second ingredient of the literary imagination of cosmopolitanism and Latin Americanism. Literary texts needed to have a common language in order to make these two principles concrete. The Spanish language turned out to be an obstacle. In the decades prior to the publication of *One Hundred Years of Solitude*, a growing number of writers were frustrated about having to write in Spanish from Spain. As Fuentes denounced, "The Spanish American does not feel that he owns a language, he suffers a foreign language, that of the conqueror, that of the lord, that of the academies. . . . The history of Latin America is that of a dis-possession of language." Likewise, critic Rama said, "The cultivated American man [feels] that he speaks, applies, manifests, exists, in a language he has not invented and that, for the same reason, does not belong entirely to him."[14]

Writers such as Peruvian José María Arguedas and Paraguayan Augusto Roa Bastos sought to overcome the obstacle of this colonial language by drawing from indigenous words, metaphors, sayings, and narrative structures. But in a region with over fifty indigenous languages, one of them could not help to build the region's literary tradition. By the late 1950s, it was clear to writers that the region's own literary language had to be Spanish but a different kind of Spanish: neo-baroque. The roots of this alternative language were in the seventeenth-century Spanish of the so-called Golden Age. Back then, Miguel de Cervantes, Luis de Góngora, Francisco de Quevedo, and Lope de Vega, among other writers, published their classic works. In Latin America, the baroque was the first regional cultural movement during the colonial era, with authors such as Fray Juan de Barrenechea y Albis, Carlos Sigüenza y Góngora, and Sor Juana Inés de la Cruz. Latin American writers from Borges to Octavio Paz to García Márquez read and admired the baroque language of their counterparts from the Golden Age. Three centuries later, writers like Fuentes praised "the [b]aroque [as] the language of our great literary tradition." Fuentes himself, Carpentier, and other writers and critics relabeled this language as neo-baroque to distinguish the Spanish of Latin American literature from the Spanish of Spain's literature. In this distinctive kind of Spanish, writers started to find a stronger Latin American identity than in their nationality. As critic Luis Harss said, referring to what some Latin American authors were trying to achieve in the 1950s and 1960s, "All these people lived more in the language than in the country." (In the 1960s censors in Spain belittled this Latin American Spanish of literary works as "Creole jargon" and tried to repress the political and cultural agenda behind this language.)[15]

Unlike mainstream literature in Spain, Latin America's neo-baroque paid attention to adjective usage (*adjectivación*) and reverie (*ensoñación*). In the 1940s it gave birth to *literatura fantástica* and "the marvelous real" (an effort to reconcile the region's realism with the marvelous in its everyday life). This language started to appear in the mid-career works of Asturias, Borges, Carpentier, Uslar Pietri, Adolfo Bioy Casares, and Pablo Neruda. Their literary language spread among the region's cultural establishment and budding writers in Julio Cortázar's and García Márquez's generations. And the diffusion of this language among them favored the success of *literatura latinoamericana* in the 1960s. (As the next chapter shows, readers, too, developed a taste for this Latin American language, which mainstream publishers favored.)

By the late 1950s, regional support for Latin Americanism and cosmopolitanism grew. The result was the collective imagination of literary works that shared an interest for "the historical formation of Latin America, the relation between that history and other mythical versions, and the contributions of both to contemporary Latin American identity."[16] These principles of cosmopolitanism and Latin Americanism permeate *One Hundred Years of Solitude*, with its synthesis of exuberant Latin American nature, neo-baroque language, and countless cosmopolitan references, from the Bible to *Don Quixote* to Faulkner's modernism.

THREE GENERATIONS COLLABORATE

Intellectual principles such as cosmopolitanism and Latin Americanism do not function automatically; they need loyal users.[17] The successful application of these principles to literary texts was the achievement of neither a group of talented authors nor of a single generation. It was the result of an unprecedented collaboration among three consecutive generations of writers, critics, and publishing industry gatekeepers. They were born between 1895 and 1936 and worked in over fifteen countries on three continents. With the assistance of critics and publishers, writers collaborated in magazines, organizations, and meetings. These platforms brought together, as if they were part of a single region-spanning tradition, literary works published in twenty countries, four centuries, and two major languages, Spanish and Portuguese. This collaboration caused a "synchronous flattening of the history of American narrative," to use the words of critic Rama. Of a similar opinion was writer Carpentier, who referred to "the coincidence at a given time, in the span of about twenty years, of a group of almost contemporary novelists."[18] Readers also started to consume the works of three generations.

A basic consensus about what counted as true Latin American literature united what I call the Short Form, Hybrid, and Novel Generations. Each generation is named after the literary format that defined the works of its most influential members.[19] The Short Form Generation was born between 1895 and 1910. Its members mostly wrote poetry and short stories. Among its key members were Borges (Argentina), Asturias (Guatemala), Nicolás Guillén, José Lezama Lima, and Carpentier (Cuba), Neruda (Chile), Juan Carlos Onetti (Uruguay), and João Guimarães Rosa (Brazil). The Hybrid Generation was born between 1911 and 1921. Its members combined the writing of short forms of literature (poetry and short stories) with long forms (books of essays and novels). This generation included Cortázar, Ernesto Sábato, and Bioy Casares (Argentina), Rulfo and Paz (Mexico), Mario Benedetti (Uruguay), and Jorge Amado (Brazil). The Novel Generation was born between 1922 and 1936. Its writers' main works were novels. The novel format defined this generation's professional identity and how readers and critics first and foremost remember these writers, who included García Márquez (Colombia), Fuentes (Mexico), José Donoso and Jorge Edwards (Chile), Vargas Llosa (Peru), Manuel Puig (Argentina), and Guillermo Cabrera Infante (Cuba).

Previous research has stressed intra- and intergenerational conflict among these writers and overlooked the depth of their collaboration.[20] Yet sustained cooperation across generations until the 1970s was key in putting Latin American literature on the map of world literature. The collaboration happened when the principles of cosmopolitanism and Latin Americanism circulated through an intricate network of strong and weak ties among generations that covered four decades and three continents. In committing to these principles, the three generations helped create an intellectual and professional space that made it possible for novels such as *One Hundred Years of Solitude* to be imagined as a cosmopolitan, Latin American work of art, not as a local or regionalist one. (The modernizing publishing industry further strengthened this network, as the next chapter shows.)

A community of readers, including the budding writer García Márquez, was the first step to create a collaborative network among generations. Writers from the three generations, as critic Harss put it, "read and admired each other. That was the New Latin American Novel of those years. In reality, it had not existed before at a continental level." A shared group of readings and favorite authors can help to unify professional literary practice. And these generations shared a cosmopolitan taste for international literature by James Joyce, Franz Kafka, Scott Fitzgerald, Marcel Proust, Virginia Woolf, Thomas Mann, and especially William Faulkner, as well as regional literature by Sarmiento, Martí, Rodó, and Darío in particular. They also read the same translations of foreign books and, collaboratively, regional authors managed these translations. Famously, Borges and his literary circle, which included Victoria Ocampo, José Bianco, and Bioy Casares, translated major modernist works of Faulkner, Woolf, and Kafka into Latin American Spanish.[21]

From the 1940s onward, informal gatherings and professional meetings strengthened ties across generations. Attending these reunions were writers as well as critics, scholars, and gatekeepers of the publishing industry. In traveling across the region, participants started to develop a common cultural agenda, and they connected it to their professional aspirations. Collaborating peers and gatekeepers also came from outside the region, in particular from Spain, the United States, and France. Mail correspondence was a site for networking, too. With the expansion of air travel, cheaper and faster airmail between major cities helped to maintain regional conversations in real time, as if they were happening in town. As an organizer of the 1962 Congress of Intellectuals in Chile, poet Gonzalo Rojas wrote, "Every week, every month I receive letters from Fuentes, Alegría, Benedetti, Bianco, Arguedas, and the others. . . . They send me magazines where the debates go on as in *Siempre!* of Mexico and others from Bogotá, Buenos Aires, Lima, and Montevideo." In 1965, when he started *One Hundred Years of Solitude*, García Márquez, like Rojas, was corresponding with other writers in Latin America and Europe. In their correspondence, writers exchanged ideas for new books and updates about their work in progress (including copies of their manuscripts). They made suggestions on how to solve a technical writing problem (such as how to find the tone of a novel), to improve writing habits, and to overcome the frightening writer's block. They shared tips on how to find the best acquisitions editors and literary agents for their work and how to market it via mainstream media. Ultimately, the writers not only exchanged trade secrets, but also they became pen pals, lending lots of emotional support coupled with professional advice.[22]

What gave this collaboration among writers a greater advantage to promote their works was the support of three generations of critics and publishers. These included contemporaries of the Short Form Generation such as Enrique Anderson Imbert (Argentina), Mexicans Luis Leal and Antonio Castro Leal, Luis Alberto Sánchez (Peru), and Arturo Torres-Rioseco (Chile), contemporaries of the Hybrid Generation such as Emir Rodríguez Monegal (Uruguay) and Roger Caillois (France), and contemporaries of the Novel Generation such as Francisco Porrúa, Carmen Balcells, Carlos Barral, Víctor Seix, Neus Espresate Xirau, and Josep Maria Castellet (Spain), Emmanuel Carballo (Mexico), Tomás Eloy Martínez, Adolfo Prieto, and Ernesto Schoo (Argentina), Domingo Miliani (Venezuela), Harss (Chile), and Rama (Uruguay). Critics and publishers collaborated with writers to connect their works to the idea of Latin America and the Western tradition. Critics, in particular, helped to internationalize what writers in the region did. For this reason, three years before the publication of *One Hundred Years of Solitude*, Rama confidently stated in a text that resonated with authors in the region: "Everything that is said about the Latin American writer concerns the writer from anywhere in the world."[23]

In practical terms, critics helped writers in three ways. First, they wrote about Latin American writers in journals and books; second, they recommended these writers' works to other writers, critics, and ordinary readers; and, third, they included these writers in courses on Latin American literature that they taught at universities in the region, the United States, and Europe. Critics Rodríguez Monegal and Rama did all three for the works of Donoso, Cortázar, Vargas Llosa, Fuentes, and García Márquez.

PARIS, A LITERARY MEETING POINT

In 1967, two popular Latin American writers, Chilean poet Neruda (of the Short Form Generation) and Mexican novelist Fuentes (of the Novel Generation) met in the fashionable Parisian restaurant La Coupole to talk, among other things, about a new Latin American novel: *One Hundred Years of Solitude*.

Fuentes praised it and compared it to *Don Quixote*, inspiring Neruda's growing interest in it. Uruguayan critic Rodríguez Monegal (of the Hybrid Generation) was also present at the meeting. He had already premiered two chapters of *One Hundred Years of Solitude* in *Mundo Nuevo*, the leading magazine of new Latin American literature, edited in Paris and distributed in over twenty countries. This literary summit of writers and critics from three different generations to talk about a Latin American best seller was unimaginable in the 1920s, when Neruda first visited Paris. Back then, most writers did not believe that Latin America had a region-spanning literature. But they believed that a stay in the city was a rite of passage for any aspiring writer. And in their exchanges with other artists, writers from the region discovered a common identity: "All Latin Americans, unanimously, found in the Paris of the twenties and thirties: their distant Latin America . . . what they have recovered in Paris is the originality of Latin America, its specificity, its accent, its unique reality."[24]

It was in Paris where Uslar Pietri talked to Asturias and Carpentier about Roh's essay on magical realism, and where they started to think of the mixture of realism and magic as the main ingredient of Latin American literature. They came to Paris inspired by what famous writers had accomplished from that city, especially Nicaraguan poet Darío, who lived there in the early twentieth century. Considered the first major regional literary figure, Darío acted as a broker of literary styles: he was a Paris-based cosmopolitan who reworked major literary trends and became a committed Latin American. After Darío's success, the idea of the cosmopolitan American author in Paris entered the imagination of Latin American writers of the three generations. These included the already mentioned Neruda, Venezuelan Uslar Pietri, Cubans Carpentier and Guillén, and Guatemalan Asturias in the Short Form Generation; Argentines Cortázar and Sábato and Mexican Paz in the Hybrid Generation; and Peruvian Vargas Llosa, Mexican Fuentes, Chilean Edwards, and Colombian García Márquez in the Novel Generation.

Several of these writers also lived in Madrid, but they did not develop a Latin American identity there. For many of them, the capital of Spain was synonymous with colonial domination, which de Torre revived after publishing his incendiary essay on Madrid as the intellectual meridian of Spanish America. Paris, on the contrary, meant openness to other artistic traditions and the possibility to affirm the cultural autonomy of Latin America. Writers seeking admission to artistic circles in Paris had to move beyond their local literary traditions and convert to Latin Americanism. They did so by embracing a cosmopolitan cultural viewpoint, discussing current affairs about the region, and commenting on the latest international and regional literature. Cuban poet Guillén (of the Short Form Generation) led one of such groups, which García Márquez joined in 1955.[25]

CULTURAL VOID AND AESTHETIC LIBERATION

"The Latin American novel," writer Vargas Llosa said in 1966, "is now on an equal footing with any other." He could make such a statement thanks to the aesthetic liberation among artists in the region from the 1940s onward. "In Latin America," as Francisco Porrúa, acquisitions editor of *One Hundred Years of Solitude*, put it, "it was considered that we were a kind of Europe and that the reputable literary models came from there. This changed suddenly . . . what happened then was a kind of awareness of a literary identity. . . . People began to consider that we had a literature here, a proper Latin American literature."[26] Two world events channeled this "awareness": the Spanish Civil War and World War II. They caused a cultural void in the region that lasted about fifteen years. This void consolidated Latin American literature as a transnational phenomenon with its epicenter in America not in Europe.

In 1936, as the Civil War was ravaging Spain and fascism was rising in Europe, Mexican writer Alfonso Reyes claimed, "Arrived late to the banquet of European civilization, [in America] we have reached our full age. Very soon, you will get used to counting with us." Reyes delivered this message to the Latin American and European attendees of an international meeting of intellectuals in Buenos Aires. His speech was immediately published by the literary magazine *Sur*, with readers across the region and Europe.[27]

Then, in 1942, two years after the Nazi invasion of France and when the Allies were losing World War II, Asturias dedicated a poem to France written from Latin America: "I sing to you, France, near the tropical blast furnaces / Where sweat flows along the skin like lizards. / I sing to you before your dead rise with resolution / In the somnambulist battle of those who are not defeated." For writers and former residents of Paris such as Asturias, World War II had a deep moral impact. For the second time in less than three decades, Europe was fighting a fratricide war. The situation was not better in Spain; the victory of fascism in the Civil War led to Francisco Franco's dictatorship. To members of the Latin American cultural establishment, World War II and the Spanish Civil War proved that the Old Continent, with its colonial legacy falling apart, no longer was a moral compass on the issues of progress and civilization. Barbarism—the same problem writers in Latin America had frequently complained about since the nineteenth century—was now rampant throughout Europe.[28]

In practical terms, the cultural void meant that neither Spain nor the rest of Europe could offer any worthy literary ideas to draw inspiration from. Western literature, as Fuentes wrote, "lost its universality." Writers in the region decided to favor their own cultural trends. This inward look boosted the region's aesthetic liberation among writers, critics, scholars, and publishers. Their liberation brought about a region-spanning Latin American literature. It was during the 1940s when writers such as Carpentier and Asturias deepened their commitment to free the novel from nineteenth-century realism, that is, from the viewpoint of the Western, bourgeois, third person, and omniscient narrator. Instead, they paid attention to local peoples—including indigenous peoples and slaves—and experimented with narrative techniques, such as mixing descriptions of reality with marvelous and fantastic stories.[29] (The inward look during this decade coincided with a sudden growth of the Argentine publishing industry; see next chapter).

Not coincidentally, it was in the 1940s when two terms that came to define the region's literature took off. The first term was magical realism, which Uslar Pietri and Carpentier started to apply to literature in 1948, as mentioned earlier. The second term was *literatura latinoamericana*. During this decade, references to this latter term as well as to *literatura hispanoamericana* and *literatura iberoamericana* grew in book publications, as figures 1.1 and 1.2 show. As a result of these region-spanning developments, scholars rightly claim that there was a mini boom of Latin American literature in the 1940s. (But they have not seen the robust connection between this early boom and the rise of these terms.) At that time, Eduardo Zalamea Borda, Uslar Pietri, Carpentier, Guimarães Rosa, Asturias, Onetti, Bioy Casares, and Borges published work that helped convince peers, critics, and common readers that "Latin America could produce great literature."[30]

During this cultural void, the search for inspiration not only turned to Latin America but also to the United States. Back then, few writers were more favorably received than Faulkner, to the point that he became a Latin American author thanks to numerous translations into Latin American Spanish (even Brazilian writers read his works in these translations). Faulkner attracted many writers for his literary language. Critics in the United States, however, disliked his language. For example, critic Allen Tate called him, pejoratively, "a Dixie Gongorist." By Gongorist, Tate referred to writer Luis de Góngora. He was active during the Spanish Golden Age and became one of

Spain's most influential poets of all time. Like Faulkner, Góngora achieved fame for his sophisticated baroque style known as Gongorism. It was an original style that used ostentatious language, embellished metaphors, and convoluted syntactical order. As Tate observed, Faulkner's complex style was similar to Góngora's. Translations of Faulkner's works into Latin American Spanish brought this aesthetic connection to the surface. And in his complex prose, reminiscent of the baroque, several generations of Latin American writers found a literary model for their own works. These writers included Jorge Icaza, J. E. Rivera, C. Alegría, Gallegos, Carpentier, Fuentes, Borges, Onetti, Rulfo, and young García Márquez. For them, Faulkner's *Latin Americanized* language was an alternative to Castilian Spanish. Such language was a true means of aesthetic liberation. As Fuentes put it, "the baroque, Alejo Carpentier once told me, is the language of the people who, unaware of the truth, seek it eagerly."[31]

García Márquez imitated Faulkner's style in his first novella, published in 1955, when he was twenty-eight. And a decade later, as he was writing *One Hundred Years of Solitude*, Carpentier and Fuentes advised him on how to use Latin American neo-baroque. Even common readers first heard about García Márquez through his connection to Faulkner. The summer of 1965, when he decided to start this novel, the magazine *Life en Español*, sold in Latin America, the United States, and Spain, mentioned his books in an article about the influence of Faulkner on Latin American writers.

THE LETTERED REGION AND THE CULTURAL COLD WAR

During World War II, unlike Europe, Latin America lived a period of relative peace and expansion of social democracy, with Mexico City, Buenos Aires, and São Paulo functioning as cultural centers. These favorable political conditions helped expand the means of cultural production, including publishing houses, translations, textbooks and anthologies, academic scholarship and literary criticism, institutes and foundations, conferences, awards, and periodicals. Under this new organizational umbrella, numerous literary publishers, critics, and scholars insisted on how unique the region's literature was—it was something different from the sum of national literatures.[32]

New and refurbished institutes and foundations dedicated to the region's culture and literature helped develop this regional literary identity. These included the Instituto Internacional de Literatura Iberoamericana and

Centro de Estudios Latinoamericanos Rómulo Gallegos. Growing international resources, including awards and fellowships, were key to removing writers' regional isolation. Up until the 1950s, most writers knew few colleagues from other countries personally. Networks were mainly individual-based, as it was the case even for famous regional writers, such as Rodó and Darío. But regular professional meetings, symposia, seminars, and conferences started to create a transnational network of writers. And many of them would identify with the idea of a Latin American literature and tried to speak with a homogeneous voice. Starting in 1954 with the first International Congress of Ibero-American Literature, meetings brought together writers and critics from the three generations and most countries in the region. Donoso, then an unknown, young writer, commented on the 1962 Congress of Intellectuals in Chile: "The topic . . . that clearly prevailed was the general complaint that Latin Americans knew European and North American literature perfectly, along with that of our countries [but] we almost completely ignored the contemporary literatures of the other countries of the continent." As part of the effort to end this regional separation, members of the three generations from twelve countries signed an open letter at the congress. "Overcoming our isolation, our mutual ignorance," their letter stated, "is to find our common, united voice and grant it the strength, presence, and dissemination that our age—and the destiny of our peoples—demand."[33]

The Cuban Revolution endorsed this idea of a region-spanning literature and offered a wealth of resources to promote it. As critic Harss said about the revolution, "The Latin American novelist is less interested in its political and economic ends than in its strength. [The revolution] is the realization of a deep socio-cultural transformation within a continent that finally begins to define itself." Casa de las Américas (literally, the House of the Americas) was in charge of spreading the cultural ideals of the revolution in Latin America. This political and cultural organization opened four months after the triumph of the revolution. It sought to achieve the region's cultural independence from outside forces and its unity according to the ideals of the revolution. To do so, it organized a regional literary award and published a magazine, *Casa de las Américas*. Already in its first issue, it featured works by members of the three generations. During the 1960s, it promoted the New Latin American Novel and it was mandatory reading for the region's cultural establishment until the revolution started to purge critical intellectuals the following decade. Also, Casa de las Américas had a library that organized café-conversatorios (coffee-round tables), in which works by Alfonso Reyes, José Bianco, and García Márquez (*Big Mama's Funeral*), among others, were read and promoted as Latin American literature. In 1968, this publisher released the first international edition of *One Hundred Years of Solitude* in its collection *Literatura latinoamericana* (including blurbs by Vargas Llosa, Rama, and the *Times Literary Supplement*). Soon, these and other cultural activities of the revolution attracted the world's attention to Latin America. As Spanish literary critic Castellet said, "Through Cuba we began to understand the Latin American phenomena and Latin American literature much better, because, first, we began to understand what we could call this dynamic and militant unity of Latin American literature." Casa de las Américas responded to this international interest by organizing big events such as the Congreso Cultural in Havana in 1968. It gathered five hundred delegates from seventy countries, such as Aimé Césaire, Italo Calvino, Carpentier, Cortázar, and Vargas Llosa.[34]

The cultural activities of Casa de las Américas strengthened the region's cultural autonomy, which in return helped with the commercial success of the New Latin American Novel. However, something of more international scale fully landed in Latin America after the revolution. As tensions between the Soviet Union and United States rose, the region became a Cold War battleground. This war was waged in the domain of politics and also of culture. And the result of this confrontation between cultural organizations outside and inside was to further develop Latin America as a lettered region.[35]

In the early 1940s, while World War II was spreading throughout Europe, the U.S. government sponsored translations of works by Latin American writers, and the State Department invited experts to lecture on Latin American literature at colleges. After the war, the U.S. government introduced the Point Four Program to counter the influence of the Soviet Union and its communism over developing and Third World countries. The U.S.-based Ford and Rockefeller Foundations seconded the efforts of the government to shape the agenda of the arts and social sciences in Latin America. Also, the Faulkner Foundation created in the 1950s the Ibero-American Novel Project. It followed the desire of Faulkner, who used part of the money from his Nobel Prize in Literature to create fellowships for Latin American writers. The goal was to promote the work of established and upcoming novelists from the region. One of its early beneficiaries was Donoso. His first novel, *Coronation*, received the 1962 Ibero-American Award from the foundation. These awards led to important professional connections and growing excitement about the future of the region's literature. Donoso himself recalled that Scottish literary scholar Alistair Reid told him that Vargas Llosa was going "to be one of the greatest novelists of his time." Reid also gave him a copy of Vargas Llosa's *The Time of the Hero*. Shortly after, in 1964, Donoso published in the leading

Chilean magazine *Ercilla* an enthusiastic book review with the subtitle "The Novel that Triumphs Worldwide."[36]

Starting in 1962, cultural philanthropist Rodman Rockefeller and editor Alfred Knopf helped fund the symposia organized by the Inter-American Foundation for the Arts. Three years later, the symposium met in Chichén-Itzá, Mexico. Among its participants were writers William Styron, Oscar Lewis, Nicanor Parra, Juan García Ponce, Donoso, Rulfo, Fuentes, Sábato, and García Márquez. At this meeting, García Márquez and Donoso consoled each other about their writer's block. Having the chance to talk about his writing problems with peers helped him, since a few weeks later he put his writer's block behind him and started working on *One Hundred Years of Solitude*. The following year, the Inter-American Foundation for the Arts changed its name to Center for Inter-American Relations and, thanks to the advice of critic Rodríguez Monegal, it shifted its focus away from symposia to the promotion of Latin American books. In ten years, the center sponsored the translation into English of fifty titles, including *One Hundred Years of Solitude*.

Like the United States, communist Soviet Union and China promoted Latin American writers. Although more research is necessary to fully understand this promotion, two of the most popular writers in the region before the 1960s, Amado and Neruda, were under the spell of the Soviet Union. Their works were translated and circulated in the countries behind the Iron Curtain as well as in China. The Soviet Union also tempted budding writers. In 1957, a thirty-year-old García Márquez traveled to Moscow to attend the Sixth World Youth Festival as a member of a Colombian cultural delegation. Four years later, the Latin American Institute opened its doors in this city. In Latin America, the Soviet Union gave not only ideological but also cultural support to the Cuban Revolution. One of its many initiatives was to fund the Cuban book industry. With this purpose in mind, a Czech-Russian book-publishing consortium started to operate on the island. Soon after, "Soviet-financed books [were] sold in South America at what we would call nominal prices, about a third of the price of Spanish books."[37]

In Spain, high-ranking officials of the Franco government were as concerned as their U.S. counterparts about the growing threat of the Cuban book industry, with its cheap pro-Soviet titles and writers. But Spanish officials were equally worried about the threat of the Rockefeller and Ford Foundations. U.S. funding for writers, books, and publishers endangered Spain's geo-cultural power over the book industry in Latin America. Thus, Spanish institutions sought to influence the region through journals such as *Mundo Hispánico* and *Cuadernos Hispanoamericanos*, organizations such as Instituto de

Cultura Hispánica, professional meetings such as Congreso de Instituciones Hispánicas, summer courses, cultural travels, and fellowships for Latin American students. Fellowships, in particular, connected Latin America to Spain by co-opting its artists, as was the case for the twenty-two-year-old Vargas Llosa, who left Peru to study in Madrid.[38]

For France, Latin America was also a target of cultural entrepreneurship. French interventions included journals, professorships, book collections, and organizations. The Maison de l'Amérique Latine was created in Paris in 1945, while the Institut Français d'Amérique Latine opened branches in the capitals of Mexico, Haiti, Chile, and Peru. The same year the prestigious Collège de France established the chair on literature and language of the Iberian Peninsula and Latin America. And France's leading literary publisher, Gallimard, created in the early 1950s the pioneering collection *La Croix du Sud*. This collection promoted the region's literature, mostly novels. Among its forty-two titles, there were indigenists, cosmopolitans, and Brazilian authors. The director of this collection was the French critic Roger Caillois. He lived in Buenos Aires as a World War II refugee. During his stay, he met Borges and his circle and became familiar with the region's literature. When he returned to France, Borges's *Ficciones* was the first volume in *La Croix du Sud*, and its publication in this collection started a national interest in Latin American writers that peaked in the 1960s. Caillois also directed UNESCO's *Collection d'oeuvre representatives*, which published works by "Ibero-American" authors. Its titles included foundational fictions from the nineteenth century such as Sarmiento's *Facundo*, groundbreaking writers such as Martí, and up-and-coming contemporary writers such as Paz. This collection promoted Latin American literature as a unified and well-established tradition.[39]

Along with the strategies of different nations, the works of several generations of scholars were important to consolidate the idea of Latin American literature. While several of the contributions cited below still understood the region's literature as a collection of national traditions, there was a growing recognition that "in a large part of Spanish-American literature there is an American spirit that differentiates it from that of the mother country," as a U.S. professor put it in 1925. This recognition that the region's literature was no longer an appendix of Spain's literature appeared in textbooks and anthologies published in and outside the region. Some of these titles are Luis Alberto Sánchez's *Historia de la literatura americana* (1937), Óscar Rafael Beltrán's *Manual de historia de la literatura hispanoamericana* (1938), Arturo Torres-Rioseco's *La gran literatura iberoamericana* (1945), *Ensayos sobre literatura latinoamericana* (1953 and 1958), *Nueva historia de la gran literatura iberoamericana* (1960), and *Aspects of Spanish American Literature* (1963), Harriet de Onís's *The Golden Land: An Anthology of Latin American Folklore in Literature* (1948), Julio Leguizamón's *Bibliografía general de la literatura hispanoamericana* (1954), the six volumes of *Diccionario de la literatura latinoamericana* (1958), Ugo Gallo and Giuseppe Bellini's *Storia della letteratura ispanoamericana* (1958), Fernando Alegría's *Breve historia de la novela hispanoamericana* (1959), José Luis Sánchez Trincado's *Literatura latinoamericana, siglo XX* (1964), Zum Felde's *La narrativa en Hispanoamérica* (1964), John Englekirk's *An Outline History of Spanish American Literature* (1965), Raimundo Lazo's *Historia de la literatura hispanoamericana* (1965), and Juan Loveluck's *La novela hispanoamericana* (1966). An important voice in this field was that of Pedro Henríquez Ureña, author of the influential *Literary Currents in Hispanic America* (1945), and arguably the first Latin American literary scholar. Among his main contributions was to develop the idea of a unified "Latin culture" that embraced Spanish and Portuguese speaking countries.[40]

Luis Harss's *Into the Mainstream* (1966) occupies a special place in this scholarship on Latin American literature. Originally published in English, it was instantly translated into Spanish as *Los Nuestros* (literally, *Ours*). This book was not an anthology of literary texts but a series of long conversations with ten writers. *Into the Mainstream* brought together as a single literary tradition, that of Latin American literature, writers from the three generations, including a Brazilian author. The selected writers were Carpentier, Asturias, Borges, Guimarães Rosa, Onetti (Short Form Generation), Cortázar, Rulfo (Hybrid Generation), and Fuentes, García Márquez, and Vargas Llosa (Novel Generation). In his conversation with Harss, García Márquez described at length and for the first time his book in progress, *One Hundred Years of Solitude*. This conversation turned out to be an unexpected means of promoting his novel, because *Into the Mainstream* became a best seller in Argentina in the months prior to the release of the novel.

Topping the consolidation of Latin American literature were major awards. In general, the impact of an award goes beyond the personal beneficiary, as it can create group closure, spark imitation, and attract the attention of publishers, critics, and scholars.[41] In 1945, Latin America received its first Nobel Prize in Literature. Chilean poet Gabriela Mistral won it just months after the end of World War II "for her lyric poetry which, inspired by powerful emotions, has made her name a symbol of the idealistic aspirations of the entire Latin American world." Indeed, for the Nobel committee, Mistral was not a Chilean but a Latin American author. This Nobel sent the message to writers in Latin America that a region-spanning literature, one that was independent from Spain, was gaining international attention among powerful gatekeepers. Barely a decade later, in 1956, the second Nobel Prize in Literature traveled to the region. The laurate was the Spanish poet in exile, Juan Ramón Jiménez. He had been publishing in the Americas for the past two decades and was involved in the region's literary scene. In 1960, only four years after J. R. Jiménez's win, poet Saint-John Perse, born in the French-American territory of Guadeloupe, received the Nobel. Partisans of a region-spanning Latin American literature such as Fuentes and Carpentier considered the Caribbean and even French Canada as part of Latin America. So for them, the Nobel given to this Caribbean poet further recognized the region's cultural independence and its autonomous literary voice. Two other Nobel awards in literature followed in the next decade or so for Asturias (1967) and Neruda (1971). According to the Nobel committee, the merit of their work was once more that it spoke for the region as a whole. Aspiring professional writers in Latin America kept up with the news about these and other Nobel winners. So did García Márquez. In 1950, when he was twenty-three years old and had published no book of fiction, he was already commenting in his daily newspaper column about the merits of Nobel laurates in Literature.[42]

Along with these Nobel Prizes in Literature, Latin American writers received a growing number of awards in the 1950s and 1960s. In 1952, Asturias won in France the prestigious Prix du Meilleur Livre Étranger (Best Foreign Book Prize) for *El Señor Presidente*, a novel about a Latin American dictator. In 1959, Vargas Llosa published *The Leaders*, which received a Spanish award named after Leopoldo Alas, one of the country's leading nineteenth-century writers. In 1961, Onetti's "Jacob and the Other" was a finalist in the short story contest recently created by *Life en Español* magazine. The same year, Borges and Irish playwright Samuel Beckett together won the Prix International des Éditeurs awarded by the Formentor Group. In 1962, as mentioned earlier, *Coronation* by Donoso received the Ibero-American Award from the Faulkner Foundation. The following year, Vargas Llosa published *The Time of the Hero*, which won the Biblioteca Breve and Crítica awards in Spain. These and other awards attracted the interest of international publishers. In 1964, U.S. publishing house Harper & Row created a division on Latin American literature. It moved fast and signed many writers from the region; a year later it had an option to publish García Márquez's next work, *One Hundred Years of Solitude*.[43] These awards also attracted the attention of region-spanning periodicals, which were key to promoting Latin American literature among hundreds of thousands of middle-class readers.

PERIODICALS FOR A NEW LITERATURE

Nowhere was the effervescence of Latin American literature more visible than in literary journals, current affairs magazines, and weekend supplements of newspapers. From the 1920s onward, a handful of literary magazines started to imagine the region's literature as a tradition that was independent from Spain and Europe. These periodicals circulated poorly among the mass public, had small print runs, and were mainly discussed in intellectual circles. But they set the foundations for a Latin American and cosmopolitan community of writers because they emphasized regional unity over difference. Their readership increased in the 1940s and especially the 1950s. Then, general interest magazines spread to cater to the literary tastes of the rising urban middle classes, following the models set by *Time*, *Newsweek*, *Life*, *L'Express*, and *Paris Match*. By the 1960s, many periodicals had become taste-making publications that promoted a regional cosmopolitan culture.[44]

For this period, some influential periodicals were *Sur*, *Panorama*, *El Escarabajo de Oro*, and *Primera Plana* in Argentina, *Contemporáneos*, *El Hijo Pródigo*, *Cuadernos Americanos*, *México en la Cultura* of *Novedades de México*, *Revista Mexicana de literatura*, *La Cultura en México* of *Siempre!*, and *Diálogos* in Mexico, *Marcha* in Uruguay, *Cromos*, *Mito*, *Crónica*, and *Eco* in Colombia, *Orígenes*, *Carteles*, and *Casa de las Américas* in Cuba, *Papel Literario* of *El Nacional*, *Imagen*, *Zona Franca*, and *Papeles: Revista del Ateneo de Caracas* in Venezuela, *Amauta* and *Amaru* in Peru, *Repertorio Americano* in Costa Rica, *Clima* in Brazil, *Ercilla* in Chile, *Asomante* in Puerto Rico, *Mundo Nuevo* in France, and *Revista Hispánica Moderna*, *Revista Iberoamericana*, and *Life en Español* in the United States. At least twelve of these periodicals, published in eight countries and distributed in more than twenty, featured or reviewed work by García Márquez before the publication of *One Hundred Years of Solitude*. Thus, thousands of readers in three continents first encountered his literary work in periodicals rather than in books.[45]

As García Márquez and his peers realized, the main advantage of these magazines, journals, and literary supplements was twofold. First, they broadened the audience for regional literature. As critic Rama wrote, "The magazines were capital instruments of modernization and the hierarchy of literary activity: replacing specialized publications intended only for the restricted cultivated public, mainly formed by writers themselves; these magazines established communication with a larger audience." Given the limited amount of space on their pages, they were the perfect vehicle to promote short literary works (poetry, short stories, and essays) as well as excerpts of forthcoming novels.[46]

Second, these periodicals reported what was really going on in literature all over the region and beyond. In these publications, regional readers could find essays about mainstream Latin American (including Brazilians), Spanish, and international writers. They published literary criticism about famous and best-selling works, news about meetings of writers, reviews of books and cultural events, news about recipients of regional and international literary awards, announcements of book releases, and letters from readers reacting to literary works. A regular section was the reportage on new and upcoming national writers and generations, and especially the interview. In these interviews, writers talked about their works and the craft of writing. The reporting also presented the writers as public figures, inserting them in the mass media commercial circuit, and sometimes portraying them as agents of social change in the region. Scores of writers embraced this promotion. Benedetti put in words what many of his colleagues thought at the time when he wrote, "The Latin American . . . writer cannot close the doors to reality." Writers, he insisted, could not waste this opportunity to influence their readers.[47]

Primera Plana was one of the general interest magazines that allowed writers to influence readers across the region. Since its creation in 1962, *Primera Plana* conducted surveys to measure its penetration among highbrow readers. By 1964, it had a weekly print run of sixty thousand copies, with an average of two hundred and fifty thousand readers. The same year critic Tomás Eloy Martínez took over. Under his leadership, *Primera Plana* gave more space to literature, including covers featuring writers from the three generations: Borges, Lezama Lima, Cortázar, Silvina Ocampo, Leopoldo Marechal, and García Márquez. It also published their work and that of Sábato, Puig, Fuentes, Macedonio Fernández, Armonía Somers, and Carlos Drummond de Andrade, among others. In October 1965, in the pages of this magazine, the term "Boom" appeared for the first time to report a "*boom* of the book" in Argentine literature. Nine months later, in August 1966, the term already applied to the region's literature: "the famous 'boom'—the rise—of the Latin American novel." That same month, members of the three generations—J. Bianco, Rodríguez Monegal, Vargas Llosa, and Fuentes—awarded for the first time the *Primera Plana* Novel Prize, which was open to any novel written by a Latin American author. The committee received sixty-four submissions, which, for them, proved the "continental renaissance of the genre [and] alluvium" of new novels. In between October 1965 and August 1966, *Primera Plana* did something else to promote another novel that was part of this "alluvium." It was the first periodical to announce in print (more than half a year before its publication) the title of García Márquez's next novel, *One Hundred Years of Solitude*.[48]

Another magazine that promoted this book as a New Latin American Novel was *Mundo Nuevo*; it did so because this highbrow literary magazine brought the sentiment of aesthetic liberation in Latin American literature to its peak. Indeed, the history of the region's booming literature "at the time it presented its most compact appearance is written on the pages of *Mundo Nuevo*." Since its creation in 1966, it called itself *Revista de América Latina*. With its headquarters in Paris and a print run of six thousand copies, this monthly magazine was for sale in twenty-three countries on three continents. "My intention," its editor Rodríguez Monegal explained, was for "the magazine to be a guide for anyone seriously interested in following the development of the latest Latin American literature."[49]

The publication of *Mundo Nuevo* had five important consequences. First, it endorsed the idea that Latin American literature was not limited to the works of a few popular writers. Second, it created a hierarchy of the good Latin

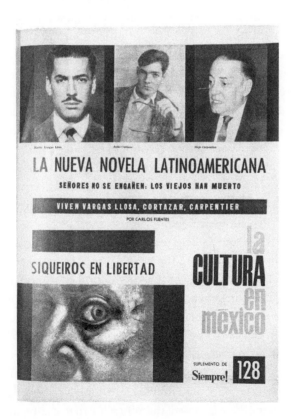

1.3 Cover of Carlos Fuentes's major essay on the rise of the New Latin American Novel.

Source: La Cultura en México (July 29, 1964).

American writers by publishing literary criticism on contemporary works from the region. Third, it favored the publication of texts that embraced cosmopolitanism and Latin Americanism. Fourth, it did not print texts by writers from Spain, except for the work of a few political exiles and outsiders. And fifth, it published mainstream international work with connections to "the Latin American reality" and was part of new trends in the novel in Europe and the United States, including works of Anglo-American modernism à la John Dos Passos or Joyce and French *nouveau roman* à la Nathalie Sarraute.[50]

Another outlet that writers and critics used to promote their agenda was the literary supplement of newspapers and magazines. The summer of 1964, Fuentes published "La nueva novela latinoamericana" ("The New Latin American Novel") in *La Cultura en México*, the literary supplement of *Siempre!* (see figure 1.3). In this art manifesto, he studied the works of Vargas Llosa, Cortázar, and Carpentier. Each of them was a best-selling member of the Novel, Hybrid, and Short Form Generations. Fuentes singled them out as the leading voices of "La nueva novela latinoamericana," which, for him, was inaugurating a new era for literature in the region. As the subtitle to his manifesto proclaimed, "Gentlemen, don't be fooled: the old [writers] have died." To prove it, Fuentes's manifesto blurred the chronological boundaries between the three generations and exaggerated the differences between these generations and older writers such as Gallegos, J. E. Rivera, and Mariano Azuela. Fuentes also connected Vargas Llosa, Cortázar, and Carpentier to modernist authors such as Joyce, Faulkner, Woolf, and Kafka. For him, these three Latin American writers were also cosmopolitan and offered an alternative to the so-called death of the European bourgeois novel. For him, key to this alternative was to put myths at the center of their works. This is why "our literature," Fuentes concluded, "is truly revolutionary."[51]

Critics like Rama and Rodríguez Monegal used region-spanning periodicals to make similar arguments. The fall of 1964, a few weeks after Fuentes's manifesto, the journal *Casa de las Américas* published a special issue on the "Nueva novela latinoamericana." It included excerpts of new work by Carpentier, Cortázar, Vargas Llosa, and other writers of the three generations, plus eight articles authored by critics and writers about recent Latin American novels such as *Explosion in a Cathedral* and *The Time of the Hero*. The issue opened with a long article by Rama entitled "Diez problemas para el novelista latinoamericano" ("Ten Problems for the Latin American Novelist"). Throughout its forty pages, he diagnosed the obstacles that the region's literature faced, especially its economic structure, the cultural elites, the public, and the publishing industry. At the same time, Rama celebrated that recent Latin

American novels were helping overcome these obstacles and pushing regional literature toward independence.[52]

In 1965, Rodríguez Monegal, then a visiting professor of literature at Harvard University, published several articles on the rise of the New Latin American Novel. He wrote "The New Novelists" and "New Latin American Writers" for highbrow journals *Encounter* and *Bulletin of the American Academy of Arts and Sciences*. And for the general interest magazine *Life en Español*, he wrote "La nueva novela de Latinoamérica" ("The New Novel of Latin America") and "Un espejo de espejos entrecruzados" ("A Mirror of Intersecting Mirrors"). In these articles, he introduced general and educated readers to the works of three generations of cosmopolitan and Latin American writers, including a brief reference to García Márquez in the last piece. The message of the critic could not be stronger: "A revolution . . . is happening in the world. For the first time in history, Latin American literature is starting to be acclaimed beyond the continental sphere." And he added, "Thanks to Carpentier and Guimarães Rosa, to Onetti and Rulfo, as to Fuentes, Cortázar, and Vargas Llosa, the Latin American novel is beginning to take wing beyond its present linguistic limits. It is being translated, discovered, and discussed, as one hears, in Europe and the United States; the prizes and the editions are beginning to multiply. . . . Perhaps not since the introduction of the Russian novelists to nineteenth-century France, or of the modern Americans into postwar Europe, have similar potentialities existed, both for Latin American writers and for their potential readers overseas."[53]

French critic Caillois expressed a similar opinion that year in an interview published in the world-famous newspaper *Le Monde*. "Latin American literature will be the great literature of tomorrow," he said, "as Russian literature was the great literature at the end of the last century, [and] the literature of North America that of the years 25–40[;] now it is the time for Latin American literature. It is the one called to give us the masterpieces that we expect." Months later, another prestigious periodical, the *Times Literary Supplement*, published an essay by English translator J. M. Cohen on the New Latin American Novel. Its opening statement stressed how much the novel in the region had changed: "Until the present decade [it was] at its best, provincial." According to Cohen, writers from multiple generations were at the center of its transformation, such as Elena Garro, Vicente Leñero, Rulfo, Carpentier, Vargas Llosa, Onetti, Fuentes, Benedetti, García Márquez, and Cortázar, author of *Hopscotch*, "the first great novel of Spanish America."[54]

Compared to what a handful of poorly distributed periodicals imagined in the 1920s, Latin American literature had traveled a long way by 1965. That year, when García Márquez started *One Hundred Years of Solitude*, the statements of writers and critics in periodicals read in more than twenty countries on three continents further convinced him that it was possible to imagine his ideas for a Caribbean story as something greater: a New Latin American Novel.

A COSMOPOLITAN AND LATIN AMERICAN NOVEL

The four decades during which *literatura latinoamericana* was imagined as a region-spanning literary tradition coincided with García Márquez's birth, literary education, publication of his early works, and release of *One Hundred Years of Solitude*. As he was growing up, three generations of writers, critics, and gatekeepers of the publishing industry collaborated to create an audience for New Latin American Novels. *One Hundred Years of Solitude* benefited from this collaboration. Over two decades of compromise across generations with the principles of Latin Americanism and cosmopolitanism made it possible for a novel about a fictional and remote village in Colombia's Caribbean region to be imagined. And imagined by its author, peers, critics, and first readers, not as a provincial work of art, but rather as a cosmopolitan reflection on Latin America's history and its place in the Western cultural tradition.

One Hundred Years of Solitude gained even more visibility because it came out at the end of this period of literary effervescence, first known as the New Latin American Novel and later as the Latin American Boom. The avalanche of best-selling novels started in 1962 with the publication of *Explosion in a Cathedral* in Cuba, *The Death of Artemio Cruz* in Mexico, and *Bomarzo* in Argentina. It continued the following year with the release of *The Time of the Hero* in Spain and *Hopscotch* in Argentina. The avalanche of best-selling titles had just started. By 1967, these and other novels paved the way to label and market *One Hundred Years of Solitude* as a Latin American novel that could easily achieve regional and international success. Thus, the claim that this novel inaugurated the age of the New Latin American Novel or Latin American Boom is inaccurate.

Counterfactually, if *One Hundred Years of Solitude* had been published in the 1920s and 1930s, it would have passed as a work of *regionalista* literature, such as *The Vortex* by J. E. Rivera and *Los Sangurimas* by de la Cuadra. If García Márquez had written his novel in the 1940s and 1950s, it would have received little regional attention and no international acclaim, which occurred with *Pedro Páramo*, the modernist novella by Rulfo, and *The Kingdom of This World*, the magical realist novel by Carpentier. At best, readers and critics would have read *One Hundred Years of Solitude* as a precursor of the New Latin American Novel, just as they read Rulfo's and Carpentier's books.[55]

One Hundred Years of Solitude, however, came out in the 1960s, when a region-spanning literature was growing and attracting regional and international readers. Being at the center of this expansion was crucial to the novel's early success. By April 1967, one month before its publication, critic Rodríguez Monegal wrote a note about it in *Mundo Nuevo* and said, "It does not represent the literature of a single Latin American nation, but of all Latin America," like the work of Cortázar, Fuentes, Vargas Llosa, Carpentier, and Sábato. A month later, the cover of *Primera Plana* magazine presented *One Hundred Years of Solitude* to its quarter of a million readers as "The Great Novel of America."[56]

CONCLUSION

Latin American literature came into existence as a region-spanning tradition in a multiethnic, multilingual, and multinational niche. Its boundaries did not match those of the Latin American region or a national literary field. García Márquez imagined *One Hundred Years of Solitude* as a work of art inside this niche. Three generations of writers, critics, and publishers embraced the principles of cosmopolitanism and Latin Americanism, which helped imagine literary texts such as García Márquez's novel. These generations' collaboration started in earnest in the 1940s thanks to a cultural void that the Spanish Civil War and World War II left in the region. This void strengthened the region's cultural autonomy by creating numerous regional and international organizations. With this cultural autonomy in full swing in the 1960s, attention to the region soared with the beginning of the Cuban Revolution. Latin America had had other moments of cultural effervescence that shaped the imagination of writers prior to the 1960s, such as *modernismo* in the late nineteenth and early twentieth centuries. But unlike previous moments, the modernization of the Spanish-language publishing industry was a central factor that helped to move ideas for works of art beyond the stage of imagination into the stage of production. As the next chapter shows, *One Hundred Years of Solitude* was also a big beneficiary of this modernization.

2

THE PUBLISHING INDUSTRY
MODERNIZES

I waited for many years for a continental editor.
For me, it is like the achievement of an old dream.

—García Márquez after signing with Sudamericana Press[1]

Whmen *One Hundred Years of Solitude* hit the market in 1967, the book industry in Spanish was booming. This situation was unimaginable for most writers and critics just a few years before. "How can literature exist," writer Mario Vargas Llosa asked, "in countries where there are no publishing houses, where there are no literary publications, where if you want to publish a book you must finance it yourself?" Although he did not mention that book piracy was also rampant in these countries, his words describe well the situation of literary publishing in most of Latin America before the 1960s. Until then, the publishing industry was small and divided into national containers. For decades, low print runs weakened the circulation of literature in the region and beyond. In Mexico and Argentina, which published more titles than the rest of Latin American countries combined, the print run of most literary books was under five thousand copies. In Spain, it was three thousand.[2]

The standard literary book faced an even harsher reality on both sides of the Atlantic: print runs of one thousand copies. Of his first book, *Los días enmascarados* (*The Masked Days*), published in Mexico in 1954, Carlos Fuentes sold all five hundred copies printed. That number was "considered a wild success," as he recalled on a TV interview with a smile on his face. "Today," he added, "a novel easily sells fifty thousand copies." This change in book sales described by Fuentes occurred abruptly in the 1960s, when García Márquez was a rising literary star. The modernization of the Spanish-language publishing industry turned the ideas and manuscripts of Latin American authors into commodities, mostly books, which consumers were eager to buy. No longer were these consumers a "lettered minority" of local edu-cated elites and peer writers. As illiteracy rates dropped across the region, these new consumers were an expanding audience of university students and middle-class readers. And this modernization meant many authors were able to live off their writing. In comparison to the publishing boom in the 1960s, "Not even Jorge Luis Borges, Alejo Carpentier, or Miguel Ángel Asturias, giants from an earlier generation," as scholar Gerald Martin puts it, "could have dreamed of such favorable terms of trade when they first came to prom-inence in the 1940s and 1950s."[3]

What usually goes unsaid is that it would have been inconceivable for novels such as *One Hundred Years Solitude* to reach the stage of production if gatekeepers of the Spanish-language publishing industry—in particular liter-ary agents, acquisition editors, and publishers—had not participated actively in the literary imagination that these writers believed in. Put differently, the organizational conditions in which gatekeepers made their decisions about what to publish mattered. And it also mattered a great deal how their deci-sions were influenced by writers' aesthetic beliefs. Therefore, these gatekeepers were not simply profit seekers; they were also believers. They came to believe in their clients' agenda for Latin American literature. And to help their cli-ents move their literary works from the imagination stage into production and circulation, gatekeepers did two things effectively. They made sure, first, that these literary works were standardized and, second, that they circulated transnationally.

Regarding standardization, gatekeepers used their resources to market the works by writers of three generations as if they belonged to a single liter-ary movement. By signing some writers (as opposed to others), gatekeepers helped to shape the literary mainstream in the region in the 1960s. This stan-dardization of the publishing agenda began the creation of a literary tradition (and region-spanning nationalism) that complemented the agenda found in region-spanning periodicals. Yet gatekeepers did more than use their resources to publish *Latin American* writers. In searching for potential artists in the region, gatekeepers were transformed by the imagination of the writers, espe-cially by the literary viewpoint of cosmopolitan Latin Americanism. Once gatekeepers believed in this viewpoint, they helped writers transform it into a commercial brand. In doing so, gatekeepers started to participate in (and influence) writers' imaginations. Thanks to this convergence between writ-ers and gatekeepers, the norms, principles, and conventions that writers had developed in the stage of imagination did not die, so to speak, in front of gate-keepers' gates. Rather, such norms, principles, and conventions became part of the imagination of gatekeepers, who ought to believe that these writers' viewpoint could give a literary work its novelty, prestige, and marketability. This convergence meant that publishers such as Seix Barral and Sudamericana and literary agent Carmen Balcells became leading advocates of the cosmopolitan Latin Americanism that defined the region's literature in the 1960s.[4]

And regarding transnational circulation, the Spanish-language publishing industry achieved an unprecedented feat: its books traveled like those in no other epoch before it. A transatlantic publishing circuit reached its peak. Writers in Latin America, aware of the prestige and larger distribution available by publishing their work with a leading Spanish press, began to do so. Thanks to this circuit, on the one hand, Latin American writers exported literary ideas and manuscripts to Spain. And, on the other hand, publishers in Spain turned them into books sold nationally and in Latin America. Under these favorable conditions, Spanish publishers produced thousands of cheap paperbacks that were sold in Spain and Latin America. A center of this transnational circuit was not in the region but in a different country and continent: the city of Barcelona. By the mid-1960s, this circuit was in full swing and readers in Spain and Latin America faced an avalanche of Latin American literary works.[5]

A DIVIDED AND LOCAL PUBLISHING INDUSTRY

Small print runs, few new literary titles, rampant piracy, and local circulation made it impossible for most authors to live off their writing in Latin America until the 1960s. The situation of the publishing industry was so negative that it reduced the achievements of the region-spanning intellectual class that emerged in the early twentieth century.[6] The audience for most literary works was mainly fellow writers, friends, literary salon attendees, and readers of local periodicals. Rather than a full-time professional, the typical author was a weekend writer. And rather than books, writers wrote for periodicals, since they were the dominant form of publication for new literary works, including novels, which often appeared in installments. Publishing with a regional press that could reach a transnational audience was a dream only within the reach of a minority of senior writers. García Márquez had to wait two decades to attain his dream of finding a Latin American publisher. As he wrote to a critic, "I was distressed to see my books in local editions, and scattered across different publishers," which hindered their regional circulation. Despite the initial success of *One Hundred Years of Solitude*, newspapers in

Peru and Colombia described readers' difficulties buying copies, due to poor book distribution or hefty importation tariffs.[7]

Given the state of the publishing industry in the region, it is not surprising that the most widespread literary form until the 1960s was the short form: poems, essays, and short stories. This state of this industry shaped what writers in the Short Form, Hybrid, and Novel Generations produced until then—each generation defined by the format of works by its most influential members. Writers had to adapt to see their works published in serial format, printed in small numbers, circulated locally and, if sold abroad, pirated. Borges, a member of the Short Form Generation, published his first book in 1923. It was a collection of poems entitled *Fervor de Buenos Aires* and was printed by a local publisher. Its print run was three hundred copies. Recalling his experience, he said, "It did not occur to me to take a single copy to bookstores, nor to newspapers, and there was no talk of success or failure." It took years to sell all the copies, mostly bought in Buenos Aires. Several of the poems in the book, for which he received no royalties, first appeared in newspapers and magazines in Spain. The debut book by Julio Cortázar, a member of the Hybrid Generation, sold two hundred copies. It was a collection of short stories entitled *Bestiary* (1951) and included "House Taken Over," a short story previously published in a small local magazine in Buenos Aires run by Borges. A decade was necessary to sell the initial print run. Another member of Cortázar's generation, Juan Rulfo, said, "I was frustrated" because "the first editions [of my short stories] were never sold. They had print runs of two thousand copies [and the ones] that circulated did so because I had given them away. I gave away half of the print run." García Márquez, a member of the Novel Generation, did the same with the copies of his first book, *Leaf Storm*. And the second, *No One Writes to the Colonel*, was originally published in a Colombian magazine, and he received no royalties for it.[8]

Although an analysis by word count would be more precise, the publishing output in number of pages by members of each generation confirms the popularity of short forms of literature before the 1960s. For the Short Form Generation, the average length of the works published between 1923 and 1959 was 151 pages. In the 1960s, when the New Latin American Novel rose, the average length went over two hundred pages, since members of this generation published more frequently and wrote longer books. Asturias, for example, published four novels, one novella, and three books of essays. Carpentier published his longest novel until then, *Explosion in a Cathedral* (423 pages). And José Lezama Lima, who for the past three decades wrote mainly poetry, published his monumental novel *Paradiso* (617 pages). In the Hybrid Generation,

Ernesto Sábato, who until 1961 had authored a novella and a book of essays, published his first novel, *On Heroes and Tombs* (417 pages). And Cortázar, known as a short-story writer, attained international recognition in 1963 with the publication of his novel, *Hopscotch* (635 pages). Likewise, the most successful members of the Novel Generation were those who adapted to the new demands of the publishing industry: long works of fiction.[9]

All three generations produced more pages because the modernization of the Spanish-language publishing industry in the 1960s motivated writers across generations to imagine longer literary works. In reality, no generation was more skillful at writing novels than the others. Before this modernization, the regional publishing industry gave more incentives to short-form writers. Those who did not conform to the industry's standards faced obscurity. The case of Leopoldo Marechal's *Adam Buenosayres* is paradigmatic. This member of the Short Form Generation dared to publish in 1948 a 741-page novel, which was the Argentine response to *Ulysses* by James Joyce. *Adam Buenosayres* had a small print run and most critics ignored it. After that, it was dormant for decades. Yet this novel became a national and Latin American best seller after the release of a new edition of ten thousand copies in 1966 by Sudamericana. Additional printings of ten thousand copies followed in 1967, 1968, and 1970.[10] Of course, this success is linked to the fact that, in between the 1948 and 1966 editions, the industry published more long forms of literature, especially novels. Thus, when in 1967 *One Hundred Years of Solitude* came out at 352 pages, it was just part of the new normal in publishing.

POLITICS, PRINT CAPITALISM, AND LATIN AMERICAN LITERATURE

The efforts from Spain to control the Spanish-language book market helped Latin American literature succeed commercially in the 1960s.[11] These efforts were politically engineered by the authoritarian regime of Francisco Franco. In 1959, the government approved the Stabilization Plan to improve the country's ailing postwar economy and to end international isolation. Three consecutive plans of social and economic development followed. These plans initiated the so-called Spanish Miracle. Book publishing, along with tourism, was deemed a priority industry for national growth, and government officials considered Latin America a key market. As an official report on foreign trade stressed in 1963, "THE FUTURE OF THE EXPANSION OF THE SPANISH

BOOK INDUSTRY rests upon the situation in the Ibero-American market, precisely where this industry is now threatened."[12] To achieve its goal, the government reformed the production and supply of raw materials for book publishing, introduced fiscal incentives for book exports, and adopted a protectionist policy against book imports from Latin America.

The Spanish government, however, had a long way to go because in 1936, when the Civil War began, exports collapsed. Publishers in Latin America filled the gap left by Spanish companies. The main beneficiary was the Argentine book industry, which boomed during the Spanish Civil War and World War II. In 1937, it produced 817 titles and 3 million copies. By 1944 it produced 5,323 titles and 31 million copies, of which two-thirds were exported. Average print runs of nonliterary books increased from 3,500 copies in 1936 to 11,040 in 1953. (Average print runs of literary works were smaller.)[13]

Spain's book exports recovered slowly after World War II. The rate of annual growth in exports between 1949 and 1959 was 16.69 percent, and it grew to 36.73 percent by 1973. The average numbers of titles also increased. The weight of books shipped to the region reveals an even more impressive growth in the exporting capacity of Spain's publishing industry. Between 1960 and 1961, there was a 183 percent increase (from 2.7 to 7.7 million kilograms) in books exported. By 1970, the amount had almost quadrupled (27 million kilograms). In total, the 1960s saw a 253 percent increase in the amount of kilograms of books exported abroad.[14] A part of this rapid growth was the transnational success of Latin American literature.

AT THE BEGINNING WAS THE PAPER

To modernize its publishing industry, Spain faced a major obstacle: paper production and supply. Research on cultural production has often overlooked the importance of raw materials, as if resources were plentiful in general. But their scarcity constrains the production of cultural goods.[15] In Spain, a chronic shortage of paper between the Civil War and the early 1960s threatened the viability of the national publishing industry. Furthermore, paper shortage remains an understudied factor in the reduction of book exports to Latin America. By 1958, the problem was so acute that the lack of raw bisulfate, a chemical needed for making paper pulp, forced Papelera Española—Spain's main paper mill—to cut its production by 50 percent. At that time, the paper-related economy was responsible for 1.2 percent of

Spain's commercial income, and 55 percent of this income came from paper used for publishing. Paper, indeed, had become a valuable commodity, and its importation for publishing purposes was taxed at an exorbitant rate: 42 to 47 percent. Given the high taxes on paper importing, publishers had to adopt a conservative publishing agenda. They refrained from printing innovative novels and new authors because those ventures were risky and unprofitable.[16]

The solution to paper shortage came from an outside agent of cultural production, the government, which adopted measures that made an immediate and long-lasting impact on the rapid modernization of Spain's book industry. To ensure that publishers bought paper in favorable conditions of quality and price, the government began to sponsor loans for paper importation and to offer tax breaks for paper used in the publishing industry. In addition, a 1962 ministerial order approved tax refunds of 5 percent for publishers to cover importation tariffs on paper. (Publishers had been asking for these refunds for almost two decades.) These fiscal incentives on paper production and supply made it possible for existing and new companies to imagine literary publishing as a profitable business. The positive results of these measures were immediate. Months after the 1962 order, *The Time of the Hero* by Peruvian writer Vargas Llosa became a best seller. It sold sixteen editions in nine years. Such sales were materially impossible in literary publishing until then. Seven years later, when *One Hundred Years of Solitude* was printed in Spain, the paper industry easily fulfilled under short notice the publisher's requests for multiple reprints of this novel; each reprint being thousands of copies. By then, paper supply and prices were no longer an obstacle to promoting new novels by little-known authors.[17]

PROTECT AND EXPAND

To support its publishing industry, the Spanish government removed another obstacle: the high cost of book distribution abroad. The government reduced postal rates, which dropped to about three and a half Spanish pesetas per kilogram for shipping books overseas, and also assumed the deficit caused by reducing the price of postal rates for book exports. Soon, the gains of Spain's book trade with Latin America exceeded any deficit the government incurred for lowering postal rates. By 1969, 82 percent of the books published in Spain were exported to Latin America. Half of them shipped to four countries: Argentina (18 percent), Mexico (13 percent), Venezuela (10 percent), and Chile (10 percent). Spain's publishing industry adapted so well to the needs of the Latin American publishing market that hundreds of books, including literary works, were printed in Spain solely to be exported and sold in Latin America.[18]

At the same time, the Spanish government restricted book imports, especially from Cuba, Mexico, and Argentina. Government officials regarded these countries as competitors because their books could impose their publishing agenda and vision of Hispanism on book markets in Latin America, Europe, and especially the United States. (Government documents described the United States as the future market of the Spanish book.) In 1959, sales for books exported to Argentina, Cuba, and Chile, including literary titles, amounted to 557 million pesetas (US$9.2 million). By 1962, sales had more than doubled: 1,200 million pesetas (US$20 million). Profits increased after the publication of most titles of the New Latin American Novel, which appeared from 1963 onward.[19]

Again, the publishing trajectory of writer Vargas Llosa exemplified the commercial success of Latin American literature published in Spain. His first book, *The Leaders* (1959), had a print run of thirteen hundred copies. More importantly, it was published shortly before the Spanish government started to reform its national book industry. The situation was quickly changing by 1963, when publisher Seix Barral released his novel *The Time of the Hero*; it had a print run of four thousand copies before becoming a best seller. His 1969 novel, *Conversation in the Cathedral*, had an initial print run of ten thousand copies. And in 1973, one hundred thousand copies were first released of *Captain Pantoja and the Special Service*. These numbers show a 7,600 percent increase in the copies printed of Vargas Llosa's books in barely a decade.[20]

This surge in sales touched other Latin American writers such as Borges, Carpentier, Asturias, and, for the first time, even young and unknown writers like García Márquez. Thus, their commercial success cannot just be explained in terms of their works' aesthetic beauty or captivating stories. Government subsidies and tax breaks for publishers in Spain made it possible in two ways: first, to produce at a low cost large-scale paperback editions destined for both the domestic and the overseas market in Latin America; second, government actions kept average book prices low. According to UNESCO statistics, between 1959 and 1976 the number of titles published worldwide increased by 77 percent. In Latin America, the two leading publishing countries, Argentina and Mexico, increased their numbers by 82 and 94 percent,

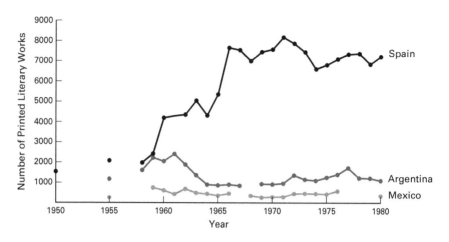

2.1 Number of literary works printed in Spain, Argentina, and Mexico (1950–1980).

Source. UNESCO Basic Facts and Figures (1952–1962) and UNESCO Statistical Yearbook (1963–1983).

respectively. In Spain, the increase was 327 percent, that is, production grew four times above the world average.[21] This tremendous growth also affected the publication of literary titles. Figure 2.1 shows the surge of these titles published in 1960, after the approval of the Stabilization Plan, and then again in 1966, after the adoption of a new law to reduce censorship. Not coincidentally, titles of the New Latin American Novel boomed during this publishing surge in Spain.

There was also a surge of publishing houses in Spain, some of which have controlled the Spanish-language market ever since: Plaza & Janés (1959), Anaya (1959), Santillana (1960), Círculo de Lectores (1962), Alfaguara (1964), Alianza (1966), Anagrama (1969), and Tusquets (1969). By 1970, there were over five hundred publishers registered. Although the majority of these publishers did not release literature, they marketed their catalogues to readers in Spain and overseas.[22]

The Spanish government's goal of entering the Latin American book market worked so well that publication of new literary titles fell by more than 50 percent in Argentina and stagnated in Mexico in the 1960s (see figure 2.1).[23] By the end of this decade, these two countries had become the main foreign consumers of books produced in Spain. Almost one in three books, including literary works, printed in Spain in 1969 was sold in these two countries. These numbers suggest that the New Latin American Novel was an idea imagined in Latin America but printed in and sold from Spain.

TO CENSOR, OR NOT TO CENSOR,
THAT WAS THE QUESTION

For the Spanish government, books were not only commodities for national economic growth. They also were political weapons to promote its vision of Hispanic culture overseas. To do so, the government began imposing a conservative agenda in the arts after the Civil War. But two decades later, government officials realized that a major obstacle to conquer the Latin American market was ideological: censorship. "There was no competition," a magazine editor wrote about publishing in Spain in the 1960s. "We all had a common enemy, which was government censorship." Since publishers could not compete against censors, their adaptation to censorship was essential to produce and sell books and other cultural goods. For this reason, a lesser-known gatekeeper—and yet a critical agent of standardization—was the Francoist censor. He made sure that Spanish readers only read Latin American literature that complied with the regime's conservative views on morality and usage of the Spanish language. In so doing, censorship influenced the contents (and sales) of what Latin American literature was.[24]

Between the late 1950s and 1976, censors rejected 65 percent of the books that publishers submitted for publication. Yet government agencies continued to warn that too much censorship only benefited Spain's competitors. In 1963, the National Book Institute produced an alarming report entitled "Spain Losing Its Book Market." Indeed, Latin American book importers and readers were suspicious of translations of foreign works printed in Francoist Spain for ideological reasons. As a Latin American literary critic put it, in the 1950s in Peru "Spanish editions of foreign books . . . were covered with dust on the shelves; we preferred to read the Germans, or English, or Russians in editions that came from Buenos Aires or Mexico."[25] (As mentioned in the previous chapter, these translations into Latin American Spanish became part of the literary imagination of numerous writers in the region, including García Márquez.)

Given this somber prospect for books produced in Spain, the government started to overhaul censorship procedures. Changes included a new printing and publishing law (*Ley de prensa*) that softened censors' screening of new publications and meant that publishing houses in Spain no longer had political obstacles to target the Latin American market. Once the government introduced these changes, readers in Spain faced, after twenty years of literary isolation, an avalanche of unknown works of Latin American literature.

This avalanche explains why the so-called Latin American Boom was partly a publishing phenomenon engineered in Spain.[26] Censors had to filter this avalanche by selecting the titles that qualified as publishable Latin American literature on Spanish soil.

In the early 1960s, the Spanish censorship office had about seventeen readers on their payroll (*lectores fijos*), including priests, law-degree holders, and higher education graduates. These readers watched out for the usual suspects: pornography, politics, and history. For example, censors forbid the publication of *Explosion in a Cathedral* (1963) by Carpentier and *The Good Conscience* by Fuentes (1960) for criticizing Spain's colonial legacy in Latin America. And, according to censors, excessive pornography made *Paradiso* by Lezama Lima unpublishable.[27]

These examples support the traditional view of censors as ideological watchdogs, a role that is well known and studied. But censors can also act as aesthetic tastemakers. This latter role is traditionally assigned to peer writers, agents, and publishers, even though censors were active in most developed countries until the 1950s, including the United States, United Kingdom, and France. Indeed, the role of censors in the promotion of certain kinds of literature and books remains largely unexamined in sociological research dealing with cultural production.[28] In Spain, censors acted as aesthetic gatekeepers by influencing what qualified as New Latin American Novels. They policed language and style. Their goal was to teach Latin American writers "how to write, how to be truly Hispanic." As gatekeepers of the purity of Castilian Spanish, censors kept Latin American Spanish to a minimum. They praised authors for what they deemed "good" writing, which helped them clear censorship faster. Censors complimented Borges's Spanish in *Dreamtigers* (1960) for being classic, Hispanic, and "erudite." Furthermore, their evaluation reports showed knowledge of an author's previous works: this new novel "is very-well written, as is usually the case with Vargas Llosa."[29]

On the other side of the spectrum were the writers using "Creole jargon" (*jerga criolla*). Censors rejected for publication books that, they claimed, had this jargon, such as Sábato's *On Heroes and Tombs* and Fuentes's *Where the Air Is Clear*, with its "incomprehensible language, full of idioms." Even copyeditors and linotypists in Spain felt compelled to protect the purity of Castilian Spanish. García Márquez was one of their victims. The text of the first edition of *In Evil Hour* (1962), printed in Spain to be sold in Latin America, was corrected into "perfect Castilian," suppressing any traces of the writer's Latin American Spanish. For government censors, not only the language but also the style of the literary work mattered. They complained that Manuel Puig's *Betrayed by*

Rita Hayworth (1968) "pretends to be modern but turns out to be dreary and unbearable" and they even scoffed at the fact that the novel "pretends to be considered part of the new Latin American narrative." But in Latin America, these and other titles sold well upon publication by region-spanning publishers. Their commercial success in Latin America confirmed the concern of government officials in Spain: strong censorship could result in loss of consumers of Spain's books in the region.[30]

The role of censors as *sui generis* collaborators in the creation of literary works has received even less attention from researchers. A beneficiary of such collaboration was Cuban writer Guillermo Cabrera Infante. In the 1960s, he submitted the manuscript of his most famous novel, *Three Trapped Tigers*, four times to censorship officials. He acknowledged that their feedback after the multiple rounds of reviews helped him improve his novel, which general-interest magazines like *Primera Plana* described to their readers (and consumers of this type of novels) as a towering product of the New Latin American Novel. Yet in Spain, the censor wrote initially, "We are confronted with a novel that imitates the modern French novel, which Sartre calls the anti-novel since it does not follow any classical rules of time, situation, and plot. Unable to master his material, the author has produced a fragmented and incoherent work." Thus, the censor first rejected Cabrera Infante's novel by claiming that it was not original enough. This is the kind of rejection—one based on originality—that researchers see as coming from insiders such as peer writers and editors, but not from censors. Yet after receiving a new submission, the censor insisted, "The novel is really illegible." To produce his judgment, the censor read the new version and revised previous censorship reports to evaluate whether the newer version showed improvements that would make it publishable. This procedure of resubmitting the manuscript to earlier reviewers is a standard practice among book editors and publishers. But it was unheard of among censors. And yet in the 1960s in Spain, this practice had a major effect on the commercial success of Latin American literature because Spain was the largest producer and consumer of Spanish-language books and the largest exporter of these books to Latin America. Censors influenced not only what Latin American consumers read, but also what people read in Spain, especially high school and university students. Only books approved by censors were added to the national educational curriculum. Thus, students in Spain started to develop a taste for literary works that were truly Latin American once censors had reviewed and approved them. They did so for *One Hundred Years of Solitude*, which became mandatory reading for thousands of Spanish students.[31]

GATEKEEPERS DISMISS A LITERARY STYLE

An aesthetic turn was also necessary for the commercial success of Latin American literature in Spain: the dismissal of social realism from Spanish literature. Social realism was a style characterized by colloquial and direct language, simple and linear narratives, sober and prosaic descriptions, and social and moralistic themes. The goal of this style was to offer a critical vision of society and compassion for the drama of the lower classes.[32] Until the early 1960s, social realism was tolerated by the government, practiced by most writers, endorsed by influential critics, and marketed by mainstream Spanish and foreign publishers.

Yet those gatekeepers that helped this style become the literary avant-garde in the 1950s dismissed it the following decade. Among its detractors were writer Juan Goytisolo, critic Josep Maria Castellet, and editor Carlos Barral. (The three were contemporaries of the Novel Generation, with whom they created strong professional ties in the 1960s.) Goytisolo started his career as a social realist with his successful novel *The Young Assassins* (1954), which the prestigious French publisher Gallimard added to its social-realist collection two years later. In 1959 in *Problemas de la novela* (*Problems of the Novel*), Goytisolo was still calling for a national literature in contact with the social reality of Spain. But soon after, he grew critical of social realism and even stopped writing fiction altogether. In 1966, in the essay "Literatura y eutanasia" ("Literature and Euthanasia"), published in the Latin American magazine *Marcha*, he denounced social realism as "incapable of capturing and expressing the novelty and complexity of the modern world [and is condemned] to the cemetery of the already made, terminated styles." He concluded that the alternative to "our stagnant Castilian Spanish language" was contemporary Latin American literature.[33]

Literary critics disapproved of social realism, too. In *Notas sobre literatura española contemporánea* (1955; *Notes on Contemporary Spanish Literature*), which censors sequestered, and *La hora del lector* (1957; *Reader's Time*), critic Castellet first supported social realism. A decade later, in his essay "Tiempo de destrucción para la literatura española" (1968; "Time of Destruction for Spanish Literature"), he wrote that it was necessary to "destroy" Spanish literature and praised the innovations of Latin American fiction. Publishers started to criticize social realism as much as writers and critics did. Editor Carlos Barral stopped publishing social-realist literature in the early 1960s as his company shifted its focus to Latin American literature. He later said that social-realist literature was "mediocre" and that the New Latin American Novel "traumatized . . . many social realists."[34]

Growing criticism from some sectors of the literary establishment made it possible to promote Latin American literature as a "challenge and alternative to autochthonous forms of fiction" in Spain.[35] Publishers such as Seix Barral started to advertise works of the New Latin American Novel as modernizers of literature in Spanish. Yet the dismissal of social realism did not translate into full support of Latin American literature by the publishing industry in Spain. Writers such as Luis Martín-Santos and Juan Benet, critics such as Rafael Conte and José Blanco Amor, and publishers such as Destino and Planeta favored alternatives that grew out of Spanish literature. Others, like Seix Barral, won the jackpot by targeting the untapped Latin American literary market.

SEIX BARRAL SETS THE AGENDA

Publishers cannot compete in equal terms with government censorship. They either adapt to it or perish. Seix Barral rejected the Franco dictatorship ideologically. But its publishing agenda conformed to the demands of censors so effectively that, in return, Seix Barral became the most influential Spanish-language literary publisher in the 1960s. From this position of power, it championed the dismissal of social realism in Spain, published European and North American avant-garde writers in translation, marketed Latin American writers internationally, and produced and exported affordable and modern-looking paperbacks.[36]

Founded in 1911 in Barcelona, Seix Barral had in the Latin American publishing market a major revenue source before the beginning of the Spanish Civil War in 1936. This experience of the prewar years became handy in 1958, when Seix Barral created a publicity department to recover its ties with the Latin American market. Its representatives toured the region and offered writers professional incentives, including stylish book design, transatlantic distribution, best-selling sales, international translations, and prestigious awards. These incentives attracted writers of the three generations, which Seix Barral marketed to Spanish and international readers as members of a single tradition: Latin American literature.[37]

To set its agenda, Seix Barral used aesthetic and ideological gatekeeping. To implement aesthetic gatekeeping, it abandoned social realism. Its acquisitions editor, Carlos Barral, admired cosmopolitan Anglo-American authors, which the company began to publish once censorship softened. He also liked baroque language, which became a trademark of Spanish literature during its Golden Age in the seventeenth century. Barral claimed to have rediscovered this language in the neo-baroque writing of cosmopolitan novels by Latin American authors in the 1960s. This renewed language became part of his aesthetic imagination. As he put it, "It was, linguistically and stylistically, a rich novel. It was like the resurgence of the Baroque."[38] In finding this aesthetic connection with the novel in Latin America, his company began promoting the neo-baroque, which, as discussed in chapter 1, was key to the region's literary independence from Spain.

Literary language was also connected to ideological gatekeeping, and Seix Barral believed in a unified literature in Spanish. So, it published writers that contributed to this literary Pan-Hispanism. By 1969, this ideological gatekeeping had taken the form of a two-hundred-page catalogue, in which the publisher claimed that literature in Spanish was "a mosaic of equidistant languages from the Castilian of the Baroque." The catalogue also stated that the company's goal was to "incorporate the values of Spanish-American narrative into our national culture."[39] The other (and more contentious) ideological filter was sympathy for the Cuban Revolution. Seix Barral published works by writers who had reservations about the revolution. But the publisher was not as enthusiastic about speeding up censorship clearance for these authors, unlike what it did for the works of Cortázar, Vargas Llosa, and Fuentes, who supported the revolution. Seix Barral's passivity delayed the publication of books by critics of the revolution, especially Cabrera Infante and Puig. And this delay did not help them to secure a position in the star system of the New Latin American Novel.

To promote its publishing agenda, Seix Barral acted on three fronts: commercial partnerships, international awards, and collections. The publisher cemented commercial agreements with major publishing houses. In 1960, Seix Barral, Gallimard (France), Rowohlt (Germany), Eiunadi (Italy), Weidenfeld & Nicholson (United Kingdom), and Grove (United States) created the Formentor Group with the goal of controlling the avant-garde in literature internationally.[40]

Regarding awards, Seix Barral established in 1958 the Premio Biblioteca Breve, bestowed first to Spanish social-realist writers. Four years later, it reinvented the award as a "transatlantic literary bridge" to promote Latin American literature in the region, Spain, and internationally.[41] The award became a magnet for Latin American writers upset with the lack of opportunity, limited distribution of their works, and small print runs in the region.

From Vargas Llosa's win in 1962 and until 1971 (except for three years), all winners of the Biblioteca Breve award were young (thirty-four years old on average) and unknown Latin American writers.

In partnership with the Formentor Group, Seix Barral created two additional awards: the Prix International des Éditeurs and the Prix Formentor. The first was given to books already in circulation and not necessarily released by publishers in the Formentor Group. Their goal was to turn this award into an opponent of the Nobel Prize in Literature. (Italian editor Einaudi actually called it the "anti-Nobel.") When first awarded in 1961, it was strategically given *ex aequo* to the world-recognized Samuel Beckett (who then won the Nobel in 1969) and to a heretofore-unknown Latin American writer: Jorge Luis Borges. "As a consequence of that prize," he confessed, "my books mushroomed overnight throughout the Western world." By 1964, he was being tapped for the Nobel Prize. The second award, the Prix Formentor, was presented to new literary works published by members of the Formentor Group. This award's goal was to advance winners to the literary mainstream and immediately translate their winning book into up to ten languages.[42]

Finally, Seix Barral also changed its literary series. The company refurbished the collection *Biblioteca Breve* (until then dedicated to social-realist titles) and created the collection *Biblioteca Nueva Narrativa Hispánica* (including Spanish and Latin American writers) and the collection *Biblioteca Formentor*. The latter collection published best-selling contemporary U.S. and European writers, began to launch works by three generations of Latin American writers, and introduced modern marketing techniques, such as appealing book design and mass-produced paperbacks. Taken together, these series became the most commercially successful outlets of avant-garde literature in the Spanish language in the 1960s.

By 1967, when *One Hundred Years of Solitude* was published, Seix Barral monopolized the market of avant-garde literature in Spanish, and had no real competitor. The fact that Seix Barral declined to publish *One Hundred Years of Solitude* is a good example of how competitors can reap the benefits from the actions of a leading player. As Vargas Llosa put it, "the Boom would have not had the impact it had without Barral." Seix Barral compelled young Latin Americans writers to embrace the New Latin American Novel, especially its neo-baroque language and cosmopolitanism. Thus, the publisher's actions paved the way for the regional and international success of books labeled by other publishers as New Latin American Novels and authored by young and unknown writers from the region, as publisher Sudamericana did in the case of *One Hundred Years of Solitude*.[43]

EXILED SPANIARDS AND THE LATIN AMERICAN
PUBLISHING INDUSTRY

Unexpected intermediaries, political exiles from Spain, facilitated the entry of Seix Barral and other publishers into the Latin American literary market. As writer Juan Carlos Onetti said, "Until the Spaniards arrived [in Buenos Aires, Argentina] there were no publishers. . . . It was difficult to find an editor."[44] The editors Onetti talked about were among the half a million Spaniards who went into political exile during the Civil War and early years of the Franco dictatorship. Refugees' presence was felt in big cities such as Mexico City and Buenos Aires and small cities such as Barranquilla in Colombia and San Juan in Puerto Rico.

Spanish exiles were not the only case of a group of immigrants who helped to activate the cultural industry of the host country.[45] What made their presence different from other groups was their influence in every sector of the publishing industry in Latin America, from paper production (paper makers, binders, printers) to book production (typographers, translators, copy editors) to sales (book distributors, sellers, stores). They also helped with agenda setting in literature by getting involved in cultural organizations, literary circles, and mainstream periodicals.[46] In the 1960s, two decades after their arrival, these refugees (and their offspring) were key in reconnecting Spain's publishing industry to the Latin American book market.

In collaboration with local cultural organizations and writers, Spanish exiles created in Latin America eleven publishing houses (eight of them were founded during the Civil War and the early years of Francoism) and helped to refurbish many old publishing houses. Thanks to this influx of exiled human capital, publishers Sudamericana, Fondo de Cultura Económica, Losada, Emecé, Era, and Joaquín Mortiz played a decisive role in the commercial success of the New Latin American Novel. Spaniards were also gatekeepers of the works of Latin American writers. Critic Guillermo de Torre, author of the controversial essay "Madrid, Intellectual Meridian of Spanish America," went into exile in Buenos Aires. There, he was a reader for Losada, founded by another Spanish exile. De Torre rejected, because of their exotic Latin American Spanish, *Final Exam* (1950) and *Leaf Storm* (1951), the first novellas of Cortázar and García Márquez, respectively.

In the 1960s, when the Spanish publishing industry was seeking to recover the Latin American book market, numerous Spanish exiles working in publishing rekindled their connections with their motherland's industry. Catalan

exile Antonio López Llausàs, the director and major stockholder of Sudamericana, secured strong ties with fellow Catalan literary agent Carmen Balcells.
A Spanish political dissident living in Bogotá since 1959, poet José Manuel
Caballero Bonald recommended García Márquez to Seix Barral and literary
agent Balcells after he won the 1962 Esso Novel award for *In Evil Hour*. Another
important action was to reactivate the transnational flow of venture capital in
publishing. In the 1940s and 1950s, Spanish exiles invested their capital in new
publishing houses in the region. But in the 1960s venture capital from Spain
returned to Latin America to be invested in new publishing ventures.[47]

Spanish exiles created journals and wrote for local and regional journals,
magazines, and newspapers.[48] They participated in literary conversations in
coffeehouses, salons, and house meetings, about which there is evidence scattered across autobiographies. These gatherings left a visible mark on many
literary works at the time. Regarding *One Hundred Years of Solitude*, García
Márquez dedicated it to a couple of Spanish exiles living in Mexico City,
actress María Luisa Elío and filmmaker Jomí García Ascot, a collaborator,
among others, of Era Press, the popular cultural supplement *La Cultura en
México*, and highbrow journal *sNob*. García Márquez also dedicated the French
version of his novel to Carmen Miracle Feliú, daughter of a Spanish exile,
and her husband Álvaro Mutis. Catalan poet Ramón Vinyes, exiled in Barranquilla, mentored the young García Márquez. Vinyes read parts of the
manuscript of his first book and helped him to choose the name of the town
where *One Hundred Years of Solitude* is set: Macondo. "[Vinyes] warned me," he
recalled, "that nobody would believe my story if I set it in Barranquilla. Furthermore, he reproached me that it was an anti-literary name."[49] Years later,
another exile Luis Vicens advised him when he signed a new contract with
Balcells, after which he started the novel. And he asked exile Vicente Rojo to
design the novel's iconic cover. In sum, Spanish exiles were present throughout the imagination and production of his novel.

MODERNIZING THE PUBLISHING INDUSTRY
IN LATIN AMERICA

While the publishing industry in Spain was crucial to the commercial success of Latin American literature, this industry in Latin America was not
simply a bystander of such success. To begin with, publishers in the region
offered deals to writers that helped a larger number of them make a living

from their books, even if contractual conditions continued to be skewed in favor of publishers. Other professional incentives for writers included royalties and literary awards such as the Xavier Villaurrutia, Casa de las Américas, Rómulo Gallegos, and Esso. (In Mexico, Universidad Veracruzana Press started to pay royalties in 1958, which encouraged García Márquez to publish *Big Mama's Funeral* with them.) Yet until the 1960s, literary titles were not central to publishers' agendas. Fondo de Cultura Económica, Sudamericana, and Emecé, among others, published mainly titles of general interest and in the human, social, and natural sciences. By the mid-1960s, as these publishing houses expanded, the increase in new literary publications authored by Latin American authors was noticeable in Argentina, Mexico, Chile, Uruguay, and Venezuela. In Argentina, *Primera Plana* reported in 1964 that numbers of new titles were up by 20 percent from the previous year. New publishing houses contributed to this increase. Joaquín Mortiz (Seix Barral's partner in Mexico) began to publish contemporary Mexican, Latin American, and international literature as well as Barral's winners of the Biblioteca Breve award. In Mexico, too, Era "emerge[d]," according to Mexican writer Carlos Monsiváis, "as a Latin American project [when] the moment of Latin America is electric."[50] (Aware of its region-spanning publishing agenda, García Márquez first reached an agreement with Era to publish *One Hundred Years of Solitude*.)

New and old publishing houses launched collections of contemporary literature to promote their titles. By the time García Márquez was living in Mexico City, University Veracruzana started the collection *Ficción*; writer Juan José Arreola subsidized the publication of *Los Presentes* in Editorial Cultura and Ediciones de Andrea; Fondo de Cultura Económica inagurated *Letras Mexicanas*, which published best-selling titles of the New Latin American Novel *Pedro Páramo* by Rulfo (1955) and *Where the Air Is Clear* (1958) by Fuentes, both rejected by censors in Spain. And Joaquín Mortiz released *Novelistas Contemporáneos* and *Nueva Narrativa Hispánica*. Yet print runs in these collections were still small. For example, titles of *Los Presentes* averaged five hundred copies, Universidad Veracruzana printed two thousand copies of García Márquez's *Big Mama's Funeral* in its *Ficción* collection, *Letras Mexicanas* released on average about two thousand copies (as it first did with *Pedro Páramo*), and Joaquín Mortiz printed between three and five thousand copies.

José Donoso, Cabrera Infante, Vargas Llosa, García Márquez, and other writers seeking to become full-time professionals voiced their concerns about the small size of editions. And they lamented that these companies were driven more by an amateur love for literature than by commercial profit. For this reason, these writers dreamed about publishing with a major Latin

American or Spanish company, even if they had to see their work delayed by censors. While looking for a publisher for his novel *Three Trapped Tigers*, Cabrera Infante knew that "the alternative would be to publish the original book in Mexico" with Joaquín Mortiz. But he also knew that "there, Seix Barral's schizoid cadavers would go to their rest on the other side of the border: death or death." Thus, Cabrera Infante and peer writers eager to join the literary mainstream preferred to adapt to censors' demands and to publish their work with a major press, rather than seeing it perish with a small one. This was also the aspiration of García Márquez. After signing the contract with Sudamericana to publish all his past and future works, he achieved, as he wrote to a colleague, "an old dream."[51]

A REGION-SPANNING PUBLISHER

"No, you cannot sell books in this country," Spanish book editor Antoni López Llausàs said regretfully after visiting García Márquez's home country, Colombia. "Let us go back to Paris even if we die of hunger." During his visit, shortly after the outbreak of the Spanish Civil War in 1936, this political exile also visited Cuba. His goal was to open a publishing house somewhere in the region. But he returned to France and worked for Hachette Press until a friend, Catalan expat Rafael Velhis, offered him the position of executive manager at a new press in Buenos Aires: Sudamericana. A decade later, he was its director and major stockholder. By then, another Spanish expat, Julián Urgoiti, was its executive manager and served as president of the Chamber of the Book in Argentina. Between 1939 and 1967, Sudamericana became the Latin American publishing house par excellence. Readers, critics, and writers associated its brand with novelty, prestige, commercial success, modern design, and affordable books. By the early 1960s, Sudamericana was actively promoting Latin American writers and contemporary foreign literature. Just days before the publication of *One Hundred Years of Solitude*, García Márquez shared in a letter to a literary critic his excitement about publishing his work with Sudamericana: This ends "a problem that you point out almost dramatically in your letter: that my friends, acquaintances, and strangers have to get my books miraculously, through the charity of other friends."[52]

In its early years, however, Sudamericana did not release many titles of Latin American literature. It mainly published academic monographs, classics, general interest books, and Anglo-American and European modernist literature.

At first, its books targeted the market of readers in Buenos Aires, had initial print runs of under three thousand copies, and only traveled abroad through networks of writers and critics. By 1959, its literature catalogue included works by some important Argentine writers (Cortázar, Marechal, Sábato, Eduardo Mallea, Manuel Mújica Láinez) and mainstream international writers such as Virginia Woolf, Aldous Huxley, Simone de Beauvoir, Lawrence Durrell, Graham Greene, and Truman Capote. Its catalogue also included Nobel laureates François Mauriac, Hermann Hesse, John Steinbeck, William Faulkner, and Ernest Hemingway. Until the 1960s, Sudamericana made its profits from literature publishing by selling international and well-established names in translation (as was the case of its competitor Emecé). Yet, when it came to Latin American authors, most of them were published at a loss. Unsold copies of Cortázar's first book, *Bestiary* (1951), were in storage for eleven years; the same happened to Onetti's works. Sales of their books skyrocketed in the mid-1960s, at the onset of the Latin American Boom.[53]

Spanish-born Francisco Porrúa was behind Sudamericana's contribution to this boom. From an early age, he developed a taste for Anglo-American novels and especially for science fiction and fantasy literature. In 1955, he founded Minotauro to publish this type of literature, back then a minor but popular genre in Argentina. Ray Bradbury's *The Martian Chronicles* (with a prologue by Borges) was its first title. Next, it published works by Cortázar, Brian Aldiss, Italo Calvino, Olaf Stapledon, and J. R. R. Tolkien. Seeing its sales potential, Sudamericana partnered with Minotauro to increase its science fiction catalogue. Sudamericana also offered Porrúa a position as one of its manuscript readers, and then, in 1962, it appointed him as acquisitions editor. Under his leadership, Sudamericana released two best-selling titles of the New Latin American Novel, in which fantasy plays an important role, Cortázar's *Hopscotch* (1963) and *One Hundred Years of Solitude*. The publication of this latter novel was also part of an expansion campaign. In 1967, Sudamericana opened new headquarters and aimed to put a book a day on the market. It could be a new title, a re-edition from its back catalogue, or a book from affiliated publishers like Minotauro.

Despite a protectionist book market and censorship in Spain, Sudamericana published its titles there. Exile López Llausàs took the lead. He rekindled his connections with the publishing industry in Barcelona, where in 1946 Sudamericana opened its franchise, EDHASA. During its first decade, it only distributed books published by Sudamericana, Emecé, and Hermes. In the 1960s, EDHASA changed its strategy and started to distribute its own titles exclusively. Now, this agent of transatlantic capitalism in publishing became a key connection between mainstream publishers on both sides of the Atlantic.[54] One of its collections, launched in 1963, had the symbolic name *The Bridge* (*El Puente*) and was edited by Spanish exile de Torre. This collection published authors on both sides of this literary bridge as well as Spanish writers in exile. Six years later, EDHASA started to print and sell on Spanish soil thousands of copies of *One Hundred Years of Solitude*.

A TRANSNATIONAL GATEKEEPER AT WORK

The rise of the literary agent, a new player of print capitalism, was essential in connecting writers in Latin America to publishers in Spain. Catalan entrepreneur Carmen Balcells played this role. Born in 1930, she belonged to the same generation of publishing entrepreneurs such as Barral, Seix, and Porrúa. She was also a contemporary of writers of the Novel Generation. She opened her agency in Barcelona in 1959, and thanks to tips from Barral and aware of the Formentor Group's agenda, she decided, "My destiny is America." She entered the publishing industry there, including trips to remote places to meet with members of literary circles, such as the Barranquilla Group in Colombia which was crucial to García Márquez's literary education. In less than a decade, she became the literary broker of the Latin American Boom, with clients such as Donoso, Vargas Llosa, Fuentes, Onetti, Cortázar, and García Márquez. Her role in the promotion of Latin American literature comes close to that of French art dealer Ambroise Vollard, who brokered the international success of impressionist art. Like Vollard, Balcells was the boundary-spanning agent in search of "creative raw material." She believed that the "indispensable raw material is the author," not the "paper."[55]

Before Balcells, most Spanish-language authors faced an unregulated professional environment fully controlled by acquisitions editors. This lack of regulation meant that average authors like García Márquez before the success of *One Hundred Years of Solitude* had to accept tough contractual conditions to publish their work. Publishers were used to negotiating with writers without intermediaries. Therefore, they regarded agents like Balcells as intruders and parasites. Publishers also detested that agents encouraged their clients to shop a manuscript around and to publish their works with different publishing houses, a behavior that Mexican publisher Joaquín Mortiz regarded as, using a sexual analogy, promiscuous. For publishers like López Llausàs at Sudamericana, the relationship between the author and the editor could not just be "exclusively commercial, but rather of friendship and mutual fidelity." As his granddaughter recalled, "The two agreed on a contract directly and one could not imagine that a writer would change his publishing house because he got 'a better deal.' . . . My grandfather organized social gatherings and luncheons in his house, attended by his writer-friends, such as Abelardo Arias, Silvina Bullrich, Marta Lynch, 'Manucho' Mújica Láinez, Manuel Puig, and many others."[56]

With the arrival of agents, writers started to break away from this old model. In the early 1960s, Fuentes was a rising star: a young and dashing full-time writer, whose regional and international success inspired budding writers like García Márquez and Donoso. Fuentes knew how important it was to have a capable agent promoting his career, so he hired New York literary agent Carl D. Brandt and recommended him to his peers; for example, he wrote to Donoso: "He is really first class, takes care of your interests as if you were his Juliet, fights for you, forces publishers to advertise the work, 'stings' critics, etc."[57] Fuentes quickly learned that the agent's job was to take power away from editors and give it to writers.

Changing this power balance was Balcells's primary goal by the time she signed García Márquez as her client. To achieve her goal, she introduced game-changing contractual practices.[58] She negotiated publishing agreements per each work that were limited by time (as opposed to contracts for life or until the edition sold out) and by national markets (before, the publisher could sell the work anywhere in the world without the author's consent). Rather, her agency enforced the delimitation of "territories" for books that circulated in and across linguistic areas; now this practice has become standard in book contracts. Balcells also asked for a strict publication schedule; if the publisher did not print the work in the period included in the contract, the author was released from the contract and would not return any advances to the publisher. She demanded a meticulous payment of forfeit royalties. She regulated author payments for sales to book clubs and similar organizations and for remainder copies. She offered a limited-time option on the author's next work. And she streamlined the publication of pocket-book editions.

Arguably, the agency's most important contractual innovation was to regulate subsidiary rights, that is, the rights paid for reproducing parts of the author's work prior to and after its publication. In the past, publishers only paid authors a small percentage, or even nothing, for such reproductions. Now, Balcells asked, in the case of prepublication, for subsidiary rights in between 50 and 90 percent of the amount received by the main publisher from the subsidiary publisher. In the case of postpublication of the author's work, subsidiary rights were around 50 percent of the subsidiary publisher's payment, whose exact amount the contract established according to the length of the text to be reproduced, format, duration, and prestige of media outlet. Under Balcells's protection, it did not take García Márquez long to understand that these rights were "a gold mine."[59]

Balcells enforced these contractual practices with Spanish-language publishers throughout the 1960s. And since she was the agent of several best-selling authors at the time, her contractual practices had a domino effect in the publishing industry internationally. By the end of the decade, her agency had turned into a powerful broker of literary excellence. As her client Donoso put it, "She seemed to hold in her hands the strings to make us all dance like puppets."[60]

MODERNIZING READERS' TASTE

In the late 1950s, when literary critic Tomás Eloy Martínez arrived in Buenos Aires, he noticed that "very few people read the great Latin American narrators [whose] books went unnoticed outside the lettered circle." He was referring to the traditional educated minority of local elites and writers—the main and only audience of most titles of Latin American literature until then. Less than a decade later, his review in *Primera Plana* magazine of *One Hundred Years of Solitude* reached over two hundred thousand readers in the region. His review celebrated this novel as part of the international success of "Latin American literature, now the most original of all literatures." What stands in between both statements made by T. E. Martínez is the modernization of readers' taste. Within a decade, habitual reading became a common practice and a sign of distinction, especially for the rising middle classes and university students. No longer could writers complain, as Vargas Llosa did, that it was impossible to receive "encouragement" to develop "an audience." "The *boom*," Cortázar believed, "was not done by editors but by readers, and who are the readers, but the people of Latin America?" This was also García Márquez's opinion: "There is no emergence of writers, but of readers. We, the novelists so requested and read today, have been working for the past twenty years." And these writers started to believe that their literature was helping readers to be aware of Latin America as a single region.[61]

Indeed, more and more readers realized that they belonged to a regional literary community and celebrated the rise of its literature. They did so, for example, in letters to the editor of magazines and newspapers. In 1965, readers of *Life en Español* in the United States, Argentina, and Mexico sent letters reacting to Emir Rodríguez Monegal's article "La nueva novela de Latinoamérica." They did not deny that the boom of the novel existed. Rather, they noticed that the critic ignored the works of more important writers such as Sábato, José Revueltas, and Luis Spota.[62] Some readers did not keep their comments to the pages of periodicals; they shared them with writers. "When my last novel was published," Uruguayan writer Mario Benedetti wrote the year *One Hundred Years of Solitude* came out,

> I received many phone calls from people I didn't know and who simply wanted to discuss with me a passage or a character in the book; several times, in the middle of the street, I was approached by strangers who had different objections or agreements about my novel. Such strangers were not the elite by the way. . . . They were simply readers, who liked or were outraged by the novel, and who wanted to compare their affinities or to state their differences, hand in hand, with the author. Such a reaction would have been inconceivable, not just ten years but even five years ago.[63]

For some critics, the sudden appearance of readers in general and of consumers of novels in particular was part of an ongoing social change in the region. There is "an urban growth that justifies the existence of the genre," Rodríguez Monegal explained, "the novel needs a society that reads it, an audience, an editorial field. It is no coincidence that precisely this boom of the Latin American novel coincides with the growth of cities, urban societies and therefore of publishers." Indeed, by the early 1960s, the region's population had grown from 140 million of two decades before to 211 million. Its expansion went hand in hand with rural exodus, improvement of living standards, increase of rates of literacy, and rise of disposable income for the consumption, for example, of literary books. In October 1965, when García Márquez had just started writing *One Hundred Years of Solitude*, *Primera Plana* magazine reported that in Argentina alone there was a 40 percent increase in sales from the previous year.[64] A year and a half later, thousands of Argentine consumers were among the first readers of his novel.

As mentioned in the previous chapter, readers first and foremost started to imagine themselves as members of a larger cultural community thanks partly to general interest magazines and newspapers. Not only did these periodicals have print runs that were ten times larger than the average literary book, but also many crossed national boundaries. In them, publishers informed readers about new literary titles, too. Best seller lists started to become common practice to influence readers' tastes, and critics like T. E. Martínez and Rodríguez Monegal developed a reputation as reviewers of mainstream Latin American literature. Simultaneously, in the region and Spain, a revolutionary publishing format made its appearance: cheap paperbacks.

Publishers designed paperbacks to reach the broadest audience possible. With the motto "The man who reads is worth more," the Continental Organization of Book Fairs (Organización continental de los festivales del libro) launched in 1956 a series of book events in Peru, Ecuador, Colombia, Cuba, Brazil, Mexico, and Venezuela. This organization also published the collection *Biblioteca Básica de Cultura Latinoamericana*, which followed "an imperative need: to spread the fundamental books of Latin American culture." It intended to do so by printing thousands of copies of affordable books. In Colombia, this collection planned to publish in 1959 twenty-five thousand copies of García Márquez's *Leaf Storm*, which hardly sold its first edition years before. Thus, García Márquez learned about the forthcoming paperback revolution several years before the publication of *One Hundred Years of Solitude*, first released as a low-priced paperback.[65]

In Argentina, Sudamericana launched *Piragua*, its collection of pocket-size books. In 1958, its titles had print runs of ten thousand copies and were sold in bookstores as well as less conventional sale points such as newspaper kiosks (the same points where *One Hundred Years of Solitude* was sold in Buenos Aires a decade later). In 1959, Editorial Porrúa of Mexico, a popular publisher of cheap paperbacks, started its best-selling collection *Sepan Cuantos . . .*, dedicated to all-time classics with prologues by Latin American authors. In Peru, the *Populibros* collection, created in 1963, sold close to one million copies its first two years. And in Spain, Alianza launched the collection *El Libro de Bolsillo* (which literally means *Pocket Book*), while paperback sales of the collection *Austral* by Espasa-Calpe rose during the 1960s.

Another important change that helped to shape readers' taste for Latin American literature was the creation of the book club Círculo de Lectores, which was inspired by the U.S. Book-of-the-Month Club and was founded in 1962 by the German Group Bertelsmann and Catalan publisher Vergara (the same year García Márquez contacted Vergara in vain to publish *In Evil Hour*). Researchers have shown that book clubs are platforms for the "sentimental education" of the reading middle classes. In Spain, this book club offered its clients a combination of best sellers and highbrow literature in attractive and affordable editions. Círculo de Lectores did so by creating its own network of agents and door-to-door delivery system. (Unsuccessfully, it tried to expand to Latin America in the 1970s.) Thanks to this book club, thousands of Spanish households saw New Latin American Novels delivered to their door for the first time ever. This was possible because Seix Barral and Balcells were on good terms with Círculo de Lectores from the start, and the book club began reprinting Seix Barral's titles and literary works by Balcells's clients. In 1966, Círculo de Lectores doubled its subscribers, from two to four hundred thousand. And in 1970, when it published its own first edition of *One Hundred Years of Solitude*, the book club was close to one million subscribers. In just three years, the Círculo de Lectores edition sold four hundred thousand copies. Since then, *One Hundred Years of Solitude* became a permanent title on its sales catalogue and one of its most profitable long-term sellers.[66]

A NOVEL ADAPTS TO THE PUBLISHING INDUSTRY

One Hundred Years of Solitude came out during a revolution of the Spanish-language publishing industry. In Spain, this industry had reached an unprecedented publishing peak of literary titles, surpassing the numbers from the United States, coming close to the United Kingdom, and closing the gap with France. Young and relatively unknown Latin American writers were experiencing aesthetic liberation, too. Publishers introduced modern strategies of book marketing. Literary agents were now negotiating better contractual conditions on behalf of their clients. Spanish exiles bridged the publishing gap between Latin America and Spain. The international audience for the New Latin American Novel was growing. And changes in readers' taste asked for modern-looking and affordable paperbacks. *One Hundred Years of Solitude* did nothing to upset this new status quo in the publishing industry. In fact, it fully benefited from it and helped to consolidate it.

Before *One Hundred Years of Solitude*, García Márquez struggled to get his literary work published. He tried publishing it in Spain, Colombia, Mexico, and France, and in different formats: books, literary magazines, and newspapers. Not only did his early literary works circulate poorly, but he also faced harsh contractual conditions like most of his peers in the region. In 1962, Universidad Veracruzana published *Big Mama's Funeral*, his first book of short stories. Its production ran into the customary obstacles so characteristic of the region's publishing industry. By contract, the publisher "acquires the literary property of the manuscript . . . property rights that will stay in place as long as the University has more than one hundred unsold book copies."

The contract stipulated that the publisher could take up to two years to publish his book and that it would be in charge of distribution. Additional proofs of the publisher's full control over the book were that it "will have, at all times, the right to make new editions of the book by just notifying the Author," it prohibited him to publish any part of the work elsewhere, and it paid the author no subsidiary rights. These tough contractual conditions soon turned into the typical nightmare for Latin American writers. First, a happy García Márquez informed a friend that the book would have a print run of five thousand copies only to find out later that the contract lowered the amount to two thousand. After its publication, he complained that distribution was terrible: only one hundred and fifty copies were sold half a year later, and he had to distribute the same number among friends and colleagues. Three years later, he was still complaining about the publisher's handling of the rights and pleaded Sudamericana to help him get the rights back. García Márquez's sorrows were not over. The book, of course, was pirated. The supplement of *Diario del Caribe* in Barranquilla published *Big Mama's Funeral* in 1964. As usual, he received no royalties.[67]

The poor circulation of *Big Mama's Funeral* and most of his early works had, of course, nothing to do with their aesthetic quality and had all to do with the local and divided publishing industry in the region.[68] The truth was that *One Hundred Years of Solitude* was set to face the same scenario. García Márquez had reached a verbal publishing agreement with Ediciones Era, which had four years earlier released in Mexico new editions of his novellas, *No One Writes to the Colonel* and *In Evil Hour*. Era's official policy was to print no more than two thousand copies of new literary titles. More fundamentally, this small, family-owned publishing company lacked a competitive international distribution. For example, its 1963 edition of *No One Writes to the Colonel* only arrived in Uruguayan bookstores two years later.

If García Márquez had honored the oral agreement with Era for *One Hundred Years of Solitude*, the publisher would have printed a small print run and used no international distributor. His first novel, which took him seventeen years to write, would most likely have attracted little attention and been framed as a Caribbean story published by a Colombian expat living in Mexico. (It was the same obscurity Cabrera Infante feared that his novel *Three Trapped Tigers* would face if Joaquín Mortiz had published it, instead of the commercial and regional Sudamericana.) Indeed, no Latin American literary title published by Era in the 1960s became an international best seller and, in the long run, oblivion was the fate of most of its titles. Thus, if Era had released *One Hundred Years of Solitude*, another book would have occupied its position as the exemplary New Latin American Novel. But, luckily for the desperate writer, Balcells and Sudamericana got involved in the novel's production.

Balcells's agency first signed García Márquez in 1962. For the next three years, it only managed the translation rights of his works worldwide. Soon after signing García Márquez, Balcells brokered the writer's first foreign contract with French publisher René Julliard for *No One Writes to the Colonel*, for which he received an advance gross payment of twelve hundred French francs, 8 percent in royalties per copy sold, and 50 percent for subsidiary rights. The print run was five thousand copies. The following year, he signed another contract with Julliard for *In Evil Hour* with similar conditions. In 1964, U.S. publisher Farrar, Straus and Giroux were interested in publishing *In Evil Hour* and asked for an exclusivity agreement to publish *The Autumn of the Patriarch* (the manuscript García Márquez had been working on before he committed to writing *One Hundred Years of Solitude*). In 1965, he signed a contract with Italy's prestigious commercial publisher Feltrinelli for *No One Writes to the Colonel* and *Big Mama's Funeral*. Both had print runs of five thousand copies. He received a combined advance gross payment of two hundred and fifty thousand lire, plus 8 percent in royalties per copy sold, and 50 percent for subsidiary rights.

The summer of 1965, Balcells traveled from Spain to the United States and Latin America to sign new clients and make more deals with publishers across the Atlantic. García Márquez signed a new contract with the agency. (As mentioned Catalan Luis Vicens, a Spanish exile and friend from Colombia, was present at the signing.) The agency now represented him in all languages, including the booming Spanish-language book market. This was great news for an author who had been seeking to become a professional writer for two decades. After signing the new contract, a cascade of publishing contracts followed. When he was writing *One Hundred Years of Solitude*, he signed contracts to publish his works in new four countries: the United States, the Netherlands, Romania, and Germany. As months of writing passed, one contract after another added to his belief that he could finally complete his first novel and become a full-time professional writer.[69]

How and why did Sudamericana approach García Márquez? Acquisitions editor Porrúa reportedly first heard about him after receiving Luis Harss's manuscript of *Into the Mainstream*, which the company published in 1966. In this volume, "[García Márquez] was next to Borges, Rulfo, Onetti, Cortázar, Fuentes, Vargas Llosa, and other great writers," Porrúa said. "That is why the first thing that came to my mind was, who is he?" Harss also gave to Porrúa copies of *No One Writes to the Colonel* and *Big Mama's Funeral*. The acquisitions editor wrote García Márquez right away. "The advantage I had over [Seix] Barral with García Márquez," Porrúa recalled, "is that I could read everything he had published before I contacted him. Thus, I expected something exceptional when he replied that the rights for his previous works were committed, but that he could send me a novel he was writing." This novel was *One Hundred Years of Solitude*, and the contact that Porrúa referred to happened the fall of 1965, under Balcells's brokerage. Once Sudamericana agreed to publish his next novel, "[García Márquez] forgot about Era, telling us," as one of its editors recalled, "that it was too small for the expectations he had placed on the novel." Publishing *One Hundred Years of Solitude* as a New Latin American Novel with Sudamericana instead ensured prestige and international sales. For the writer, this was a life-changing professional step. "García Márquez told me," critic T. E. Martínez wrote, "that, when he received the letter of acceptance from Sudamericana, he regarded it as a command, as an order of destiny. Something that definitely marked in his life a before and after."[70]

Why did Porrúa react so positively to a novel he had not even seen? Simply put, García Márquez's novel adapted to the gatekeeper's taste. Porrúa was an enthusiast and publisher of books of chronicles, science fiction, and fantasy literature. The themes in *One Hundred Years of Solitude*, the chronicle of a family saga with fantastic events, complied with Porrúa's literary agenda. He had already published the chronicles and neo-fantastic fiction of Cortázar, whose novel *Hopscotch* became a best seller, Durrel's *The Alexandria Quartet*, Bradbury's *The Martian Chronicles*, and several works of Latin American writer Onetti. Thus, contrary to the legend of a bankrupt García Márquez sending the manuscript to a tentative publisher and betting everything on it, Porrúa knew it was coming his way for a year. He did not blindly take a chance with *One Hundred Years of Solitude*.[71]

There is not enough evidence to fully explain why Seix Barral did not publish this novel, especially since Balcells was aware of the publisher's promotion of Latin American writers. García Márquez certainly offered the novel to Seix Barral. In a letter to Fuentes in November 1965, García Márquez asked for his advice: Should he opt for Sudamericana or Barral? Fuentes had no doubts: Barral. "Sudamericana," he explained to García Márquez, "puts your work to circulate only in the Latin American world . . . with Barral you have already made your way to translations and presence in Europe and the United States." García Márquez asked for Fuentes's recommendation because he was already in conversations with both publishers and wanted to make the best decision. But Seix Barral finally declined to publish it. According to Carlos Barral, he did so "because of a misunderstanding.

I did not answer a telegram punctually, and neither because of an editorial error nor because of a clumsy reading of the manuscript—which I never saw—as has been maliciously claimed."[72]

This statement agrees with the available evidence. In the fall of 1965 and under Balcells's watch, Barral probably received a telegram or letter from García Márquez offering *One Hundred Years of Solitude* to him. So, the writer approached Barral—as he did with Sudamericana—when he had just started the novel, not with a full manuscript in hand. In October, he was already talking with Barral. But that ceased by February 1966, the same month he asked Fuentes to send three chapters of the book to Sudamericana (after first giving them to Fuentes to know his opinion). Nowhere in this or other letters did García Márquez mention anything else about conversations with Seix Barral. By then, Sudamericana was his preferred publisher. Why? García Márquez was not only interested in finding a publisher for his novel in progress. He wanted to sign with one publisher that could reunite all his books, currently scattered among local publishers. Sudamericana accepted this condition by March 1966. Indeed, two months before, Guillermo Schavelzon, acquisitions editor of the Argentine publisher Jorge Álvarez, traveled to Mexico City. Looking for new clients, he met with García Márquez, who told Schavelzon that he was working on a "long-term project." The writer offered Schavelzon the rights of *Big Mama's Funeral*. They signed a publishing agreement. But sometime in March, the writer asked Jorge Álvarez to cancel the agreement. He had already reached a better deal with Sudamericana, which would publish all his works, including *One Hundred Years of Solitude*. Thus, this evidence suggests that the novel was not finished when Sudamericana decided to publish it. And Barral's practice, moreover, was to look at full manuscripts, not book proposals or advance chapters. More fundamentally, in terms of aesthetics and commercial impact, Barral did not know García Márquez's work that well in 1966. (His wife, Yvonne Hortet, who was a literary agent, apparently did.) And also, García Márquez did not fit Barral's taste, which was quite different from Porrúa's. Whereas Porrúa saw in this novel a Latin American family saga full of fantasy, Barral might have seen García Márquez as a rural, regionalist writer and not as an urban novelist. Barral preferred publishing stories centered in cities.[73]

Even if Seix Barral did not publish *One Hundred Years of Solitude*, the company did something essential for its success: it set the conditions for its diffusion in Spain as a New Latin American Novel. As such, this novel easily bypassed censorship and was marketed to middle-class and college audiences. For the past seven years, the reading public had steadily developed a taste for books marketed as New Latin American Novels, many of which Barral published. The commercial success of *One Hundred Years of Solitude* overseas further sped up censors' approval. The Spanish government did not like the idea that best-selling books from the Latin American market would leave small profits to the national book industry. As a result, EDHASA, Sudamericana's branch in Spain, started to print and sell García Márquez's works in the country.

Under the new guidelines set by the printing and publishing law of 1966, censors found nothing that was ideologically punishable in *One Hundred Years of Solitude*. According to them, "it does not defend a thesis but . . . simply describes unsuitable situations without approving or condemning them." Censors, in fact, praised its objective storytelling. It pleased them that *One Hundred Years of Solitude* did not contain the kind of Creole jargon they had to correct. Rather, the novel used a classic and even archaic language that adapted to censors' taste for good Castilian Spanish. Thus, the censor concluded, "As a novel, it is very good." It is worth pointing out that censors framed *One Hundred Years of Solitude* neither as fantasy literature (as it was originally received, see chapter 4) nor as magical realism (as it was labeled later, see chapter 6). Instead, they referred to it as a realist novel. As the censor wrote in a report, it offers "the most exact idea possible of the low and middle-class Spanish-American society."[74] Furthermore, censors did not pay attention to magical events in the novel at all. This is important because it shows that a preexisting cultural framework influenced the evaluation of censors. And they evaluated the novel based on the literary style that dominated their cultural framework: Spain's down-to-earth social realism.[75] Meanwhile, on the other side of the Atlantic, this novel attracted the attention of Sudamericana's acquisitions editor because it reminded him of fantasy literature. In sum, the opposite reactions of gatekeepers to this novel are a telling example of how aesthetic interpretation can be in the eye of the beholder and not automatically be present in the text itself.

One Hundred Years of Solitude bypassed official censorship in Spain, but not that of self-appointed censors. José Vernet Mateu, a resident of Barcelona, wrote a harsh letter to the Francoist Minister of Information. He complained about the popularity of this "repugnant . . . disgusting book." His letter reveals the obstacles that this novel would have faced if it had been published in Spain before the printing and publishing law of 1966. "I wonder," Mr. Vernet wrote, "in my ignorance as a simple man in the street, how is it possible for a book so filthy, so destructive of Christian morality, so brutalizing to have found an expedite path toward publication in Spain?" And he added that he did not understand that this book "could serve as a required textbook for sixteen-year-old boys, to whom it literally corrupts and brutalizes."[76] So he urged Francoist censors to sequester the book. Mr. Vernet was not off target. *One Hundred Years of Solitude* contains sexually explicit passages, critical comments about the Catholic Church, and descriptions of incest, authoritarian military actions, and violence that astonished readers. (Communist censors deleted incestuous passages in the Soviet Union, but not in Francoist Spain.) Counterfactually, if this novel were published in Spain before the law of 1966, it would have faced tougher censorship. At that time, as in the case of Cabrera Infante's *Three Trapped Tigers* and Donoso's *The Obscene Bird of Night*, its publication could have been delayed and *One Hundred Years of Solitude* could have lost the momentum of the New Latin American Novel. Instead, this book fully benefited from it.

CONCLUSION

Government officials (censors included), publishers, literary agents, book distributors, and booksellers in Latin American and Spain collaborated in the publication of *One Hundred Years of Solitude*. They helped to produce this novel from multiple centers, especially Mexico City, Buenos Aires, Barcelona, and Madrid. In other words, they were agents of transatlantic print capitalism whose boundaries did not match those of a Latin American field of cultural production, a national publishing industry, or the conventions of a single art world. Rather, these agents repeatedly crossed regional, national, and local boundaries. Their fluid transnational circulation is key to understanding the production of *One Hundred Years of Solitude* and its immediate success—not just regionally, something materially impossible for most novels before the 1960s, but also internationally. For this reason, no single field, cultural industry, or art world could control the production of this novel or any major New Latin American Novel. Instead, *One Hundred Years of Solitude* arose in a transnational niche in which the cosmopolitan Latin Americanism of his peer writers shaped the imagination (and hence the taste) of gatekeepers such as publishers Sudamericana and Seix Barral and literary agent Carmen Balcells. This cosmopolitan and Latin American viewpoint adapted perfectly to the demands of the modernizing Spanish-language publishing industry and its growing audience of students and middle-class readers. *One Hundred Years of Solitude* proved to be the most exact of matches for this industry.

3

A NOVEL IN SEARCH OF AN AUTHOR

The book was not coming out, I couldn't do it.

—García Márquez on *One Hundred Years of Solitude*[1]

García Márquez first imagined *One Hundred Years of Solitude* in 1950. He struggled to finish it for the next seventeen years. Conceiving a work of art, included this novel, is hardly the offspring of a solitary act of inspiration. Conception in art is a collaborative venture—no artist imagines a work of art alone. García Márquez imagined the novel that would become *One Hundred Years of Solitude* over the course of almost two decades and during that time he joined groups of artists in Colombia, France, Venezuela, and Mexico, plus short stays in the United States, England, and Italy.[2] Yet having an idea for a work of art and discussing it with collaborators does not ensure that it will come into being one day. As the previous chapters showed, the passage of *One Hundred Years of Solitude* from an idea to a book, from the stage of imagination to the stage of production, happened as Latin American literature grew into a region-spanning movement and the modernizing Spanish-language book industry created a market of best sellers for Latin American novels. For these reasons, *One Hundred Years of Solitude* is the work of García Márquez as much as the novel and its author are the work of a booming Latin American literature and publishing industry.

This chapter shows how García Márquez's imagination took form, especially from 1950 to 1965, that is, from when he conceived the idea for a novel about a family and its house in a village to when he had the professional tools to turn this idea into a publishable book. During those years, he learned vital skills from his work in journalism, cinema, advertising, and literature. In the meantime, he also wrote several drafts of "The House," the story that evolved into *One Hundred Years of Solitude*, and he published three novellas, one book

Table 3.1 García Márquez's locations from birth up to publication of *One Hundred Years of Solitude*

Location	Year
Colombia (1927-1955)	
Aracataca	1927-1929
Barranquilla, Aracataca	1929-1930
Aracataca	1930-1936
Sincé	1936-1937
Aracataca	1937-1938
Barranquilla	1938-1939
Sucre, Barranquilla	1939-1942
Zipaquirá, Bogotá, Sucre	1943-1944
Magangué	1944
Zipaquirá, Bogotá, Sucre	1945-1946
Sucre, Bogotá[ab]	1947
Bogotá,[ab] Cartagena,[ab] Sucre, Barranquilla[ab]	1948
Barranquilla,[ab] Sucre, Cartagena[ab]	1949
Barranquilla,[ab] Aracataca	1950
Barranquilla,[ab] Cartagena[ab]	1951
Barranquilla,[ab] Aracataca	1952
Barranquilla,[ab] Departments of Cesar, La Guajira, and Magdalena	1953
Bogotá,[ab] Barranquilla,[ab] Medellín,[b] Department of Chocó[b]	1954
Bogotá,[ab] Barranquilla[a]	1955
Europe (1955-1957)[b]	
Paris, Geneva, Venice, Rome, Vienna, Warsaw, Kracow, Auschwitz, Prague	1955
Paris[a]	1956
Paris,[a] Heidelberg, Frankfurt, GDR (Weimar, Buchenwald, Leipzig, East Berlin), West Berlin, Prague, Moscow, Volgograd, Kiev, Budapest, Ujpest, London	1957
Latin America (1957-1967)	
Caracas	1957
Caracas,[ab] Barranquilla,[a] Cartagena	1958
Caracas,[ab] Havana, Bogotá,[a] Barranquilla[a]	1959
Bogotá,[a] Barranquilla,[a] Havana, Mexico City	1960

Location	Year
Barranquilla,[a] Bogotá,[a] New York City,[b] Pennsylvania, Maryland, Virginia, North Carolina, South Carolina, Georgia, Alabama, Mississippi, Louisiana, Texas, Mexico City,[abcd] Veracruz[c]	1961
Mexico City,[abcd] Panamá, Chichén Itzá, Acapulco, Pátzcuaro[c]	1962–1965
Mexico City,[ad] Cartagena, Barranquilla,[a] Bogotá,[a] Aracataca, Valley of Upar	1966
Mexico City,[a] Buenos Aires, Caracas, Bogotá,[a] Lima, Cartagena	1967
Europe	
Barcelona[a]	1967

Source: Gabriel García Márquez Archives, HRC; García Márquez 2001a; García Márquez 2002; Martin 2009.

[a] García Márquez joined an art circle.
[b] Worked as a journalist.
[c] Worked as a scriptwriter.
[d] Worked in advertising.

of short stories, and over five hundred journalistic pieces. He created professional ties in six countries that nurtured his creative vision, gave him firsthand experiences for stories, and granted him privileged access to influential gatekeepers in publishing. But he also worked hard to become a professional writer. For years, fiction writing was a part-time endeavor for which he received no royalties. By 1965, after years of learning and setbacks, leading peers finally recognized him as an "integrated professional [with the skills] necessary to make it easy to make art."[3] An international network of collaborators was central to achieve this recognition. They helped him to transform his literary imagination into the professional conventions he needed in order to be a full-time writer capable of producing *One Hundred Years of Solitude*.[4]

PLACES, NETWORKS, SKILLS, AND CONVENTIONS

García Márquez was once an anxious aspirant writer. Traditionally, would-be writers must learn several skills in order to become literary authors. To attain these skills, they need to convert them into professional conventions accepted by peer writers, gatekeepers of the publishing industry, and critics. Mastering these conventions gives writers access to professional resources and opportunities for advancement. Since some conventions are more difficult to master than others, the more difficult the convention, the more likely that its practitioner would attract the attention of vested groups in that professional activity. But if socioeconomic obstacles get in the creator's way, skill learning becomes more difficult, as it did for the young García Márquez.

He was born in 1927 into a lower-middle-class family. His birthplace, Aracataca, was then an impoverished rural village in free fall after the abrupt end of its booming banana plantation economy. Aracataca is located in Colombia's coastal region facing the Caribbean. But at this time, it was isolated; it was about a week's travel away from Bogotá, the country's capital and major cultural hub. Yet in this remote village, he accumulated literary capital for his future works thanks to the experience of living in his maternal grandparents' house until the age of nine and in the company of several older members of his large family. After leaving that house, he joined his parents and six siblings (who numbered ten by the time he started college). He also discovered his father had five children out of wedlock. Many years later, as he faced the typewriter, the author was to transform those memories of his childhood and family into most of the stories and characters in *One Hundred Years of Solitude*.[5]

In his early years, his low social status and rural origins were obstacles. Despite being a very good student, his background prevented him from receiving a scholarship to study in a high school for elite students in Bogotá. Rather, the teenager was sent to a nearby town, Zipaquirá, where socialist-leaning teachers moved his artistic impulses away from drawing, then his main interest, to literature. They introduced him to Colombian literature (especially the works of the avant-garde poetry group called *Piedra y cielo*; Sky and Stone); contemporary Spanish and Latin American poets such as Federico García Lorca, Pablo Neruda, and Ramón Gómez de la Serna; writers of Spain's Golden Age literature, such as Miguel de Cervantes, Luis de Góngora, and Pedro Calderón de la Barca; and best-selling fantasy and adventure fiction for teens, such as works by Jules Verne, Mark Twain, and Alexandre Dumas. During his high school years, García Márquez, under the pen name of Javier Garcés, published several poems that followed the conventions of *Piedra y cielo* poetry in the school magazine and the newspaper *El Tiempo*. His first pieces of journalism, published in 1948, were also under the influence of this style that "sought new [literary] images to defamiliarize reality." Along with other influences that he picked up later on, it became typical of his prose to use literary images in ways that could help readers see everyday life anew. Yet nothing in his literary education at this point made him unique from other students. He was simply a creative and talented student on a scholarship, who had the typical difficulties of a shy teenager to blend in socially. In his case, some of his peers looked down on him as a *pueblerino* for his provincial and rural roots.[6]

The twenty-year-old García Márquez began his writing career as a journalist. For aspiring writers, success in journalism was the best way to publish literary works in a region with a divided and local publishing industry. For fifteen years, from 1948 to 1963, his tasks in journalism were various, including writing daily news coverage, headlines, notes, columns, reportages, and film reviews. He also worked as an editor for newspapers (including tabloids), cultural supplements, and general interest magazines. Over those years, he acquired valuable professional skills for a writer: from data gathering for stories to design, editing, and marketing. And he learned and practiced such skills in Bogotá, Cartagena, and Barranquilla (Colombia), Paris, Eastern Europe, London, Caracas, New York, and Mexico City. The downside was that he could not write fiction full-time until the mid-1960s. He wrote his short stories and novellas either at night, after the newspaper was sent to press, or at home on weekends and holidays.

First Steps in Bogotá

Unlike his peers Jorge Luis Borges, Julio Cortázar, Mario Vargas Llosa, José Donoso, or Carlos Fuentes, García Márquez received no support from family wealth or prestigious institutions so that he could turn literature into his main occupation. He was the first of eleven siblings and expected to be the family's breadwinner along with his father. In 1947, he started a law degree at the National University of Colombia in Bogotá, as his father dictated. A law degree was then one of the means of upward social mobility in the country if one wanted to join the ruling elite. But he was not a committed student. He was more interested in the arts. Yet even gaining admission to Bogotá's art circles was difficult for him because of his provincial origins, lack of economic means, bohemian lifestyle, shabby appearance, and status of *costeño* (the derogatory way in which people in the capital often refer to people from the Caribbean coast). He hung out with journalists and writers who eventually gave him access to these circles.[7]

One of his *costeño* friends introduced him to Eduardo Zalamea Borda, a modernist writer and author of *Cuatro años a bordo de mí mismo* (*Four Years Aboard Myself*, 1934), a Colombian version of James Joyce's *Ulysses*. Zalamea Borda was the editor of *El Espectador*. In the pages of this national newspaper, he had recently made a call to young writers to send him short stories, a little cultivated genre in Colombia. (Young writers were fascinated by poetry and so was García Márquez then.) Borrowing techniques from Franz Kafka's modernist fiction, García Márquez sent the short story "The Third Resignation," which the newspaper published in its weekend literary supplement. He published another two short stories influenced by Kafka's fantastic style and the intellectualism of literary circles of Bogotá. On April 9, 1948, presidential candidate Jorge Eliécer Gaitán was assassinated in the capital. What followed was El Bogotazo, violent riots that destroyed much of the city and made it unsafe for a college-age García Márquez to stay. He returned to the Caribbean coast and more importantly to his culture.

Between Cartagena and Barranquilla

If El Bogotazo had not occurred, García Márquez would have continued studying law, pursuing his career in journalism, and writing "intellectual" short stories. To his family's dismay and anger, he dropped out of law school to be a journalist and to write fiction. He worked full-time for the newspapers *El Universal* in Cartagena and *El Heraldo* in Barranquilla between 1948 and 1953. He also joined two collaborative groups that left a lifelong mark on his creative imagination.[8] It was while he was living there and returning to his Caribbean roots that he first imagined the novel that became *One Hundred Years of Solitude*.

García Márquez soon built bridges between journalism and literature. He used his columns to develop and publicize his literary agenda among readers. His earliest statement on literature appeared in his column "La Jirafa" ("The Giraffe") published in the Barranquilla newspaper *El Heraldo* on April 24, 1950. He was then at work on his first novella. In his column, he stated, "There has not yet been written in Colombia a novel evidently and fortunately influenced by Joyce, Faulkner, or Virginia Woolf." In another column printed the following year on February 9, he said that Faulkner, Kafka, and Woolf were his favorite writers and added, "My greatest aspiration is to be able to write like them." In between these two columns, on June 3, 1950, he published "La casa de los Buendía: apuntes para una novela" ("The Buendía House: Notes for a Novel"). This was his first known attempt at writing *One Hundred Years of Solitude*. The commercial success and the consecration of several of the abovementioned writers during García Márquez's formative years shaped his literary imagination. He wanted to be as influential as they were. And he knew that to achieve such an influence he had to reach multiple audiences. He already had them in mind when writing his first novella. In an interview, he said, "It is a work that the public can like . . . that will be popular and that, therefore, will demonstrate that the contemporary novel can reach the masses . . . drivers, shoe shiners, lottery vendors."[9]

Reaching the masses the way García Márquez wanted was impossible at the time in Colombia. When he started working as a journalist in 1948, the government had suppressed civil rights, turned to authoritarian rule, and in the end fell into a military dictatorship that lasted five years. Among its anti-democratic actions, the government imposed censorship to control printed media nationwide. Government decrees in 1949 created the Office of Prior Censorship, which authorized censors to scrutinize the contents of any periodical before publication. Not coincidentally, García Márquez's first known piece of journalism was about the military curfew in Cartagena. At this moment, different "teachers" trained him on how to deal with censorship. At *El Universal*, his supervisor was managing editor Clemente Manuel Zabala. "A reporter," García Márquez recalled, "finds a good editor and can move forward professionally." At first, Zabala edited García Márquez's writing every day and taught him, pen in hand, what could be written and how to write it. Next, he witnessed a government censor's actions in the newspaper's headquarters every day after 6 p.m. The censor read the next day's edition before it went into print. Thus, the budding writer also saw how the censor (a special kind of gatekeeper, as shown in the previous chapter) edited his writing by removing what could upset the government. Finally, the text was sent to the newspaper's proofreaders, where García Márquez learned additional editing skills. This extra learning opportunity happened in a casual and unintended way; the journalist often hung out at bars with proofreaders and linotypists after closing hours, since he stayed up until late at night to work on his short stories and novellas.[10]

During the years García Márquez lived in Cartagena and Barranquilla, he wrote nearly four hundred pieces of journalism. Most of them required censors' approval. As he soon realized, censorship "was a creative challenge," as he put it. Among his creative solutions was to write with an "objective" narrative style that would give censors the impression of mere fact reporting. This daily routine of dealing with censorship taught him useful skills: how to see his own writing as an outsider and how to use the outsider's view to edit his work before submitting it for review. Years later, in the newspaper *El Espectador* of Bogotá, he had a reputation among his peers for delivering very polished originals after obsessive rewriting and copyediting. He also started to transfer these skills to his literary writing, especially to anticipate and overcome criticism from gatekeepers in publishing and educated readers of his work. As he said about his writing ethic after publishing his first book, "It is necessary to write a lot, delete, edit, tear apart many sheets, so that one can finally bring to the editor a few pages."[11]

García Márquez also faced censors as a fiction writer. Before publishing his third novella, *In Evil Hour*, he had to convince the priest Félix Restrepo, President of the Colombian Academy, that the novel's text was decent. The priest was not really acting as a political censor but more as a moral one. He wanted García Márquez to remove obscene words—among them *masturbation* and *contraceptive*—from the text. But the writer fought back; he knew how to handle the censor. As he explained to a friend, he sent to the priest "the most Jesuit-like letter I could conceive" to tell him that he would change nothing. In this letter, he wrote one of the things the priest wanted to hear: I am "a good Christian." And he went on to explain to the priest that he wrote his "social" novella with the goal of describing "a disturbing social reality that I have known firsthand in some villages of Colombia." In other words, he told the priest that he was not inventing anything, but simply reporting facts; precisely, what he learned to do as a journalist in order to bypass government censors. García Márquez convinced the priest, who authorized the publication of his book. Five years later, he used the same narrative style in *One Hundred Years of Solitude*. The novel, in the words of censors in Spain, has no "thesis." Rather "it just describes situations," as it were a piece of reporting journalism. Mastering these writing skills helped him secure censors' approval in Spain and also in Argentina, where *One Hundred Years of Solitude* was first published.[12]

Along with censors, several of his friends in journalism, who were also writers, collaborated in García Márquez's education. At *El Universal* he befriended Héctor Rojas Herazo and Gustavo Ibarra Merlano. The first wrote rural stories influenced by realism, regionalism, and Faulkner. The second was a poet inspired by ancient Greek literature and especially by Sophocles. Along with siblings Ramiro and Óscar de la Espriella, the three men met at bars and coffee shops, where they talked about women, politics, journalism, and literature. Thanks to this group of friends in Cartagena, García Márquez first encountered the works of Sophocles, Nathaniel Hawthorne, Herman Melville, Edgar Allan Poe, Gómez de la Serna, Faulkner, and Woolf, among others. As mentioned earlier, the last two were the subject of several of his newspaper pieces at the time. By then, journalism and literary writing started to become inseparable for García Márquez. Although the city of Cartagena was not as culturally dynamic as Bogotá, it was an important regional hub. Zabala, Rojas Herazo, and García Márquez attended a talk by leading Spanish poet and Góngora scholar Dámaso Alonso; García Márquez shared with him some of his writing. He also praised the works of his friends from his daily column.

He wrote a review of the book of poems by Rojas Herazo, *El rostro de la soledad* (*The Face of Solitude*). In his opinion, "La casa entre los robles" ("The House among Oak Trees") was the most beautiful poem in the book. These and other reviews reveal that early on themes such as solitude and the family house were becoming an integral part of García Márquez's literary imagination.[13]

In 1950, the journalist left for the nearby city of Barranquilla in search of a better salary. He worked for the newspaper *El Heraldo*, which paid him one peso daily. He also joined the so-called Barranquilla Group. Its members were mainly amateur writers and visual artists, who met regularly between 1944 and the late 1950s. They were followers of mainstream North American and European modernist fiction; several of them had already read García Márquez's short stories in *El Espectador*. The fact that he used literary techniques imported from modernism facilitated his admission to this group.

As the Cartagena Group did, the Barranquilla Group supervised García Márquez's literary writing. It oriented his professional readings toward cosmopolitan works of ancient Roman and Greek literature and modernist Western literature. The group helped him financially and lent him books that the impoverished journalist could not afford to buy. It was "a time of . . . discovery," García Márquez explained. "Not of literature! But of literature applied to real life which, after all, is the big problem of literature." Unlike what happened to the shy and awkwardly dressed writer in Bogotá, he did not feel outclassed or a cultural outsider in Barranquilla. As a member put it, he "was the [most] provincial of the group" and they did not share his lower middle-class background or rural origins.[14] But culturally, García Márquez was a *costeño* just like most members of the group. Indeed, Barranquilla is less than 150 kilometers away from García Márquez's birthplace. Thus, his closest group of friends (who even became characters in *One Hundred Years of Solitude*) shared his culture and bohemian lifestyle. Regular participants during García Márquez's stay in this city included writers Alfonso Fuenmayor, Germán Vargas, and Álvaro Cepeda Samudio, painters Alejandro Obregón and Noé León, and photographer Enrique Scopell. Writer and Spanish exile Ramón Vinyes—the character of the wise Catalan in the novel—often led their conversations on journalism, literature, arts, and politics.[15]

Their conversations were not just about local arts but also cosmopolitan debates about the literary mainstream. Germán Vargas advised the owner of El Mundo bookstore, one of the group's meeting points, on book selections for its customers. To do this, Vargas read magazines and newspaper supplements such as *El Hijo Pródigo* from Mexico City and *Sur* and *La Nación* from Buenos Aires at the bookstore. Thanks to this up-to-date bookstore, the group received a regular flow of international and regional literary journals and works by Latin American writers such as Cortázar, Borges, Neruda, and Felisberto Hernández as well as foreign writers such as Kafka, Joyce, Faulkner, Hemingway, Woolf, Jean-Paul Sartre, Albert Camus, Graham Greene, Aldous Huxley, Katherine Mansfield, William Saroyan, Erskine Caldwell, Sinclair Lewis, and John Dos Passos. Group members also exchanged books they had read. And as copies passed from one member to another, readers could see the handwritten highlights and comments of other members, and sometimes they added their own opinions, continuing their conversations about literature. For a budding writer like García Márquez, such conversations on the printed page were key to learning firsthand why certain passages attracted more attention than others and to understand how writers crafted them.[16]

More importantly, the Barranquilla Group (and also his friends in Cartagena) advised García Márquez on how to draw inspiration at different levels from other writers. The plot, techniques, and contents of *Leaf Storm*, García Márquez's first novella, show his assimilation of the group's conventions about how to write literature. He started to write *Leaf Storm* in the late 1940s and published it in 1955. This novella combines the dramatic fact of an unburied corpse, taken from Sophocles's *Antigone*, the Ancient Greek classic from the fifth century BC, and Faulkner's modernist techniques and style in *As I Lay Dying* (1930).[17] The choice of *Antigone* was not an accident. Multiple versions of this play were available in the region because, since the nineteenth century, major writers had imagined it as a Latin American tragedy.[18] In 1951, when García Márquez was writing his novella, Argentine writer Leopoldo Marechal premiered a successful adaptation in Buenos Aires, entitled *Antigone Vélez*, which was set in the Argentine lowlands known as the Pampas. Whereas *Antigone* was a model of Latin Americanism, Faulkner's *As I Lay Dying* served as a model of cosmopolitanism. Thus, the choice of this novel was not an accident either. Faulkner's story is set in the imaginary Yoknapatawpha County. The story is narrated from fifteen different points of view, using stream of consciousness and interior monologues, among other techniques. García Márquez's *Leaf Storm* is his first book set in the imaginary village of Macondo (the center of most of his fiction until after the publication of *One Hundred Years of Solitude*). The story is narrated from three points of view and uses Faulknerian stream of consciousness and interior monologues.[19]

Regarding the novella's style, group members helped García Márquez develop it. Its style, naturalist and descriptive, had to be different from the subjectivity narrative of writers like Marcel Proust or the omniscient narrator as in the works of Gustave Flaubert. Rather, García Márquez (and the group) followed Faulkner's style. In one of his first interviews, he proudly stated that he wanted to do something "similar to Faulkner's in his work *As I Lay Dying*." [20] In reality, what he did was not so original. Faulkner was a highly acclaimed author in Latin America and winner of the 1949 Nobel Prize in Literature. As shown in chapter 1, Faulkner not only influenced García Márquez's local literary groups in Barranquilla and Cartagena but also shaped senior, mid-career, and emerging writers in the region that the young García Márquez read during his formative years: Juan Carlos Onetti (Uruguay), João Guimarães Rosa (Brazil), Ernesto Sábato (Argentina), Juan Rulfo (Mexico), Alejo Carpentier (Cuba), Fuentes (Mexico), and Vargas Llosa (Peru). By the time García Márquez started writing *One Hundred Years of Solitude*, he was friends with most of these writers or had met them at professional conferences. They, in return, praised how he had drawn from Faulkner's style in his work.

García Márquez did not learn on his own how to follow Faulkner's writing method; members of the Barranquilla Group used it in their own writing as well. "We were seeing a reality," the writer recalled, "and we wanted to tell it and we knew that the European method did not work, nor the traditional Spanish method; and suddenly we find out that the most appropriate to tell this reality is the Faulknerian method. At the end, this is not very unusual because I don't forget that Yoknapatawpha County has shores in the Caribbean Sea; so he is a Latin American writer somehow."

Reframing Faulkner as a Latin American writer helped García Márquez understand at the onset of his career that local Latin American stories and cosmopolitanism were not opposites in literature. As he said after publishing *Leaf Storm* in 1955, "My novel es *costumbrista*," a style that tells stories grounded in everyday life, customs, and manners. For him, "*Don Quixote* is *costumbrista*. . . . So, I can call *costumbrista* any work that has the same purpose, that is, one that makes the local known within the universal." He added that he had just started writing a new novel, *Los catorce días de la semana* (*The Fourteen Days of the Week*), which would be also *costumbrista* in its universal dimension. Ten years later, in 1965, when he started writing *One Hundred Years of Solitude*, the idea of a universal *costumbrismo* was fully rooted in his literary imagination. As he then explained in an interview, every great novelist is "in a certain sense regionalist. And even more *costumbrista*." [21]

For a young writer interested in rural realist fiction, the discovery of the *Latin American* Faulkner was crucial in his literary education. With the assistance of his friends in Cartagena and Barranquilla, García Márquez made the connection between the rural south of the United States in Faulkner's work and his personal experience growing up in the rural village of Aracataca.

To further understand these connections, he visited other parts of the Magdalena Department, the Valley of Upar, and La Guajira as an itinerant book salesman in 1953 and 1954. "These trips," he indicated, "ended up revealing to me the magic of a world without which my novels would not have been possible today." The importance of the rural in his literary imagination was quite clear in the titles and contents of his novellas at the time. A draft of *Leaf Storm* was supposedly called *Ya cortamos el heno* (*We Already Cut the Hay*) and his third novella, *In Evil Hour*, was first entitled *En este pueblo de mierda* (*In This Shit-Heap of a Town*).[22]

Along with Faulkner, Hemingway was another writer who helped García Márquez imagine life in a literary way. As he said, "Hemingway taught me that you can invent whatever you want, as long as you make people believe in it." He learned from Hemingway that key to the creative process was the manner in which a story is told, not just the story itself.[23] And again his friends in Barranquilla and Cartagena helped him to write like Hemingway, as he intended, for example, in "The Woman Who Came at Six O'Clock." He published this short story in 1950. But his friends were not convinced by it. They advised him to soften the pornographic tone and rework the dialogue and the ending. In their opinion, these changes were necessary if he wanted to achieve Hemingway's objective style, which only describes the characters and their conduct as an observer would see them. To comply with how his collaborators interpreted Hemingway's style, García Márquez could not write about the character's interior world and subjectivity, something that he did in some of his early short stories inspired by Kafka's style. The only thing that García Márquez could do was to stick to the facts that the writer could see, as if he were a news reporter. Following his friends' feedback, he revised the short story and published it again two years later in the literary supplement of *El Espectador*. On the same page, he published "Auto-Crítica" ("Self-Criticism").[24] In this letter, he apologized to readers for writing dialogue that was too correct and whose style was more similar to Hemingway's than to his. Therefore, the publication of "The Woman Who Came at Six O'Clock" and "Auto-Crítica" was a pivotal moment in his education as a writer. With the help of his collaborators, he was learning how to apply the literary styles of different authors to his work. By 1952, he could combine Hemingway's realism with the fantastic elements that appeared in Kafka's *The Metamorphosis* (which he read in Latin American Spanish). This combination of realism and fantasy became a key feature of the style of *One Hundred Years of Solitude*.

Along with Hemingway and Faulkner, other writers were a part of García Márquez's literary imagination: Woolf, Huxley, Caldwell, Dos Passos, Joyce,

Sherwood Anderson, Teodoro Dreiser, Robert Ripley, and Curzio Malaparte.[25] He read works by most of them in translations into Latin American Spanish. This detail is important because, like sculptors draw inspiration from live models, his friends recall that García Márquez copied by hand or memorized paragraphs from several of these literary works, such as Woolf's *Orlando* and Joyce's *Ulysses*, which inspired him for aesthetic and technical reasons. Passages from these and other works then lived in his literary imagination and in the imagination of his Latin American peers. The fact that these writers and their works inspired many of García Márquez's peers secured his admission a decade later into literary circles that controlled the New Latin American Novel. These circles included Fuentes—a fan of Faulkner's novels and whose style he followed in his own writing—and Carpentier, who was a fan of *Antigone* and published enthusiastic reviews of representations of this play in Cuba and Haiti in the 1940s and 1950s. García Márquez met both of them in Mexico City, and they became collaborators in the making of *One Hundred Years of Solitude*.

Drawing inspiration from a writer's style is one thing, but doing it effectively is another. To ensure that he used the techniques from these writers correctly, García Márquez began to do something he repeated for the rest of his professional life: he shared his writing in progress with different audiences. He read fragments of "The House" and *Leaf Storm* to his siblings and friends. He would ask them specific questions that ranged from soliciting their advice on whether a word or sentence was necessary to their opinion about the general argument of the text. He also gave his manuscripts to collaborators such as Germán Vargas (to whom he dedicated *Leaf Storm*) and Alfonso Fuenmayor, who assisted him with syntax and proofreading of his texts. He used the technique of sharing his work obsessively during the writing of *One Hundred Years of Solitude*.[26]

García Márquez was learning how to get his work published along the way, because the Barranquilla and Cartagena Groups did not limit their efforts to talk about literature. They also sought to promote their literary agendas in periodicals. For this reason, García Márquez got involved with at least two short-lived publishing ventures, *Comprimido* in Cartagena and *Crónica* in Barranquilla. *Comprimido* claimed to be the world's small newspaper, with a trim size of seventeen by thirteen centimeters and only eight pages in length. For the first time, García Márquez worked as newspaper chief editor. The mission of *Comprimido* was to deliver news to readers in an enjoyable, fast, and compressed manner. But this free newspaper, which printed about five hundred copies daily, lasted only six issues. Next, he worked, along with Fuenmayor, as managing editor of *Crónica*. Local in scope and circulation, this weekly magazine had a print run of two thousand copies, most of which went unsold. It lasted fourteen months and published fifty-two issues. *Crónica* printed sports news, short fiction by the members of the Barranquilla Group (García Márquez included), and North and Latin American writers.[27] But besides these opportunities, the Cartagena and Barranquilla Groups could not help García Márquez publish his literary work with a commercial press.

His first main publishing opportunity came through the poet Álvaro Mutis, about whose work García Márquez wrote in his column in 1951. They became lifetime friends and collaborators. About that time, Mutis told him that an acquisitions editor from Losada, the prestigious Argentine publisher, was looking for new talent in Colombia. García Márquez asked his group friends and one of his siblings for help polishing a book manuscript. Losada received at least two submissions: *El Cristo de espaldas* (*Christ on His Back*) by Eduardo Caballero Calderón and *Leaf Storm*. It only published the former. Losada's manuscript reader, the critic and Spanish exile Guillermo de Torre, rejected *Leaf Storm* because, in his opinion, the Spanish language in this novella was too exotic, along with other flaws. According to the reviewer, these flaws were so obvious that he advised García Márquez to quit writing altogether. This rejection was a major blow for the twenty-four-year-old writer. His group of friends had to convince him that his novella was good, regardless of the gatekeeper's opinion. "Everyone knows that Spaniards are stupid," said Cepeda Samudio to his saddened friend. Counterfactually, had not García Márquez received emotional support from friends in Cartagena and Barranquilla, he might have quit fiction and stuck to daily news coverage and the occasional short story published in a newspaper, as he had done until then. But these groups trained him on how to borrow techniques from classic and mainstream contemporary writers. They also moved him away from intellectual short stories by showing him how to connect fiction writing to real-world life experiences. By the time he left the Caribbean, he had a lifetime connection to these collaborators, who were key supporters as he wrote *One Hundred Years of Solitude*.[28]

The Journalist Succeeds in Bogotá

Back in the country's capital, García Márquez tried his luck at journalism. He worked for the national newspaper *El Espectador*. During these years, he had his first major success, but it was as a news reporter, not as a literary writer. In 1955, he published "The Odyssey of the Surviving Shipwrecked Sailor from the A.R.C. Caldas," a reportage that told the story of a Colombian sailor who survived on a life raft on the open sea for ten days without food and water after his ship capsized in heavy waves in the Caribbean. It ran as a series of installments for fourteen consecutive days. It was "the biggest print run any Colombian newspaper has ever published," as reported to García Márquez's biographer Gerald Martin. To imagine this story, he repeated the writing formula that he learned in writing *Leaf Storm* under the supervision of the Cartagena and Barranquilla Groups. He used as his models an Ancient Greek classic and a successful, contemporary literary work. The first model was Homer's *Odyssey*, and the second was Hemingway's realist novel *The Old Man and the Sea* (1952), which he read in the magazine *Life en Español* in 1953 translated into Latin American Spanish. By writing with such a formula, García Márquez turned what was supposed to be a simple reportage of a shipwrecked sailor into a literary experiment. It is worth noting that José Salgar, the newspaper editor who assigned García Márquez the story, claimed that he had "more brilliant and more skillful journalists" to write it. After the success of that story, García Márquez received an offer to publish his first book and moved away from daily news coverage to writing journalistic series (*series periodísticas*). In these series, García Márquez continued to combine fact reporting with a literary style. Since he could not find a publisher for his new fiction writing, these series were key to his professional growth. Between 1955 and 1959, they were also his only means of literary expression (more on this below).[29]

While he improved his skills as a reporter, García Márquez learned another set of skills from writing film reviews. As a film critic for *El Espectador*, every week he reviewed an average of three movies released in Bogotá. He worked as a critic for about a year and reviewed all kinds of films, from Hollywood and Disney blockbusters to Latin American films and European independent movies. Film reviewing helped him to think about character construction, storytelling, editing, and other technical aspects that he commented on repeatedly.

He developed a special taste for films of Italian neorealism. After World War II, it was one of the most influential trends in cinema. He was attracted to the ways in which neorealism portrayed the lives of the working class and ordinary people facing dire situations as well as magical events. He wrote enthusiastic reviews of the now classic neorealist films *Bicycle Thieves*, *Miracle in Milan*, and *Umberto D.*, among others. About *Bicycle Thieves*, he concluded, it is "the most humane film ever made." About *Miracle in Milan*, he wrote a long and detailed review rather than his customary review of three films in one piece. He was fascinated by its seamless combination of fantasy and reality.

As he put it, this movie "is quite a fairy tale, but set in an unusual environment, and it mixed, in a real manner, the fantastic and the real, to the point that in many cases it is not possible to know where the one ends and where the other begins." At several points in this review, he also pointed out specific examples of how the film made it possible for viewers to believe that the most fantastic of events were completely normal for the characters. And about *Umberto D.*, he wrote, "Its greatness lies in the fidelity with which it resembles life. [Vittorio De Sica and Cesare Zavattini] have shown the tremendous pathos present in the simple act of going to bed."[30]

Thanks to his writing as a film critic, García Márquez learned about the conventions of cinematic language and storytelling, conventions that enriched his literary imagination. And thanks to his writing on neorealist cinema in particular, he nurtured a sensibility for fantastic events happening in ordinary, daily situations. This mixture of magic and reality was crucial to the imagination he needed in order to write *One Hundred Years of Solitude* and became the basis of his own magical realist style.

Although García Márquez could not find publishers for his work, he started to win literary awards. In 1954, he won a short story contest organized by the National Association of Writers and Artists of Colombia. He wrote the award-winning story "One Day after Saturday" in 1953 and it came out the following year in *Magazín Dominical*, the Sunday literary supplement of *El Espectador*, which had published several of his short stories. "One Day after Saturday" tells the story of a half-crazy priest who helps a poor young man leave the village. In this story, Macondo appears for the first time in his writing. But with a crucial difference: Macondo is not yet the name of a village but of a hotel. Central characters in *One Hundred Years of Solitude* participate in the story, especially the widow Rebeca, and Colonel Aureliano Buendía and his brother José Arcadio Buendía are mentioned. Several characters feel solitude (the overarching theme in his future novel) and live in an area of constant heat. In addition, unusual and fantastic events that appear in *One Hundred Years of Solitude* are first narrated in the story, such as the unexplainable death of dozens of birds, the scary presence of the Wandering Jew, and the strong smell of gunpowder on the corpse of Arcadio Buendía. After the award, this story was included in *Tres cuentos colombianos* (*Three Colombian Short Stories*), a book featuring this short story and those of the two runners-up, Guillermo Ruiz Rivas and Carlos Arturo Truque. In the Introduction, the members of the award committee said that García Márquez's "style suits the game of his imagination."[31] With this statement, the committee wanted to praise him for incorporating in Colombian literature some recent trends in contemporary fiction. The other two writers were closer to the traditional *costumbrista* style. Yet this book, unlike his reportage of the sailor, attracted little interest.

His novella *Leaf Storm* attracted a bit more interest. Some critics praised what members of the award committee liked about his short story: for the first time, a work of Colombian literature applied the writing techniques and themes present in Faulkner's novels. Critic Alonso Ángel Restrepo wrote, "*Leaf Storm* will divide the history of our national novel into two stages: the one before this work and the one that will follow." Other critics believed the opposite. An anonymous reviewer criticized it harshly. For him, it reflected the poor state of national literature: "prizes have been given to vulgar and despicable books such as one entitled *Leaf Storm* in which words repeat again and again in each chapter because of the shortage of materials. . . . It is not fair that this shitty novella is qualified as the last word." And, regarding its contents, critics saw the novella as a rural, local story from the country's backward banana region. In reality, the book had little impact beyond art circles in Bogotá. Poor distribution, not surprisingly, did not help. The publication and trajectory of the novella was typical for the average literary book produced in Latin America before the publishing boom of the 1960s. Ediciones S.L.B., the small publisher in Bogotá that released *Leaf Storm*, disappeared shortly after its creation. By contract, S.L.B. agreed to publish four thousand copies. Most likely, it ended up cutting the print run to a quarter of that or less. By contract, too, the publisher was responsible for distributing the book in Colombia and in any Spanish-speaking country. But the truth was that García Márquez had to rely on friends for distribution and sales.[32]

In short, by 1955, only journalism, not literature, had improved García Márquez's professional standing. His reportage on the shipwrecked sailor succeeded not just because of the formidable story of the sailor's odyssey at sea, but also because it actually uncovered a case of corruption and smuggling in the navy. This discovery proved to be politically dangerous. President and military dictator Gustavo Rojas Pinilla had decorated the surviving sailor. Fearing retaliation from the government, *El Espectador* sent García Márquez to Europe for a few weeks as a foreign correspondent. A few weeks turned into years.

Becoming a Latin American Writer in Paris

García Márquez worked as a correspondent for *El Espectador* in Europe from July 1955 until January 1956, when the military government closed the newspaper down for political noncompliance. He decided to stay in Paris until the end of 1957. To survive, he worked as a freelance writer for media in Colombia, Peru, and Venezuela. He also collected used bottles and newspapers for cash, performed as a street singer, and received money and food from friends. Sometimes he went days without eating. Once, as he confessed to one of his siblings, he took party leftovers from a friend's garbage can. This kind of economic hardship, as the Barranquilla and Cartagena Groups taught him, was the perfect real-life experience that, if imagined as a literary plot, could be the basis of a powerful fiction story. So, he found the inspiration for his next story in his daily life, especially as he obsessively awaited for paychecks in the mail for his freelance writing. This theme of waiting for a letter that may never arrive became the basis of the plot for *No One Writes to the Colonel*. His second novella tells the tragic story of a retired and impoverished colonel. He fought in the civil war alongside Colonel Aureliano Buendía, and for years he waited in vain for his war pension to arrive.[33]

Before García Márquez imagined the plot for this novella in Paris, he worked for *El Espectador* from Rome between July and December 1955. He managed to do so before the newspaper closed down and he ran out of money. There, he also studied scriptwriting and montage at the Centro Sperimentale di Cinematografia (Experimental Film Center). This center was then under the influence of screenwriter Zavattini, one of the leading proponents of the neorealist movement in Italian cinema. *No One Writes to the Colonel*, which García Márquez started after his stay in Rome, was the first of his literary works in which the conventions of cinema were key to crafting the story. To imagine it, he opted for direct and unadorned language, a trademark of neorealism's cinematic language. As mentioned earlier, he first studied the narrative techniques of cinema in his film reviews for newspapers. Before he left for Europe, he also collaborated with members of the Barranquilla Group in the production of *The Blue Lobster*, a silent short movie based on a script by García Márquez and Cepeda Samudio.[34] When he arrived in Rome, he was convinced that the narrative techniques of cinema would allow him to communicate his ideas to larger audiences, and he desired to make movies. (On his interest in filmmaking, he was no different from other members of his generation, especially Fuentes, Vargas Llosa, Guillermo Cabrera Infante, and Manuel Puig.) For this reason, he tried to extend his stay in Rome and sought contacts with Cinecittà, then one of the world's leading and largest film studios. But this project fell through and he moved to Paris.

A few weeks later, in January 1956, he found out about the closure of *El Espectador* in Colombia. Out of a job, instead of returning to his home country, he decided to commit to literature as a full-time professional writer. He was motivated to do so. Like previous generations of Latin American writers, living in Paris was a mandatory rite of passage. For them, Paris was the place where writers could nurture their literary imagination. They absorbed themes and motives from the life of a city that had influenced the imagination of classic works of the Western literary tradition, from François Rabelais's *The Life of Gargantua and of Pantagruel* to Honoré de Balzac's *The Human Comedy* to Hemingway's *The Sun Also Rises*.

In Paris, García Márquez worked on the manuscript of "The House" and the story for *In Evil Hour*. But another story developed and grew into *No One Writes to the Colonel*. As in Cartagena and Barranquilla, he did not write in isolation; collaborators gave him feedback as he wrote. Among the collaborators who helped him in Europe were, in particular, Colombian artists Plinio Apuleyo Mendoza and Guillermo Angulo. (They became life companions and gave García Márquez emotional and professional support during the writing of *One Hundred Years of Solitude*.) For feedback on *No One Writes to the Colonel*, he also reached out to the Barranquilla Group. He knew little about cockfighting, which is central to the story, so he sent a questionnaire to group member Enrique Scopell, a cockfighting aficionado, who helped him with fact checking. García Márquez continued to rely on this kind of research assistance during the writing of *One Hundred Years of Solitude*.[35]

His time in Paris shaped his imagination in another way. For the first time in his life, he was exposed to cosmopolitan Latin Americanism. He met with Latin American writers and artists from different generations, and they sometimes gathered around Cuban poet Nicolás Guillén. In his conversations with peers from different countries in the region, García Márquez started to comply with a belief shared by his peers: Latin American literature was not a collection of national literatures but rather a literary tradition built on the existence of a Latin American nation. He also realized that there was an audience for this kind of region-spanning literature. In short, in Paris, he began to convert to "Latin American 'continental nationalism,'" which he fully embraced after arriving in Mexico City a few years later.[36]

His Parisian stay planted the seeds of his Latin American literary imagination, but it was a complete failure to promote this imagination in the region. He had no access to publishers, as was the case for most Latin American writers from previous generations who had lived there. He tried without success to publish *No One Writes to the Colonel* in French. He sent the manuscript in Spanish to Mendoza and to his Barranquilla Group friend Germán Vargas, asking for help. But they could not find a publisher. The cultural magazine

Mito published it in full in 1958, without García Márquez's consent and without paying him royalties. He had to wait four year to see *No One Writes to the Colonel* published as a book, and again, only an obscure publisher agreed to release it. No major press, it seemed, wanted to publish the writer.[37]

A Freelance Journalist in Caracas

García Márquez left Paris in December 1957 after his friend Mendoza offered him a job in Caracas, Venezuela, as editor for *Momento*, a major news magazine. Half a year later, he lost his job when his friend quit his post after a political argument with the magazine's chief editor. The best job García Márquez could find was tabloid journalism. He worked as editor in chief for *Venezuela Gráfica*, also known as "Venezuela pornográfica" because of its sexually charged covers of lightly dressed women. Thanks again to Mendoza, he also worked as a freelancer for *Élite*, a leading news magazine with a weekly print run of one hundred thousand copies. He wrote ten reportages, most of them about Venezuelan society and politics.[38]

While working as a journalist, García Márquez attended a series of lectures on the art of short story writing, given by Dominican Juan Bosch Gaviño, at the Universidad Central de Caracas. The instructor was in political exile and had by then become a well-known writer of short stories with explicit social themes. The year García Márquez attended these lectures, Chilean critic Ricardo Latcham published his influential *Antología del cuento hispano-americano contemporáneo* (*Anthology of the Contemporary Spanish American Short Story*). His book praised Bosch Gaviño for his "mastery as a short story writer, thanks to which he appears in the main anthologies of the continent with brief and dramatic short stories or peasant tales." Bosch Gaviño's expertise on how to write rural short stories helped García Márquez, who at the time was working on *Big Mama's Funeral*, a book of short stories set in the countryside.[39]

Another political exile García Márquez met was Colombian journalist José Font Castro, who, like his compatriot, left the country due to political censorship. In the company of Font Castro and Mendoza, García Márquez hung out at Gran Café de Sabana Grande, a mandatory meeting point for journalists, writers, and painters. There, he saw members of the Sardio Group. This art group functioned very much like the Barranquilla and Cartagena Groups, discussing books, arts, and politics in a bohemian environment. In theory, Sardio could not have been a better fit for García Márquez. Like groups he joined before, Sardio rejected provincial forms of literature and favored its modernization following the conventions of new European literature. Sardio's cosmopolitan imagination and leftist inclinations should have secured García Márquez's admission to the group. But Sardio was oriented to French literature, while García Márquez was more attracted to Anglo-American writers. This difference was an important divide in the imagination of the group and the writer.[40]

During his time in Venezuela, the Sardio Group published five books, all by Venezuelan authors.[41] It also released *Sardio*, a bimonthly literary magazine; it included literary texts by Venezuelan, Latin American, and international authors, as well as notes on films, paintings, and books. It published no works by García Márquez. Yet its second issue premiered a fragment of a novel in progress, *Explosion in a Cathedral*, which years later had a major influence on the imagination and writing of *One Hundred Years of Solitude*. Its author, Cuban Carpentier, had lived in exile in Caracas for the past fourteen years. It is unclear whether the two writers met back then. Given the impact that his novel had on García Márquez in 1964, it is unlikely that the fragment published in *Sardio* attracted his attention in 1958. The fact that he might have overlooked this fragment is not as surprising because the framework of imagination that helped him make sense of Carpentier's book—the framework of the New Latin American Novel—had not fully surfaced in 1958. And when it appeared, it did so in Mexico City, not in Caracas. Only when the ideas of the New Latin American Novel spread throughout Latin America and when Carpentier became part of García Márquez's network in Mexico City in the 1960s did he make sense of *Explosion in a Cathedral* as a cosmopolitan and Latin American reflection about Caribbean history that could help him imagine and write *One Hundred Years of Solitude*.

During his time in Caracas, the daily reality for García Márquez was not the imagination of new literary works but the writing of reportages. He could only write fiction after working hours and on weekends and holidays. In this way, he wrote his third novella, *In Evil Hour*, and the majority of the short stories in *Big Mama's Funeral*. He continued to share his manuscripts for feedback with his connections. Ramón J. Velásquez, director of *El Mundo* newspaper and a political historian, read *No One Writes to the Colonel*, and journalist Ángel Rivero read several of his short stories. Despite these and other good connections, the literary standing of García Márquez in Caracas was weak, as proved by the fate of his short story "Tuesday Siesta." He wrote it during his Easter vacation in 1958 and then sent it to the short story contest organized by *El Nacional*, a top newspaper in the country. His close Venezuelan friend and writer Miguel Otero Silva presided over the jury. Yet his submission was not even long-listed for the award, proving him that his network in Venezuela was weaker than previous networks. Aware that he had no chance as a professional writer in Caracas and with a potential job in his home country, he left after a bit more than a year. He was no longer making these decisions alone; in March 1958, he had married Mercedes Barcha after a three-year, long-distance engagement. She was not only Colombian but also a *costeña*, so they had the same cultural background. Barcha became one of his closest collaborators and a deep influence on the writer as he imagined *One Hundred Years of Solitude* as a Latin American novel deeply rooted in Colombia's Caribbean region.[42]

Working for the Cuban Revolution from New York

After Caracas, García Márquez returned to Colombia. One of his cherished ideas was to open a film school in Barranquilla modeled after the Centro Sperimentale di Cinematografia in Rome. He and his Barranquilla Group friend, Cepeda Samudio, wrote a detailed project for the school. If he had stayed in Barranquilla and opened the school, he could have ended up making movies and being a journalist; the road taken by Cepeda Samudio. But a world historical event altered García Márquez's plans: the Cuban Revolution of 1959. Thanks again to Mendoza, who was in contact with Cuban agents, García Márquez started to work in Bogotá for Prensa Latina, the official state news agency of Cuba, founded after the revolution. The same year his first son, Rodrigo, was born. Between his job and family obligations, García Márquez had little time to write and only managed to draft the story "Big Mama's Funeral."

Two years later, in 1961, Prensa Latina appointed him chief of its headquarters in New York City, and he moved there with his family. This new job, he complained, was time consuming. He started at 10 a.m. and often stayed until 4 a.m. He had no time for fiction writing. His wife complained, too. She said that his writing, in addition to the long hours at work, was affecting their marriage. As García Márquez put in a letter to his Barranquilla friend Germán Vargas, living like this was "impossible" and could only lead to "madness or divorce." He was hoping to finish revising *In Evil Hour*, then entitled *A la buena de Dios* (*God Would Tell*), for an award submission. His correspondence mentioned no other literary project, not even "The House." His letters with friends of the Barranquilla Group and Mendoza dealt mostly with Cuban-American politics and the production of a documentary about the Barranquilla Carnival. And he grumbled repeatedly about how little time he had to work on the documentary, including the fact that he had to disassemble his editing studio every time he got some work done to prevent his son Rodrigo from messing with the equipment.[43]

The demands of his job for Prensa Latina and family responsibilities left him no time for joining artistic groups either. But thanks to his job he made new connections that proved useful years later, especially Mexican writer Juan García Ponce, a gatekeeper who helped him access the cultural circles in Mexico City, and Chilean writer and critic Luis Harss, who interviewed him at a key juncture in the making of *One Hundred Years of Solitude* and helped circulate chapters of his novel in progress among Latin American publishers and writers.[44]

In April 1961, halfway through García Márquez's stay in New York, the United States launched the Bay of Pigs invasion, an unsuccessful military operation in Cuba. After this event, the work environment in the New York office of Prensa Latina became increasingly tense. He resigned a month later, afraid that political purges of revolutionaries in Cuba would reach him. He was also fed up with full-time journalism. Instead of returning to Colombia, he decided to move to Mexico City. To get there, he and his family took a bus south through the United States. They did so after the Freedom Riders started their rides on interstate buses into the segregated southern states. In Mississippi and other states, he saw firsthand the efforts of civil rights activists to end racial segregation. This rural, socially divided, and violent territory was the land of Faulkner's imagination. García Márquez noticed the literary similarities between Faulkner's land and his own land in Colombia's Caribbean region. He could see that the characters, themes, and situations of Faulkner's novels were not so distant from his native Aracataca. On the bus, he thought about his future, too. As his correspondence shows, he was not optimistic about it. In a letter written days prior to his trip to Mexico City, his mood was somber, "the prospects, to be concrete and without literature, do not seem to be very good."[45] Things turned out to be completely the opposite.

Becoming a Professional Writer in Mexico City

García Márquez could not foresee that the death of a writer would secure his admission into Mexico City's exclusive cultural circle just days after leaving the United States. The dead was Ernest Hemingway. García Márquez learned about his passing upon arriving in the city in early July 1961, and he quickly wrote the essay "A Man Has Died a Natural Death" for *México en la Cultura.*

Thus, his first piece of writing on Mexican soil was included in the literary supplement of *Novedades de México*, a leading national newspaper that reached over one hundred thousand readers weekly among the middle and upper classes.[46] This magazine featured his essay in a special issue on Hemingway with several collaborations, including one by Spanish exile and writer Max Aub. García Márquez had spent the last decade reading Hemingway's works, writing about them and his life, and especially studying his writing techniques and applying them to his own work in fiction and in journalism. Hemingway, in short, had become one of the voices in his literary imagination. This connection and knowledge about him paid off for García Márquez. His essay gave him access to "literary circles" and to befriend "the cream of the intelligentsia," to whom he gave copies of his books.[47] His network of Colombian friends in town, which included Mutis, Angulo, and Rodrigo Arenas Betancourt, also helped him access cultural circles.

More broadly, his arrival in Mexico could not have been more fortunate since the country was undergoing rapid economic and social modernization, including the expansion of its culture industry. Mexico City now rivaled Madrid, Paris, and Havana in attracting the Latin American intelligentsia and offered its members financial and organizational incentives. García Márquez was one of its beneficiaries. He had full access for the first time in his career to influential gatekeepers in cinema and literature. Mexico City had the largest film industry in the Spanish-speaking world and was about to become one of the centers of the New Latin American Novel.

This mixture of personal and external circumstances had three effects on García Márquez. First, he deepened his commitment to writing Latin American literature. Second, he could finally work as a full-time writer. And third, he adapted his literary style to suit the demands of the New Latin American Novel. The network that channeled these effects was the so-called Mafia (*La Mafia*). This group was born in the early 1960s as a Latin American Bloomsbury. The original Bloomsbury was a group of influential artists and intellectuals in England that included Virginia Woolf, John Maynard Keynes, and E. M. Forster, among others.[48] In the case of the Mafia, its members were mostly Mexican artists and intellectuals, and its leader was best-selling writer Carlos Fuentes. He played "a major role in bringing García Márquez to world attention," as he did for writers like Donoso.[49] Fuentes worked tirelessly to connect them to gatekeepers of the publishing industry in and beyond Latin America. He could do this so successfully because he had a vision. He was a leading ideologue of the New Latin American Novel and claimed that the literature of the region was no longer peripheral or inferior to its French,

American, or Russian counterparts. For him, not only was Latin American literature more central, but also its novels were changing world literature. He believed wholeheartedly that it was because writers in the region had found the balance between cosmopolitanism and Latin Americanism. These two principles finally complemented each other. It is important to point out that Fuentes promoted his vision in two ways: as a writer and as a critic of mainstream contemporary literature. In his own literary works, he imagined his international best seller *The Death of Artemio Cruz* (1962) as a hybrid of Latin American and cosmopolitan influences. The former included *Journey Back to the Source* by Carpentier and *The Underdogs* and *Pedro Páramo* by Mexican writers Marino Azuela and Rulfo, respectively. The latter included Orson Welles's *Citizen Kane* and Faulkner's writing techniques of multiple voices and perspectives. (García Márquez had used these techniques in *Leaf Storm*.)

As a literary critic, Fuentes launched a campaign to put Latin American cosmopolitanism at the center of the region's literature. Two essays stand out among his numerous writings of literary criticism. In 1962, he published a four-page essay entitled "Faulkner: entre el dolor y la nada" ("Faulkner: Between Pain and Nothingness"). It came out in the supplement *La Cultura en México*—the successor to *México en la Cultura*—and it was included in a special issue as an homage to the recently deceased writer. In his essay, Fuentes argued that the cosmopolitan Faulkner was also a Latin American writer (a belief that García Márquez nurtured after joining the Barranquilla and Cartagena Groups). And Fuentes credited Faulkner for helping him to find the connection with the language of neo-baroque. According to Fuentes, this poetic and elaborate kind of Spanish was the true language of Latin American literature. Two years later, he published another influential essay in *La Cultura en México*, "La nueva novela latinoamericana" ("The New Latin American Novel"). Written as an art manifesto, he proclaimed that the cosmopolitan and Latin American works of Vargas Llosa, Cortázar, and Carpentier were the beginning of a new era for the region's literature.[50]

Fuentes started to promote this vision in his thirties, when he was already a mainstream professional writer and best-selling international author. He was also married to Rita Macedo, a famous Mexican actor, which facilitated his easy access to the country's powerful film industry. By the time García Márquez arrived in Mexico City, Fuentes was in an advantageous position to recruit collaborators to the Mafia. Among its members were the poet Mutis, García Márquez's close friend, as well as new and established Mexican and Latin American writers such as Mexican Rulfo and Chilean Donoso, artists such as Spanish filmmaker Luis Buñuel, critics such as Emmanuel Carballo, and film producers such as Gustavo Alatriste.[51] Most members were also in their thirties, quite mobile internationally, and hence they often extended invitations to visit Mexico City to prestigious non-Latin American writers, scholars, donors, and publishers.

When Fuentes and García Márquez met, it was love at first sight. As a friend put it, García Márquez was "mesmerized" with Fuentes. Years before they met, Mutis, who moved to Mexico City in 1956, gave Fuentes a copy of his friend's *Leaf Storm*. So even before they met, Fuentes was promoting García Márquez's work by publishing several of its short stories in *Revista Mexicana de Literatura*. Fuentes also recommended his colleague's work to gatekeepers such as Argentine critic Emir Rodríguez Monegal, just months before he became chief editor of *Mundo Nuevo*, the magazine of the New Latin American Novel, which also championed the promotion of *One Hundred Years of Solitude* before its release.[52]

Beyond the affinity between the two writers, García Márquez met the criteria for admission to the Mafia. First, its members admired innovative modernist writers like Faulkner, Hemingway, Woolf, and Joyce for their approach to novels. Second, Mafia members were leftists and supported the Cuban Revolution with enthusiasm. And third, they produced their own version of the cosmopolitan Latin Americanism that previous generations of writers initiated in the 1920s; thus, the Mafia rejected literary works that were too provincial or focused on indigenous peoples. García Márquez met all admission requirements. First, the Barranquilla and Cartagena Groups cultivated his taste for modernist writers and helped him to effectively bring modernist writing techniques to his fiction. Second, he had just worked for revolutionary Cuba's news agency. And third, in Paris, he had started to develop a cosmopolitan Latin American viewpoint.

The Mafia offered García Márquez a full professional setting for the first time in his career. Suddenly, he occupied a privileged position now that commercial publishers in Latin America, Europe, and the United States were becoming increasingly interested in Latin American writers as a group. For example, the summer of 1965, when he was about to start writing *One Hundred Years of Solitude*, he attended a conference in Chichén Itzá, Mexico. Attendees included writers Fuentes, Rulfo, Sábato, Donoso, Nicanor Parra, Augusto Monterroso, Lillian Hellman, and best-selling anthropologist Oscar Lewis. International gatekeepers of the publishing industry also attended: William Styron (co-founder of the prestigious *The Paris Review*), Rodríguez Monegal (editor of the upcoming *Mundo Nuevo* magazine), publishers Alfred Knopf and Seix Barral, literary agent Carmen Balcells, and donor Rodman

Rockefeller. Thanks to professional meetings like this one, García Márquez further understood what kind of novels publishers were looking for and readers were consuming. He also learned about the direction in which the literary market was going, as he heard peers talking about their work in progress (and he told them about his writer's block with a novel about the village of Macondo and the Buendía family). An interview he gave months later shows that he had acquired an insider's knowledge about the state of Latin American literature. It was precisely at this moment when he started writing *One Hundred Years of Solitude* and was struggling to change his literary style to adapt it to the demands of international gatekeepers and readers (more on this in the next chapter).[53]

However, the professional path of García Márquez in Mexico City could have gone in a completely different direction. He arrived in the city without a work visa and worked illegally for a few months. Spanish exile Max Aub, who read his essay on Hemingway's death, hired him to teach a course on Colombian literature for Radio Universidad. Then, he found a job as editor of magazines *Sucesos para Todos* and *La Familia*.

Sucesos para Todos was the weekly with the broadest circulation in the country. It featured easy-to-read and engaging texts and images about international and national news, historical events and characters, and literature and art. It also had sections of humor, horoscope, TV channels, and so on. *La Familia* was a popular monthly magazine among middle-class housewives. It included, among other items, sections on domestic economy, marriage, cooking, health, hygiene, and childrearing. García Márquez's friend, Mutis, arranged an interview between him and businessman Gustavo Alatriste, who had just bought both magazines. Alatriste hired him and sponsored his work visa. He was looking for an all-terrain editor and journalist, whose job was to manage the production of the magazines and to increase sales. García Márquez modernized the magazines, opting for more visual layouts and creating new sections. In addition he did a significant amount of anonymous writing and selected for publication short pieces by classic writers like Rubén Darío, Santa Teresa de Jesús, Antonio Machado, and García Lorca. Excerpts of *One Thousand and One Nights*, an important influence in García Márquez's imagination and in *One Hundred Years of Solitude*, were published in *Sucesos para Todos* for months in 1962. In *La Familia*, he added notes about popular figures such as Shakespeare and Chaplin and a section on "sentimental literature." For both magazines, he supervised the work of linotypists and printers, with whom he hung out after hours, as he did back in Barranquilla and Cartagena. Four years later, several of these workers attended the first public reading of *One Hundred Years of Solitude*, when he was testing people's reactions to the novel among the broadest possible public before sending it to the publisher.[54]

García Márquez's work for these magazines paid off, especially for *Sucesos para Todos*, whose sales rose and by May 1962 was selling over seventy thousand copies weekly. His executive position was well paid and easy for him because he had learned the necessary professional skills in Colombia and Venezuela. Indeed, after interviewing García Márquez for the job, Alatriste said to Mutis about his friend, "This guy's too good." So the overqualified García Márquez could have done magazine journalism for life. His correspondence reveals his satisfaction with a good, middle-class life. But he was ashamed of working for these magazines. He regarded this job as the lowest form of journalism. For this reason, he made sure that his name never appeared as a staff member in any issue and that he signed no text with his name. Although he felt that magazine journalism was humiliating, the truth is that it equipped him with a powerful professional skill: he learned firsthand about the taste of the rising urban middle class in Mexico and abroad since *La Familia* also had an international edition sold in other Latin American countries. The middle classes were, then, the main consumer of New Latin American Novels. He had no other choice but learn about their taste if he wanted to keep the job. He had to understand what kind of contents sold (and did not) to increase magazine sales.[55]

García Márquez took the job in *La Familia* and *Sucesos para Todos* to support his family and to enter the Mexican film industry. The magazines' owner, Alatriste, was one of Mexico's leading film producers. (Like Fuentes, he was also married to another famous Mexican actor, Silvia Pinal.) In particular, he was the producer of *Viridiana* and *The Exterminating Angel* by Spanish filmmaker Buñuel. The movies won awards at the Cannes Film Festival in 1961 and 1962, respectively. Buñuel lived in Paris from 1925 to 1930, where he made his first films under the influence of French surrealism. This surrealist style also influenced Latin American writers Carpentier, Arturo Uslar Pietri, and Miguel Ángel Asturias, who lived in the city at the same time as Buñuel. This style was the basis of magical realist art mixing realism and the fantastic (see chapter 1). The surrealist cinema of Buñuel—in which mundane, real events turn into sometimes magical and sometimes absurd situations—was making its way into the literary imagination of artists like Fuentes, García Márquez, and others. So García Márquez did not wait long to reach out to the filmmaker with ideas. In 1962, he sent him a script for a comedy, "Es tan fácil que hasta los hombres pueden" ("It's so Easy that Even Men Can"). Simultaneously, he wanted to use Mexican cinema to promote his poorly received literary work. For example, he tried to sell the rights of *No One Writes to the Colonel* and found a purchaser. Other producers were interested in adapting *Leaf Storm* and four short stories in *Big Mama's Funeral*. But all these projects fell through. Finally, in April 1963, after almost two years of magazine journalism, he became "a professional writer," as he happily told in a letter to a friend.

This career move occurred when Alatriste requested García Márquez to write two film scripts full-time for a year, meaning that he would no longer work as magazine editor.[56]

Alatriste knew that García Márquez was a skillful writer of rural stories. He had already written three novellas set in the Colombian countryside and the year before he published a book of short stories with a similar setup. During his Easter vacation in 1963, he wrote a script provisionally entitled *El Charro* (*The Cowboy*), which two years later came out as *Tiempo de Morir* (*Time to Die*). This film tells the story of a cowboy who returns to his home village after eighteen years in prison and faces death threats from the sons of the man whose assassination put him behind bars. Alatriste was persuaded by this powerful story. García Márquez's skills at writing stories set in the countryside became handy as he was asked to adapt other Mexican stories as well as his own stories, which was how scriptwriting offered him a new way of learning about the literary techniques of other writers. In 1964, he had already read Rulfo's *Pedro Páramo* and was also adapting one of his short stories, *El Gallo de Oro* (*The Golden Cockerel*), to cinema. His close reading of Rulfo's writing helped him see a connection between the Mexican and Colombian countryside. And the writer who helped him bridge the connection between these two Latin American settings was once again Faulkner, whose writing techniques Rulfo used in his own work. For García Márquez, this learning experience was useful in adapting one of his short stories into a film: *There Are No Thieves in This Village*. Its cast included several members of the Mafia—Rulfo, Buñuel, Leonora Carrington, Carlos Monsiváis, and García Márquez himself.

As with his literary writing, García Márquez did not venture into scriptwriting alone. Fuentes collaborated with him on the adaptation of *The Golden Cockerel* and other scripts. Their collaboration led to hours of conversations about the craft of writing and the technical differences between literature and cinema. And as García Márquez did with his literary manuscripts, he mailed his film scripts to friends in Barranquilla for feedback. His experience in cinema also expanded his professional network. Involved with the Mexican film industry was a couple who had a crucial influence on the imagination and writing of *One Hundred Years of Solitude*: the García Ascots, Jomí and María Luisa, to whom he dedicated his novel.[57]

Despite all his connections and skills as a scriptwriter, García Márquez did not succeed in the Mexican film industry, although he did get close. In the early summer of 1963, he was planning a trip to Los Angeles to search locations for the two movie scripts he was working on for producer Alatriste. García Márquez knew this was a great opportunity. As he wrote in a letter to his friend and writer Mendoza, if these scripts worked, "I will be on the other side" and "I will get a good name in Mexican cinema, and then I will have no problems." By September 1963, he already had his eyes on Hollywood and he wrote to his friend that he was becoming fashionable in film and receiving money. But his situation changed suddenly. Alatriste started to have problems financing his films. So he told García Márquez that he would continue to sponsor his work visa but he had to find a job elsewhere. Thanks to his Mafia friends, he found a job in the advertising agency Walter Thompson. But working in advertising was a major setback for him. A few months before, he had been a "professional writer" for the first time after decades of hardship and he was even dreaming about Hollywood.[58]

For any author aspiring to become a professional writer, an advertising job would have been a terrible career move. For García Márquez in particular, advertising brought back sad memories. When he arrived in Mexico City in 1961, he did some work for an advertising agency without a work visa and even took a one-month job as the editor of a supermarket magazine. Then, he found the job in Alatriste's magazines for which he was overqualified. He could not afford to be choosy with a pregnant wife and a three-year-old son. His second son, Gonzalo, was born in early 1962. By the end of the next year, he lost his job with Alatriste. Now, he was an adman. As his friends recall and his correspondence suggests, the unsuccessful scriptwriter and struggling fiction writer grew anxious and depressed about his future.

But his advertising job, like his magazine journalism, was another opportunity to learn new skills that entered the writing of *One Hundred Years of Solitude*. He became familiar with cutting-edge marketing techniques used to attract the attention of a rapidly expanding Mexican middle class, the preferred consumer of New Latin American Novels. He had already started to learn how to talk to this audience as the editor of *La Familia* and *Sucesos para Todos*. By 1966, when he was writing *One Hundred Years of Solitude*, he was quite skillful at marketing himself and his work:

My name, sir, is Gabriel García Márquez. I'm sorry: I don't like the name either.... I was born in Aracataca, Colombia.... My sign is Pisces and my wife is Mercedes. Those are the two most important things that have happened in my life, because thanks to them, at least until now, I've managed to survive by writing. . . . My true vocation is that of magician [but] I've had to take refuge in the solitude of literature. . . . In my case, being a writer is a huge achievement because I'm very bad at writing. I've had to subject myself to an atrocious discipline in order to finish half a page after eight hours of work. . . . I'm so stubborn that I've managed to publish four books in twenty years. . . . The fifth [*One Hundred Years of Solitude*], which I'm writing right now, is coming out slower than the others, because between my debtors and a neuralgia I have very little free time. I never talk about literature because I don't know what it is, and besides I'm convinced that the world would be the same without it. On the other hand, I'm convinced that it would be completely different if the police didn't exist. I think, therefore, that I'd have been more useful to humanity if instead of being a writer I were a terrorist.[59]

This is how García Márquez presented himself to readers of *Los diez mandamientos* (*The Ten Commandments*). This volume included his short story "There Are No Thieves in This Village" (adapted into a film a few months earlier) and those of another nine Latin American writers of three generations. This book, an inexpensive paperback, became a best seller in Argentina in the months prior to the release of *One Hundred Years of Solitude*. This was the first time hundreds of potential consumers of his fifth book came across the name of a writer who introduced himself as someone who disliked his name, was a very bad writer, did not know what literature was, and believed he should be a terrorist. These, of course, were not simple personal facts but an author's biography infused with literary catchphrases, the same kind of marketing catchphrases that have made the prose of *One Hundred Years of Solitude* so entertaining to its millions of readers. As the next chapter shows, he used his marketing skills to write his novel as a best seller. Learning marketing conventions such as slogan design proved to be quite advantageous for him when his goal was to get readers to turn to the next page. He also built on his marketing skills to advertise the novel in unconventional ways. Statements such as "my wife writes my novels" made the headlines of Latin American newspapers during his book tour in Latin America in August and September of 1967.

García Márquez knew that publicity was key to creating a literary brand. Fuentes helped him learned this new skill. Each one of Fuentes's novels was a media event and so were the novels by other New Latin American Novel writers such as Vargas Llosa. García Márquez started to correspond with him no later than January 1966. Two months later, García Márquez declared, "I like publicity. I love to see my picture . . . in a European newspaper." The following month, he explained in a letter to Mendoza that writers had to control the means of literary communication, which was what *Mundo Nuevo* magazine sought to do—to shape the way in which readers had to consume Latin American novels. García Márquez was so skillful at putting to work the skills he learned from his job in advertising that some opponents started to call him "García Marketing."[60]

Before *One Hundred Years of Solitude* brought him success, García Márquez had no time to write literature. From 1962 to 1965, he worked as a magazine editor, scriptwriter, and publicist and was also the father of two children. Months passed and his anxiety grew, as he could not write anything new for publication. In June 1963, he declined an invitation from leading Colombian intellectual Germán Arciniegas. He told him that he had written no literature in two years, and that it was impossible to do it now because he was really busy writing several film scripts for the next twelve months. When he had time and the mind to do so, he worked sporadically on the story that would become *The Autumn of the Patriarch*. When Alatriste told him to find another job in the fall of 1963, he kept his hope of working in cinema by collaborating on several scripts with Luis Alcoriza, a Spanish exile and scriptwriter for Buñuel. (García Márquez gave Alcoriza the corrected galley proofs of *One Hundred Years of Solitude* as a gift to thank him for his help during these difficult moments.) In 1964, things only worsened. The U.S. government denied García Márquez a travel visa and by September 1965 Buñuel had clearly distanced himself from Alatriste. García Márquez had no other choice but to return to literature. His next project was *One Hundred Years of Solitude*. Counterfactually, if he had succeeded in the Mexican film industry, he would not have written it. But during the fall of 1965, his personal situation and the state of the New Latin American Novel were both quite different than two years before, when he lost his scriptwriting job. Back then, a gloomy García Márquez confessed in an interview with literary critic Emmanuel Carballo, "The biography of Colonel Aureliano Buendía . . . will never be written." After thirteen years, he had finally given up on writing *One Hundred Years of Solitude*.[61]

THE TRANSNATIONAL LIFE OF A MANUSCRIPT AND ITS TROUBLED WRITER

Before 1965, *One Hundred Years of Solitude* was just a group of loosely connected ideas in manuscript form. Inside this changing manuscript, which some years was five hundred sheets long and others was eight hundred, García Márquez mined ideas for three novellas, one book of short stories, and dozens of journalistic pieces. Upon his arrival in Mexico City, he continued to refer to "my old project of a book of fantastic short stories," for which he had "six or seven ideas." One of these stories was about the "social drama of a poor town." He had imagined some of these ideas for years and he eventually merged them into a single narrative: *One Hundred Years of Solitude*. The novel's original idea came to him around 1950 when he was a member of the Barranquilla and Cartagena Groups: a story that would take place inside a house. "I wanted," as he said, "the story never to come out of it; the town, the country, the world would be known through the reflections that entered into the house; through the family members that inhabited it; generations and generations would pass but always inside the house." Not surprisingly, the original manuscript was titled "The House." He carried it with him to six countries on three continents and discussed it with members of all the art circles he joined.[62] So how did his transnational movements, skills acquisition, and networks shape the evolution of the manuscript between 1950 and 1965?

In February 1950, the twenty-two-year-old writer traveled to his hometown of Aracataca for the first time since he was about ten years old. It was a transformative moment for his literary imagination. Childhood memories of his grandparents' house, family stories, and the town came back to life vividly. After his return from Aracataca, he started writing and publishing fragments of "The House." At this stage, it was "the story of a family told during the time the house lasted." He ended up saving this idea for the final novel, except for the fact that the story begins before the family has built the house, an idea he borrowed from Carpentier's novel *Explosion in a Cathedral* (see next chapter.) The first of these fragments appeared in June 1950. It came out in *Crónica* magazine and was titled "The Buendía House: Notes for a Novel." As its opening passage shows, the main character is the house: "The house is fresh; wet at night, even in the summer. It is in the north, at the end of the only street in town, elevated on a high and solid concrete curb. The doorjamb high, without stairs; the long hall noticeably unfurnished, with two full-length windows onto the street, is perhaps the only thing that distinguishes it from the other houses in town."[63]

The piece, 771 words in total, opens with two paragraphs that describe the house's location and its size, layout, objects, and atmosphere. Next, it introduces the character of Colonel Aureliano Buendía, who has just returned from the civil war, in which, we are told, many of the Buendías died. The rest of the text describes the reconstruction of the house after the war. In general, a strong feeling of nostalgia and the passage of time impregnate the text. Along with references to the house, the colonel, and the Buendía family, the piece refers to key elements in *One Hundred Years of Solitude*: the ever present rain and wind, the suffocating heat, plaster figures of saints, and the destruction of the family house. There are, of course, meaningful differences. Solitude (Soledad) is the name of Colonel Buendía's wife. In the novel, solitude is not a character but the main theme. There are meaningful absences, too. The village has no name.

"The Buendía House: Notes for a Novel" was the first of at least fifteen pieces published in 1950 and 1951 that might have come from the manuscript of "The House."[64] As mentioned earlier, before *One Hundred Years of Solitude* became a novel, it was a group of loosely connected ideas. And these early pieces of "The House" confirm this impression. They read more as small vignettes of daily life in a rural village, in which the narrator seems to be a child. Arguably, García Márquez was adopting the viewpoint of a child to recall more easily his childhood memories of people, scenarios, and events in his hometown of Aracataca. These pieces also include for the first time characters that appear in *One Hundred Years of Solitude*, such as Remedios, Rebeca, and Meme, as well as others that finally never developed, such as Evangelina and Natanael. The texts contain elements that would be central in his novel: the sudden passage of time, a deep feeling of nostalgia for the past, characters leaving and returning to the family house, the permanent heat and dust in the village, the division between the world of men, who are absent and violent, and the world of women, who are domestic and active (especially by taking care of the household), and characters that seem to have been alive forever.

Based on these published fragments, "The House" was, stylistically, a work of rural realist fiction with undertones of U.S. gothic fiction. The presence of the gothic in García Márquez's writing has not really been studied, as researchers and readers have paid more attention to magical realism. Yet references to ghosts and the supernatural abound not only in the surviving texts of "The House" but also in numerous columns and short stories that he published during his early years of journalism in Cartagena and Barranquilla; he even published a play in three acts called "El congreso de los fantasmas" ("The Congress of Ghosts"). In particular, in the surviving texts from "The House," a boy is abandoned in a closet of the house, dust accumulates on things over the centuries, a daughter preserves clean clothes of her dead mother in a trunk, there is a "mysterious silence" in the house latrine, two chairs in the living room are the only surviving "beings" after the passage of the "great wind," and a nephew writes a letter to an aunt who died twenty years ago. The rural gothic is also present in several surviving manuscripts that García Márquez wrote in the early 1950s, especially in two unpublished short stories: "Olor antiguo" ("Old Smell") and "El ahogado que nos traía caracoles" ("The Drowned Man that Brought Us Snails"). (The latter short story includes a character named Úrsula acting as head of the family, as she does in *One Hundred Years of Solitude*.)[65]

García Márquez did not imagine these stories on his own. The rural gothic was a theme present in several of the works that the Barranquilla and Cartagena Groups recommended García Márquez to read. One of these works was the nineteenth-century novel *The House of the Seven Gables* by U.S. writer Nathaniel Hawthorne. As the next chapter explains, when García Márquez was writing the first chapters of *One Hundred Years of Solitude*, he continued to imagine that the gothic undertone of "The House" should be part of his novel.

In 1952, García Márquez claimed to have visited Aracataca again. His description of his hometown aligns with the ideas present in his texts from "The House," especially references to the passage of time and death. "I just returned from Aracataca," he wrote, and "it continues to be a dusty village, full of silence and dead people. Bleak; perhaps too much, with its old colonels dying in the backyard, under the last banana bush, and an impressive number of sixty-year-old virgins, rusty, sweating the last vestiges of sex under the drowsiness of two in the afternoon. This time I ventured to go, but I think I will not return alone."

He wrote this description in the letter "Auto-Crítica," which, as mentioned earlier, he published during a transformative moment in his education as a writer: his new trip to Aracataca and the nearby region of Valley of Upar. In his letter, he announced that he was planning to use the materials of these visits for "The House," a novel of seven hundred sheets that he was working on and expected to finish in two years.[66]

His friends in Cartagena and Barranquilla recall that the "tenacious" García Márquez was writing the novel and walked around with a portfolio full of sheets, which he claimed was his novel. For feedback on his text in progress, he relied on friends in his two groups and common readers such as his sister Aida. To these collaborators, he read out loud fragments of the manuscript and questioned them about whether a given sentence or word was necessary to maintain the narrative flow. But he soon started to face technical problems and had to put the manuscript aside. "My great difficulty," he said, "was always to find the tone and the language for this story to be believed. I was moving forward when I concluded that the book was not coming out, I couldn't do it, I really didn't have enough maturity, neither the technical knowledge, nor the experience; I was full of limitations of many sorts to be able to write a book in which everything happened."[67]

The limitations García Márquez faced were not only technical but also professional; no press wanted to publish his work. Had he managed to publish "The House" in the 1950s, it would have faced the same path of *Leaf Storm* and *No One Writes to the Colonel*. Those two books were released by small publishers and had limited distribution in Colombia and none in the rest of Latin America. They received some national recognition but nothing international. The early works of García Márquez were also facing history. Colombian literature was a minor player in the region's literature, unlike Mexican or Argentine literature. No work of Colombian literature succeeded internationally before *One Hundred Years of Solitude* did, with the exception of novels *María* (1867), whose success was greatly due to its serialization in newspapers, and *The Vortex* (1924). Thus, had García Márquez published "The House" before the 1960s, critics and readers would not have received it as a New Latin American Novel. Rather, they would have labeled it as a work of Caribbean literature with mixtures of gothic and rural realism. Instead, the manuscript and the writer left for Europe in 1955.

In Paris, García Márquez resumed work on "The House." One of the things he did was soften the influence of Faulkner and start to add the sober language of Hemingway and Italian neorealism. He also began work on the story for *In Evil Hour*. Yet another story, that of *No One Writes to the Colonel*, emerged with force. And he decided to follow that thread rather than "The House" or *In Evil Hour*.[68] When he arrived in Mexico City, he had in mind a collection of fantastic stories, including one with "flying carpets," which he abandoned. By 1963, he started to work occasionally on the idea that would become *The Autumn of the Patriarch*, which he set aside in 1965 to work on the manuscript of *One Hundred Years of Solitude*.

Despite his personal and professional hardships, García Márquez overcame in Mexico City the two most important problems that had blocked his imagination and forced him to put the manuscript of "The House" aside. The first was that he did not have people to actively promote his work. The second was that he did not know how to write a novel. The organizational problem was solved when he joined the Mafia and he received support from important gatekeepers of the publishing industry, especially the literary agent Balcells and Sudamericana Press, as shown in the previous chapter. Regarding the technical problem, before 1965, García Márquez's writing oscillated between two styles: the journalistic and the literary. Throughout the 1950s, his journalistic style became more narrative (an important skill for reporting on current affairs). Simultaneously, his literary style became more and more terse and parsimonious. This duality of styles meant that,

before 1965, García Márquez used his literary skills more freely in his reporting than in his fiction writing.

Only when he started *One Hundred Years of Solitude* did he realize that
he had put too much pressure on himself to write his fiction in a style that
was not fully his. He had written *Leaf Storm* in the baroque style of Faulkner. Then, from the mid-1950s onward, he opted for more simplicity and
removing all ornaments, as Gertrude Stein and his revered Hemingway had
done for the American style. García Márquez also admired the capacity to
describe bare life in movies of Italian neorealism. So, he set to follow the
same style in *No One Writes to the Colonel*, *In Evil Hour*, and most of the short
stories in *Big Mama's Funeral*. He stripped down sentences and made them
less poetic, overlaying them with the narrative directness of newspaper writing. For this style, he also found inspiration in Hemingway, who, like him,
worked as a journalist.

In his journalistic writing, García Márquez did the opposite: he drew from
literary techniques. Given the success of his reportage about the odyssey of the
shipwrecked sailor, he discovered the power of writing journalistic reportages
with a literary prose. He continued to use this formula in his freelance pieces
for *Momento* and *Élite*, which were published in Caracas. The style in these
pieces, reminiscent of Faulkner, mixes short and long subordinate and main
clauses. In these journalistic pieces, he started to overcome the technical problems with his style that paved the way for the writing of *One Hundred Years of
Solitude*. To illustrate this point about the similarities between the style of his
reportages for *Élite* and the novel, compare one passage on page 30 of "Nagy:
¿héroe o traidor?" ("Nagy: Hero or Traitor?"), a reportage on the Hungarian
Revolution and execution of Prime Minister Imre Nagy, and the opening sentence of *One Hundred Years of Solitude*.

On the banks of the Danube, in front of the ruins of the Elisabeth Bridge
blown up by the Germans, an official van with two loudspeakers spread all
day proclamations against Nagy. (Length in Spanish: 29 words.)

Many years later, as he faced the firing squad, Colonel Aureliano Buendía was
to remember that distant afternoon when his father took him to discover ice.
(Length in Spanish: 28 words.)

These passages have a similar rhythm and follow the same structure: three
interconnected clauses. First, there is a short introductory clause: "On the
banks of the Danube" and "Many years later." Next, the second intermediate

clause opens with the same preposition in Spanish: "in front of" ("frente"). The goal of the second clause is to complement the first clause with more precise information. And finally, the main informative clause follows. It explains the action involving the main actors and, to do so, the clause uses a similar sequence: character, time, and character. In the *Élite* reportage, the sequence turns into the van, all day, and Nagy. In *One Hundred Years of Solitude*, the sequence is the colonel, distant afternoon, and father, plus an object: ice. In both passages, the first two clauses compel readers to travel; in the *Élite* reportage they travel in space and in *One Hundred Years of Solitude* they travel in time and space. García Márquez was able to create this sequence in the first two clauses of the reportage using sixteen words. He only needed eight words, that is, half, to do the same in the novel. When compared, these passages are telling proof of how much his writing technique improved over the years and how much it was due to his writing of literary reportages.

The duality of his journalistic and literary style is even more apparent if we compare a passage from his *Élite* reportage on Nagy, written in 1958, and a passage from his novella *No One Writes to the Colonel*, written the year before.

> In the freezing fog of November, those two men who had fought together, who had suffered together and together had triumphed and had been defeated, went out at dawn on two different paths. Nagy to the Yugoslavian embassy, Nadar to power.

> Sabas opened a cupboard in the office wall. He uncovered a jumbled interior: riding boots piled up, stirrups and reins, and an aluminum pail full of riding spurs. Hanging from the upper part, half a dozen umbrellas and a lady's parasol. The colonel was thinking of the debris from some catastrophe.[69]

The passage in this reportage reminds us more of a Faulkner novel, with its poetic language and rhythmic combination of verbs. The passage from his novella resembles more direct and concise fact reporting, as if we were reading (or watching) a sober description of events. On a personal level, this duality of styles, between the baroque narrative flow of his reportages and the terse literary language of his fiction writing, tormented García Márquez for almost a decade. He grew anxious and unhappy writing in both worlds: journalism and literature. His solution to his growing anguish was to stop writing fiction and reportages and to commit his time and energy to scriptwriting.

During his two years away from journalistic and fiction writing, García Márquez underwent a period of profound reexamination of the craft of writing. In a letter to his friend Mendoza, he confessed that did not know how to distinguish between the short story, the novella, and the novel.[70] Indeed, he had never published anything longer than two hundred pages. His uneasy answer to this technical problem was to undertake his first novel. He could so in 1965, when he overcame his stylistic corset and freed his literary imagination. By then, his literary imagination experienced two key changes. First, he understood how to write cosmopolitan Latin American literature and second, for this to happen, he had to change his literary style. Regarding the first, as late as 1962, García Márquez was neither perceived as a writer of New Latin American Novels nor did he think of himself as one. He knew really well the literary traditions of Colombia, Spain, France, England, and the United States. But he arrived to Mexico City not knowing the work of writers of the New Latin American Novel, such as Rulfo and Fuentes. As a member of the Mafia, García Márquez met Rulfo, whose novella *Pedro Páramo* had a deep impact on the imagination of *One Hundred Years of Solitude*, and he became one of Fuentes's friends, whose professional mentorship was decisive for him.

Second, García Márquez transformed his writing style. As he did when he was a member of the Barranquilla Group, he adapted to the literary constraints imposed by the Mafia Group in Mexico City. His correspondence reveals how his professional circle compelled him to rethink the content of his literature. He made clear that he was starting to distance himself from his home country, Colombia, and was open to the culture of Mexico, a country "full of incredible things," as he put it. These incredible things started to enter his imagination. During a visit to Michoacán, he saw Indians "weaving straw angels, [on] whom they put dresses and shoes from the region. There I came up with an idea that seems good to me." This idea was the basis of his short story "Blacamán the Good, Vendor of Miracles," while other ideas found their way into *One Hundred Years of Solitude*.[71]

CONCLUSION

Between 1948 and 1965, García Márquez learned skills for his literary work from a disparate array of sources, especially journalism, scriptwriting, and advertising. Showing that he was able to turn his skills into conventions accepted by peers and professionals was critical to his admission into six art groups on three continents. He never violated the conventions of any of these collaborative circles but rather followed them closely. After his admission to an art group in Mexico, García Márquez became part of a small pool of writers eligible for a privileged position in the more visible and far-reaching art world in Latin America: the Mafia. This group was different from other circles he had joined before. Thanks to the Mafia, by 1965, he was an integrated professional eagerly putting his skills to work on his first novel, *One Hundred Years of Solitude*.

4

NETWORKED CREATIVITY AND
THE MAKING OF A WORK OF ART

Now I realize that they were all working on *One Hundred Years of Solitude*.

—García Márquez on the writing of his novel[1]

The fall of 1965, when García Márquez sat down to write *One Hundred Years of Solitude*, the words that describe how he felt are identical to the ones he used to remember his feelings when he was writing his first book, *Leaf Storm*: "I see him perfectly: he is a [thirty-eight]-year-old man, who believes that he will not write anything else in his life, that this is his last chance, and tries to put everything, everything he remembers, everything he has learned of techniques and of literary wickedness in all the authors he has read." García Márquez was, indeed, doubtful about his commitment to writing *One Hundred Years of Solitude*. His doubts had grown into a dreadful writer's block. Critic Emir Rodríguez Monegal saw it firsthand: "When I met Gabo in Mexico, in 1964, I saw a man who lived in hell for not being able to write the great novel that he has thought out and written mentally even in its smallest details." A few months later, writer José Donoso ran into the same anxious man at a professional conference. García Márquez's correspondence with fellow writer and friend Plinio Apuleyo Mendoza is also honest about his angst for not being able to succeed as a fiction writer. And as literary critic Emmanuel Carballo put it, "He was not famous." The best he had managed to achieve was a reputation among "intelligent people of Mexico, Latin America, and Spain," he added. Carballo was the person to whom an unhappy García Márquez confessed in a 1963 interview that he would never be able to write *One Hundred Years of Solitude*. After repeated setbacks, he turned his back on literature and believed his future was in script-writing. "Cinema is much more noble and reproductive than literature," he explained to a friend in 1965. "Imagine that I am now receiving ten thousand pesos for reviewing a script. And to think that I have wasted so much time of my life writing short stories and reportages. Besides, everything in literature seems to be already written. . . . Literature is great to enjoy as a reader . . . not as a writer."[2]

Months later, not only did García Márquez return to literature with unprecedented energy, but the product of his work was *One Hundred Years of Solitude*. How did it happen? This chapter shows how García Márquez's imagination finally took form and paved the way for the production of the novel. As shown in the previous chapter, he first imagined it when he was twenty-two years old, but despite several attempts, he did not have the necessary skills to turn his ideas into a publishable novel. Writing the final draft of *One Hundred Years of Solitude*, rather than a bout of inspiration, was an act of networked creativity. He was at the center of a network of relatives, friends, peers, and gatekeepers who closely supervised the progress of his manuscript and secured its production and initial reception as a best-selling New Latin American Novel. This networked creativity, which moved the novel from imagination to production, was the real force behind the making of *One Hundred Years of Solitude*.[3]

Five triggering events during the summer and fall of 1965 brought García Márquez back to fiction writing. First, in July, the critic Luis Harss interviewed him for a book of conversations with ten Latin American writers. Second, also in July, García Márquez signed a comprehensive contract with literary agent Carmen Balcells, who, aware of the international boom of Latin American literature, had traveled to the Americas to recruit as many clients as possible for her agency. Third, at the end of August, García Márquez attended a momentous talk by his mentor Carlos Fuentes on how to become a best-selling cosmopolitan and Latin American writer. Fourth, between August and October, international media outlets such as *Life en Español*, the *Times Literary Supplement*, and *Papel Literario* published articles on new and old Latin American writers, and García Márquez was one of them. And fifth, for the first time in his life, he signed book contracts with major international, commercial publishers to print all his previous and future work in Spanish and English, including his next novel, *One Hundred Years of Solitude*.

All these events resonated with García Márquez like never before because 1965 was the year when he became an integrated professional. He was convinced that he had the skills and connections to write a New Latin American Novel. He knew in depth the works of famous international writers—especially William Faulkner, Virginia Woolf, and Ernest Hemingway—that other successful writers of New Latin American Novels were using as models in their best-selling works. Furthermore, García Márquez had direct access to several of these Latin American writers, including Fuentes, Donoso, Alejo Carpentier, Mario Vargas Llosa, and Juan Rulfo, for technical consultation and feedback on his literary ideas and manuscripts. Once he believed that he could write that kind of Latin American novel, he ensured that his venture was bulletproof. He adapted his literary style to meet the aesthetic requirements of New Latin American Novels as well as the commercial expectations of the publishing industry. At the same time, peers and gatekeepers intentionally labeled him a Latin American writer, rather than a rural Colombian author.

A LATIN AMERICAN WRITER IS BORN

If García Márquez had not been labeled a Latin American writer in the 1960s, *One Hundred Years of Solitude* would have passed as yet another of his Colombian stories about a rural Caribbean town in the banana region. By 1965, he was aware of this problem. He was "at once mesmerized and horrified by the progress his contemporaries were making." On July 7, *La Cultura en México* featured writer Vargas Llosa on its cover alongside a seven-page interview. The cover presented him to the supplement's tens of thousands of readers as "the young man who at twenty-five won a first place in the Latin American novel." Fuentes and Donoso were also publishing best-selling books—launched as New Latin American Novels—with major commercial publishers, while García Márquez had only written poorly sold novellas with amateur publishing houses.[4]

Afraid of missing out on commercial success, his insecurity deepened. None of his books published before he moved to Mexico City in 1961 promoted him as a Latin American writer. Even the collection *Biblioteca Básica de Cultura Latinoamericana*, which published the second edition of *Leaf Storm* in the late 1950s, regarded him as a prominent Colombian writer, but said that his book was only "transcendental for the Colombian novel." The way his few readers at the time could make sense of him was just that: a Colombian writer of rural stories. Peers, critics, and journalists also understood him that way. In 1958, Chilean writer Ricardo Latcham selected García Márquez's short story "Monologue of

Isabel Watching It Rain in Macondo" for his best-selling *Antología del cuento hispanoamericano contemporáneo* (*Anthology of the Contemporary Spanish American Short Story*). Latcham praised how the author portrayed "tropical life." But nothing in the text justified labeling him something other than a Colombian writer. In 1961, Latcham published an essay on recent Colombian literature in *Marcha*, the leading weekly general interest magazine in Uruguay with regional circulation. He called García Márquez the most important young Colombian writer and again did not think of him as a Latin American author. The following year, in 1962, *In Evil Hour* won the Esso Prize, awarded to the best novel in Colombia. The Sunday literary supplement of *El Tiempo*, one of the country's leading newspapers, published the first pages of the novella and an interview with the author. At this time, even García Márquez did not think of himself as different from a Colombian novelist; nowhere in the interview did he present himself as a Latin American writer or referred to the New Latin American Novel. The following year, in 1963, Ernesto Volkening, a German literary critic living in Colombia, published in the highbrow literary magazine *Eco* (with the subtitle *Journal of the Culture of the West*) the essay "Gabriel García Márquez o el trópico desembrujado" ("Gabriel García Márquez or the Unbewitched Tropic"). Once more, another critic did not frame him as a Latin American writer but as a "writer of the tropics."[5]

The labeling of García Márquez as a Latin American writer started in Mexico City, then one of the centers of the New Latin American Novel. Only when influential writers, publishers, and critics started to imagine his early works as Latin American—as they were doing for other authors—did he manage to write his future work as Latin American literature in order to market it to a wider regional and international audience. In 1962, Universidad Veracruzana Press published his first book in Mexico, *Big Mama's Funeral*, which was also the last book of fiction he wrote before *One Hundred Years of Solitude*. He did not intentionally imagine *Big Mama's Funeral* as a New Latin American Novel because he wrote most of it before joining the Mafia, his network of collaborators in Mexico City and thinkers of the New Latin American Novel. Rather, he imagined and wrote it as a collection of Colombian rural short stories. Yet something began to change in terms of how to present the writer to his readers. The book's back cover stated that the short stories in his book "reflect the entire tragedy of Latin American nations." It added that, although García Márquez's fiction centered on Colombia, its lessons extended beyond that country and even the region. His fiction was concerned with the "universal problem [of] man," as present in the writings of other writers that influenced him, especially Faulkner, Woolf, and James Joyce. Thus, under

García Márquez's watch, this publisher labeled his work as that of a cosmopolitan and Latin American writer. A year later, in 1963, Mexican publisher Era, which promoted the work of Mafia Group members, published the second edition of *No One Writes to the Colonel* in its collection *Letras Latinoamericanas*. The back cover presented García Márquez not as a Colombian ruralist author but as a "renovator" of Latin American letters and, furthermore, as one of the "great narrators of our language." In 1966, Era reprinted the novella with the same description of the writer. The same year, it published a new edition of *In Evil Hour*, and its back cover presented him as a writer whose sober style "recreat[ed] aesthetically the Latin American reality."

The labeling of García Márquez as a Latin American writer also happened in highbrow literary magazines such as *Revista Mexicana de Literatura* and in popular cultural magazines such as *La Cultura en México*. Not only did these periodicals label him a Latin American writer, the author himself started to imagine his work as Latin American. In an interview with Mafia Group member and critic Carballo, who later collaborated on the writing of *One Hundred Years of Solitude*, García Márquez said that, with his fiction, he was trying to solve "the most salient vice in Latin American fiction: rhetorical leafiness (*frondosidad retórica*)."[6] His goal was to tell stories "in a direct, clear, and concise way." But as he soon realized he did not have to solve this vice to stand out as a true Latin American writer. He simply had to accept that vice and, seamlessly, bring it into his narrative; something he had never done before in his fiction (but he did partly in his reportages, see chapter 3). To accomplish this, as explained below, he changed his literary style to find a balance between economic and rhetorical language. The result was *One Hundred Years of Solitude*.

Critics beyond Mexico City also started to label García Márquez a Latin American writer. So did leading Uruguayan critic Ángel Rama, who was in close contact with Mafia Group leader Fuentes. In *Marcha*, the magazine where Latcham wrote about García Márquez as a young Colombian author in 1961, Rama referred to him three years later as "one of the inventors of the new artistic expression of the continent." Rama's description of García Márquez's style was remarkably similar to Latcham's descriptions in 1958 and 1961. For both critics, he was a rural, regionalist, realist novelist and a chronicler of the Colombian *violencia*, the period of nation-wide violence that started after the riots of El Bogotazo. But what changed between Latcham's and Rama's interpretation of García Márquez's work was the ascent of the New Latin American Novel in the early 1960s. For Rama, his works were both Latin American and cosmopolitan. He belonged to the tradition of Latin American writers exemplified by Rómulo Gallegos and José Eustasio Rivera and simultaneously his writing was comparable to that of cosmopolitan writers such as Faulkner, Hemingway, Honoré de Balzac, and Anton Chekhov. Rama's support went beyond his essays of literary criticism; he also published García Márquez's works. In October 1965, Rama's Uruguayan publishing company, Arca, released a new edition of *Leaf Storm* in its collection *Nueva Narrativa Latino-americana*. The back cover put García Márquez "among the renovators of the Latin American novel." After the release of this edition, Uruguayan writer Mario Benedetti published a laudatory review of García Márquez's books in *Marcha*, including Arca's *Leaf Storm*, and called him "one of the names of contemporary Latin American letters."[7]

By the time García Márquez was writing *One Hundred Years of Solitude*, publishers in the region had already labeling him a Latin American author. In 1966, the Argentine publisher Jorge Álvarez included his rural realist short story "There Are No Thieves in This Village" (taken from his book of Colombian and rural short stories *Big Mama's Funeral*) in *Los diez mandamientos* (*The Ten Commandments*). This book was an anthology of short stories published in the collection *Narradores Americanos*, which featured writers from three generations and presented them as part of a region-spanning literary movement. Strategically, García Márquez marketed himself in his short bio as a writer working "in the solitude of literature."[8] In this way, he advertised the major theme of his novel in progress. The same year, he was included in the Latin American volume *Into the Mainstream*, edited by Harss. Following Fuentes's recommendation, Harss interviewed García Márquez. (They first met in 1961, when García Márquez worked as a journalist in New York.) This volume marketed ten writers of three generations as leaders of a region-spanning Latin American literature. Harss presented García Márquez as the member of a "loosely knit group of young internationalists . . . whose work is changing the face of our literature." In the interview, García Márquez said he was a Latin American writer and stated that "the ebullience of the Latin-American novel is the only answer today to the sterility of the French *nouveau roman*—and he is fiercely proud of it."[9] He also promoted his next novel, *One Hundred Years of Solitude*. Sudamericana released *Into the Mainstream* in 1966 and, like *Los diez mandamientos*, it was a best seller in Buenos Aires in the months prior to the release of *One Hundred Years of Solitude*.

The labeling and visibility of García Márquez as a Latin American writer grew in highbrow journals, general interest magazines, and newspaper supplements that circulated beyond Latin America and the Spanish language. As part of the rise of the New Latin American Novel, *Life en Español* (August 2, 1965), the *Times Literary Supplement* (September 30), and *Papel Literario* (October 31) published articles on new and old Latin American writers, including García Márquez. By then, he already knew that, a few months earlier, French critic Roger Caillois stated in an interview in the French newspaper *Le Monde* that Latin American literature was "the literature of tomorrow." García Márquez also believed this claim by October 31, when he was at work full-time on *One Hundred Years of Solitude*. On that day, Venezuelan newspaper *El Nacional* published an interview with him in its Sunday literary supplement, *Papel Literario*. In the months before and after his interview, this supplement published work by and interviewed mainstream regional and international authors such as Vargas Llosa, Julio Cortázar, Rafael Alberti, Camilo José Cela, Samuel Beckett, Allen Ginsberg, and Pier Paolo Pasolini. For García Márquez, who lived in Caracas six years before and still remembered how one of his short stories lost *El Nacional*'s literary award, this full-page interview in its Sunday supplement proved how much his literary standing had improved since then. And it did so, not because he had published new fiction (in fact, he had published nothing new for the past three years) but because of the boom of Latin American literature. *El Nacional* interviewer, Venezuelan critic Domingo Miliani, presented García Márquez as a cosmopolitan writer, "a novelist who has begun the ascent to universality." And the author promoted *One Hundred Years of Solitude* as a Latin American novel in progress.[10]

To imagine his writing as Latin American, García Márquez asked his peers, such as Fuentes, what people said about his work. More importantly, he read closely literary criticism about his own work. He started to keep copies of this criticism and sometimes added his handwritten opinion about the critique. These copies eventually filled twenty-one large size scrapbooks in his personal archives. One of the essays he liked the most was written by Volkening, who published an essay on García Márquez's works just before the release of *In Evil Hour*. Volkening decided to supplement his essay with a book review that criticized the novella's shortcomings. For the critic, the book was more a series of loosely tied "fragmentary" scenes rather than a clearly connected narrative. García Márquez took note of Volkening's comments. His next book, *One Hundred Years of Solitude*, did not suffer from the problem highlighted by the critic, as the scenes were part of a narrative whole. Volkening's criticism of García Márquez, with whom he was in contact, exemplifies the collaborative environment that helped him improve his creativity and writing.[11]

Critics also helped García Márquez further understand not just his technique but his literary agenda. The abovementioned critic Rama wrote about his works: "In all of them, we are told the same repeated, obsessive theme: life in a small Colombian town, Macondo (which comes, of course, from

[Faulkner's] Yoknapatawpha [County]), with its repertoire of hopeful, miserable, hallucinated, humble neighbors, all caught up in the tiny hopes of small town life." With statements of this kind Rama laid out for García Márquez a literary agenda in which his ruralism was not provincial but cosmopolitan. This rural cosmopolitanism matched well the principles of cosmopolitanism and Latin Americanism that gatekeepers like Rama and Fuentes had been promoting since 1964. Months later, García Márquez started to write *One Hundred Years of Solitude* as a cosmopolitan and Latin American story set, once again, in the small town of Macondo. But now life there would be more cosmopolitan than ever. So, this kind of literary criticism informed and guided his choices about the professional steps he needed to take when writing his work and approaching gatekeepers' tastes. To make sure he was on the right track, he asked Carballo, at the time Mexico's leading literary critic, to give him weekly feedback during the writing of *One Hundred Years of Solitude*.[12]

MAKING THE PUBLISHING DEAL

In the summer of 1965, Carmen Balcells traveled from Spain to the United States and Latin America to sign new deals with writers and publishers. She arrived in Mexico City on July 5, and her visit was dutifully reported in the cultural supplement *La Cultura en México*. From 1962 until that summer, she had negotiated on behalf of García Márquez the translations of his works, but on that visit she met the writer for the first time and they signed a new and more ambitious contract that had her representing him in all languages, including the booming market of literature in Spanish.[13] For García Márquez, this contract was a professional breakthrough. Under Balcells's brokerage, he secured a steady income of royalties and subsidiary rights for his works for the first time in his life. Allegedly, after signing the deal with his agent, he took his family on a vacation to Acapulco and, on the road, had his famous epiphany: the first sentence of the novel came to him from nowhere as a cow crossed the road in front of his car. In reality, his true epiphany was the prospect of a stable financial and professional career as a writer who was also the breadwinner of the family.[14] He just needed to start writing new work again given the momentum of the New Latin American Novel and the determination of Balcells to sell the rights of his past, present, and future works. The novel he had struggled to write for the past fifteen years had to be written. Now or never.

Yet, if this triggering event alone could not convince him that he could finally write that novel, other events happened between July and October. The time for *One Hundred Years of Solitude* had finally come. The same month García Márquez signed the deal with Balcells, he was interviewed about his career and works by critic Harss, who selected him for *Into the Mainstream*. Inclusion in this volume was another career-defining moment for García Márquez. It attracted the attention of the gatekeepers in Argentina and the United States that published this volume. By October, two major publishers interested in the booming Latin American novel were knocking on García Márquez's door for the first time in his career. One publisher was Sudamericana, which had released several best-selling titles of Latin American literature over the past five years. The second publisher was New York-based Harper & Row, which opened a branch for Latin American literature in 1964 and was signing many writers from the region. Both publishers realized that García Márquez was the most unknown of the authors featured in the Harss volume. They also realized two things. First, García Márquez was together with Latin American writers whose works were already international best sellers. And second, his works—published locally and untranslated into English—were too good an opportunity to miss; none of them was a best seller yet. Once Sudamericana and Harper & Row approached him, García Márquez understood that his long-awaited opportunity to become a professional writer had come, and he immediately committed to writing full-time the type of New Latin American Novel that these publishers produced. He wrote *One Hundred Years of Solitude*, released by Sudamericana in 1967 and by Harper & Row in 1970.

Francisco Porrúa, the acquisitions editor of Sudamericana, received three novellas by García Márquez from Harss. "I discovered there," said Porrúa, "that it was really worth publishing him in Argentina, where he was unknown" and decided to contact him. García Márquez replied, "I am, indeed, working on my fifth book: *One Hundred Years of Solitude*. It is a very long and complex novel on which I have put my best expectations." He intended to finish it in five months. (It took him fourteen.) García Márquez signed the contract for *One Hundred Years of Solitude* on September 10, 1966. The conditions in the contract reveal that the Balcells Agency had not yet developed all its power as a broker. In fact, the publisher retained significant control over the novel, such as the rights to sell it in the Spanish language throughout the world. (This power relationship changed greatly after the success of the novel; see chapter 5.) This contract included an advance of US$500 and a royalty of 10 percent of the retail price of all copies. The subsidiary rights were in the hands of the publisher, who was obliged to share them equally with the author. The contract indicated neither the print run nor the selling price. But it meant substantial progress from earlier contracts shown in the previous chapter. First, Sudamericana only owned *One Hundred Years of Solitude* until its first edition was sold out. Second, the books released by Sudamericana, unlike those of Era (with whom the author had a previous publishing agreement for the novel), circulated in Latin America, North America, and Europe. And third, Sudamericana had a reputation for publishing novels and original literature by Latin American writers.[15]

The initial contract with Harper & Row was not a great deal for García Márquez. Dated October 5, 1965, it included the publication of all his previous fiction: three novellas and one book of short stories. As royalties, he received an advance of US$1,000, plus 8 percent of the retail price for the first five thousand copies sold and 10 percent after passing that amount. When he knew about the conditions, he supposedly said to Balcells, "This contract is a piece of shit." He was not mistaken. He was aware of the advantageous contracts that his peers were signing at the time. In comparison, in 1958, Simon & Schuster acquired Joseph Heller's classic *Catch-22* for US$1,500 and Obolensky bought Fuentes's *Where the Air Is Clear* for US$500. Nine years later and for just US$1,000, Harper & Row acquired four books and was granted "a first option on the next book by the author," *One Hundred Years of Solitude*. Yet, this company put García Márquez's work on the path of global circulation in the "English language throughout the World," which included the market in the "British Commonwealth, Empire, and trusteeships." From this large market, he would receive 50 percent from the sale of subsidiary rights. The amount went up to 70 percent for the sale of serial rights after publication to a newspaper syndicate and to 90 percent for serial and broadcasting rights before publication. Then, as the date of publication in Spanish approached, publisher Coward-McCann tried to buy the publication rights of *One Hundred Years of Solitude* in English; Balcells used this new offer to get "a big advance" from Harper & Row for the novel.[16]

Without Balcells's brokerage, the novel's fate would have been quite different. Before she visited Mexico City, García Márquez had reached a "verbal agreement" to publish *One Hundred Years of Solitude* with Era, even though he knew their books had limited circulation outside Mexico. If Era had published his novel, it would have printed two thousand copies, most of which would have been available in Mexico. As an Era novel, *One Hundred Years of Solitude* would not have transformed García Márquez into a full-time writer. Rather he would have continued to work as a journalist and scriptwriter, while writing literature part-time. (An attempt to publish this novel with Seix Barral fell through; see chapter 2.)

García Márquez only made the decision to work full-time on *One Hundred Years of Solitude*, when interest from major commercial publishers in the novel was apparent and when he knew he could write and deliver it within seven months,[17] a reasonable amount of time to live on credit and let bills accumulate. More than ever, his dream of becoming a professional writer was literally at his fingertips. He just needed to sit down in front of his typewriter and write *One Hundred Years of Solitude*. He did not do so in solitude.

IMAGINING A LATIN AMERICAN NOVEL

When García Márquez began *One Hundred Years of Solitude*, he was a member of a multinational, multilingual, and multicultural network of cosmopolitan and Latin American artists and critics (see figure 4.1). Thanks to this network, he learned about the international success of the New Latin American Novel. As Fuentes told him in a letter sent from Paris, "If there is something I know, it is that Europe (I already knew it about the United States and we have

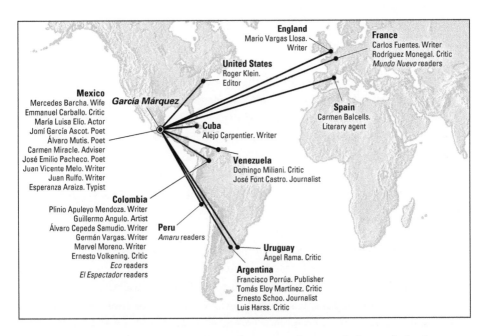

4.1 García Márquez's network during the writing of *One Hundred Years of Solitude*.

Source: Gabriel García Márquez Papers, HRC; García Márquez 2001a; Martin 2009.

talked about it) is wide open to Latin American literature. . . . We have taken the bull by the horns and it is not the time to fall asleep or get distracted." Learning from Fuentes and others about the success of the region's literature unblocked García Márquez professionally. "We, Latin American writers," he said in a letter to a fellow author in Colombia, "have the guts" to write whatever we wanted to. He was fully informed that New Latin American Novels were competing against international novels for the most prestigious awards. That is why a euphoric García Márquez predicted in a letter to his friend Mendoza that "very soon a big hit (*trancazo*)" would come out of this region.[18] Little did he suspect that it would be his own novel.

His correspondence between 1961 and 1965 reveals that he started to believe that Colombian literature belonged to Latin American literature. As shown earlier, he used media to promote his commitment to the New Latin American Novel. In the interview with Miliani, published when he was writing *One Hundred Years of Solitude*, he assessed the health of the Latin American novel. "It is very good," he said. "Carlos Fuentes, from Mexico, has finished *El sueño* (*A Change of Skin*); Mario Vargas Llosa, from Peru, has finished *The Green House*; Alejo Carpentier, from Cuba, has finished *El año 59* (*The Rites of Spring*); Julio Cortázar, from Argentina, has finished a more powerful book than *Hopscotch*." In sum, García Márquez understood what the market was consuming and, more importantly, he knew what its future direction would be, as he again explained to Miliani:

> Each of these writers published, in the last two years, a novel that competed with the best in Europe and is already translated into the most important languages. They have achieved something that seemed impossible: world critics pay attention to us; publishers in foreign languages pay advances for works yet to be written; Spanish print runs sell out faster and in greater numbers. Until recently we wrote for our friends. And this, in a way, was very comfortable. Now, we are aware that we write for a crowd of merciless strangers.[19]

He knew that New Latin American Novels were easily marketable, international commodities for the consumption of the growing reading classes. It was this in-depth knowledge of the present and immediate future of Latin American literature that compelled him to write *One Hundred Years of Solitude*. Yet firsthand and inside knowledge was, of course, not enough to write a best-selling novel. His contemporaries Adriano González León in Venezuela, Álvaro Cepeda Samudio in Colombia, and Elena Garro in Mexico, among others, knew that, to succeed commercially, their works had to comply with the cosmopolitan and Latin American principles of the New Latin American Novel. Here, García Márquez's network made a difference in imagining *One Hundred Years of Solitude* as a New Latin American Novel. Thanks to this network, he received advice on solving technical problems at the level of ideas, format, and style in his novel.[20]

To solve these problems, García Márquez used conventions by peers such as Carpentier, Cortázar, Fuentes, Rulfo, and Vargas Llosa; all of them leading members of their generations. García Márquez did not select these writers and their works by chance. In his private correspondence, he was already aware of the fact, months before he started *One Hundred Years of Solitude*, that the novels *Explosion in a Cathedral*, *The Death of Artemio Cruz*, *Hopscotch*, *Pedro Páramo*, and *The Time of the Hero*, were published to great regional and international success. For this reason, the text of *One Hundred Years of Solitude* went as far as to mention characters from the first three novels: Lorenzo Gavilán, Rocamadour, and Victor Hughes. By so doing, García Márquez signaled to peers and gatekeepers of three generations—Carpentier, Fuentes, and Cortázar—that *One Hundred Years of Solitude* wanted to belong and expand this Latin American tradition. To do so, he had to follow the conventions of what his peers saw as original and commercial Latin American writing.

How did *One Hundred Years of Solitude* follow such conventions at the level of ideas? García Márquez had already read Fuentes's manifesto "La nueva novela latinoamericana" ("The New Latin American Novel"), in which he explained that the successful novels of Carpentier, Cortázar, and Vargas Llosa were putting myths at the center. García Márquez also talked to Mexican writer Rulfo, who participated in activities of the Mafia Group and whose rural stories García Márquez had adapted into film scripts. Regarding format, he was up to date about what his colleagues were working on and what their format was: 700-page novels. Never before *One Hundred Years of Solitude* had García Márquez written something that long. Fuentes, a prolific writer of novels, mentored him on how to write his work in such a format, not only by talking to him about the novel as a format, but also by sharing with him the drafts of his work. When he was starting *One Hundred Years of Solitude*, García Márquez read Fuentes's novel in progress, *A Change of Skin*, published by Seix Barral and winner of the prestigious Biblioteca Breve award. At the same time, Donoso, who was living in Fuentes's house, was writing another novel, *Hell Has No Limits*. The two writers, members of the Mafia, helped García Márquez overcome his fears and doubts about how to write a novel. Finally, regarding style, he abandoned his spare social realism and searched for a mixture of reality and fantasy for his new writing. He talked to a collaborator who had mixed both successfully: Carpentier. He visited Mexico City often and his influence on García Márquez's novel proved to be crucial in terms of format and ideas (more on this below).[21]

The final trigger in García Márquez's imagination was a talk by Fuentes on August 26, 1965. This talk was part of a cycle entitled "Narradores ante el público" ("Narrators before the Public") sponsored by the prestigious Instituto Nacional de Bellas Artes in Mexico City. During his talk, Fuentes recognized Latin American writers from the two previous generations and his own generation as influencers on his writing. In front of a packed audience, he praised "my friend" García Márquez, whom he considered a member of the literary avant-garde in Latin America along with Cortázar, Vargas Llosa, and Donoso and internationally along with Saul Bellow, William Styron, Norman Mailer, and Günter Grass, writers with whom Fuentes was in "direct dialogue." Here, he was seamlessly labeling García Márquez as a Latin American and cosmopolitan writer. He also said that he lived off his books, which at this moment were published in up to fourteen countries. And he proclaimed that writers should not be ashamed of publicizing themselves and with the help of their friends.[22]

Among the Mafia members who attended the talk was a hesitant García Márquez. He had just started writing One Hundred Years of Solitude part-time. But Fuentes's passionate words about his friend, the craft of writing, and international success were truly cathartic. After the talk, the Mutis family invited several Mafia members to eat at their place. An almost-levitating García Márquez started talking to guests about key characters and events of the novel he was imagining. One of them was Spanish exile María Luisa Elío, who said to him, "Tell me more, tell me more, and then he kept telling me.... I listened to him all night." Elío was so enthusiastic about his stories that she became one of his closest collaborators as he wrote the novel, to the point that he dedicated it to her.[23]

A few hours before, Fuentes had once more said that myths were a fundamental ingredient of any literary work. And now García Márquez was telling the mythical story of Macondo to a hypnotized Elío. About a month later, when he had figured out the structure of the novel, he also reported to critic Miliani that his untitled novel was cosmopolitan, and it contained the "authentic values in Latin American life." He imagined cosmopolitanism and Latin Americanism coming together in Macondo. As he said a few months later in another interview, this town was such a cosmopolitan place that "it can exist anywhere in the imagination . . . it can be here [in Cartagena, Colombia], it can be in Paris. It's something like the 'microcosm' of man."[24] In short,

Macondo was at once in the most cosmopolitan of cities and also a Latin American city. And vice versa: Paris and Cartagena were in Macondo.

THE WRITER AND THE MANUSCRIPT

"I remember quite distinctly," García Márquez confessed, "the day that with enormous difficulty I finished the first sentence and I asked myself, terrified, what the hell came next. In fact, until the galleon was discovered in the middle of the jungle [halfway through chapter 1] I didn't really think the book would get anywhere." Once he was certain that the novel was going somewhere, he quit his job in an advertising agency and stopped collaborating with Luis Alcoriza on two film scripts. Quitting was the last step into a situation of *modeled uncertainty*, since he was already in conversations with publishers about his next novel. As time passed, he had to make financial sacrifices, including pawning family possessions. But he was not a bankrupt writer. He had found, to paraphrase Virginia Woolf, a social room of his own to write undisturbed. The Mafia Group, the Balcells Agency, and his close friends created a patronage system to support his writing project financially, professionally, and emotionally. In September 1965, he retreated from regular paid work and lived mostly on credit until August 1966, when he finished the manuscript.[25]

First of all, García Márquez had to decide which novel to write. In late 1964, about eight months before he started *One Hundred Years of Solitude*, he was working on at least two things: on the movie script for *Presagio* (*Omen*), "the story of a town that is coming to an end," and a novel about a dictator. In May 1965, the script for *Presagio* was not finished, and he had also changed the novel's plot: it would instead be about the "solitude" of a despot.[26] Thus, by mid-1965, he had three themes on his writing desk: solitude, a town in disarray, and a despot. During the summer and early fall, he realized that he could blend these three themes in a single novel.

In addition to combining themes for the novel, García Márquez abandoned his creative habits of the past two decades. Until then, he had done most of his writing after working hours. Now, he shifted to daytime work. To write his novel full-time, he adopted an office schedule, writing daily from about 8–9 a.m. to 4–8 p.m., including most weekends. He created a work environment conducive to enforce discipline and minimize distractions. He started with his own body: he wore overalls while writing. Then, he and his wife arranged a separate small room on the ground floor. His work space was about seventy-five square feet, with a window onto the backyard and a small bathroom. The space had a few dozen books on shelves, a couch, and a table with his typewriter. On the wall, along with two posters and a few photos, as the novel advanced, he stuck charts with the history of Macondo and the genealogy of the Buendía family. To further enforce discipline, he cut off his social and even family life. "My children . . . remember me as a man who was locked in a room and never left." As the critic Carballo put it, he wrote "like a crazy person. He did not do anything else. He stopped seeing friends."[27]

During the writing process, he kept notebooks to keep track of the plot,

> When I finished the book, I had at least forty of these notebooks. Because I was typing chapter three, but in the notebook, I was already in chapter twelve, chapter fifteen, because the book was taking me at high speed. I couldn't let it escape, so in the school notebook I wrote the diary of the book, because at any time, when I needed to know where the story was going, I checked the notebook, do you understand? Interviewer: But, did you write sentences, ideas, as writers usually do? García Márquez: No, none of that. I was controlling the structure of the book in the notebook. I needed to know if so-and-so was so-and-so's grandson or great-grandson, or great-great-grandson, because I got confused and then I referred to the notebook where everything was very clear. I even made a family tree, but I destroyed it.[28]

When he was stuck, could not write anything new, or was feeling lazy, he copied entire chapters again to keep the rhythm going. He relied on the best possible technological and human resources that he could afford then. He started typing the novel on a Torpedo—a portable mechanical typewriter—but ended up writing most of it on a Smith Corona Electric, one of the first portable electric typewriters, which allowed him to write faster and with fewer typos. He also hired a professional typist, Esperanza Araiza, who had typed novels for Mafia members, to make clean copies of his work in progress and the final manuscript. Thanks to her assistance, García Márquez focused on writing and wasted no time typing clean copies of the originals, which were full of his numerous handwritten corrections.[29]

How did the manuscript develop over time? In July 1965, when Harss interviewed García Márquez for *Into the Mainstream*, he confessed that he was blocked. But in a letter to Harss written four months later, he was "on top of the world." The book, he continued, "is literally gushing from me, without any problems of words." And, he added, "I am very happy with it." Indeed, he was happy because, among other reasons, the text would be as long as the standard

New Latin American Novel: four to five hundred sheets. (The final manuscript is four hundred and ninety sheets long.) At first, he wrote it quickly. When Miliani interviewed him in September (the interview was published in October), he was in the initial stages, and the novel was yet untitled. This coincides with Elío's testimony, who said that when he talked to her about the novel in late August, he only "had written points but nothing more." He came up with the title at some point between the interview with Miliani and a letter he sent to Fuentes in October asking for his opinion on the title. By early November, he had written half of the novel, and was planning to have eight hundred sheets in total. In sum, he did most of the foundational writing for the novel between August and November 1965.[30]

After the initial burst, however, he started to struggle to work on the novel full-time. In December, he complained that the novel "moves at a snail's pace." He had to work on it part-time to attend to "everyday needs" and to do some film projects so that his family could eat. In January 1966, he resumed work on the novel full-time. But again, he had to stop in mid-February, precisely when the novel was moving forward, although "it gets longer and longer." That month, he flew from Mexico to Colombia to present the movie *Time to Die*, for which he wrote the script, at the Cartagena Film Festival. Upon his return to Mexico City, a month later, he regretted that the trip was a "foolishness" that delayed the completion of the novel by two months and only increased his doubts about its quality. "This time I cried in rage," he told Vargas Llosa. "I wrote two horrendous chapters to catch up with the story, and then I destroyed and remade them again." From then onward, he locked himself up and did not stop until he finished the novel. Due to his seclusion, "we are living kind of miraculously," while he received constant requests to write "rubbish" that could alleviate his financial situation. But he turned them down these offers and lived off the checks the literary agent sent and the support of his friends and neighbors.[31]

García Márquez was growing anxious, since writing the novel was taking him longer than expected. To soothe his frequent bouts of insecurity, in early 1966, he sent three chapters of the novel to Harss along with the timeline and the family tree. He asked Harss to give them to Fuentes next, to whom García Márquez explicitly asked in a letter, "I am really interested in your point of view." Fuentes not only gave García Márquez his opinion, but also circulated the chapters among Latin American writers in Paris, before he sent them to Sudamericana, as García Márquez instructed him to do.[32]

The anxious writer started to test the reactions of readers to his novel as early as May 1996, three months before he finished writing it. For the next few months, seven chapters of the novel premiered in magazines and newspapers. It was the first time in his career that he had published work in progress. He was very worried, but at the same time confident. He was closely imitating a convention set by writers of New Latin American Novels such as Donoso, Fuentes, Cortázar, Vargas Llosa, and José Lezama Lima. They all promoted their forthcoming work in mainstream, region-spanning publications. On June 15, García Márquez did a public reading of several fragments of the novel, too. The event was part of "Narrativa latinoamericana y otros trazos" ("Latin American Narrative and Other Traces"), a series of talks to promote new Latin American works. His reading went so well that five days later he was still euphoric in a letter he sent to Guillermo Angulo in Colombia. He told his friend that the novel was 700 sheets long, and he was about to finish it. He had money and believed that he was going to make a living as a literature writer not as a scriptwriter. His euphoria was also related to the success of the New Latin American Novel about which he knew from correspondence with peers, such as Fuentes, who was then in Paris and equally excited about its success. García Márquez made Fuentes's words his own when he said to Angulo, "The Latin American novel is at a moment when one cannot go to sleep." And at the end of the letter, he wrote he was happy about the fact that *One Hundred Years of Solitude* was going to be published during this thriving moment for the region's literature.[33]

A month later, on July 22, he had finished the writing, with a total of five hundred fifty sheets. He was ready to work with the typist on editing the final manuscript for the publisher, as he explained in a letter to Mendoza. To Fuentes, he wrote, "I feel [the novel] turned out better than I expected." Insecurity, however, returned soon and stronger than ever. In another letter to Mendoza on August 24, a somber and exhausted García Márquez confessed not knowing what would happen with the novel, of which the typist was finishing a clean copy. He shared his angst with Fuentes, too: "Suddenly, I was terrified, as if I had really said nothing in [those] sheets, and I locked myself up with the neurotic purpose of doing the novel again in a different way." At the end, he only made a few big cuts and cleaned up the text. The result was a manuscript of four hundred ninety sheets, which took him about fourteen months of work. (He yielded an average of one sheet or between two hundred and fifty and three hundred words per day.) In late August or early September, he sent the manuscript from Mexico City to Sudamericana in Buenos Aires. But his insecurity still lingered: "I am . . . waiting for the readers of Sudamericana to tell me that it is shit." He did not have time to worry too much because he had to start cancelling debts right away, including rent payments, groceries bills, etc.

He used the publisher's advance payment and resumed work in advertising and other jobs. He was still under the spell of *One Hundred Years of Solitude*, though, to the point that one of his anonymous writing gigs at the time for the chemical company Celanese was entitled "5000 Years of Celanese Mexicana" ("5000 años de Celanese Mexicana").[34]

Only in retrospect, after the novel's success, García Márquez said, "It was a great time . . . because I was writing like a train. That is the best thing that can happen to a writer." But the truth is that he wrote most of it under a lot of stress. He smoked about sixty cigarettes per day (twenty thousand in total) to write the novel, and took passiflorine, a natural medicine, to lessen his anxiety. A neighbor remembers seeing a restless García Márquez often seated on the street curb in front of his house and smoking non-stop. Meanwhile, his wife Mercedes developed a stomach ulcer. Her husband's anxiety peaked in March 1967, when he sent the final galleys to the publisher after a previous set of galleys got lost in the mail. He suffered from an episode of nervous arrhythmia while driving on a highway in Mexico City and had to pull over to the side to calm down. This was one of several moments in which he asked himself, his wife, and his friends, "What am I going to do if the novel is bad?"[35]

NETWORKED CREATIVITY

The previous pages may have given the impression that García Márquez's literary writing was the product of an author's solitary endeavor. But the writing of *One Hundred Years of Solitude*—and of most works of professional literature—was far from being such a product. Other contemporary novels by Fuentes, Donoso, or Vargas Llosa were produced in collaboration, too. A testimony of such collaboration is the surviving correspondence among these writers. Donoso, for example, received feedback on his work in progress from critic Rodríguez Monegal. In his letters, Fuentes commented on the development of *One Hundred Years of Solitude* in one paragraph and in another explained to García Márquez his ideas for a text in the stage of imagination. Then, García Márquez replied to Fuentes with suggestions for his text and also thanked him for the feedback on *One Hundred Years of Solitude*, which was then moving from the stage of imagination to the stage of production. In a similar way, in person, over the phone, or by mail, and alone or in groups, García Márquez received feedback from relatives, friends, peer writers, literary critics, publishers, and common readers. So constant was their feedback that the imagination and writing of his novel was more like the act of distributed cognition and agency that I call networked creativity. Thus, networked creativity can serve as another antidote to the arguments of those who claim that a major work of art is the product of an artist's creative genius. The reality is that over a dozen individuals worked closely for *One Hundred Years of Solitude* as it was being written. They began to do it in earnest after Fuentes's talk in August 1965, when García Márquez's stories convinced his friends of the Mafia that he should work full-time on the novel. "Everyone agreed to give him peace, time, and love. And thanks to that—mainly to his family and friends—that novel was written," as a witness put it. The emotional support that ran through the veins of García Márquez's local and international network boosted the confidence of the insecure author as he wrote his first novel, helping him maintain a state of creative flow for over a year. "Very soon I realized," he said, "that everyone's reactions and enthusiasm were illuminating the gorge leading to my real novel." He acknowledged their emotional and personal support by including both explicit and hidden references to his family, friends, and peers in Latin American and Europe. "*One Hundred Years of Solitude*," as he confessed, "is full of signs to my closest friends, signs that only they can discover."[36]

Many of these friends met at 19 Cerrada de La Loma, García Márquez's house in an up-and-coming middle-class neighborhood. They affectionately called his house "the cave of the Mafia." Friends and peers with links to the arts visited him to check on the novel's progress. Others in Latin America and Europe gave feedback that not only motivated García Márquez to keep writing but also helped him solve multiple technical problems. In the early fall of 1965, he had to work out the problems of tone and style. Regarding tone, "I was unhappy," he stated, "with my novel because I couldn't find the tone." He compared it to a similar problem in music composition, as in Beethoven's Violin Concerto in D major. "I believe that Beethoven could not have composed that concert if he had not found the exact tone: D major; if he had composed it in any other tone it would not have come out." In the case of *One Hundred Years of Solitude*, the solution came when he understood that the tone had to be purely narrative. A few months earlier, he advised his colleague Mendoza (who like García Márquez at the time was writing a novel about a dictator) to write the text "as Cervantes wanted it."[37] In his opinion, his friend had to write in the classic baroque language of the Spanish Golden Age, that is, the kind of neo-baroque language that writers like Vargas Llosa and Carpentier were promoting as truly Latin American. This was the tone García Márquez himself used in *One Hundred Years of Solitude* a few months later. Journalist José Font Castro, one of his collaborators from his time in Caracas, came to Mexico City and he recalled the moment when,

> I listened to, in the company of Álvaro Mutis, the first chapter of *One Hundred Years of Solitude*. Read by Gabo in a classic Spanish accent 'because I have discovered—he explained—that the best way to tell all these crazy things is to assume the same style of the Spanish narrators of chivalry novels. They tell the most incredible things, described from the outside, without showing any amazement and without frowning a single facial nerve.'[38]

In *One Hundred Years of Solitude*, he mixed this classic narrative tone with the more popular and familiar tone that his maternal grandmother used to tell him stories when he was a child. In his novel, "facts are not told as they happened, but as my grandmother believed that they happened." And he added, "She believed that everything was possible, to the point that she lit candles to the saints so that a benevolent and very real telegraphist did not pass through her house; although he had the unbelievable name of César Triste (Caesar Sad), about whom people said that he was born and grew up with a pig's tail." This was going to be the novel's tone. Thanks to it, "fortunately for me, in this book, carpets fly, Don César Triste has a pig's tail, the dead raise, cards predict the future." For this reason, he insisted that, even though he narrated fantastic events, they were grounded in a real imagination: "the true world in which you and I grew up," as he wrote to Mendoza.[39]

Regarding García Márquez's technical problems with the novel's style, the solution came when he read *Explosion in a Cathedral* by Carpentier, a New Latin American Novel set in the Caribbean region. In his pioneering manifesto "The New Latin American Novel," Fuentes praised Carpentier's novel by highlighting specific passages, such as these two:

> Esteban felt disconcerted by the incredible servility of a vigorous and lively mind, which could yet be so completely given over to politics that it shied away from a critical examination of the facts, and refused to acknowledge the most flagrant contradictions.

> The doctor tried a new treatment, which had worked wonders in Paris in curing eyes affected by the Egyptian Disease: the application of bleeding lumps of fresh veal.[40]

Carpentier's passages and the way Fuentes interpreted them as new Latin American literature helped García Márquez gain insights into his own style. Fuentes published his manifesto on July 1964. The same month, an amazed García Márquez wrote to Mendoza about Carpentier's novel. He called it "a masterpiece of universal literature." Spanish exile Federico Álvarez recalled running into him at the time: "He told me, delighted, that he had just read *Explosion in a Cathedral* and that he had destroyed the two hundred sheets he had already written of his novel in order to start it again." Indeed, Carpentier's novel had an immediate impact on García Márquez: it *Latin Americanized* his literary imagination, paving the way for *One Hundred Years of Solitude*. As mentioned earlier, in 1964, he was working on the novel of the dictator. But after reading Carpentier's novel, his goal was to find a middle point between Carpentier's and Hemingway's styles, a compromise between, on the one hand, the neo-baroque and magic Latin American language of Carpentier and, on the other, the concise and realist cosmopolitan language of Hemingway. He knew that it could be done.

Thanks to the Barranquilla and Cartagena Groups, he learned how to adapt Hemingway's style to his own work, and thanks to the Mafia Group, he had full access to Carpentier. For example, Carpentier helped him understand the importance of writing in an archaic language. As García Márquez explained in a letter, "[Carpentier] told me that in *Explosion in a Cathedral*, he does not use a single word that did not exist in the seventeenth century, no words created after the seventeenth century." And he did something similar in *One Hundred Years of Solitude*. "Yes," he admitted, "I was very careful with the evolution of language, so the flavor of my book is not the same at the beginning as at the end." Their conversation on language helped García Márquez believe that he was writing in "a language that was not ours, a borrowed language." That complaint was made by Carpentier and Fuentes, and their solution was to write in Latin American Spanish, as García Márquez did in the novel.[41]

Carpentier's rhythmic style also made its way into the writing of *One Hundred Years of Solitude*. Of course, it was not an imitation since García Márquez cut down on Carpentier's tendency for using many adjectives and, instead, opted for Hemingway's succinct style. Finding the balance between styles was his personal *aesthetic liberation*. As he explained in the Miliani interview, right after starting *One Hundred Years of Solitude*, "For me, this is a liberation, after four books repressed by the chastity belt of rigor and the poor reality of notaries." In his novel, everything was now going to be "Pantagruelic." The novel would merge, he said to the interviewer, "traditional common places: rhetoric, exalted sentimentality, abuse of telluric elements, melodrama, soap opera."[42]

Rhetoric, which he criticized earlier as a vice of the region's literature, had by now become one of the key ingredients in his novel.

Carpentier's novel was also an exemplar for García Márquez because it helped him solve another major problem that a New Latin American Novel like *One Hundred Years of Solitude* had to face: how to merge history and myth. Carpentier's novel combined historical facts and mythical stories surrounding the spread of the cosmopolitan ideas of the French Revolution in the Caribbean. Ever since García Márquez first imagined his novel, history was a central component. There are references to characters of a family in the eighteenth century in texts that he published as early as 1950 from the manuscript of "The House." His interest for this century was, of course, another similarity with Carpentier's novel. Writing history from a literary angle must have been a part of their conversations. At the same time, Carpentier was already the leading figure of the marvelous real, a way of writing that merged fantasy and reality. García Márquez found in Carpentier's interest for the marvelous real another technique to merge the history of the Buendía family and myths about the Caribbean village of Macondo. Counterfactually, had García Márquez not read *Explosion in a Cathedral* and talked to Carpentier about it, *One Hundred Years of Solitude* would have not been written or at least not with the scope the author had imagined for his novel over the years.

Along with feedback from influential writers, García Márquez relied on collaborators of the Mafia. Several helped him as research assistants:

> I said to José Emilio Pacheco: "Please do me a favor and study for me how exactly was the whole thing of the philosopher's stone," and then I put Juan Vicente Melo to investigate plant properties and gave him one week. I asked a Colombian: "Please, do research for me about what all the problems of civil wars in Colombia were about," I asked another one for the greatest amount of data about federal wars in Latin America, and I always had friends doing such tasks for me; all the poetic work, for example, that Álvaro Mutis did for me, is invaluable. . . . Now I realize that *they were all working* on *One Hundred Years of Solitude*.[43]

They worked for him, researching and fact gathering, so he did not have to stop writing. The information selected by collaborators influenced García Márquez's writing about herbs, historical events, wars, and other topics as well as his use of poetic language. And after being transformed into literature fiction, the information and language from his collaborators prompted new questions from the busy writer and led to new creative occasions to investigate these and other topics. In this way, collaborators participated in the act of networked creativity that underlaid the imagination and writing of *One Hundred Years of Solitude.*

Networked creativity also occurred as the writer gathered feedback on what he wrote. He reached out to friends either on the phone or face-to-face and at the end of his writing day, on weekends, or when he was stuck. Along with his wife Mercedes, two couples and Mafia members were at the center of this creative network: the abovementioned poet Mutis (close friend, reader of manuscripts, and unofficial literary agent for the past ten years), his wife Carmen Miracle Feliú, actor María Luisa Elío, and her husband film director and writer Jomí García Ascot. Elío recalled, "Since Gabo did not go out, we went to see him every night. We arrived around eight o'clock. . . . And there we met with the Mutises." They talked about the novel, and "Mutis," García Márquez said, "begins to circulate, enriching it with his imagination, the version [of the story] I gave him; which, over time, comes back to me augmented and improved. More than once it happens that this renewed version that I receive is better than mine; and then I replace it."[44] Often, García Márquez phoned Elío to get her input. "I stayed at home a lot," she said,

> He used to call me. Gabriel told me: "I'm going to read you a little piece, to see what you think." And he read me a little piece. He called me and said: "I'm going to explain to you how the aunts are dressed. What else would you put on them? What color do you think the dress should be?" And we talked. Or he would say: "Look, I have put this word here but I don't know what it means. Did your aunts say so? Because mine did."

Elío read chapters of the novel as García Márquez finished the drafts, too. In short, she was a collaborator regarding "life experiences" and also helped with her viewpoint of an educated female reader. García Márquez's wife, Mercedes, collaborated with him in a similar way. He read his work to her and she would say things like "that was not exactly like that" or "that is not said like that." She collaborated as a language and fact checker, like Elío, and especially as a cultural translator of his region of origin. In this way, his wife confirmed that his use of language and descriptions of characters and events were grounded in their own Caribbean culture.[45]

As part of his strategic approach to feedback, García Márquez shared, both out loud and on paper, his work with friends to test their reactions as potential readers. As he reported in a letter about what he did with guests in the Cave of the Mafia, "I brought together the most demanding, expert, and candid people and read them another [chapter]. The result was great, above all because the chapter I read was the riskiest: Remedios the Beauty's ascent to heaven."

He took this step because he wanted to write a novel with multiple levels. As he explained, "A person without literary education reads the novel for what is happening there, just to know what happens to this character and how another one is faring. So, this public reads it as an adventure novel. And there is another public that sees different things, and then there is a third literary public."[46]

In writing *One Hundred Years of Solitude*, García Márquez also added feedback he received from literary critics. When he joined the Mafia Group, he met an influential gatekeeper, Emmanuel Carballo. This key collaborator was Mexico's top critic. He wrote incessantly about contemporary Latin American and international literature for mainstream professional journal *Casa de las Américas* and general magazine *La Cultura en México*. Carballo was also an important gatekeeper of the publishing industry, since he was then married to the owner of Era, Spanish expat Neus Espresate.[47] The fact that García Márquez and Carballo belonged to the same generation helped strengthen their professional and personal ties. Carballo had interviewed García Márquez for *La Cultura en México* in 1963, after the release of Era's edition of *No One Writes to the Colonel* and during one of García Márquez's hardest professional moments. When he started working on *One Hundred Years of Solitude*, he asked Carballo if he would read his novel in progress. "He chose me," Carballo recalled, "because he knew that I was relentless, that if I didn't like something, I will tell him." He accepted García Márquez's request and commented on the manuscript from beginning to end. The procedure they followed was quite straightforward:

> [García Márquez] brought me the first installment of what he was writing. . . .
> He brought me sheets every Saturday until he finished [the novel], and he
> asked me: "What flaws do you find? Tell me what things you don't like, why
> you don't like them." . . . I didn't have to do anything but just tell him: "It's
> splendid, this character is growing, you're putting this one aside, I don't know
> why but in the next few weeks you will tell me why you're doing it."

A witness of their collaboration, Mexican journalist Carlos Ferreyra, reported that when García Márquez first approached Carballo with chapters in progress, the latter said: "My God, Gabriel, no one can understand this!" One of the things Carballo did was help him with punctuation to make the text more readable. Indeed, as shown below, the final manuscript had almost two hundred and fifty changes in punctuation, starting with the famous opening of the novel.

García Márquez knew that Carballo was a careful reader. Their collaboration was labor-intensive. Every week, Carballo read a chapter in progress: I read "the chapter, two, three times (this will take me a week) to talk about it with him the following week. . . . We talked about the characters. They were our friends. We talked for two, three hours, but not at the level of teacher and disciple but from friend to friend." For Carballo, this was clearly a collaborative work. "This work was finished, and our friendship ended. The year *we were working together* was a very beautiful year." This means that, when they met, they worked for hours on about twenty sheets, which is five sheets below the average length of chapters in the manuscript. (To thank him, García Márquez gave Carballo a copy of the final manuscript.) The result of their labor-intensive collaborative work was that Carballo helped him see inside his novel through the eyes of an expert and leading literary critic as he was writing it. For this reason, Carballo acknowledged, "All my suggestions were already there in the novel." This was possible because, while at his writing desk, García Márquez would recall the critic's recommendations and criticism on previous chapters. More broadly, their collaboration challenged the traditional view of the critic as someone who delivers a critical opinion about a work of art only after it is imagined and produced. Indeed, the case of this and other New Latin American Novels analyzed in chapter 8 shows that a critic can be a collaborator involved in the imagination and production of the work of art, not just in its reception via book reviews. After Carballo influenced García Márquez's imagination during the production of the novel, he acted as a regular critic, wrote a review, and tried to shape the reception of the novel by writing a review.[48]

The author benefited from the feedback and viewpoint of another collaborator who read all his drafts: the typist. Esperanza Araiza became a member of his collaborative network. She had typed best-selling works of the New Latin American Novel by Fuentes and Rulfo, and because of this García Márquez hired her. Thanks to her professional experience, she had developed tacit knowledge about what made these novels click. As she worked with him on the manuscript, she did not limit her input to typing and polishing grammar and syntax; she asked him questions about what certain characters would do and, in this way, another creative collaboration ensued.[49]

García Márquez used the approach of the serialized novel (made famous by nineteenth-century writers such as Dickens and Pérez Galdós) to test his work in progress with different collaborators and to try out alternative scenarios or paths a certain character could take. He studied audience reactions and adapted their recommendations. For this reason, his friend Mutis kindly reproached him after reading the final version of the novel, "Ah, but you are a bastard, this is not what you told me." Elío also said that numerous ideas and versions of events he tested with her did not make it into the final novel. As his literary agent described it, he did "as if he was conducting a general test in order to see how I reacted." Years later, García Márquez offered more details about this technique: "What I told [the audience] has nothing to do with the final result of the story. I told them something different of what I'm actually writing. This is a technique that I have to test the stories, and it allows me to see people's reactions, to know what they are thinking, how they feel the plot and whether what I'm telling hypnotizes them."[50]

Yet García Márquez was aware that excitement about his work in progress could distort the opinions of his closest collaborators. So, he tested other live audiences. In Mexico City, he gave a public reading of his work in progress in June 1966, when he was still three months away from submitting the manuscript to the publisher. Among his guests were "people of all cultural and social levels," including students, secretaries, friends from the film industry and marketing, colleagues, intellectuals, and "typographers and linotypists from the printing workshop" of magazines *Sucesos para Todos* and *La Familia*. He decided not to read a single chapter (the standard practice). Rather, "I selected paragraphs from different chapters because I really wanted to know if the idea [for the novel] was good and not something that Álvaro Mutis planted in my head." This public reading was also important for emotional reasons: it released tension at home. "[My wife Mercedes] had been taking care of the household for at least one year, so that I could write, and on the day of this public reading the expression on her face assured me that the book was heading where it had to."[51]

He tested the novel in progress with people from other Latin American countries who visited Mexico City. As mentioned earlier, he invited Font Castro to his place and, together with Mutis, he heard the first chapter of the novel and gave him feedback on it. Despite the long distance, he sought as much feedback as he could from transnational collaborators. He sent the first three chapters to Harss in Paris. Harss passed them to Fuentes, who talked about them to other Latin American writers and critics. "I told Monegal yesterday," Fuentes wrote to García Márquez, "in an interview for *Mundo Nuevo*, that Latin America, culturally, has gone from the utopia of foundation to the epic of incarnation and from the latter to the myth of re-cognition, of re-conquest: your sheets are the three things." And to help the insecure writer and friend, Fuentes added, "Your first 70 sheets of *One Hundred Years of Solitude* are masterful, and whoever says or insinuates otherwise is a mother-fucker." Fuentes told him that with this novel he was entering the "no-man's land" of great writers such as Faulkner, Jorge Luis Borges, Franz Kafka, Mark Twain, and Graham Greene. Once more, Fuentes was labeling García Márquez a cosmopolitan Latin American writer. Fuentes kept encouraging him until the final stretch. When García Márquez was struggling to finish it, he wrote, "What you tell me about *One Hundred Years of Solitude* is wonderful. Bravo maestro. Nothing should stop you."[52] He also received feedback from Colombia from his friend Mendoza on the first chapter of the novel, which premiered in *El Espectador* in May 1966. "It makes me very happy what you say about the chapter. . . . That's why I published it," because he was uncertain about the quality of the novel. Not all feedback was necessarily positive, but it was useful. Harss reacted coldly to it: "I thought it was a kind of long anecdote, too funny to be taken seriously." Finally, García Márquez took the manuscript with him the only time he left Mexico City during the writing of his novel. He traveled to Colombia in February 1966, where he met with friends of the Barranquilla Group, who helped him to figure out certain parts of the novel, such as the ending.[53]

As mentioned earlier, he premiered one third of the novel in periodicals that circulated in up to twenty-two countries and reached multiple audiences from ordinary readers to the cultural intelligentsia (more on this below). Some of them gave him feedback, as he wrote in a letter to Fuentes: "The advances in *Mundo Nuevo*, *Amaru*, and *Eco* have fared very well: I receive letters from unknown enthusiasts from all places."[54]

After submitting the manuscript to Sudamericana, García Márquez continued to revise the text as he received feedback from more collaborators. In a letter to his friend Angulo in December 1966, he gave precise instructions about the order in which each friend in Bogotá and Barranquilla should read it and asked for their opinion on technical matters. One of them was Germán Vargas, who recalled, "He sent me a copy of the manuscript of *One Hundred Years of Solitude*, asking me for my opinion about it, especially in regard to the insertion of reality in the novel. . . . I reply to him that his way of mixing the fictitious and the real was very good." Manuscript revision continued until March 1967, when he sent the galleys to Sudamericana. Even then, the manuscript was still circulating among friends, and reactions were more positive than he anticipated. Yet he was afraid about what they could say, and hoped "that *they do not change it*, too much."[55]

EDITING, EDITING, EDITING

After receiving the first copy of *One Hundred Years of Solitude* from the publisher, García Márquez destroyed all materials that he produced while writing the novel. These included about forty notebooks with daily notes, diagrams, family trees, partial drafts, and all manuscripts, except for the last one. As described in the previous section, constant transnational feedback helped García Márquez make changes as he was writing the novel. This section analyzes several key changes in the text to better understand the creative process behind the writing of *One Hundred Years of Solitude*. To do so, I built on *critique génétique*—an approach that studies the genesis of a manuscript through its different versions.[56] What I did was to compare the following versions of the novel: the final text in the first edition of the book published in 1967, the three surviving carbon copies of the final typescript of 1966, the seven chapters of the novel premiered between May 1966 and May 1967, and the 181-page galley proofs of March 1967.[57] Changes across the different versions of the novel revealed that García Márquez relentlessly edited the text until the end while informing collaborators about what he was doing. "I just finished editing the galley proofs of *One Hundred Years of Solitude*," he wrote to Vargas Llosa. "The novel has no taste for me anymore, but instead of changing everything, as I desired the nights of insomnia, I decided to leave everything as it was."[58] These editing changes are important to show how an artist's network collaborates in the creative process of a work of art.

Style Variants

The book that García Márquez started to write was a gothic novel. In his interview with critic Miliani in October 1965, he said, "This is the closest definition that I can give of the book I am writing: it is a gothic novel in the tropics." His description of the novel as gothic is not only puzzling but also has gone unnoticed by scholars. Why was *One Hundred Years of Solitude* at first a tropical gothic novel? The trajectory and readings that are part of the writer's imagination help explain it. When he was growing up in his grandparents' home, his grandmother often told the unruly boy scary stories about ghosts living in the house and coming out at night. She warned him that they would come to chase him if he did not behave. This motive of the haunted house in the author's imagination was present in the Harss (July 1965) and

Miliani interviews. To Harss, he said, "[My grandparents] had an enormous house, full of ghosts. . . . In every corner there were skeletons and memories, and after six in the evening you didn't dare leave your room. It was a world of fantastic terrors." Along with his childhood experiences, his early readings in the late 1940s included Nathaniel Hawthorne's *The House of the Seven Gables*, Faulkner's novels, and Kafka's *The Metamorphosis*. These works feature gothic themes that appeared in García Márquez's writing from the beginning of his career. His first published short story, "The Third Resignation" was about a dead boy who told his story from the coffin where he continued to grow. As shown in the previous chapter, gothic elements appeared in several of his early short stories, journalistic pieces, and unpublished manuscripts. Furthermore, the surviving fragments of the manuscript of "The House" also had gothic components.[59]

Some critics noticed a gothic undertone in other works published before *One Hundred Years of Solitude*. Ángel Rama described his short stories in *Big Mama's Funeral* as "phantasmagoric" and explained that this book was a shift from "realism to phantasmagoria." Likewise, critic Volkening referred in an essay to the character of the rooster in *No One Writes to the Colonel* as "phantasmagoric." And the title of his essay stressed the connection between the writer, the Caribbean region, and the occult: "Gabriel García Márquez or the Unbewitched Tropic."[60]

The gothic theme of the haunted house was not exclusive to García Márquez's imagination. It was present, for example, in the work of some of his collaborators, such as his friends of the Barranquilla Group and the Mafia. After years of delays, in 1962 Cepeda Samudio published *La casa grande*, a novella that contained gothic elements, such as the story of a declining family and its house (more in chapter 8). In 1965, in a public talk attended by García Márquez, Fuentes mentioned his childhood fascination with gothic novels and the supernatural. During the talk, he also said that *Pedro Páramo* by Rulfo (whose rural stories and characters Fuentes and García Márquez had adapted into scripts) was "a story of ghosts told by ghosts." After several years in the making, García Márquez's collaborator Mutis published in 1973 *The Manor of Araucaima*, a gothic novella set in a house in the Caribbean.[61]

If we keep in mind the presence of the tropical gothic in García Márquez's imagination, it is possible to understand that multiple characters, situations, and settings in *One Hundred Years of Solitude* are in fact gothic-like. Only a slight twist in the narrative tone is necessary to notice them. These are a few of them: the ghosts of dead people walked in the house for generations; Macondo was first a remote village, set apart from civilization and surrounded by tenebrous marshes and an aggressive jungle; in this jungle, there was a ghost-like galleon, abandoned miles from the coast; the plague of memory sickened the entire population of Macondo, which acted like zombies; Melquíades the gypsy and some of his alien science and objects scared Macondo for years; José Arcadio died mysteriously and his corpse had a persistent odor of gunpowder that people could smell from afar; the goat-like wandering Jew terrorized Macondo residents; flocks of birds suddenly attacked the town; termites and enormous red ants ate the Buendía house for years; the threat of giving birth to a son with a pig's tail tormented the family for generations; ants ate up the body of the last Buendía, a baby born with a pig's tail; and a biblical hurricane destroyed Macondo. In hearing this description of characters and events, someone who has never read *One Hundred Years of Solitude* could perfectly think that those features belong to a gothic novel.

In 1965, when he started to write the novel, he remained loyal to the gothic elements that he imagined in 1950. But as he worked on the manuscript and talked to collaborators about it, the gothic evolved into a mixture of the real and the fantastic. He lessened the gothic facts in the text by adding clarifications that turned into pedestrian events what otherwise could be scary. The appearance of the first ghost, Prudencio Aguilar, was crucial in order to set the tone for the rest of the novel. The patriarch of the Buendías, José Arcadio, killed Aguilar in a duel. Days later, the ghost of Aguilar appeared in the Buendías's house. The first sentence about this event describes Aguilar as a traditional ghostly apparition. "He was livid, a sad expression on his face, trying to cover the hole in his throat with a plug made of esparto grass." The next sentence is key because it describes how José Arcadio's wife, Úrsula, reacts to the ghost's presence. She does not scream or run away, a typical reaction after seeing a ghost. Aguilar's ghost "did not bring on fear in her, but pity." So, adding this sentence was strategic because it changes the readers' interpretation of what otherwise could have been read as a gothic scene. Thus, there is no scary moment because the ghost turns into a sad and human being. In addition, García Márquez never used the word ghost in the description of this scene. He only mentioned the character's name, as if he were a real, living person. Stylistic choices of this kind throughout the novel disguise any direct gothic interpretation and make possible the seamless cohabitation of the real and the fantastic on the same narrative plane, as the writer intended. This stylistic shift allows readers and critics to interpret characters, situations, and settings in the novel not as gothic or creepy but as humorous, fantastic, or magical realist.[62]

Plot Variants

In moving away from the gothic, García Márquez also changed important components of the plot. César Triste was a kind of Sack Man with a pig's tail about whom the young García Márquez heard scary stories from his grandmother. During the early stages of writing the novel, the pig's tail turned into a humorous and fantastic idea. Instead of being the frightening attribute of a potential secondary character, his tail was now the driving idea of the plot—the fear of giving birth to a son with such a tail. This fear remained until the end of the story, when the last Buendía was indeed born with a pig's tail.

At first, García Márquez had no title for the novel. He wrote to Fuentes in October 1965 that he just come up with *One Hundred Years of Solitude* and asked for his opinion about it.[63] In the Miliani interview, done a few weeks earlier, the writer said that his novel in progress had no title. This seems true because of the way he summarized the plot:

> It is the public and private history of a family in some Caribbean town, of their greatness and misery, of their deserved frustrations, of their tragic destiny from the times of the colony to the present. The first generation of this family founded the town, the second was ruined by the War of Independence, the third organized thirty-two civil wars and lost them all, the fourth revolted the workers against the injustices of the banana company and the result was a massacre, the fifth conquered power without intending it and did not know what to do with it, and the sixth became extinct in the nostalgia of its past greatness. The last of the line shot himself tormented by solitude, in a town already transformed into a big and hot African city, where nobody knew who he was. In the absence of a name, the authorities placed on his grave the number of the judicial file.[64]

Major elements of the novel were already present in this summary of the plot. It was a historical narrative set in the Caribbean that spanned several centuries, clearly showing the author's debt to *Explosion in a Cathedral*. But other major elements were absent. García Márquez mentioned neither the fear of incest nor the names of the village and the family. Remarkably, the novel's hero, Colonel Aureliano Buendía, was missing. However, these elements were no longer absent in November 1965. In a letter to Harss, García Márquez explained that his novel "[is] not just the story of Colonel Buendía, but that of his whole family, from the founding of Macondo to the day the last Buendía commits suicide a hundred years later, putting an end to the line." Another key addition to the plot was the repetition of characters' names generation after generation: "In the hundred years of history there are four José Arcadio Buendías and three Aurelianos." In his letter to Harss, García Márquez also mentioned Macondo as the location of the novel.[65]

These differences suggest that he figured out between October and November how to insert the colonel in the novel.[66] And he solved this at the same time he was working on the preparatory notes for *The Autumn of the Patriarch*. This further suggests that, during this time, he realized what *One Hundred Years of Solitude* was going to be about and separated the character of Colonel Buendía from the main character of *The Autumn of the Patriarch*. These two breakthroughs helped him understand that *The Autumn of the Patriarch* and *One Hundred Years of Solitude* were two different novels, not a single one. He also realized that the story would not begin during the colonial era but with the foundation of Macondo. This decision shortened the novel's time span from three or four centuries to a bit over one hundred years and hence the plot's length was reduced by half.[67]

By the fall of 1965, the novel's ending was still underdeveloped. In the Miliani interview and the Harss letter, the novel ended when the last Buendía committed suicide. Yet he killed himself in different ways. In the Miliani interview, he shot himself and was buried in an unmarked tomb, and in the Harss letter he committed suicide because the motive of the pig's tail had moved to the center of the plot: "the tragic fate of the last suicidal Aureliano, who is born to solitude with an old family stigma: a pig's tail." It is important to underscore that, in both versions of the ending, the town of Macondo survived the death of the last Buendía. In the final version, the town disappears along with the Buendías. The ending only changed after García Márquez's trip to Colombia in February 1966. He traveled to his hometown of Aracataca with his friends Angulo and Cepeda Samudio. They revisited the locations of his fictional Macondo, including his grandparents' house. One of the subjects of conversation with his collaborators was *One Hundred Years of Solitude* and his next film script, *Presagio*, which he put on hold to work on his novel. During his visit, a creative connection appeared between his novel and the film script: he decided to use the ending of *Presagio* for the novel. In the script, the town is condemned to disappear after everybody leaves. This also became the fate of Macondo in the novel. Only the last Buendía stayed behind to witness the town's disappearance, when "a storm happens and takes everything with it," as he explained to a journalist at the end of his visit. Counterfactually, had García Márquez finished the script for *Presagio* in early 1965, part of *One Hundred Years of Solitude* could have become a movie. Instead, García Márquez and screenwriter Alcoriza worked on this script for about four months. Then García Márquez "disappeared," as Alcoriza put it, to write his novel.[68]

Character Variants

Changes in the text affected both main to minor characters and early- to late-appearing characters. The novel's hero, Colonel Buendía, mentioned in the opening sentence, was not going to be a central character at all. As shown earlier, García Márquez did not even refer to him in the Miliani interview. Rather, the colonel's role was going to be secondary, as he had been in previous works. He would simply pass through Macondo during the wars. But during the writing, García Márquez decided that Colonel Buendía would be born in Macondo, although it was unclear which son of the founders would be the colonel: José Arcadio or Aureliano. In terms of character development, the colonel died earlier in the novel, and García Márquez brought him back to life. After talking to his collaborator Elío, the writer understood that he had to "give the story another twist so that he is not dead." By the time García Márquez traveled to Colombia, the colonel's death was very similar to the death of the last Buendía described in the Miliani interview. The colonel died anonymously: "the dead is buried with the file number." In the final version of the novel, the colonel died peacefully when he was urinating under a chestnut tree.[69]

Another main character, Remedios the Beauty, originally had a different name: Rebeca de Asís. García Márquez probably recycled this name from the novella *In Evil Hour*. The choice of Rebeca maintained the rule of repeating characters' first names across generations, as choosing Remedios did. And her original last name, de Asís, implies a more religious rather than sensual character, for it brings to memory the character of Saint Francis of Assisi. These changes suggest that beauty might have not been Remedios's defining attribute in an initial version of the novel. Furthermore, in an earlier version Remedios (or Rebeca) ran away with a lover, instead of ascending to the sky. This version would have left the novel without one of its "riskiest," as the writer put it, and most memorable passages. Before setting on the final version, García Márquez tried yet another one: Rebeca died and her dead body ascended to heaven in front of many people. In the final version, the character (with a new name, Remedios) ascended to the sky alive and in front of only two relatives.[70]

Changes in Manuscripts and Galley Proofs

The three copies of the final typescript of 1966 and the galley proofs of 1967 contain handwritten corrections. The analysis of the changes across these documents and the final text of the novel published in 1967 revealed several editing patterns:

(1) *Archaisms.* As García Márquez learned from a conversation with Carpentier about the use of language in *Explosion in a Cathedral*, he wanted the language and the style to be more archaic at the beginning of *One Hundred Years of Solitude*. For example, he used "grande alboroto" (uproar), 1967 novel, p. 1, instead of "gran alboroto", typescript, p. 1. Language became more modern with the passage of time, that is, as generations passed. For example, "instrumentos músicos" (musical instruments) in chapter 1 of the typescript was again "instrumentos músicos" in chapter 8 of the typescript (p. 174), but not in the final text, which has the more modern "instrumentos musicales" (p. 130).

(2) *Rhythm.* The typescript contains more than two hundred changes in punctuation. Over 90 percent of these changes involved adding or suppressing commas or removing periods to join two paragraphs. This is apparent from chapter 1 onward. In the typescript, García Márquez suppressed six periods in the first six sheets (the equivalent to the first three pages of the final novel). He did so to introduce the story in a single narrative block, with the goal of maintaining readers' attention. Words were also chosen to convey a certain rhythm. As mentioned above, critic Carballo helped García Márquez with punctuation to make the text more readable.[71]

(3) *Concise language.* García Márquez edited the text word by word and sentence by sentence. Regarding word editing, he eliminated what did not help to move the action forward or clarify it. One telling example is the reference to "amber substance," which appears on chapter 1 when the young Colonel Buendía is about to discover ice. In the first version of this event, the one that premiered in the newspaper *El Espectador* on May 1, 1966, the colonel's father drank "una copa de la azucarada substancia color de ámbar" ("a glass of the sugary substance of amber color") (p. 10e). Then, in the typescript, the writer removed the reference to the taste of the substance and shortened the sentence by typing: "una copa de la substancia color ámbar" ("a glass of the substance of amber color"). But during a revision of the typescript, he decided to cross

out the sentence and handwrote an even shorter description: "una copa de la substancia ambarina" ("a glass of the amber substance"). And in the final text, it became "una copa de la sustancia ambarina." (He removed the letter *b* from the word substance.) Regarding sentence-by-sentence editing, he suppressed several to speed up the action. For example, he did this before an important event: the massacre of the striking banana workers in chapter 15. He also crossed out half a page of the typescript (pp. 456–57). He did this in order to remove the references to literature classics made by his Barranquilla Group friends. During their conversation, they called Cervantes and Shakespeare "asshole" and "motherfucker," respectively, out of admiration for them.

(4) *Consistency*. Here, García Márquez edited single words as well as entire paragraphs. For example, on page 108 of the galley proofs, he added one hundred and twenty new words to describe how Colonel Buendía cried inside Úrsula's womb. With these words, he wanted to clarify the reason for the colonel's weeping: it announced his innate solitude and incapacity for love that explain many of his actions later in life (typescript, p. 293; novel, p. 214). This kind of editing also sought to ensure consistency in the words he used for key events. The famous "firing squad" of the opening sentence reappears several times in the novel. In one case, the typescript refers to it as a "wall" (paredón), a word that García Márquez eliminated and replaced with "firing squad" (pelotón). Word choice was also necessary to respect the historical sequence of the evolution of Macondo from a tiny settlement to a large town to its collapse. Thus, the writer crossed out in the typescript the word "city" (ciudad) to refer to Macondo in chapter 3. Instead, he used the word "field" (campamento). This latter word described more accurately the urban development of Macondo at this moment in the novel.

(5) *Syntax*. Changes appear throughout the typescript and reveal García Márquez's obsession with and excellent command of editing his own writing. He learned this skill while working as a journalist and magazine editor, as shown earlier.[72]

Changes in Premiered Chapters

The seven chapters of *One Hundred Years of Solitude* that premiered in printed media further proved that the opinions of collaborators in García Márquez's transnational network informed the writing and revision of the manuscript.

When compared to premiered chapters 1 and 2, the final text of *One Hundred Years of Solitude* contains forty-two and fifty-one changes, respectively. Several of these changes are key to the construction of the novel. In premiered chapter 1, readers could easily identify Macondo as a village in Colombia. This version included precise references to its location: "to the west [there were] the dunes of the Magdalena River" of Colombia. But the final text of the novel did not include this and other geographic references. Giving no specific information about the location of Macondo increased its isolation and also its Latin American and universal appeal. With this change, García Márquez sought to create the impression that Macondo could be a cosmopolitan and typical village in any Latin American country, and even in Paris, as he explained in an interview in 1966. This change helped readers universalize Macondo (see chapter 6).

Another important change had to do with the birth of Colonel Buendía, which García Márquez rewrote. In the final version, the colonel "had wept in his mother's womb and had been born with his eyes open," while in the premiered chapter 1, the novel's hero received a non-heroic treatment: the midwife "smacked his bottom three times, energetically" to get him to cry. As indicated above, to be consistent with this change, García Márquez added in the galley proofs six sentences to chapter 13. These new sentences reminded readers that the colonel cried inside her mother's womb.

A residue of the original, gothic tone in the novel had to do with the destructive action of termites (*comején*) and "enormous red ants." In early versions of the text, the termites appeared already in chapter 1. García Márquez kept them there until the version premiered in *El Espectador* in May 1966. In this version, "termites undermined the foundations of the house" from chapter 1 onward. During revisions, the writer removed this sentence from the manuscript. (His collaborator Mendoza was among those who read and commented on the *El Espectador* version.) García Márquez did so for the sake of narrative consistency. Such early references to termites eating the foundations of the house would lessen the impact that its future decay due to the presence of termites could have on readers. These references would also lead to inconsistencies because the fact that termites ate the house from the start contradicted the splendor that the house and the village experienced by the middle of the novel before their rapid decline. For this reason, the first reference to termites only appeared halfway the novel (chapter 9) and more often from chapter 17 until chapter 20. In these last four chapters, the growing presence of termites, along with that of "enormous red ants," added drama and suspense to the end of the story, when ants eat the last Buendía. The nature and amount of these and other changes, especially in premiered chapters 1 and 2, confirm that after May 1966 and until he finished revising the galley proofs, he continued to edit the text with the help of collaborators. His goal was to remove any inconsistencies that contradicted the narrative. As his correspondence reveals, these changes led to a substantial reduction of pages. In a letter to Colombian journalist Guillermo Cano in April 1966, he said that the manuscript would be eight hundred sheets long and, when he finished it five months later, it ended up being just under five hundred.

MARKETING THE NOVEL

How much does a cultural good owe its success to a favorable moment? For *One Hundred Years of Solitude*, such a moment was central to its success. To cash on the momentum of the New Latin American Novel, García Márquez's book benefited from a transnational, prepublication advertising campaign in newspapers and magazines. These periodicals targeted four different audiences: intelligentsia (highly educated readers), critics, peer writers, and common readers. The marketing campaign for the novel, remarkably, lasted the same time García Márquez spent writing the novel. The prepublication campaign ran from May 1966 to May 1967 (thirteen months), while he wrote the novel approximately between August 1965 and August 1966 (thirteen months). After this long campaign, by the time of its publication on May 30, 1967, consumers of New Latin American Novels had high expectations.

Advance chapters of the novel were key to promoting it among its potential consumers. Argentine critic Ernesto Ayala-Dip recalled that in Buenos Aires in 1966, "I first read the first chapter or the second chapter of *One Hundred Years of Solitude*. For us, reading it was almost a real epiphany. . . . I was then . . . nineteen years old and when I read those first two chapters I did nothing else. Those living in these circles in Buenos Aires and I were desperately hoping to get the novel to read it."[73]

As table 4.1 shows, with the publication of advance chapters, García Márquez wanted, first, to test audience reaction to the novel and, second, to insert it in the commercial circuit of the New Latin American Novel. Thus, one third of *One Hundred Years of Solitude* was available to readers in over twenty countries in Latin America, North America, and Europe, including international general interest magazines, avant-garde literary journals, and the Sunday edition of national newspapers.

Table 4.1 Chapters of *One Hundred Years of Solitude* premiered before its publication.

Date	Publication (Issue), Place	Chapter	Changes[a]	Audience	Major themes in the chapter
1966/May/1	*El Espectador*, Colombia	1	42	M	Intro to Macondo and the Buendía family (first two generations)
1966/August	*Mundo Nuevo* (2), France	2	51	I, C, P	Founding of Macondo; Buendía's fear of incest; José Arcadio's genitals
1967/January	*Amaru* (1), *Peru*	12[b]	3	I, P	Remedios the Beauty's ascent to heaven; Macondo's banana fever
1967/February	*Eco* (14:4), Colombia	17	8	P, C	Ursula's death; Macondo's decline
1967/March	*Mundo Nuevo* (9), France	3	12	I, C, P	Insomnia plague in Macondo
1967/March–April	*Diálogos* (2:3), Mexico,	16	6	I, P	Four-year rain in Macondo; Aureliano Segundo ruined
1967/May/5	*Marcha* (1351), Uruguay	16[b]	13	M	Four-year rain in Macondo
1967/May/23–29	*Primera Plana* (230), Argentina	7[b]	0	M	Colonel Buendía's wars; death of his father and Macondo founder

Notes: M = Mass readers, I = Intelligentsia, C = Critics, P = Peer writers

[a] Including only from word and/or sentence replacement and/or suppression.

[b] Fragment.

People García Márquez had met over the last twenty years in Europe, North America, and Latin America published articles, reviews, and notes to create momentum for his novel before its release. These collaborators made sure not to simply refer to it as a rural novel set in Colombia's tropical Caribbean region but, more ambitiously, to label it a New Latin American Novel. As table 4.2 shows, reviewers did so by connecting it to major works in other literary traditions, from *One Thousand and One Nights* and *In Cold Blood* to major writers such as Thomas Moore and Faulkner. These reviews confirm that critics act as brokers in the creation of literary value. However, what is less known is how much the creation of this value can rely on an author's network, including peer writers who pass as critics.

In *La Cultura en México*, the supplement of a magazine with one hundred thousand weekly readers, a key writer in García Márquez's network, Fuentes, wrote the first book review of *One Hundred Years of Solitude*. As the first critic of the novel, he had a clear goal: to promote it as yet another successful New Latin American Novel, even if García Márquez had not finished it yet. Fuentes based his review on seventy sheets and alerted readers that this "novel in progress [was] masterful." He also praised García Márquez's neo-baroque language and added that his colleague was writing "[America's] history," in which myths played a central role. Macondo, for him, was "Site of the myth." And this village and the Buendías were similar to Comala and the Páramos, the village and the family in the Latin American best seller *Pedro Páramo*. Fuentes also connected the story in *One Hundred Years of Solitude* to cosmopolitan authors such as Faulkner and his fictional Yoknapatawpha County, calling García Márquez's Macondo the "Colombian Yoknapatawpha."[74]

In April 1967, one month before the novel's release, another best-selling New Latin American Novel writer, Vargas Llosa, acting as a literary critic, was cited in an anonymous book review published in *Primera Plana*. Vargas Llosa, in a friendly way, challenged Fuentes's opinion about *One Hundred Years of Solitude* and argued that it was more like a novel of chivalry set in Latin America. With that reference, Vargas Llosa connected the novel to the literary milieu of *Don Quixote* and the Spanish literature of the Golden Age. He reiterated his opinion in a review published after the novel's release in the avant-garde literary magazine *Eco* (which months earlier premiered one chapter of the novel). Neither Fuentes nor Vargas Llosa limited his actions to a book review. In private, they corresponded with García Márquez and gave him professional and emotional support as he was writing the novel. Fuentes, for example, informed him about people's excitement about the novel: "When is *One Hundred Years of Solitude* [going to be] published? Everyone who reads

Table 4.2 Reviews and notes about *One Hundred Years of Solitude* published before its release.

Date	Author	Title	Publication (Issue), Place	Main audience	Books and authors indexed
1966/June/29	Carlos Fuentes[a]	García Márquez, *Cien años de soledad*	*Siempre!* (679), Mexico	M, I	Gallegos, J. E. Rivera, Faulkner, Borges, Paz, Carpentier, Cortázar, *Pedro Páramo* by Rulfo, *Utopia* by Moore
1966/July	Fuentes & Rodríguez Monegal[b]	La situación del escritor en América latina	*Mundo Nuevo* (1), France	I, C, P	Joyce, Gallegos, Rivera, Faulkner
1966/August/7	García Márquez	Desventuras de un escritor de libros	*El Espectador*, Colombia	M	*In Cold Blood* by Capote, Camus, Sartre
1966/December	Luis Harss	Gabriel García Márquez o la cuerda floja	*Mundo Nuevo* (6), France	I, C, P	Donoso, Fuentes, Vargas Llosa, Joyce, Kafka, Faulkner, Woolf, *The Plague* by Camus
1967/February	Valencia Goelkel	Editorial	*Eco* (14:4), Colombia	P, C	Vargas Llosa, C. Alegría, Carpentier, M. Vallejo, C. Calderón
1967/April	Germán Vargas[c]	Autor de una obra que hará ruido	*Encuentro Liberal*, Colombia	I, C	*The Green House* and *The Time of the Hero* by Vargas Llosa, Faulkner, Woolf
1967/April/18–24	Anonymous	Amadís de Colombia	*Primera Plana* (225), Argentina	M	*Amadís de Gaula*, *Hopscotch* by Cortázar, *The Green House* by Vargas Llosa, *Explosion in a Cathedral* by Carpentier, *The Death of Artemio Cruz* by Fuentes
1967/June/20–26	Ernesto Schoo	Los viajes de Simbad García Márquez[d]	*Primera Plana* (234), Argentina	M	*One Thousand and One Nights*, *Gargantua*, *Pantagruel*, *Mrs. Dalloway* and *Orlando*, Faulkner, Kafka
1967/June/20–26	Tomás Eloy Martínez	América: la gran novela[d]	*Primera Plana* (234), Argentina	M	*Calila e Dimna*, *Conde Lucanor*, *Mío cid*, *Amadís*, Güiraldes, Gallegos, Azuela, Rivera, Macedonio Fernández, Artl, Borges, Cortázar, Vargas Llosa, Onetti, Guimarães Rosa, Carpentier

Notes: M = Mass readers, I = Intelligentsia, C = Critics, P = Peer writers

[a] La Mafia Group leader.

[b] *Mundo Nuevo*'s chief editor.

[c] Barranquilla Group member.

[d] Scheduled to coincide with the book's release, but postponed for technical reasons.

your instalments in *Mundo Nuevo* is speechless. [Novelist] Beatriz Guido and [film director] Torres Nilsson [from Argentina] have just written to me in this regard." In public, "Mario [Vargas Llosa]," as literary critic Rodríguez Monegal witnessed, "has been one of the most active promoters of *One Hundred Years of Solitude*, since the manuscript started to circulate in Paris."[75] Thus, Fuentes and Vargas Llosa, acclaimed producers of New Latin American Novels, helped best position this novel in the literary market before its publication. In the process, their reviews shaped the opinions of critics and common readers who were yet to read it.[76]

In Colombia, García Márquez's collaborators also marketed the novel before its publication. It is "the best Colombian novel written in the last quarter of the century," Barranquilla Group member Germán Vargas proclaimed in his review, "Autor de una obra que hará ruido" ("Author of a Work that Will Make Noise"). And he quoted Vargas Llosa's review, saying "it is the best thing that has been written in many years in the Spanish language." Germán Vargas wrote that his friend's book was a cosmopolitan Colombian novel that happened in a "*costeño* town" with connections to Faulkner's literature. To further impress readers, Vargas mentioned that publishers in up to five countries would publish the novel and that, in the United States, publishers Harper & Row and Coward-McCann were competing for it, offering up to US$10,000, a sum never seen before for a Colombian literary work. Vargas's review appeared in the first issue of *Encuentro Liberal*, a modern-looking general interest magazine for the middle classes; one of García Márquez's collaborators, Mendoza, was its executive director. Even García Márquez, when he was about to finish the novel, wrote the essay "Desventuras de un escritor de libros" ("Misadventures of a Book Writer"). It came out in *El Espectador*, the same newspaper that in May had published the first chapter of his novel. His essay began with the following statement: "Writing books is a suicidal job." Here, he followed the strategy of Fuentes and Vargas Llosa about the importance of influencing the media as a writer of New Latin American Novels. This strategy also helped maintain momentum for the work in progress among readers of these novels and international best sellers, such as Truman Capote's *In Cold Blood*, which he mentioned in his essay.[77]

The imminent publication of *One Hundred Years of Solitude* helped García Márquez expand his network and strengthen connections, including writers and critics from three generations: Carpentier, Rama, Benedetti, Nicolás Guillén, Roberto Fernández Retamar, Miguel Otero Silva, and Juan Liscano. Behind the scenes, he relied on this network to influence the initial reception of the novel. He authorized Volkening, a critic he trusted, to promote the novel as he wanted.[78] He sent letters to critics and peers across the region, two being critic Pedro Lastra in Chile and Germán Vargas, his friend in Colombia. A comparison of the letters reveals that García Márquez followed a script with his collaborators to ensure the best possible launch for his novel in Latin America:

> Send to Paco Porrúa, at Sudamericana Press, a very precise list of the critics and journalists who should receive advance copies to ensure a good book launch in Chile. On this list, of course, you put your name at the top. [Letter to Lastra]

> Make a quick list, but very precise, of the critics and journalists of Colombia who should receive an advance copy so that the book launch is perfectly covered. You put your name on top of the list, of course, and try not to miss a single shot. [Letter to Vargas][79]

Five months before its release, *Mundo Nuevo* premiered in full Harss's interview with García Márquez. (Soon after, it also appeared in *Into the Mainstream*, the best-selling volume of interviews with Latin American writers.) An endnote indicated that *Mundo Nuevo* had premiered the second chapter of *One Hundred Years of Solitude* in August 1966 and that Sudamericana would publish it in 1967. *Mundo Nuevo*'s editor, literary critic Rodríguez Monegal, was first introduced to the works of García Márquez by Fuentes in 1964. Two years later, Rodríguez Monegal said to the writer, with whom he had regular correspondence, that he was "one of the greatest propagandists of the novel after having read only one chapter." He said so to Porrúa, the novel's acquisitions editor, who had just read the full manuscript: "How I envy you! . . . Now, you already have the book and you are the first Columbus to arrive at this completely new world."[80]

Along with *Mundo Nuevo*, *Primera Plana* promoted the novel because of its commercial partnership with Sudamericana. In its April 18, 1967, issue, *Primera Plana* added Harss's *Into the Mainstream* to its best-seller list. Above this list, the magazine announced the release of *One Hundred Years of Solitude* and cited Vargas Llosa's endorsement. This announcement also put the novel at the level of other best-selling Latin American novels, such as *Hopscotch*, *The Green House*, *The Devil to Pay in the Backlands*, *Adam Buenosayres*, *The Shipyard*, *The Death of Artemio Cruz*, and *Explosion in a Cathedral*. Thanks to these novels, the announcement claimed, the region's literature was becoming a phenomenon similar to the U.S. novel of the 1920s, led by Hemingway, Scott Fitzgerald, and Gertrude Stein. In late May 1967, a week before the novel's release,

4.2 Cover of *Primera Plana* dedicated to García Márquez and *One Hundred Years of Solitude.*

Primera Plana premiered chapter 7 and announced that the novel was being hailed as "one of the best works of fiction ever published in America." In mid-June, when the magazine dedicated its cover to Gabriel García Márquez (see figure 4.2), its hundreds of thousands of readers in the region read the main cover line: "The Great Novel of America." The accompanying interview, conducted in the Mutises's house and with the presence of María Luisa Elío and Mercedes, García Márquez's wife, publicized to an international audience that this book would be the "baptismal font [of the] New American Novel." The journalist added that the first edition was already sold out.[81] In the interview and cover photo, García Márquez branded himself a cosmopolitan Latin American writer. And he connected his writing to that of major writers such as Hemingway and to Latin American literature. Following the interview was a laudatory review by critic Tomas Eloy Martínez, who compared the novel, as table 4.2 shows, to the works of cosmopolitan and Latin American writers.

The evidence so far might suggest that *One Hundred Years of Solitude* received unusual media coverage before and upon its release. But the truth is that "García Márquez was no special case in this regard," as *Mundo Nuevo*'s editor put it, "because this was what I had been doing for other writers, Reinaldo Arenas, Manuel Puig, Severo Sarduy, and Guillermo Cabrera Infante among them." The same goes for *Primera Plana*, which said that *The Time of the Hero* by Vargas Llosa was "one of the greatest Latin American novels of all time" and *Three Trapped Tigers* by Cabrera Infante was "expected to become the most shocking invention of Latin American narrative in recent times."[82]

Sudamericana's release of *One Hundred Years of Solitude* on June 5, 1967, was not unusual either. The publisher followed the same marketing strategy used for other books. It was sold in bookstores, newsstands, and entrances to subway stations in order to reach the broadest possible audience. As general manager Vidal Buzzi put it, "Television was economically unthinkable. . . . So the usual ads came out in literary supplements of newspapers and in some magazines." Announcements of this kind started to appear no later than June 6. *Primera Plana* printed one in its June 8 issue. It appeared in a tiny spot of an omnibus advertisement that featured ten books, including *Cosmicomics* by Italian writer Italo Calvino and *La Femme au petit renard* (*The Woman with the Little Fox*) by French author Violette Leduc (whose *La Bâtarde* [*La Batarde: An Autobiography*] was a best seller a year earlier in Argentina). Sudamericana included *One Hundred Years of Solitude* in its collection *Great Novels* (*Grandes Novelas*). The book's paper quality and appearance, which followed the publisher's norm, were quite "modest." It was a softcover paperback of 352 pages that sold for an affordable 650 Argentine pesos (US$1.8). The back cover presented García Márquez in an unassuming way, too. It described him as a writer born in Colombia and as the author of several books, all of them connected to an "obsessive theme: the imaginary life and landscape of Macondo." *One Hundred Years of Solitude* was just the "complete history of Macondo."[83]

PUTTING EXPECTATIONS IN CONTEXT

Those involved in the production of *One Hundred Years of Solitude* did not expect much of it. As this section shows, preexisting conditions shaped the expectations of individuals and organizations about this novel. To begin with, neither García Márquez nor his collaborators, starting with María Luisa Elío herself, anticipated a major success. "I thought the book was really good. But

I'll be frank," she said, "to *that* degree, no." Asked if he thought the novel could become a best seller, Porrúa, Sudamericana's acquisitions editor, replied, "No, I didn't think about that." His company released an initial print run of eight thousand copies. Given the good sales for Latin American novels at the time, the company calculated that this novel would be available for sale for six to twelve months and then disappear from view as other New Latin American Novels were published. As with most of these novels, *One Hundred Years of Solitude* should not have had a second printing.[84]

García Márquez was "really scared" when he learned his novel would be released in Spain and France and that publishers in the United States were competing for it. He feared that it would not sell. As he wrote to a literary critic, my novel "represents my great hope to escape the anonymity in which I have been writing for twenty years." For him, this hope consisted of selling most copies of the first printing. Since he wrote it as a New Latin American Novel, good regional sales would attract a mainstream publisher in Spain to import and publish the novel. International recognition would follow with translations into English, French, German, and Italian. To hit the jackpot in 1967 was to receive one of the coveted literary awards of the Spanish language, the Biblioteca Breve, Rómulo Gallegos, Casa de las Américas, or Formentor. With this kind of success, García Márquez thought he could use *One Hundred Years of Solitude* as a "trampoline" for other writing projects.[85]

In reality, he had serious doubts, which he often shared with his collaborators, about the quality of the text. "When I read what I had written so far I had the demoralizing feeling of being involved in an adventure that could be either fortunate or catastrophic." After finalizing the manuscript, his mood could not be more somber. "The problem is mine," he confessed to Mendoza, "that after so many years of working like an animal, I feel overwhelmed with fatigue, without clear perspectives, except in the only terrain that I like and does not feed me: the novel."[86] Little did he expect that the sales of a single book would do that for him for the rest of his life.

Since he believed he could not live off writing full-time after finishing the novel, he planned to write columns for the Colombian newspaper *El Tiempo*. He declined an offer to move to Paris and work as editor for *Mundo Nuevo*. Instead, he returned to advertising and scriptwriting, including three film projects with Alcoriza. The University of California at Berkeley invited him to lecture on the New Latin American Novel; an invitation he wanted to use to write *The Autumn of the Patriarch*. Only as the day of publication of *One Hundred Years of Solitude* approached did he start to believe that perhaps he could secure an income from Sudamericana and Harper & Row if he wrote a book per year.[87]

INITIAL CIRCULATION AND SALES

One Hundred Years of Solitude was a success upon publication, but at first it was far from a resounding one. *Tomorrow I'll Say, Enough* (1968), by Argentine Silvina Bullrich and published by Sudamericana, sold forty thousand copies the first month, while *One Hundred Years of Solitude* sold ten thousand in three weeks. In fact, the initial success of this novel owed less to actual sales and more to the rapid diffusion of reviews about it in literary and general interest magazines and newspapers' cultural supplements. These reviews increased the regional demand for the novel. They also revealed how much the region was now culturally connected and capable of circulating news more rapidly than before the 1960s, when communication and book distribution were slower and more local. For this reason, news about the novel's success spread faster than readers' access to it. Indeed, two problems that stopped the distribution of successful books in previous decades also slowed down the early circulation of *One Hundred Years of Solitude*. The first problem was poor regional distribution, including that of New Latin American Novels. Only seventy copies (0.8 percent) of the first printing made it to bookstores in Caracas, Venezuela. In García Márquez's home country, Colombia, tariff problems made it quite difficult to acquire copies from the start. In Lima, Peru, newspapers informed the public that, four months after its release, the book had sold forty thousand copies in Argentina but could not be found in Lima, despite import requests from booksellers. Half a year after its publication, a journalist reported that two thousand copies were finally for sale in Lima's bookstores. The second problem was faulty paper supply, a serious obstacle in Spain the previous decade and still ongoing in Mexico and Colombia (see chapter 2). The second printing of ten thousand copies left the publisher in Argentina without paper and "without printing quotas." Thus, for two months, "all of Latin America talked about *One Hundred Years of Solitude*, but people could not buy it because it was not in bookstores." Luckily for this novel, the modernization of the region's publishing industry reached a point that permitted it to quickly surmount these two perennial problems.[88]

Overcoming these obstacles was possible because of other best-selling books that preceded *One Hundred Years of Solitude*. Its success in Argentina was similar to that of *Hopscotch* (1962) and *Bomarzo* (1962), also published in Buenos Aires by Sudamericana. Five years later, when *One Hundred Years of Solitude* came out, the publishing industry in the region and Spain was in full swing, New Latin American Novels were featured regionally and internationally, and their audience was growing. Sudamericana released a new edition of *Bomarzo* in mid-1967 (at the same time as *One Hundred Years of Solitude*), and it immediately rose to the number one position in *Primera Plana's* best-seller list.

One Hundred Years of Solitude also entered the literary market when there was little competition against the New Latin American Novel, and this movement's agenda was starting to pay off commercially.[89] Promoting this agenda were writers such as Fuentes, Vargas Llosa, Carpentier, and Cortázar, publishers such as Sudamericana, Seix Barral, and Joaquín Mortíz, critics such as Rodríguez Monegal, Rama, and Carballo, and periodicals such as *La Cultura en México, Primera Plana,* and *Mundo Nuevo.* Writers, publishers, critics, and periodicals in the United States, France, Spain, England, and Italy were also interested in New Latin American Novels. Their attention proved that Latin American writers had succeeded at positioning their literary products as a viable commercial alternative to the dated European bourgeois novel, social realism in Spain, the *nouveau roman* in France, and indigenism in Latin America. By 1967, indigenism had become a marginal style among writers and a commercial failure for publishers in the region. The market shifted to the kind of cosmopolitan Latin American works written by Borges, Cortázar, Fuentes, and Manuel Mújica Láinez, among others. In Spain, social realism no longer received support from mainstream Spanish publishers, as critic Josep Maria Castellet stated in a Latin American conference in Caracas in 1967. In France, the moment of the *nouveau roman* had passed. There, the national best seller in 1967 was *Friday, or, The Other Island,* an anti-*nouveau roman* novel, which also won that year's prestigious Grand Prix du Roman of the French Academy. And in other European countries, influential authors such as Günter Grass and Natalia Ginzburg wrote about the death of the bourgeois novel.

The success of the New Latin American Novel in general and the year-long prepublication campaign for *One Hundred Years of Solitude* yielded great results. As mentioned, the novel came out on June 5 with a print run of eight thousand copies. During its first week, it sold eighteen hundred copies. By the end of the second week, when *Primera Plana* featured García Márquez and his novel on its cover, sales tripled. The edition sold out by week three. The second printing of ten thousand copies, with a new book cover by Mafia member Vicente Rojo, was issued on June 30. (Rojo sent the artwork on time to be the first cover of the novel, but the package got lost in the mail, and Sudamericana's designer Iris Pagano rushed to create a cover for the first printing that featured a galleon lost in the middle of a jungle.) Starting in June and except for one week, *One Hundred Years of Solitude* stayed on the best-seller list of *Primera Plana* for fifty weeks. And except for the first two weeks of August, the novel was in the number one position for twenty-one consecutive weeks between June and November 1967.

For the first and second printings, sales were mainly confined to Buenos Aires. As demand for copies was rising, Sudamericana's publishing strategy changed in August. It decided to include advertisements of the novel, especially in *Mundo Nuevo* and *Primera Plana*, in which three top Latin American writers, Cortázar, Fuentes, and Vargas Llosa, praised it and labeled it a cosmopolitan and Latin American novel. The third and fourth printings were released in September and December, with print runs of approximately twelve thousand copies each. At this time, more copies reached Latin American readers beyond Argentina. The publisher also put out a recording of García Márquez reading the first chapter as part of its collection of literary works read by their autors. Famous Argentine journalist Ernesto Schoo, who interviewed the author in *Primera Plana* in June, wrote the introductory note. (In Mexico, Universidad Nacional Autónoma released a similar disc and critic Carballo wrote the introductory note.) A few months later, Sudamericana published new editions of *No One Writes to the Colonel* and *In Evil Hour*, which quickly landed on *Primera Plana's* best-seller list." And García Márquez went on a Latin American speaking and book tour between August and September of 1967, visiting Buenos Aires, Caracas, Lima, and Bogotá.[90]

During the tour, Latin American media interviewed García Márquez, and he used his advertising skills to promote the book by making shocking statements. For example, he said that he would stop writing novels, belittled *One Hundred Years of Solitude* as a "dead lion" (meaning that it no longer interested him), claimed his wife actually wrote it, and stated that it was just the story of a family who did not want to have a child with a pig's tail. "That's it. The rest are adornments." He also went on the offensive, defending his book as a New Latin American Novel and branding himself as a Latin American writer. He stated that he belonged to a group of writers whose goal was to write the novel of the "continent." In addition, he used his identity as a Latin American writer and the success of his novel to create group boundaries. He praised Carpentier, Fuentes, Cortázar, and Vargas Llosa, criticized Gallegos, Asturias, José María Arguedas for their "Europeanist indigenism," and changed his opinion about Borges: he was "completely insubstantial." (The year before he had called Borges "essential.") He extended his criticisms beyond the region; he attacked the French *nouveau roman*, which "cared nothing or little about content," and declared that the most important literary phenomenon was "the Latin American novel." He noted that the decay of the novel in Western countries helped attract attention to the Latin American novel. In sum, during the book promotion, he implemented Fuentes's and Vargas Llosa's mentoring strategies on how to use mainstream media to publicize the agenda of the New Latin American Novel (now so closely tied to his own novel).[91]

By May 1968, a year after its publication, Sudamericana had issued seven printings and Cuban organization Casa de las Américas published its own edition in the collection *Literatura latinoamericana*. In total, the novel had sold almost one hundred thousand copies. By then, everybody knew that such numbers were unprecedented for a newly published Latin American book. Fake news and rumors about the novel's print runs and actual sales increased expectations among potential readers in the region. For example, Peruvian media reported three months after its release that it had sold forty thousand copies, when it had probably sold half. Soon, the novel's record sales numbers attracted the attention of regional and international magazines and newspapers, such as the *Times Literary Supplement* in England and *Le Monde* in France. For the past five years or so, they had reviewed New Latin American Novels not yet translated, as they did with *One Hundred Years of Solitude*.[92]

In Spain, García Márquez's early works entered the book market after requesting permission for importation. In 1967, the country imported twenty-five copies of *In Evil Hour*, twenty-five of *No One Writes to the Colonel*, fifty of *Big Mama's Funeral*, and just fifty of *One Hundred Years of Solitude*. Requests to import these works rose to thousands of copies a year later. Then, the Spanish government, seeking to protect its national book industry, turned García Márquez into a "Spanish" author, as it did with other best-selling Latin American writers such as Borges and Vargas Llosa. This label meant that García Márquez's works had to be published by a company that paid taxes on Spanish soil, so Sudamericana started to print all his works with its branch EDHASA. In January 1969, it requested to print five thousand copies at a selling price of 180 pesetas (US$2.5). Three months later, it demanded to reprint another ten thousand copies. And just a week later, it asked for permission to publish another reprint. In five years, the EDHASA edition sold over one hundred thousand copies. And in 1970 the Círculo de Lectores book club released its own edition, which by 1974 had sold over four hundred thousand copies. By then, the novel was in its way to becoming one of Spain's literary best sellers of all time.[93]

INITIAL RECEPTION

How did professional writers, critics, and common readers receive *One Hundred Years of Solitude* during its first year on the market? Book reviews played a crucial role because they helped direct consumers' taste toward this cultural good. As shown above, Fuentes, Vargas Llosa, and Germán Vargas, among other collaborators, reviewed this novel months before its release, and their opinions about it influenced how initial reviewers made sense of it. This suggests that pre-labeling (or the way a product is talked about before its release) can influence reception and meaning-making by others, especially critics.[94] During the novel's first year, at least thirty-nine reviews were published in twelve countries. These reviews highlighted four aspects. First, *One Hundred Years of Solitude* was a New Latin American Novel written by a Latin American author. Second, the novel had a unique style that portrayed central features of the region. Third, it was not an aesthetically innovative but rather a traditionalist work of art. And fourth, it was mainly a humorous book.[95]

1. *A New Latin American Novel Written by a Latin American Author.* This pattern across reviews confirmed that, had the book not been framed as a New Latin American Novel, its fate would have been quite similar to García Márquez's previous works. Pinto, writing for *Expreso*, stated that the book had a place next to other Latin American novels. In *Análisis*, an anonymous Argentine reviewer labeled it "the most important novel in America [and one that] reflects Latin America." As a Peruvian reviewer put it, it contains "a magical-mythological-realistic universe, which sums up Latin America." For a *Primera Plana* reviewer, connecting the novel to the *Summa Theologica*, a major work of Western culture, it was "more than a book; a Summa Mythological of the continent."[96]

Favorable endorsement about the novel's Latin Americanism came from reviewers across the ideological spectrum. In a conservative Catholic newspaper, García Olaya confirmed that *One Hundred Years of Solitude* was a Latin American novel. Furthermore, aligning with Fuentes's, García Márquez's, and Vargas Llosa's literary agenda, García Olaya claimed that the New Latin American Novel was the only answer to the "sterility of the *nouveau roman*." His opinion was shared by Marxist literary critic Rama, who said that *One Hundred Years of Solitude* was a Latin American novel that "corrects the course [of the modern novel] in a severe and sudden way." Likewise, liberal critic

Rodríguez Monegal claimed in *Mundo Nuevo* that the novel "truly is one of the most unique feats of [the] present-day Latin American novel." He added that with García Márquez, who followed Faulkner, Latin American literature had left behind the times of dated writers such as Gallegos and Rivera. (In a letter, García Márquez had already told Rodríguez Monegal, following Fuentes's recommendation, that he wanted to overcome the writing of Gallegos and Rivera in particular.) Rodríguez Monegal added that García Márquez's use of time was similar to Shakespeare's *Hamlet*. And he concluded that the novel's vision applied to "all of Colombia and the entire universe." Even nonreaders were willing to praise the novel upon publication. As did communist Miguel Otero Silva, who stated at a crowded international conference in Caracas, Venezuela, that this novel (without reading it) occupied "a first row in the Latin American novel."[97]

The release of the novel in 1967 coincided with Asturias's Nobel Prize in Literature and Borges's Norton Lectures at Harvard University. These events did not go unnoticed by reviewers, such as Peruvian newspaper *La Prensa*, which celebrated that "1967 was the year of literary consecration for Latin America." Thus, for Peruvian journalist Orbegozo, writing for *El Comercio Gráfico*, the commercial success of *One Hundred Years of Solitude* proved that there was a real Latin American boom in literature. This opinion extended beyond reviewers in the region. As British reviewer Jean Franco wrote for the *Times Literary Supplement*, this book is "one of the greatest novels in Latin America to this day." This statement echoed again the opinions of Fuentes and Vargas Llosa before its publication. Likewise, the anonymous reviewer of *Atlas* magazine presented it as a Latin American novel, whose success explained why Latin American literature "now appears to be the most original of all the world's literature." Along with this review, *Atlas* translated for the first time into English two passages of the novel: the founding of Macondo and the ascent to the sky of Remedios the Beauty.[98] These and other reviewers stressed that myths were at the center of the novel. And this interpretation also aligned with the way Fuentes and Vargas Llosa wanted the novel to be read upon its release.

Several reviewers argued that *One Hundred Years of Solitude* was basically a Colombian novel, while acknowledging that it opened Colombian literature to the world. This was Ayax's opinion, who said that this book was superior to famous New Latin American Novels *Hopscotch*, *The Time of the Hero*, and *Where the Air Is Clear* but not *Explosion in a Cathedral*. Only one reviewer, Peruvian José Miguel Oviedo, openly claimed that *One Hundred Years of Solitude* was a universal novel because it captured "the eternal human tragedy."[99] As chapter 7 shows, universalization became a trend once cultural brokers outside Latin America appropriated the novel and once the label New Latin American Novel fell into oblivion.

2. *A Novel with a Unique Style.* In the year following its publication, reviewers and common readers struggled to make sense of its style. There was no agreement on how to label it. Or to put it differently, they agreed on only one thing: its style was not magical realism. Neither the author nor Sudamericana's acquisitions editor thought that the novel was an example of magical realism. "My idea at that time," the editor said, "was that this novel was a wonderful example of what was once called the chronicle. I did not think about the magical." Likewise, collaborators who helped produce the novel had different views about its style. These collaborators were Carballo, who read the manuscript in weekly installments, Germán Vargas, reader of the manuscript and member of the Barranquilla Group, Rodríguez Monegal, the critic who promoted the novel in *Mundo Nuevo*, and Jomí García Ascot, the friend who visited the writer at home and to whom the novel is dedicated. For Carballo, the writer "jumps cleanly from reality to imagination, from traditional realism to a realism made with the best elements of the contemporary novel." For Vargas, this novel combined real events with "fantastic elements." For Rodríguez Monegal, "the unreality [of] the novel mixes natural episodes with supernatural episodes." And for García Ascot, "it is the first global crystallization of [the] real-fantastic."[100] Magical realism, the term used to label *One Hundred Years of Solitude* globally, was introduced afterward to interpret this novel's style (see chapter 6).[101]

Only four reviewers connected this novel to Carpentier's "marvelous real," the term now considered an early version of magical realism.[102] (García Ascot was one them.) One reviewer indicated that García Márquez's realism was "at times magical." And reviewer Alone in Chile denied that the novel could be interpreted by using both terms: "it is not realism but magic."[103] Yet despite the strong association of this novel with magical realism, only one reviewer, and not an influential one, Mexican critic Luis A. Domínguez, clearly linked *One Hundred Years of Solitude* to this style: "magical realism found in García Márquez a high exponent." And the only reviewer who called him a "magical realist" was Peruvian Mario Castro Arenas, who added that García Márquez did so "a bit like Carpentier but without the baroqueness."[104] In reality, reviewers did not "miss" the magical realism of *One Hundred Years of Solitude*. Rather, in the context of 1967, magical realism was not yet the way to make sense of the novel. Let us remember that in their "review" of this novel, censors in

Spain overlooked references to fantastic events in the book. Instead, they read this novel as a Latin American work of social realism.

How was then *One Hundred Years of Solitude* labeled its first year? Initially, most reviewers referred to it as a mixture of fantasy and reality: "harmonious mix of imaginations and realities," "mixes the myth . . . with a more concrete reality," "brings reality and unreality together," "the magical and the fantastic absorb the everyday life," and "the fictitious with the real," among others. Several reviewers elaborated on what kind of realism the novel captured: "innate realism," "descriptive realism," and banal "suprarrealism." Other reviewers preferred to obviate any reference to realism. Juan Toro Martínez labeled its style "narrative humor" (on narrative and humor, see below) or highlighted, as the *Atlas* magazine critic did, the novel's baroque style as a characteristic of "our America" and as the most appropriate to narrate the reality of the region. Finally, Manuel Pedro González wrote that the novel was an "unclassifiable work." Outside Latin America reviewers also struggled to make sense of the novel stylistically. Jean Franco, the reviewer for the *Times Literary Supplement*, indicated that "neither realism nor naturalism had provided a satisfactory style for a continent." In his review for *Le Monde*, scholar Claude Fell called the novel an example of "the marvelous symbolic." And in Spain, reviews referred to "unreality" and noticed that "surrealism operates with real events."[105]

3. *A Traditionalist Work of Art*. Reviewers were more in agreement about the technique of *One Hundred Years of Solitude*. Yet most of them initially believed the novel was not an original work of art but rather traditional, even anachronistic, if compared to other contemporary works. This is particularly surprising because, over the past six decades, global readers have regarded it as an innovative work of fiction. Yet during its first year, an anonymous Colombian reviewer wrote that the novel did not have "an original structure and technique." Reviewer Carmen Llorca, a Spanish historian, argued, "With García Márquez, the novel becomes the novel again: with its human beings, its environment, its plot, its wonderful language, its incredible clarity." And she concluded that its style was "classicist." For another reviewer, García Márquez, as a traditionalist writer, "restores to the narrative genre all its historical value, of whose validity there were doubts." Likewise, reviewer Oviedo stated, "Its technique is much simpler and more transparent than that of many novels written today. The story is virtually linear." Spanish reviewer Pere Gimferrer claimed *One Hundred Years of Solitude* had little resemblance to the works of Cortázar and Vargas Llosa. It was more similar to chivalry novels and the classic *One Thousand and One Nights*. (On this comparison, Gimferrer echoed the

interpretation offered by Vargas Llosa before the novel's publication.) Whereas some critics chastised *One Hundred Years of Solitude* for its archaism, others such as Carballo and Rodríguez Monegal argued that the novel's archaism was its originality. Carballo indicated that while its "anachronism" is striking at first, "García Márquez seeks and achieves originality using seemingly reactionary ways." Rodríguez Monegal also referred to its "anachronism."[106]

4. *A Humorous Book.* Several of its initial reviewers claimed that the novel was humorous, agreeing with the author's original intention.[107] Yet as it became a classic, it gained an aura of gravity that compelled readers to approach it solemnly. This change in the reception of the novel, first, proves that popular interpretations of a work of art can disappear or be turned upside down in the long run. And, second, it highlights the limited impact of reviewers' opinions on readers' reactions over time. Once more, Fuentes inaugurated the way of framing the novel as humorous. In his review, he wrote that García Márquez "turns the evil [of our history] into humor." He reiterated his opinion in another piece: it was "one of the funniest books ever written in Latin America." For the *Times Literary Supplement* reviewer, it was a "comic masterpiece" and he added that "comic exaggeration is the keynote of the style." Writer Roberto Burgos Cantor also highlighted the "humor." A Venezuelan reviewer lamented that, unlike in García Márquez's novel, "humorism is absent from the majority of our best American writers." Among the dissenting voices, the critic Montero Castro mentioned that the novel was sad, tragic, and even depressive.[108]

Finally, *One Hundred Years of Solitude* was the target of severe criticism from the start. The harshest critiques came from reviewers who shared García Márquez's culture. Colombian reviewer Eduardo Gómez dismissed the writer for being a *costeño* (a native of Colombia's Caribbean coast) and ridiculed his book as a "*costeña* novel." For him, it was a clear example of "escapist literature," "*costumbrista*," and "easy humor." (Even this negative review picked up the book's use of humor.) According to Gómez, the weakest point in the book was the "mixture of fantasy and reality," and concluded that he had written "a prosaic saga." Another Colombian, a common reader named José María Coneo, sent a letter to the editor of a national newspaper to dismiss the novel as the work of a "communist." He argued that the true work of "pure imagination" was *The Vortex*, a 1924 novel by Colombian J. E. Rivera. García Márquez's network came to the rescue to refute this kind of criticism. Three months after its publication, *El Espectador* denounced a campaign against *One Hundred Years of Solitude*. The newspaper claimed that the novel was falsely accused of being "pure propaganda" and the "product of a self-eulogizing 'maffia' promoted by pro-Castro communists." Even the journalist and writer Jorge Zalamea released an open letter, defending García Márquez from its critics and accusing them of not having read the novel.[109] (As chapter 7 shows, this kind of entrenched criticism helps works of art to become classics.)

UNDERSTANDING THE SUCCESS OF A BEST SELLER

Buenos Aires, August 1967. Two months after the release of *One Hundred Years of Solitude*. A woman carries her shopping bag. Among the groceries is a copy of the novel. Although this event is most likely another legend surrounding the book's success, it has, as all legends do, some truth to it. In the 1960s, books like this novel were becoming everyday commodities for middle-class readers in the region. The success of this novel clearly built on this larger social transformation, as it also did on the modernization of the Spanish-language book industry and growing international attention to the New Latin American Novel. Those involved in the imagination and production of the novel (and even some scholars) have often attributed the novel's success to pure luck. Sudamericana's acquisitions editor stated that success "happened by chance." Yet he was clearly aware that "chance" was part of "a series of causes that came together at a certain time." Preceding the release of *One Hundred Years of Solitude* was an avalanche of best-selling Latin American novels as well as successful African and Caribbean literature (especially the works of Derek Walcott and Chinua Achebe) from the late 1950s onward. So, this novel built on the commercial and literary attention paid to non-Western novels that exploded in the postcolonial world during a moment of crisis of the Western novel. This novel's success, then, was the result of a Matthew Effect over a cultural object. This effect suggests, to put it simply, the rich get richer and the poor get poorer because the rich have an accumulated advantage in society. When *One Hundred Years of Solitude* came out in 1967, it benefited from the advantages accumulated by the international success of the New Latin American Novel and the modernizing publishing industry in Spanish. Counterfactually, had it been published a decade earlier or later, another Latin American work would have been in a more advantageous market position to succeed the way García Márquez's novel did.[110]

The analysis in this chapter and previous ones showed that *One Hundred Years of Solitude* was carefully crafted in a niche. This finding questions the tendency to speak of this novel as an innovative and revolutionary work of art that took Latin America and the rest of the world by storm. García Márquez and his collaborative circle of close friends, peer writers, gatekeepers of the publishing industry, and critics in Latin America, North America, and Europe imagined, produced, and circulated his novel as a commodity that closely adapted to the demands of the market for best-selling literary works, the aesthetics of successful mainstream mid-century Western literature, and the principles of a Latin American literary tradition.

One Hundred Years of Solitude appeared at the peak moment of collaboration between three generations of Latin American writers. García Márquez's multigenerational ties included friends, writers, and critics. By 1967, these collaborators had become gatekeepers that controlled mass media and highbrow publications as well as professional literary magazines, in which they enthusiastically promoted this novel. Aesthetically, *One Hundred Years of Solitude* was published at the epicenter of a dislocation of literary styles.[111] In Latin America, indigenism did not manage to become a region-spanning literary movement. In Spain, there was disenchantment with social realist narrative. In Europe, critics saw the sterile French *nouveau roman* as a sign of what was wrong with the novel as a bourgeois genre. In the United States, with the Beat Generation on its way out, there was no major literary movement that garnered the attention of readers and the support of commercial publishers. The opposite was true of Latin American fiction. Authors from three generations were writing literature that a modernizing publishing industry in Spanish marketed as fresh and original to the rest of the world, which transformed the New Latin American Novel into a sought-after literary commodity during the second half of the 1960s. In addition, with the Nobel Prize in Literature awarded to leading Latin American writer Asturias in 1967, *One Hundred Years of Solitude* could not fit better the climate of the international literary market. Its supporters proclaimed that this book freed the novel from the impenetrable *nouveau roman*, boring social realism, and narrow-minded indigenism, and celebrated its connection to the Great American Novel.

The semantic structure of *One Hundred Years of Solitude* matched the ideas and conventions of the New Latin American Novel.[112] The novel was quite different from what García Márquez had written previously; never before had he written anything longer than two hundred pages. By 1964, his network made him aware that the market for successful New Latin American Novel demanded works over five hundred pages. *One Hundred Years of Solitude* conformed to this demand. In 1965, he sat down to write his first novel. In the process, he rejected his early realist style and instead embraced neobaroque language, which best-selling authors like Fuentes and Carpentier were promoting as an essential feature of Latin American literature. Furthermore, they and other collaborators mentored García Márquez on how to use this Latin American language in his novel. Conforming to other demands of the New Latin American Novel, this book placed myths at the center of the story. Finally, rather than embracing the experimental techniques of contemporary novels, *One Hundred Years of Solitude* opted for a conservative approach: a return to narrative storytelling.

Finally, a macro historical transformation helps to further understand the success of the novel. I call it the World We Have Lost Effect, after Laslet's book mentioned below. This effect was quite perceptible in literature and social and human science writing in the 1960s. The novel was released at the end of a decade of increasing grief (and also nostalgia) for the disappearance of precapitalist cultures in the face of rapid industrialization of Western societies.

This social change sparked an interest in oral tradition and preindustrial societies. Increasing even more this interest in the preindustrial past was the decolonization movement and critics of Western science, capitalism, and imperialism in the years before and after 1967. Literature from decolonized and Third World countries, including Latin America, had steadily gained an international audience since the mid-1950s. It included Achebe's *Things Fall Apart* (1959), Tayeb Salih's *Season of Migration to the North* (1966), and Wole Soyinka's translation of Daniel O. Fagunwa's *The Forest of a Thousand Daemons* into English in 1968. In these novels, as in *One Hundred Years of Solitude*, traditional life in villages and the impact of outside modernization played a major role.

Likewise, in academia, philosopher Michel Foucault denounced the evils of Western science in *Madness and Civilization* (1961); historian Peter Lastlet reflected on how the arrival of industrialization affected the English family structure in *The World We Have Lost* (1965); sociologist Pierre Bourdieu published his first works on rural villages in the Kabylie and Collo regions in Algeria (1958, 1963, 1964); and anthropologist Clifford Geertz published studies on traditional societies in Java (1960, 1963, 1964). Similarly, historian Eric Hobsbawm in *Primitive Rebels* (1959) analyzed precapitalist forms of social resistance; historian E. P. Thompson (1963) published his pathbreaking account on the making of the working class in capitalist England; historian Carlo Ginzburg released his investigation of agrarian cults of fertility in *The Night Battles* (1966); anthropologist Oscar Lewis introduced the concept of culture of poverty in his best-selling study of a Mexican family in *The Children of Sanchez* (1961), which sold over one hundred and twenty thousand copies in Latin America after its release in Spanish in 1965;[113] anthropologist Carlos Castaneda sought to recover non-Western forms of science in

The Teachings of Don Juan (1968); and Claude Lévi-Strauss became the world's most famous living anthropologist for his studies on indigenous cultures as in *The Savage Mind* (1962).

One Hundred Years of Solitude was another of these reflections about a lost world. Its initial success is owed to the story's overarching theme of the rise and fall of a traditional Latin American village, as witnessed by readers of the growing urban middle classes in a region immersed in the shift from rural to urban societies. Having grown up in an agrarian village that decayed after a failed industrialization, García Márquez was sensitive from an early age to the theme of sudden capitalist transformation and aware of the literary potential of decaying villages. As he explained in an interview at the age of twenty-eight, "it has a special charm, an inexplicable, poetic mystery, what is happening in the villages that are coming to an end. . . . Villages like Macondo are not the same as before."[114] His interest in the decline of rural societies had already entered his imagination by the mid-1950s. This interest again took written form for him in 1967, at a moment when leading fiction writers, anthropologists, sociologists, historians, and others had been writing about that theme for over a decade. At this level, too, the publication of *One Hundred Years of Solitude* aligned with market tendencies which bolstered its initial success as a best seller in Latin America and beyond.

CONCLUSION

One Hundred Years of Solitude is a novel about solitude, but its author experienced very little of it as the making of this work of art was a collaborative enterprise. García Márquez's family, friends in several countries, the Mafia Group in Mexico, and the Balcells Agency in Spain created a patronage system to support him. They helped him retreat from paid work and live on credit for months. Furthermore, they checked on the progress of his manuscript as he wrote the story he first imagined seventeen years before. Whether locally or internationally, daily or monthly, orally or on paper, a transnational network of collaborators gave feedback to García Márquez on the novel as he was writing it. Collaborators also helped him promote his book as a New Latin American Novel, which increased its commercial appeal to contemporary readers. Thus, the making of *One Hundred Years of Solitude* was, at its core, an act of networked creativity because collaborators had a decisive influence on how the author imagined and made this work of art.

PART II

BECOMING
A GLOBAL CLASSIC

E ach literary classic becomes one in its own way. Yet literary classics are all alike in a particular way: they have a life that goes beyond their pages. *One Hundred Years of Solitude* started its life as a best seller. It had a favorable mix of admiring and contentious book reviews, sold thousands of copies locally and abroad, secured its rapid translation into English, French, and other major literary languages, and was named Book of the Year in several countries. This novel should also have experienced the usual death of a best seller, as the attention of critics and readers moved onto newer literary works. But something happened that no one expected: *One Hundred Years of Solitude* started to live a longer life. How did this happen to a novel so firmly imagined, produced, and circulated as a New Latin American Novel? *Bomarzo, The Green House, A Change of Skin,* and *Explosion in a Cathedral* were equally successful contemporary novels. Yet readers' interest in these and other literary works diminished when the moment of the New Latin American Novel passed. *One Hundred Years of Solitude*, on the contrary, has become one of the top best-selling literary works of all time. It has sold more than fifty million official copies worldwide in over forty-nine languages.[1]

Why has interest in *One Hundred Years of Solitude* lasted? Scholars, especially in literary studies, have argued that García Márquez's novel was aesthetically superior to its contemporaries. But the previous chapters have shown that aesthetics alone cannot explain how this novel became a best seller. The same argument applies to any explanation of how it became a classic. Did this novel, instead, attain classic status because powerful organizations, such as universities and publishers, and individuals, such as critics and celebrities, favored it over other novels? No, they are also not the main reason for this novel's long-lasting appeal. During the research for this book, I repeatedly faced this paradox: as *One Hundred Years of Solitude* rose to classic status globally, this status depended less on continuous endorsement from powerful organizations and individuals and more on support from scores of cultural brokers. Among these brokers, along with the ones just mentioned, I found individuals such as common readers, nonreaders (people who talk about a book without reading it), editors, teachers, peer writers, reviewers, booksellers, translators, artists, bloggers, journalists, priests, businesspeople, war refugees, guerrilla fighters, influencers, and politicians. Acting as cultural brokers, I found organizations such as language academies, awards, bookstores, book clubs, private foundations and companies, nonprofit organizations, national governments, job market search portals, mass media, and social media platforms. And I also found objects such as literary works, merchandising, computer software, buildings, public squares, statues, and works of art. Thanks to their brokerage, *One Hundred Years of Solitude* has become a global classic.

In the following chapters, I offer data for the period 1967–2020 in over forty-five languages and from more than ninety countries to show how these brokers have used this novel across cultural and national boundaries. Something they have done is to refer to Macondo, Colonel Aureliano Buendía's discovery of ice, and Remedios's ascent to heaven, among other notable parts of the story. The first generation of readers who consumed the novel kept doing this long enough for new generations of cultural brokers to do it, too. They encountered the novel and appropriated it. And when new generations of cultural brokers continue to adopt a work of art, they extend its life. They do so by using the work of art in ways its creator intended and, crucially, in ways he did not intend nor could imagine. Acting together, these traditional and unexpected ways are key to uprooting (or disembedding) the work of art from its niche.[2]

This analysis helps to expand the range of cultural brokers involved in the making of classics. This expansion is important because researchers have overemphasized the brokerage of literary critics and scholars. New research shows that their taste can diverge from the taste of those that ought to consume the consecrated work (especially common readers). Indeed, new studies suggest that traditional practices of cultural consecration are declining in countries such as the Netherlands, Germany, France, and the United States. This means that the taste of a prestigious scholar may turn literary works into canonical texts in schools, colleges, and so on. But the scholar's taste on its own is not sufficient to reach a wider range of cultural brokers. Literary critics write reviews of books that can lead to boosts in sales. But one thing is that critics' endorsement can increase sales and another thing is that their opinions create classics. In reality, critics (and their criticism) do not outlive classics, yet classics outlive their critics. Who can recall, for example, the names of the first critics of *Madame Bovary* or *Lolita* and especially what they wrote in their reviews? To make the decision to read or talk about *One Hundred Years of Solitude*, a reader in Kuwait today is not going to be influenced by what critic and Harvard professor Robert Kiely wrote in his review for the *New York Times* in 1970 or by what literary critic Frederic Jameson stated about this novel half a century later. Researchers have exaggerated the brokerage of critics and scholars because, among other reasons, it leaves a visible paper trail. But the rise of social media and other digital platforms is correcting this view of cultural brokerage. Online readers, nonreaders, and consumers now leave a visible trail that is revealing previously unseen (as well as new) practices of cultural brokerage by millions of anonymous people and small organizations.[3]

There is no one-size-fits-all explanation of how a work of art turns into a classic, but its ascent to glory must involve at least two important steps. First, the creator of the work of art and the creator's collaborators lose control over the long-term trajectory of the work. As I describe in the next chapter, that loss of control refers to the collapse of the niche in which the work of art was imagined, produced, and initially circulated. And second step, as chapter 6 shows, many cultural brokers step in and appropriate the work of art.[4] *Hamlet*, Beethoven's *Fifth Symphony*, and *Guernica*, are among the hundreds of works of art that have transcended their niche thanks to their appropriation by cultural brokers, spanning multiple generations and eras. Thanks to their brokerage, a work of art such as *One Hundred Years of Solitude* enters the life of a person who overhead a conversation about the novel at a coffee shop, influences the writings of Chinese writer and Nobel laureate Mo Yan, adorns the home page of Google as one of its creative Doodles, inspires the script of a Hollywood movie, becomes a person's most liked or disliked review on one of Amazon's dozen stores worldwide, or serves as a weapon of political resistance in the Middle East. And as these and other forms of appropriation happen again and again, generation after generation, the work of art acquires one of the most recognizable characteristics of the classic: its power to enter our lives in ways that can be entirely different from those imagined by its creator.

5

CONTROVERSY, CONFLICT, COLLAPSE

I have the impression that . . . the boom can be split into two.

—Mario Benedetti[1]

Witnesses reported that García Márquez's face was covered in blood. He had arrived a few minutes earlier to the lobby of a movie theater in Mexico City to attend a film preview. Writer Mario Vargas Llosa was in attendance, too. When he saw his friend García Márquez, he punched him in the face and knocked him to the ground. Bleeding and in shock, García Márquez was taken away. The true cause of Vargas Llosa's punch remains a mystery to this day. But it ended the friendship between two of the most popular writers of the Latin American Boom. Famous as this incident is, it was not an isolated event. In reality, it was part of a chain of events that happened mostly throughout the 1970s and destroyed the niche that made it possible to imagine, produce, and circulate novels like *One Hundred Years of Solitude* as international best sellers of Latin American literature.[2] As the words of Uruguayan writer Benedetti quoted above show, a year after this novel's publication, several writers started to fear that the Latin American Boom, which was crucial to bring to life dozens of New Latin American Novels, was disintegrating.

Not coincidentally, Benedetti was among those who attacked the Boom. In 1968, he criticized the meetings of intellectuals in the Parisian restaurant La Coupole, where months before writers Pablo Neruda and Carlos Fuentes and critic Emir Rodríguez Monegal met and praised *One Hundred Years of Solitude*, then hot off the press. Benedetti lamented that the Boom had become too commercial. His solution, as other writers, publishers, critics, and readers did, was to distinguish between the good Boom writers—ones who were talented, politically committed, and sought no publicity, such as Julio Cortázar—and the bad Boom writers—ones who were political traitors, products of public-ity, and contentious, such as Guillermo Cabrera Infante.[3] Controversies only grew and grew. In 1971, writer Miguel Ángel Asturias caused an international scandal after backing the accusation that *One Hundred Years of Solitude* was a plagiarism of a novel by Honoré de Balzac. Two years later, writer Jorge Luis Borges, a major beneficiary of the Boom, had García Márquez's book and others in mind when he said regretfully, "Literature is going through a very unpleasant commercial stage. People see a book and do not buy it unless they see on the cover [the names of publishers] Emecé, or Losada, or Sudamericana, nor does anyone want to publish if they are not paid half a million pesos." He added, "Nobody thinks that the books that sell a lot are good. It's all a matter of fashion, a kind of mania to read what others read."[4]

These cases of increasing confrontation among writers reveal an important shift in the imagination, production, and reception of Latin American works shortly after the release of *One Hundred Years of Solitude*. Controversy and con-flict started to replace collaboration and compromise as the conditions that buttressed the rise of the New Latin American Novel, the modernization of the publishing industry in Spanish, and the imagination of novels such as *One Hundred Years of Solitude*. In other words, dissonance (an overlooked mecha-nism of cultural circulation that ranges from conflict to obliviousness) started to uproot this novel from its niche. Simply put, new generations of readers stopped reading this book as a novel associated with the New Latin American Novel and were more likely to read it as something like world literature. Dis-sonance also meant associating García Márquez's novel with a narrow group of writers, the genuine Boom writers, rather than as the offspring of collab-oration among three generations of writers, critics, and gatekeepers of the publishing industry.

A LATIN AMERICAN NOVEL?

"Today . . . there is not what we could call a Latin American novel," critic Luis Harss stated in 2008. He had been, in 1966, the editor of *Into the Mainstream*, the best-selling book of interviews with Latin American writers of three gen-erations. Today, he continued, "There is a literature in Spanish language, with good and bad writers. We should think of Roberto Bolaño, so acclaimed in Spain and the United States."[5] Coming from Harss, this statement made it clear that the New Latin American Novel was a thing of the past and that

Latin American literature no longer was synonymous with a group of artists from different generations united by common aesthetic principles. This shift in the region's literary imagination started from the 1970s onward, and it had four dimensions. First, political events in Latin America separated authors. Second, there was a growing disagreement about the idea of Latin America. Third, the labels New Latin American Novel and Latin American Boom were challenged or simply rejected. And fourth, *One Hundred Years of Solitude*, according to numerous critics, came to exemplify what was wrong with the region's politics and culture.

1. Politics and Literature: A Widening Gap. Dictatorships and military interventions started to spread to several Latin American countries, especially Chile, Guatemala, Nicaragua, Uruguay, El Salvador, Brazil, and Argentina. For most Latin American writers, who embraced literature in the 1960s as a tool of social change, rising political authoritarianism revealed that literature could not help transform Latin American society. To the shock of many, Borges, then a famous writer and a contender for the Nobel Prize, famously welcomed the Pinochet dictatorship after the coup d'état against Salvador Allende's democratic government in Chile. The Cuban Revolution, which brought writers together, started to censor dissenting artists. In 1966, the Cuban government criticized poet Neruda, a fervent communist, for attending a New York meeting of PEN, the prestigious international association of writers, which was regarded from Cuba as a bourgeois literary circle. The government also criticized Fuentes, another supporter of the revolution, for attending the event. As a result, both writers distanced themselves from the revolution, never again setting foot on the island. (Neruda also attacked Fidel Castro and fellow generation member Alejo Carpentier.) Censorship in Cuba of José Lezama Lima's novel *Paradiso* (hailed as a masterpiece by supporters of the New Latin American Novel, see chapter 8) put more writers on the fence about the revolution. The worst was yet to come.[6]

The Padilla affair was "the single most important crisis in Latin American literary politics in the twentieth century, one which split both Latin American and European intellectuals down the middle." The affair ended the support of most writers for the Cuban Revolution. Indeed, it created enmities that writers took to their graves. (Divisive Cuban politics might have motivated Vargas Llosa to punch García Márquez in the face.) It started in 1968 when an international jury awarded Cuba's fourth national prize for poetry to dissident writer Heberto Padilla. So Castro sequestered the jury to force its members to change their minds. They did not. Three years later, he arrested

Padilla and accused him of being a spy and CIA collaborator. The detainee was forced to recant; his statement of self-criticism reminded many witnesses of Stalin's political purges in the Soviet Union. Latin American, Spanish, and other international intellectuals published an open letter in the famous French newspaper *Le Monde* asking Castro to free Padilla. Signatories included Vargas Llosa, Cortázar, Fuentes, García Márquez, Octavio Paz, Plinio Apuleyo Mendoza, Josep Maria Castellet, the brothers Luis and Juan Goytisolo, Jean-Paul Sartre, Simone de Beauvoir, Italo Calvino, Marguerite Duras, Alberto Moravia, Allen Ginsberg, and Susan Sontag, among others. Castro was furious and neutrality was no longer an option. Latin American writers had to take a side on the issue of literary freedom and political commitment. On one side, writers such as García Márquez and Cortázar ended up supporting Castro. On the other side, Vargas Llosa, Paz, Mendoza, Cabrera Infante, and Jorge Edwards, among others, denounced Cuba's fall into a dictatorship.[7]

This ideological division deepened as new authoritarian regimes on the right and on the left mushroomed in other parts of the region. These entrenched ideological alliances among Latin American writers had rippling effects in the publishing industry, network, friendships, and the status of several New Latin American Novels, including *One Hundred Years of Solitude*. Some critics of Castro's regime understood any form of praise for this novel as an ideological endorsement of the Cuban ruler. Being such a divisive novel in the region at that time further increased its long-term visibility; other books slowly receded into the background.

The slow dissolution of a unified Latin American agenda in literature also happened at conferences and in other professional gatherings. Whereas in the 1950s and 1960s these meetings helped develop a regional identity among writers, critics, and gatekeepers of the publishing industry, by the late 1960s, ideological factions began to emerge. In his reply to Paz's personal inquiry about the Segundo Congreso Latinoamericano de Escritores to be celebrated in Mexico City in March 1967, Fuentes wrote, "I do not want to exaggerate. I have a bad feeling about all the official establishment that supports it. . . . They invited no one with prestige: neither Vargas Llosa nor Cortázar nor García Márquez nor Donoso: nobody dangerous, nobody independent. Names to sugar the pill, yes: Neruda, Pellicer, Arreola, Rulfo."[8] Asturias was also in attendance. The congress sought to create a "Latin American cultural community," including a "Latin American Community of Writers," to be based in Mexico City. Most Cuban writers present at the congress boycotted its creation. For them, such a community could reduce the influence that Casa de las Américas, sponsored by Castro's government, wanted to exert over the region's writers, literature, and the arts.

In sum, deteriorating political conditions increased pessimism in the region about the continuity of the political and aesthetic message underlying cosmopolitan Latin America literature as a literary movement. The ideological conflict across the three generations worsened, and any effort to create a region-spanning literary agenda was doomed to fail. These changes meant that new generations of readers could no longer read *One Hundred Years of Solitude* as a novel associated with the aesthetic, political, and cultural agenda of the New Latin American Novel, which no longer existed.[9]

2. *A Changing Idea of Latin America and Its Literature.* The aesthetic liberation of the 1960s promoted the idea of Latin America as a regional unit. But writers who were not published as part of the New Latin American Novel or as Boom authors refused to endorse in their writings this regional view of Latin America. Peruvian writer José María Arguedas, a supporter of indigenism (which in literature emphasized the indigenous legacy), argued that the way in which the New Latin American Novel defined Latin America was too exclusive and forgot other social and literary realities. In 1968, he confronted Julio Cortázar, then a best-selling Latin American writer living in Paris for the last two decades. In his discourse "No soy un aculturado" ("I Am Not Acculturated"), which Arguedas gave upon receiving the Inca Garcilaso de la Vega Prize (named after a famous writer of mixed-race origin), he defended indigenism against the cosmopolitanism of New Latin American Novel writers such as Cortázar. In particular, Arguedas criticized him for his snobbish universalism and for dismissing writers who highlighted the provincial in their works. Arguedas stated that he was proud of being "a provincial writer" and added, "We are all provincial, Don Julio." Cortázar replied in 1969 from the pages of the cosmopolitan *Life en Español* magazine. He openly belittled writers like Arguedas as "provincials of folk obedience." The two writers' controversy created divisions that forced other publications, as well as writers, to take sides. Vargas Llosa, a fellow Peruvian, sided with Cortázar and for years criticized Arguedas's writing as too ideological, naive, and provincial. Scholars also had to take sides. Spaniard Manuel Pedro González wrote in a volume on the Spanish American novel that in *Hopscotch*, "everything is bastard, spurious, and counterfeit." For him, the real model was Arguedas, whose *Deep Rivers* stood as "one of the most accomplished novels that indigenism has produced so far. And yet, this exceptional work is barely known in America,

and critics have ignored it outside of Peru and Argentina, where it appeared, while they have clamorously praised Vargas Llosa's [*The Time of the Hero*]."[10]

Arguedas was not alone in his criticism. From the 1970s onward, others denounced that the Latin American, cosmopolitan view of the region did not seem natural; it was simply dogmatic. It was "the political project of Creole, mestizo elites," which included writers such as Asturias, Fuentes, Cortázar, Vargas Llosa, García Márquez, and José Donoso. These writers claimed that they were writing the novel of America. Critics, on the contrary, believed that the view of Latin America in their novels perpetuated the ideology of the Creole elite that took power in the region after its independence from Spain. This ideology imposed the social inferiority of indigenous peoples, blacks, and African slaves. Since these ethnic groups, critics argued, were excluded in the literature of the 1960s, Latin American literature did not capture their experience and literary voice. Critics explained that Creoles invented the concept of "Indian," which did not represent the real voice of Latin America. Years later, the success of Rigoberta Menchú's autobiography was in part due to this denial of the Creole voice in New Latin American Novels and the prospect of a Latin American literature that really included the indigenous experience. In addition, other groups who challenged the boundaries of Latin American literature were Brazilians (who complained that the term *latino* excluded them) and writers from Latin America living and publishing in the United States in English or Spanish. Political exiles were critical, too. For Cuban writer Cabrera Infante, an exile in London, Latin America itself was the "most absurd" term to refer to the region. "What does the adjective Latin mean here? . . . That we are descendants of Rome? . . . Are Haitians Latinos? Is America Latin? Is Latin the word Latin? Nobody knows." He stressed the differences between nationalities in the region: "Brazil does not resemble Venezuela or Colombia or Peru." Furthermore, he rejected his own trajectory in the 1960s, when peers and publishers saw him as a rising star of the Latin American Boom. "I was not a Latin American writer," he said. "I can't admit to being called *latino*."[11]

As a result of these and other controversies, an important shift occurred in the region's literary imagination: the idea of the multiplicity of Latin America replaced that of regional unity. Argentine scholar Walter Mignolo refuted the universalism of the term Latin America, Peruvian scholar Antonio Cornejo Polar emphasized the region's cultural and literary heterogeneity, and Argentine scholar Alejandro Losada published works about the social history of Latin American *literatures*. To prove that there were multiple Latin Americas, some researchers, for example, showed that nineteenth-century Cuban writer José Martí had a different view of *latinidad*. His view did not support the link between the region's Latin roots and ancient Greeks and Romans. Instead, Martí found *latinidad* in the region's indigenous peoples, especially the Mayas, Aztecs, and Incas. Similarly, Afro-Andean and Afro-Caribbean intellectuals also refurbished the idea of *indo-latinidad* and *afro-latinidad*. Others highlighted the contribution of Peruvian writer José Carlos Mariátegui in the 1920s, when he promoted in the literary magazine *Amauta* a definition of the region based on its indigenous cultures. Other critics, as Cabrera Infante did, denied the idea of a *Latin* America, but they went farther. They offered the term "Indo-America" or even criticized indigenism because it was still in the hands of Creoles rather than indigenous writers. Leading indigenist writer Arguedas, they claimed, was neither an Indian nor of Indian descent.[12]

On the other side of the spectrum, powerful cultural organizations continued to endorse the idea of one Latin America literature. In 1974, UNESCO published a collective volume entitled *América en su literatura* (*America in Its Literature*), and its editor, César Fernández Moreno, defended the regional concept of Latin America. UNESCO's endorsement of a single literary tradition in the region continued in the 1990s and 2010s. It co-sponsored *Archivos*, a collection of critical editions of over sixty major works of Latin American literature. This collection sought to create a genealogy of classic books and authors prior to and during this literature's consecration in the 1960s, including works by writers that critics would see as Creoles, such as Cortázar, Asturias, Arguedas, Juan Rulfo, Álvaro Cepeda Samudio, Juan Carlos Onetti, Clarice Lispector, and Ernesto Sábato, among others. Latin American scholars such as Arturo Ardao declared that the region had attained "universality." Along these lines, they celebrated its presence in the life and writings of major authors, such as Marcel Proust, while others such as writers of the Crack (an anti-Boom movement) announced the end of Latin American literature.[13]

Over the years, *One Hundred Years of Solitude* has remained visible in these debates and controversies as the novel that partisans and critics of the idea of a Pan-Latin America argue about. For critic Ángel Rama, the success of this novel certified the existence of the region's "own literary system" and the recognition of "the Latin American singularity." However, since the 2010s, the view that there are Latin American literatures has continued to gain currency.[14]

3. Normalizing the New Latin American Novel and Latin American Boom. Parallel to controversies about the idea of Latin America and its literature, there was a tendency to normalize the region's literary Boom. Like the angry young men in Great Britain, the *nouveau roman* in France, and the Beat Generation in the United States in the 1950s, the New Latin American Novel and

the Latin American Boom of the 1960s stopped being a novelty and became
"normal" literature.[15] The fact that they became normal did not mean they
were not controversial. Quite the opposite; they were the subject of heated
clashes among writers, including those whose success had been built on the
international circulation of Latin American literary works. The 1967 Nobel
Prize in Literature winner, Asturias, accused Boom writers of being "publicity
products." Borges stated, "The whole issue of the Latin American Boom is
very childish." Carpentier declared, "I have never believed in [its] existence."
Cabrera Infante criticized the term as an Argentine invention: "What is the
Boom? I do not know. But I do know what it is not. It is neither a literary
movement nor a new conception of the novel nor the conscience of America
that mumbles in Spanish." He added that the "Boom . . . was just a club—not
always of gentlemen [and] was always an obscene noise in the world of letters,
pure publicity." Vargas Llosa himself, one of the ideologues of the New Latin
American Novel and a member of the Boom, claimed they were simply "a
group of writers." And Donoso, another Boom member, attacked the works
of Cortázar, Fuentes, and Vargas Llosa for being excessively cosmopolitan and
for their obsession with form and language experiments. Furthermore, new
generations of writers criticized the Boom. In 1969, young Colombian novelist
Óscar Collazos started another controversy. In his essay "Encrucijada del len-
guaje" ("Language Crossroads"), he confronted fellow writer Cortázar because,
he claimed, his recent work was out of touch with the reality of Latin America. Vargas Llosa was another of his targets. They both replied to Collazos and
reaffirmed their compromise with the reality of the region as writers who
thought of themselves as true revolutionaries.[16]

Attacks came from non-Latin American writers, too. In France, leading
novelist Philippe Sollers, aware of the growing commercial success of the
New Latin American Novel in his own country, warned about the threat of
"Latin-centrism." Italian writer Carlo Coccioli was more explicit in his criticism. In 1971 he published an incendiary article in the literary supplement of
the French newspaper *Le Figaro*. "In Latin America, there is a literary mafia,"
he wrote. "This mafia terrorizes Latin American literature today. . . . If John
Doe (Perico de los Palotes), a simple Venezuelan pawn of the mafia, publishes
thirty verses in Caracas, Octavio Paz, the great maestro, proclaims gently in
Mexico or in the Left Bank [of Paris] that these thirty verses are a cathedral."[17]

In Spain, writers were skeptical when they were not simply against the
Boom. In 1967, José María Gironella sent a private letter to literary critic Guillermo Díaz-Plaja, in which he criticized the latter for praising Latin American writers in an essay published in the influential Spanish newspaper *ABC*.

In 1970, Gironella made public his criticism in an article in the same newspaper, expressing his disillusion with the famous works of García Márquez, Vargas Llosa, and Cortázar, whose language was full of "idiomatic baroqueness." And he put down all Latin American literature as a product of the colonies. Like Gironella, writer Víctor Zalbidea concluded that this literature was simply marginal. Another controversy exploded at the time in the literary supplement of the newspaper *Informaciones*, when writer Alfonso Grosso attacked several Latin American writers. He called Cortázar a "writer from the Third World" and considered García Márquez a "bluff," whose novel *One Hundred Years of Solitude* was unreadable after two pages. Writer Antonio Martínez Menchén joined this controversy and voiced his dissatisfaction with Latin American novels, which he saw as pure merchandising. In 1970, he extended his disapproval in the book of essays *Del desengaño literario* (*Of Literary Disillusion*). Other writers, on the contrary, preferred to defend the quality of Spain's literature. For leading social realist writer Juan García Hortelano, *El Jarama* by Rafael Sánchez Ferlosio and *Time of Silence* by Luis Martín-Santos were as good as Cortázar's books. Also, the decline of censorship in the arts in Spain made it possible to praise writers in exile after the Civil War, whose works were unknown. Their rediscovery in the 1970s, as Spain moved into democracy, gave additional ammunition to those who attacked the Boom.[18]

Critics were equally divided about the Boom. Whereas Rama was one of its most devoted ideologues and promoters, M. P. González, as mentioned above, chastised Cortázar and Vargas Llosa for going too far in their desire to renew literary techniques. In his opinion, they ended up writing pastiches of modernist literature. José Blanco Amor, an Argentine critic, turned violently against Boom writers in his controversial essay "El final del 'boom'. Terrorismo literario en America Latina" ("The End of the 'Boom': Literary Terrorism in Latin America"), which appeared in newspapers in Spain and Argentina and soon after in a book. Blanco Amor celebrated the death of the Boom, certified by the publication of *The Autumn of the Patriarch*, García Márquez's first novel after *One Hundred Years of Solitude*. This critic referred to Cortázar, Vargas Llosa, Fuentes, and García Márquez as a mafia. "How is it possible," he wondered, "that we have fallen into this Kafkaesque trap? . . . The 'boom' was born due to a political-commercial arrangement and grew up undermining all principles. . . . The vociferous apparatus of the 'boom' applied a censorship method against authors that did not integrate the team: silence."[19]

Another controversy was about whether the Boom was dead or not. In 1972, Rodríguez Monegal, former editor of *Mundo Nuevo* and then literature professor at Yale University, published a history of the Boom, *El boom de la novela latinoamericana* (*The Boom of the Latin American Novel*). In his book, he proclaimed, the Boom was "dead." The same year, Donoso released *The Boom in Spanish American Literature: A Personal History*. For him, the Boom was certainly dead. Contrary to their opinions, Rama (another ideologue of the New Latin American Novel) argued that the Boom continued beyond 1972. Donoso, however, insisted in burying it. In 1981, in his roman-à-clef *The Garden Next Door*, he described the Boom through the eyes of Julio Méndez (modeled after Donoso himself), a writer who is confused and frustrated by his lack of literary success. He belittles the fame of the writers he envies—Fuentes, Vargas Llosa, Cortázar, and García Márquez—calling the last a "false god."[20]

Debates about the New Latin American Novel and Boom have continued well into the twenty-first century, and *One Hundred Years of Solitude* remains at their center. Did that book bring the Boom to a close and was "the Boom as a literary phenomenon but also as a commercial and media phenomenon . . . essentially Gabriel García Márquez" and his best-selling novel?[21]

4. *The Specter of Macondism.* Since the early 1970s, *One Hundred Years of Solitude* has been accused of Macondism. This word refers to a stereotypical view of Latin America as an undeveloped land where magic and tradition rule over reason and progress. Macondism has become a widespread and contentious representation of Latin America as an exotic land of magical realism. In this regard, Macondism has similarities with Orientalism, Western culture's patronizing view of Middle Eastern, Asian, and North African cultures, and with Bovarysme, a person's tendency toward escapist daydreaming and avoidance of everyday responsibilities, attributes of the character of Emma in *Madame Bovary*. According to its critics, Macondism represents the land of Latin America as full of antediluvian nature, people of biblical age, flying carpets, and virgins ascending to heaven. Critics of this stereotype argue that *One Hundred Years of Solitude* contains no literary facts but rather is pure ideology. As such, it gives global readers a false image of the region as rustic, traditional, and underdeveloped. The enduring impact of Macondism has influenced the creation of anti-*One Hundred Years of Solitude* literary movements, such as the McOndo Generation in the 1990s. Its members offered a polar opposite view of the region, one that is urban, modern, and globalized.[22]

In sum, controversies and conflicts surrounding *One Hundred Years of Solitude* (or the ideas and people who collaborated in its making) have turned this novel into a monument that obstructs the view of what lies behind it, especially in literature. This novel does so to the point that even its harshest critics, such as the McOndo writers, come together as a generation with the explicit goal of burying this novel and instead only make it more visible and appealing for new generations of readers.

A NOVEL WITHOUT COLLABORATORS

Since the collapse of the Boom, no other Latin American novel has received support comparable to what *One Hundred Years of Solitude* obtained in 1967. The Boom's dissolution did away with the professional and intellectual collaboration that marked the rise of the New Latin American Novel. Collaboration evolved into competition among subgroups and individuals. Tensions and ruptures immediately began to surface.[23]

Group Closure. The rise of the New Latin American Novel movement was not, of course, free of internal criticism. But it did not threaten its continuity.[24] In a letter to Rodríguez Monegal, critic and University of Texas professor Ricardo Gullón explained his reservations about the flagship magazine of new Latin American literature, *Mundo Nuevo*: "The fact that I disagree with some opinions is necessary and convenient. I really hate conformism, and I believe that, quite the contrary, we should insist on promoting dialogue as much as possible." Other examples of correspondence and exchanges in magazines confirm that Gullón's attitude was quite the norm for most of the decade.[25] However, tension increased in the late 1960s as the number of writers seeking to benefit from the market for the New Latin American Novel grew. Collaborators turned into rivals, and soon they segmented into factions. Lists of writers further increased rivalries. Writer Benedetti started to publish his views on the good and bad Latin American writers. Donoso, in his book on the history of the Boom, decided who the founding fathers, major stars, and minor stars of the Boom were. In return, he was attacked for excluding the contribution of Asturias, Carpentier, Sábato, and Leopoldo Marechal, among others. Spanish-language publishers such as Seix Barral, scholars such as Gustav Siebenmann and Rama, and journalists such as Rita Guibert also published their own lists.[26]

From 1968 onward, a group of writers presented themselves as true representatives of the New Latin American Novel. They did so from Barcelona, a center of the publishing industry in Spanish and a city with dozens of agents and publishing houses. The group included García Márquez, Vargas Llosa, and Donoso, plus regular visits from Cortázar and Fuentes. They often met to support each other's work at public events. In Barcelona, group members joined the high society of leftist and anti-Francoist intelligentsia known as the *gauche divine* (Divine Left). Its meetings included Spanish writers, artists, critics, entrepreneurs, and publishers. Members of this exclusive society argued that the works of post-Boom writers were inferior to those of Boom writers. They made such statements to further promote the presence of the genuine Boom writers in Barcelona. As shown earlier, the view that this group was really a mafia (because the prestige of its members no longer was based on innovative and successful literary works) became popular and the subject of debates in Latin American and Spanish newspapers. Writers who until the 1960s were considered part of the New Latin American Novel felt excluded and went on the offensive.[27]

When García Márquez joined the group of Boom writers, his presence in Barcelona strengthened the visibility of *One Hundred Years of Solitude* as a best seller in Spain. Thanks to the *gauche divine*, he had access to more publishers. One of them, Tusquets, released in 1970 his first work after his best-selling novel: *The Story of a Shipwrecked Sailor*. This book version of a successful reportage written in 1955 was available as an inexpensive pocketbook and became a best seller. The same year, the Spanish book club Círculo de Lectores, based in Barcelona, released its own edition of *One Hundred Years of Solitude*, which also became a best seller. So successful was García Márquez's affiliation with the Boom writers that the media and publishers appropriated him as a Spanish author and *One Hundred Years of Solitude* as a Spanish novel.[28]

The group of genuine Boom writers started to receive honorary degrees worldwide and their members became almost pop culture icons. Soon, some of them realized they had more to gain individually than collectively, so they stopped meeting regularly, left Barcelona, and eventually withdrew from the group. In the years to come, they toned down the impact that this group and the New Latin American Novel had on their international success; they created their own individual spaces of influence and quickly criticized former colleagues if they stepped into their spaces. Donoso, who recommended his U.S. editor buy Cortázar's *Hopscotch* in the 1960s, accused him a decade later of being an intellectual snob and tried to downplay his originality. At the center of his criticism of a former colleague was not only irreconcilable differences about Latin America and literature's role in public life: it was also jealousy. Donoso was envious of his peer's success.

Controversies among writers and their factions received ample media attention. *One Hundred Years of Solitude* was at the heart of several disputes. Yet being there ensures a work's visibility over time and facilitates its appropriation by cultural brokers unrelated to the work's making. For example, if a highly reputed writer, such as a Nobel laureate in Literature, promotes the controversy, the work in question becomes more visible. After Asturias received the Nobel Prize, García Márquez provoked him by claiming that Asturias's most influential work *El Señor Presidente* was "bullshit." García Márquez could have chosen as the target of his criticism other famous novels based on dictators. But he was strategic. With his attack, he sought to promote his upcoming novel, *The Autumn of the Patriarch*, a story about a Latin American dictator. Asturias retaliated by giving credit to the accusation made in 1969 by journalist Luis Cova García, who claimed that *One Hundred Years of Solitude* plagiarized Balzac's novel *The Quest of the Absolute* (1834). The journalist explained that Balthazar Claës, the leading character in this novel, is obsessed with alchemy and scientific discoveries, as José Arcadio Buendía is in *One Hundred Years of Solitude*. The fact that Asturias backed this accusation caused an international uproar in the media. Writers had to take sides, and further division ensued. The publishing establishment and mainstream media ultimately dismissed the accusation. But this controversy has resurfaced over the years, as critics of *One Hundred Years of Solitude*, such as Colombian writer Fernando Vallejo, do what García Márquez did to *El Señor Presidente*. They attack *One Hundred Years of Solitude* to erode its status and to attract attention to their work.[29]

Borges criticized *One Hundred Years of Solitude*, too. He said, "You can get rid of fifty years" of the story. In reality, this statement is false. (He praised the novel publicly; see chapter 8). Yet this fake statement keeps circulating in print and on the Internet as if it were true. And more importantly, it informs the ways in which new generations of readers approach the novel. New writers attacked their seniors as well. Of García Márquez, Argentine Manuel Puig wrote, he is like "Elizabeth Taylor: 'beautiful face but terrible body.'"[30]

Fueling these attacks among writers was competition over resources, prestige, and jobs. In 1969, the wife of Argentine writer Ernesto Sábato asked Chilean critic Pedro Lastra to publish a special issue of the journal *Coral* dedicated to her husband's work, just like the one about *One Hundred Years of Solitude*, which featured twelve essays and reviews by prestigious critics and writers from five countries. The issue did not appear and Sábato, for this and other reasons felt excluded and eventually joined the ranks of writers against the New Latin American Novel. Sábato and many others witnessed how the success of *One Hundred Years of Solitude* and other New Latin American Novels created a small market for prestigious visiting positions at U.S. universities such as Harvard, Princeton, Yale, New York,

and Iowa. Their writers-in-residence programs offered beneficiaries a stable income to teach and write full-time. Competition for these positions
quickly ensued. They were given primarily to novelists and fiction writers:
Donoso, Borges, Fuentes, and Vargas Llosa, among others. (The University
of California at Berkeley invited García Márquez to lecture on the New
Latin American Novel but he declined the offer.) Those who practiced other
literary formats, especially poets, felt marginalized and grew resentful of the
mainstream New Latin American Novel.[31]

In the 1970s and 1980s, criticism came from a group of people excluded
from the literary establishment: women. The New Latin American Novel
sought to be a true *Latin American* movement. For this reason, it included
Brazilian writers. But it ignored most female writers, and there were plenty.
Silvina Ocampo, Clarice Lispector, Elena Garro (considered a precursor of
magical realism), Silvina Bullrich, Marta Lynch, Beatriz Guido, Nivaria
Tejera, Sara Gallardo, Elena Poniatowska, Marta Traba, and Rosario Castellanos collaborated in the circles of writers in Paris, Mexico City, and Buenos
Aires. (Garro and Poniatowska were collaborators of the Mafia, the group
that helped García Márquez write *One Hundred Years of Solitude*.)

Several women had already gained celebrity in the 1940s, but even they
were not included. In the 1960s, women were left out of the majority of
groundbreaking publications on the rising New Latin American Novel such
as Fuentes's manifesto "The New Latin American Novel," Casa de las Américas's special journal issue on the subject, Rodríguez Monegal's essays for *Life en
Español* magazine, or Harss's book *Into the Mainstream*. Several of these publications played a major role in bringing the unknown García Márquez (and his
forthcoming novel *One Hundred Years of Solitude*) to world attention. They also
cast Latin American female writers out of the spotlight, making them invisible and unnoticed. So, the New Latin American Novel looked like boys' club,
a view that scholarly research and popular opinion repeated. Mainstream publishers ignored women as well. In 1969, when the most famous novels of the
Boom had been published, Seix Barral's catalogue only listed two Latin American female novelists, Marta Traba and Ana Mairena. Likewise, the awards
that helped to promote the New Latin American Novel went to male writers.
The first female writer ever to win Seix Barral's Biblioteca Breve was Cuban
Spaniard Nivaria Tejera in 1971, but that was when the company had started
its decline. Before Tejera, the closest a woman got to the award was in 1960,
when Mairena was a finalist for her novel *Los extraordinarios* (*The Extraordinary Ones*). This happened two years before Vargas Llosa's win for *The Time
of the Hero*, which history books claim was the beginning of the New Latin

American Novel. Had Mairena won, the history of Latin American literature would have been different.

The mainstream tendency to ignore female writers started to correct itself in the 1970s, when more women were present in the publishing industry. For example, Sudamericana and two other publishers printed in Spanish over half a dozen of books by Brazilian writer Clarice Lispector, then a client of Carmen Balcells. Yet the support of two key gatekeepers of the publishing industry, Sudamericana and Balcells (which were critical to the making of *One Hundred Years of Solitude*), did not help Lispector or other female writers achieve similar success. A key factor was also the endorsement of literary critics, who overwhelmingly supported the (male) New Latin American Novel. Lispector did not participate in the stereotypical representations of gender that prevail in Latin American novels such as *One Hundred Years of Solitude*. Hence, (male) critics framed her work as "'feminine' writing." With the exception of Gabriela Mistral (because she was a Nobel laureate), critics silenced women in their anthologies of the region's literature, or women were the subject of scholarship that by default labeled (and separated) them as feminine writers.[32]

However, in the 1980s, there were new efforts to rediscover or promote the work of female writers who were active before the New Latin American Novel, including María Luisa Bombal, Armonía Somers, Teresa Hamel, Marta Brunet, Ana Mairena, Claribel Alegría, Marta Jara, and Silvina Bullrich, along with efforts to publicize the works of female writers during the Boom. At the same time, some gatekeepers tried to brand Latin American female writers as a collective: Isabel Allende, Luisa Valenzuela, Rosario Ferré, Elena Poniatowska, Cristina Peri Rossi, and Diamela Eltit, among others. Yet this attempt did not coalesce into a literary movement. In the 1990s, criticism of male dominance in the New Latin American Novel peaked, especially from female writers. In "The Bitches' Colloquy," Ferré famously denounced that male Latin American writers portrayed female characters as stereotypically weak. She added that male critics "have always been dominant in Latin America. It hasn't been until recently that a group of female critics has emerged in our countries, and they have stood out for the excellence of their work."[33] Ferré protested the exclusion of female writers from the Latin American canon. Literary anthologies by Rodríguez Monegal, Enrique Anderson Imbert, Jorge Lafforge, and John Brushwood, which canonized *One Hundred Years of Solitude* as the best novel of the period, included no women.[34] Paradoxically, this novel was more visible than others because it became the favorite target of female criticism, given its status as the most famous work of the New Latin American Novel. Furthermore, the imitation of this novel became an indicator of success for female writers. The debut novels of Isabel Allende and Laura Esquivel—*The House of the Spirits* (1982) and *Like Water for Chocolate* (1989), respectively—imitated *One Hundred Years of Solitude*, especially its magical realist style and the story of the family saga. Their success as international best sellers (and years later as blockbuster movies) secured their authors' careers as writers. And these novels' success helped make *One Hundred Years of Solitude* more visible to new generations of cultural brokers.

As the previous paragraphs have shown, the closure of the Boom also affected *One Hundred Years of Solitude* and started a solo career for its author. García Márquez acknowledged the influence of the New Latin American Novel over his novel the first few years. Then, he started to downplay it. He did so with books such as Carpentier's *Explosion in a Cathedral*, which he admired and built on to write his novel. In 1976, a journalist asked him, "I have read that . . . when *Explosion in a Cathedral* was published you destroyed dozens and dozens of chapters of the work you were writing. Is it true?" García Márquez replied, "No, it is not true the way you put it. *Explosion in a Cathedral* appeared when *One Hundred Years of Solitude* was very developed. And the first thing that surprises me is that there was a conception of the novel identical to mine, and, of course, since they coincided so much, I was forced to change mine, because it would have seemed as if I had copied *Explosion in a Cathedral*, a novel for which I feel a great admiration. Alejo [Carpentier] goes deep into the Caribbean . . . and since it is an area that is common to us, we agree on many aspects."[35] In reality, as shown in the previous chapter, García Márquez did the opposite, for he found in Carpentier's novel a model upon which to write his novel.

Despite closure, breakup, and conflict, two goals united Boom writers: to present themselves as the beginning of something new in literature and to select successors to perpetuate their literary legacy. In 1977, for example, Fuentes declared on Spain's national television, "My generation and the one that preceded me, I am talking about the fathers of the modern Latin American literature, Borges, Carpentier, Onetti, we have all had a very clear awareness that we are not the culmination of anything, but the beginning of something." For him, their works were a radical break in the region's literature. But when he talked about the new literature that followed him, he said that it simply was a continuity of the New Latin American Novel. Likewise, Donoso publicized Cuban exile and poet Reinaldo Arenas as one of the talented post-Boom writers. The result of these and other interventions is that García Márquez, Vargas Llosa, and Cortázar in particular have overshadowed younger talents, making it more difficult for them to secure a prestigious position in the regional and international literary market.[36]

A NOVEL WITHOUT PERIODICALS AND PUBLISHERS

Controversies and conflict also affected periodicals and publishers that promoted new Latin American literature. They became weapons of ideological confrontation rather than the vehicles for building the community of Latin American artists they had been in the 1960s. Periodicals across the region, in particular, published heated exchanges among writers, sending the message to their readers that new and established generations of writers were divided about what the goals of literature in the region should be and especially how to achieve them.

Periodicals

A handful of general interest and literary periodicals shaped and controlled literary taste in the 1960s. These publications had broad region-spanning readership and a clear agenda: the promotion of a specific kind of Latin American literature. They constructed and promoted novelty in a particular way that helped standardize readers' taste. From the 1970s onward, however, growing competition in the periodicals market and ideological conflict among writers led to the multiplication of publications, each with a smaller readership.

Since its creation in 1965, *Mundo Nuevo* magazine offered the "most compact appearance [of the region's literature]," Donoso claimed. And it did so "until Emir Rodríguez Monegal resigned from his post," which he did for ideological reasons. The magazine received funding from the Ford Foundation and the Congress for Freedom of Culture; the latter was secretly funded by the CIA. The news spread quickly throughout Latin America. García Márquez, one of the beneficiaries of *Mundo Nuevo*'s and Rodríguez Monegal's enthusiastic endorsement of *One Hundred Years of Solitude*, publicly stated that he had been "cuckolded" by the magazine and its editor. Next, the writer, as others did, severed professional ties with them. After the *Mundo Nuevo* controversy, promoters tried to launch another cosmopolitan and Latin American magazine based in Paris that would bring writers together, but their initiative only caused further ideological conflict. The summer of 1970 in Avignon, France, leading members of the literary establishment—García Márquez, Vargas Llosa, Donoso, Fuentes, Cortázar, and Juan Goytisolo—met to create a magazine. Conflicting views on Cuba surfaced as soon as they started to disagree on the magazine's name: *Libre* (literally, *Free*). After its launch in 1971, the outbreak of the Padilla affair turned the magazine into an impossible project to sustain and it disappeared the following year, after only four issues.[37]

The above-mentioned controversy between Arguedas and Cortázar was featured in the magazines *Amaru* and *Life en Español*, with other media reprinting their debate. Arguedas had published an excerpt of his novel *The Fox from Up Above and the Fox from Down Below* in *Amaru*. It also printed Arguedas's discourse "I Am Not Acculturated." Cortázar replied in 1969 from the pages of the cosmopolitan *Life en Español*. That mainstream, region-spanning magazines served as weapons to magnify their conflict was unusual. Until then, these two magazines had enthusiastically promoted Latin American writers. In 1965, readers of *Life en Español* learned in two reportages about the rise of the New Latin American Novel, as proved by the international success of works by writers of different generations and countries in the region. The literary journal *Amaru* premiered in 1967 for its highbrow readers one chapter of *One Hundred Years of Solitude*. But the Arguedas-Cortázar controversy created divisions that forced other publications as well as writers to take sides. Vargas Llosa, a fellow Peruvian, backed Cortázar and attacked Arguedas. And Colombian writer Collazos started his controversy with Cortázar and Vargas Llosa in *Marcha*, the Uruguayan and region-spanning general interest magazine that promoted New Latin American Novels such as *One Hundred Years of Solitude*. Other media in the region reprinted this new controversy.[38]

As with publishing houses, the commercial success of Latin American literature multiplied the number of new magazines and newspapers. Critic and *Primera Plana* editor T. E. Martínez, who once was so passionate about the success of Latin American novelists, regretted in 1970 that magazines went too far in promoting many overrated writers and works. They no longer created the conditions for collaboration—only confrontation—to attract sales and readers. Critic Harss alerted readers to this growing division: "The threads of interests from before, which during a time of euphoria seemed surpassed, have been replaced by today's clans. . . . False alarms, pseudo-events, and inflated reputations abound—thanks, in part, to the illiteracy of trendy magazines."[39]

At the same time, magazines that promoted a region-spanning view of Latin American literature started to disappear. As mentioned, rumors that the CIA secretly financed *Mundo Nuevo* damaged its prestige among writers and readers, and it ceased to exist in 1971. In 1969, *Primera Plana* interrupted its publication due to military censorship and closed its doors four years later. Fernando Benítez, founder and editor of *La Cultura en México* left the cultural supplement in 1971, and a new editorial board with a different understanding of Latin America (and its literature) took over. In Uruguay, *Marcha* closed in 1974, a year after the coup d'état. Other publications from the 1960s continued promoting a Latin American message, but writers and readers regarded it as too ideological, especially the journal *Casa de las Américas*, which Castro's communist government sponsored.[40]

Publishers

In 1968, García Márquez threatened to sue Era if it did not transfer the publishing rights of several of his works to Sudamericana. Just five years earlier, Era had saved the writer's career at a critical moment by publishing new editions of two of his novellas, which had sold poorly when they were first published. Some of its staff members were García Márquez's friends and had collaborated with him on *One Hundred Years of Solitude*, which he had first promised to Era. In reality, though, his threat was hardly an exception; it just showed how much the success of his book and other New Latin American Novels transformed the publishing industry and how conflict could detach a cultural object from its niche. The success of *One Hundred Years of Solitude* compelled many writers in the region to seek ways to reach large international audiences. And more publishing houses tried to sign these writers and market them as Latin American authors. Publishers did not do this because they had a vision for the region's literature (as Seix Barral did) but because they wanted to cash in on the regional and international success of Latin American literature; they hoped that one of their books could also hit the jackpot. This increasing competition eroded the control over the literary mainstream by a handful of publishers and gatekeepers. In the 1960s, their intervention helped standardize literary publishing by making sure that Latin American writers and their works were marketable as part of a shared literary vision and not just as single books. But in the early 1970s, the result of rising competition was that no single publisher in Spain and Latin America controlled the literary avant-garde as Seix Barral and Sudamericana did throughout the 1960s. Hence, books were put on the market as individual commodities, not as products of a larger literary movement. Fragmentation at the top of the Spanish-language publishing industry meant that it was impossible to absorb and bring together dozens of new works under a literary brand that could be easily marketed to regional and international audiences.[41]

Also, growing democratization in Spain made it possible to publish works written in exile by Max Aub, Francisco Ayala, Luis Cernuda, Rosa Chacel,

Ramón J. Sender, Pedro Salinas, and other Spanish writers. Publishers released books and anthologies that featured work by these writers, starting with Rafael Conte's *Narraciones de la España desterrada* (*Narrations of Exiled Spain*). The publishing industry in Spain started gravitating toward this new market. At that moment, the market for Latin American writers had become saturated, as the 1971 Nobel Prize in Literature to Neruda demonstrated. During this decade, exports of the publishing industry in Spain to Latin America became stagnant at 44 million kilograms. Governments in the region challenged Barcelona's control over the publishing industry in Spanish. In 1965, books made in Mexico generated only 20 percent of the national revenue from book consumption; the remaining 80 percent came from imported books, especially from Spain and Argentina. To stop this flight of capital, the Mexican government introduced protectionist measures. They sought to reduce imports of foreign books and to stimulate the national publishing industry.[42] Other governments soon followed. As figure 2.1 in chapter 2 shows, this protectionism in the 1970s had a visible impact on the Spanish-language publishing industry, which remains understudied. But clearly one of its consequences was that mainstream publishing houses in the region committed more to the consolidation of national literatures than to Latin American literature, contrary to what they did in the 1960s.[43]

Seix Barral. This company's publishing agenda created favorable market conditions for the circulation of *One Hundred Years of Solitude* in Spain as a best-selling Latin American novel. During the 1960s, the company faced no competition in the country in implementing its agenda because it tapped a market of forgotten writers and competing publishing houses did not catch up until the early 1970s. At that point, larger and established publishers such as Planeta and Destino (which mainly published social realist writers) and newcomers such as Alianza, Alfaguara, and Tusquets started to publish their own Latin American writers. They also released work by Spanish writers that imitated Latin American writers.[44]

Along with external competition for writers and readers, Seix Barral faced growing internal tension. In 1967, Víctor Seix, the managing director, died, and the communist leanings of Carlos Barral, the acquisitions editor, created more problems with the Spanish government. (The Formentor Group, one of Seix Barral's initiatives to control the literary mainstream internationally, was also reproved by the government as communist propaganda machine, and the Group's awards ceased to exist the same year.) The Seix and Barral families clashed over control of the firm, and in 1969 Carlos Barral launched his own publishing venture, Barral Editores, which further antagonized the conflict with Seix Barral because Barral Editores wanted to take with it best-selling Latin American writers such as Donoso, García Márquez, and Vargas Llosa. Two years later, the publishers finally separated. This split "ruined the most influential platform for the internationalization of Latin American literature," as Donoso put it.[45]

One Hundred Years of Solitude helped speed up the split. Seix Barral wanted to award the Biblioteca Breve prize to this novel in order to cash on its best-selling success in Spain and Latin America. To do so, it had to change the rules of the prize because only novels published the previous year were candidates. So, *One Hundred Years of Solitude* would have received the 1969 prize two years after its publication. This plan created yet another controversy surrounding the novel and cast doubts on the seriousness of the prize. The publisher had to stop its plan. Three years later, it even discontinued the prize that cemented its reputation. The split also had rippling effects in the Latin American publishing industry. In 1963, Carlos Barral and the Seix brothers owned 23 percent of the shares of Mexican press Joaquín Mortíz. As analyzed in chapter 2, the penetration of Spanish print capitalism into the Latin American publishing industry helped standardize the literary agendas of commercial publishers on both sides of the Atlantic. But by 1974, Seix Barral had sold its shares of Joaquín Mortíz. A decade later, Seix Barral, which no longer was a central player in the publication of mainstream literature, was absorbed by Catalan book conglomerate Planeta.[46]

Sudamericana. This company's fate was similar to Seix Barral's, and the success of *One Hundred Years of Solitude* was part of it as well. In 1969, unable to cope with demands for more copies (which had to be printed in Argentina and exported to Spain) and to obey Spanish authorities, Sudamericana authorized its Spanish branch, EDHASA (and soon after the subscription book club Círculo de Lectores), to publish larger print runs. Then, "the novel became a household item." Its success eclipsed all future publications. As Porrúa, the novel's acquisitions editor, confessed years later, "I think *One Hundred Years of Solitude* has become my last name." Thus, it is not surprising that he sought to downplay his role and that of Sudamericana in the success of the book, just like writers did with their affiliation to the Boom. "I repeat: the editor did little," Porrúa said. "Transforming the view of what the Latin American novel was at that time was the book itself, *One Hundred Years of Solitude*. Everything moves around that, the object, the work." Porrúa left his post in 1971, when Sudamericana—just like Seix Barral in Spain—was facing increasing market fragmentation and competition. Relations between Sudamericana and García Márquez deteriorated in 1972 because of the publisher's handling of the novel.

The author kept complaining that the market in Latin America demanded more copies than the publisher was printing. Three years later, he found out that the publisher was actually printing more copies but not declaring them. Sudamericana had underreported sales of over eleven thousand copies of the book and it had paid no royalties to the author for any of them.[47] Sudamericana agreed to pay García Márquez but ties were broken. Fraud had replaced collaboration. In the 1980s, the Bertelsmann Group, one of the world's largest mass media conglomerates, acquired Sudamericana.

Balcells Agency. García Márquez's literary agent discovered the fraud after traveling to Buenos Aires and auditing Sudamericana's book sales reports. Balcells grew more powerful thanks to the avalanche of sales and translations of *One Hundred Years of Solitude.* She started to challenge the balance of power between authors and publishers. In Spanish alone, the book had already sold almost one million copies in its first seven years. Between 1969 and 1973, the number of translations grew from four to twenty. By 1982, the year García Márquez received the Nobel Prize, the novel had been translated into another fifteen languages. By then, a total of thirty-five translations had added transnational value to the product. The quality of a translation can favor the success of a literary work, and critics, readers, and García Márquez himself praised Gregory Rabassa's translation of the novel. It is also remarkable that neither pirated nor flawed translations of this novel have stopped its global success.[48]

Balcells marketed several of his Latin American clients as a group of genuine Boom writers to increase their reputation and sales. When this group dissolved for political reasons, the agency shifted its strategy and started to attract new writers who could imitate *One Hundred Years of Solitude* in particular and Boom novels in general. The agency also detached the novel from Sudamericana by liberating its foreign rights and negotiating with European and American publishers independently. Since then, the novel's rights have been sold to publishers that pay the best price. As a result, it has become available in multiple formats (from trade paperbacks to scholarly editions) released by competing publishers, sometimes in the same country. And in 2019, it sold to Netflix the rights for the first screen adaptation.[49] The agency's strategy has ensured that, since the 1980s, *One Hundred Years of Solitude* remains more visible and available transnationally than competing Boom novels.

Weeks before her death, Balcells admitted to have "leveraged *One Hundred Years of Solitude* again and again to 'make a secret deal' with publishers worldwide, granting them the rights to new books only if they amended their individual contracts for Gabo's book—so that rights to it would revert back to the agency." The publication of new books by García Márquez allowed her to do so. As of 2008, his works represented 36.2 percent of the agency's business volume.[50] This shows how *One Hundred Years of Solitude*, produced by Balcells, has come to shape the agency's publishing agenda. Simply put, the prestige of this cultural object now dictates the strategy of an organization that collaborated in its production. Eventually, as classics outlast the gatekeepers that help to produce them, this novel will be fully uprooted from the agency.

CONCLUSION

The collapse of the niche responsible for the imagination, production, and early circulation of a literary work is an important step for the work to start climbing the ladder to classic status. This niche includes people, organizations, ideas, conventions, norms, rules, and objects involved in the work's making. Over time, these collaborators are criticized or simply forgotten. And the result of this collapse is that work more representative of that niche stands as a landmark of the moment. That was the case of *One Hundred Years of Solitude*. It started to outgrow and outlive several of the collaborators involved in its making. In the process, this novel acquired a life of its own; it was no longer labeled a New Latin American Novel, no longer associated with a network of writers (but rather it was the isolated product of a single writer), and no longer controlled by a single publisher. Collaborators stopped influencing the life of this cultural good, which expedited the way for the intervention of cultural brokers.

6

A NOVEL WITHOUT BORDERS

His world [in the novel] was mine.

—Salman Rushdie on *One Hundred Years of Solitude*[1]

T he explosion reportedly occurred at 9:56 p.m. CDT on April 20, 2010, and what followed was one of the worst oil spills in history. The center of the explosion was the Deepwater Horizon, a drilling rig platform of the multinational oil and gas company British Petroleum (BP). When the platform exploded, the company was drilling in the Macondo Prospect. Why did the prospect have that name? Two years before, a group of BP engineers decided to name it after the village in *One Hundred Years of Solitude*. What they did was not unusual.

Oil fields have technical names, but energy companies also designate them in creative ways. MC252 is the technical name for the Macondo well. The fact that this prospect in the Gulf of Mexico was the site of a historical environmental catastrophe increased, by pure chance, the meaningfulness of *One Hundred Years of Solitude*. Nowadays, this event is known worldwide as the Macondo blowout. Naming things related to this event after Macondo did not end there. An anti-pollution chamber designed to contain the spill was called the Macondome. The reference to the village compelled others to find connections between the event and other parts of *One Hundred Years of Solitude*. Some media referred to the accident as a case of "tragic realism" (in connection to the novel's magical realist style) and as the "pig's tail of the Petro-World" (in reference to the book's end, when the last member of the Buendía family is born with a curse, a pig's tail). Of course, calling this prospect Macondo or coining the expressions Macondome, "tragic realism," or "pig's tail of the Petro-World" was not García Márquez's choice nor a decision of his literary agent, a mainstream publisher, or an influential critic. Naming things in the world after this novel with the goal of seeing that world in a new and yet familiar way was the choice of cultural brokers. Thanks to their brokerage, Macondo has acquired a new meaning related to a familiar phenomenon: environmental catastrophes. Now some groups even refer to environmental accidents as Macondo-type events; a way of labeling events that an urban studies scholar sees as part of the Macondoization of the world. The Macondo blowout also touched the lives of ordinary people, such as Natalie Smith, who worked as operations coordinator for BP in the Macondo response, as she mentions in her LinkedIn profile. Seven years later, on October 30, 2017, *Time* magazine reminded its millions of print and online readers about the historical event. The following year, so did *Oyla*, a popular science magazine for youngsters published in Kazakhstan, with a print run of twenty thousand copies. Although readers of these publications might never have heard of *One Hundred Years of Solitude*, the actions of BP engineers, environmental groups, scholars, job seekers, magazines, and other cultural brokers make it possible for Macondo (and the novel where this village is set) to develop meanings that extend beyond fiction and enter people's lives in unexpected ways.[2]

As this chapter shows, the Macondo blowout is just one of the ways in which *One Hundred Years of Solitude* has attained a life outside its pages, the kind of life that literary classics have. Other practices that have contributed to this novel's classic status are the diffusion of legends and myths surrounding its making, its association with a particular style (magical realism), the comparison of this novel to other works of art, its transformation into objects and merchandise, and even the ascent of its author to classic status. Carrying out these practices are cultural brokers acting sometimes in isolation, sometimes in collaboration, and sometimes in conflict. Taken together, they have created different ways of reading, feeling, and talking about this novel. And these new ways have detached this novel from its niche of imagination, production, and early circulation. Cultural brokers, in sum, have made it possible for *One Hundred Years of Solitude* to be a novel without borders.[3]

MYTHS AND THE CREATION OF A CLASSIC

Myths are a powerful way of creating classics. One thing myths do is replace the conventional with the extraordinary. They replace the pedestrian acts of the people involved in the imagination and production of the work of art with the story of the genius and the belief that the making of the work was inevitable and even miraculous. For this reason, it is hard to find a classic that is not connected to some kind of myth. Artists themselves are often vested in myth creation by circulating legends. García Márquez was no exception. As *One Hundred Years of Solitude* became a commercial success, he started to disseminate legends about himself and the making of the novel.

One of these legends refers to the novel's opening sentence. Over the years, the author offered several versions of how he wrote it. He said he had written nothing in five years, and then suddenly he experienced a marvelous epiphany. When he was on his way to Acapulco for a family vacation, the initial words of a novel descended upon him from nowhere. He felt that the rest of the novel was so clear in his mind that he could have dictated it to a typist right there. Instead, he canceled the family vacation, rushed back home to Mexico City, and wrote nonstop in his studio for eighteenth months until he finished the novel. While this is a wonderful story, the evidence analyzed in chapter 4 suggests that it is a legend. In the years leading up to that point, he had been working on and off on another novel. Thanks to his literary agent (with whom he just signed a contract that summer) and other professional contacts, he knew it was the ideal time to work on the novel he had imagined for more than a decade. He also knew he could easily pitch it to several publishers as a trendy New Latin American Novel—then a sought-after product in the international literary market. The reality is that it took him two weeks to write the opening sentence. After that, he was unsure how to write the rest of the novel.[4]

García Márquez and his collaborators disseminated different versions of his epiphany even before *One Hundred Years of Solitude* was published. Germán Vargas, his friend from the Barranquilla Group, did that in his review of the novel. So did media, critics, and scholars over the years; some even invented new details about the epiphany.[5] As a result, the story of how he came up with the idea for the novel has become a myth that different cultural brokers continue to use and reinvent. For example, on August 30, 2018, TED Conferences LLC released "Why Should You Read *One Hundred Years of Solitude?*" This global media organization offers talks under the slogan "ideas worth spreading." This 2018 talk belonged to TED-Ed, the company's youth and education initiative. Widely circulated on the Internet, the talk attracted over a quarter of a million views the first twenty-four hours on Facebook alone. The images and narrative of the video (available in twenty-one languages) reproduce the myth about García Márquez's epiphany. "Myths worth spreading," too, would describe more accurately what this TED talk has done for the novel. Although it is factually incorrect, the video plays an important role in perpetuating among new generations the romantic view of the genial writer of the classic after falling under the spell of the muses. Finally, the video promotes the availability of this novel on Audible, a global seller and producer of spoken content.[6] Neither TED nor Audible existed when *One Hundred Years of Solitude* was first published. But six decades later they are on the novel's list of new cultural brokers.

García Márquez also invented multiple (and contradictory) versions about how he wrote the rest of the novel. In an oft-cited interview with Mexican writer Elena Poniatowska, he stated, "I never read them anything [from *One Hundred Years of Solitude*] because I do not read to others absolutely anything I am writing about."[7] This statement mirrors the old and popular myth of the artist who spent a long time in almost solitary confinement in order to single-handedly create a revolutionary work of art that shocked the world. The reality is that *One Hundred Years of Solitude* was the product of networked creativity. He read and shared in person and by mail the manuscript in process with critics, peers, and friends on three continents. And he often included their feedback to the text. But as in the case of his epiphany, García Márquez's statements about how he wrote the novel have turned into myths that cultural brokers have re-elaborated over the decades.

There are also different legends about the publication of the manuscript. One legends says that sending the manuscript to Sudamericana in Argentina was not a done deal. Rather, García Márquez was hoping that the acquisitions editor would take a gamble on the novel. The truth is that he had already reached an initial agreement with the publisher the year before. Another important component of this legend is that of the penniless writer. After months of full-time writing, he arrived at the post office and realized he did not have enough money to send the full manuscript from Mexico to Argentina. So, he divided it into two parts. And even though he sent the second part by mistake, it did not matter. Once the acquisitions editor received it, he was so astonished by the text that he sent García Márquez the money to mail the rest. Another version claims that the writer had to pawn several of his domestic possessions and his wife's jewels. With this money, he sent the other half to the publisher the next day. However, the story of the divided manuscript did not appear until four years after the novel's publication, when García Márquez had already given dozens of interviews. And he started to say he had sent the second half of the novel by mistake only in 1976, almost a decade after its publication.[8] As in the cases above, scholars, critics, journalists, and common readers have reproduced and added new and mythical details to this story. For example, in 2016, more than one million readers of the five international editions of *Vanity Fair* magazine could read in the article "The Secret History of *One Hundred Years of Solitude*" that García Márquez visited the pawnshop on multiple occasions.[9] And as new people learn about this legend and others, some of them feel compelled to repeat (or reinvent) such legends and, in doing so, become new brokers of the novel's classic status as myth makers.

A GLOBAL AND MAGICAL REALIST NOVEL

One Hundred Years of Solitude is a Caribbean story. It is mostly set around the Ciénaga, an area located in Colombia's coastal region facing the Caribbean Sea. But García Márquez imagined it as a Latin American story. As he put it, "Everything I wrote are experiences drawn from the peoples of Latin America; they are truths, they are blindingly obvious . . . and thus my novel may seem like a poetic transposition of the history of Latin America."[10] In agreement with the author's goal, numerous cultural brokers in this region have imagined his novel as neither a Caribbean novel nor a Colombian one but as the history of Latin America. Yet the different ways in which these brokers interpret a work of art are crucial to expand its reach. Decades later, they have used the language of genetics to make sense of the novel. For Jewish Mexican scholar Ilan Stavans, it has become part of the DNA of Latin America. At the same time, statements about the novel's Latin Americanism are compatible with its cosmopolitanism. For example, some scholars have interpreted Macondo as "a synthesis of all Latin American history [and simultaneously] the story of Macondo is that of mankind." Some writers consider the novel to be about the history of the region, while they connect José Arcadio Buendía's efforts in divination to the argument about the rise of modern science made by philosopher Michel Foucault in *The Order of Things*. For another writer, the novel treats myths in similar ways to the ideas of famous anthropologist Claude Lévi-Strauss about the myth. For other cultural brokers, the fact that *One Hundred Years of Solitude* is a "Latin American work" is more of an accident because it belongs to the older tradition of family saga books.[11]

Publishers have also helped uproot *One Hundred Years of Solitude* from its Caribbean setting. They have marketed it in ways that match readers' taste. In the United States, readers have imagined this novel as a story about a banana republic with similarities to William Faulkner's American South. In France, the novel is seen by many as the Rabelaisian alternative—characterized by unruliness and exuberance—to the Cartesian cogito—defined by rationality and order. In Spain, *One Hundred Years of Solitude* was included soon after publication in the tradition of novels from the Golden Age in the seventeenth century, and in Italy it was sold as the new *Don Quixote*. In revolutionary Cuba, readers welcomed García Márquez's novel as a tale of redemption and revolutionary struggle. In China, readers have connected this novel to the eighteenth-century classic *Dream of the Red Chamber* due to clear similarities: ample number of characters (some with identical names), members of two clans mixing constantly, a beautiful woman who exits the novel mysteriously, and the overarching story of a declining family saga. In the Soviet Union, readers linked *One Hundred Years of Solitude* to the nineteenth-century tradition of total novels led by Leo Tolstoy and updated by Boris Pasternak. And postcommunist Russians linked the novel to the works of writers who suffered political repression under communism, such as Mikhail Bulgakov. In the so-called Third World, readers found it meaningful in the 1980s and 1990s to approach the story of Macondo as mirroring the fate of the Third World at large (like similar works by contemporary Indian, Nigerian, South African, and Caribbean writers), and others believed this story "taught Western readers tolerance for other perspectives," as Ghanaian-born writer Nii Ayikwei Parkes put it.

Other brokers, on the contrary, changed their minds over time. In 2009, Francisco Porrúa, the novel's acquisitions editor, stated, "Yes, I viewed it as very Latin American [in the 1960s, but] today I think it is a very Caribbean work."[12] Changes of this kind are normal as cultural brokers appropriate *One Hundred Years of Solitude* in new ways. Thus, some features that were specific to the novel's imagination and initial circulation moved to the background and others come to the forefront. Its humor and its narrative anachronisms are now secondary. And one feature that went almost unnoticed upon its publication is now crucial to explain its global circulation and classic status: magical realism.

One Hundred Years of Solitude is a clear example of how associating a work of art with a style is key to its consecration as a classic. For more than five decades, cultural brokers have appropriated this novel as the best work of magical realism worldwide. In this case, too, the brokers are diverse, from anonymous readers to national governments to celebrities. And their reach is multidimensional, from local book clubs to global media. The outcome of their separate and uncoordinated actions over time and across national boundaries is that they help other brokers imagine *One Hundred Years of Solitude* as the literary work that (incorrectly) invented magical realism.[13] Furthermore, mass readers and numerous educated readers continue to (again incorrectly) make sense of García Márquez's six-decade-long writing career and his entire oeuvre as a magical realist.

Venezuelan writer Arturo Uslar Pietri is credited for popularizing the term magical realism in Latin American literature. He first mentioned it in an essay published in 1948. (Not coincidentally, a Venezuelan critic was the first to call García Márquez a "magic realist," see chapter 4.) Yet neither a writer not a Latin American coined this term. German art critic Franz Roh first introduced *magischer Realismus* into language in 1925. He used it to understand the future of pictorial arts in Europe after expressionism. Other critics used his term in similar ways for the next decade or so. But in Latin America, another member of Uslar Pietri's generation (and his friend), Alejo Carpentier, coined an analogous term, the marvelous real (*lo real maravilloso*), in an essay also published in 1948. His contribution was to apply this term to the reality of Latin America as a whole, not just to a single country, religion, ethnic group, or literary tradition. For Uslar Pietri and Carpentier, along with their friend and writer Miguel Ángel Asturias, the mixture of reality and the fantastic was a key strategy to achieve the independence of Latin American literature. In the 1950s, the literary imagination surrounding magical realism and the marvelous real were spreading among a minority of writers, critics, and the cultural intelligentsia in Europe, Latin America, the Caribbean, and the United States. Yet this literary imagination only became a novelty for commercial publishers and mass readers after the release of *One Hundred Years of Solitude*.[14]

Understanding the history of the term *magical realism* is important because the construction of an aesthetic category like this one has detached the cultural good *One Hundred Years of Solitude* from its niche.[15] Neither García Márquez nor his closest collaborators had magical realism in mind when he imagined his novel nor did its acquisitions editor refer to magical realism to market the book. The editor in fact stated, "The term 'magical realism' still seems to me a bit contradictory."[16] Despite his and other people's reservations about this term, since the 1970s transnational audiences have started to believe that *One Hundred Years of Solitude* invented magical realism. The following decade a global explosion of magical realism occurred in Spanish and soon after in other major literary languages, such as English, French, and German. As figure 6.1 shows, the term *magical realism* started to appear more frequently in printed publications in these languages as the success of the novel continued. Also, thanks partly to the Nobel Prize awarded to García Márquez in 1982, the aesthetic agenda of magical realism became a formula imitated and turned into "an aesthetic form easily translatable to the most diverse cultural locations."[17]

By the late 1990s, new generations of readers, writers, and critics began to imagine magical realism as "a universal tendency." This term was then so

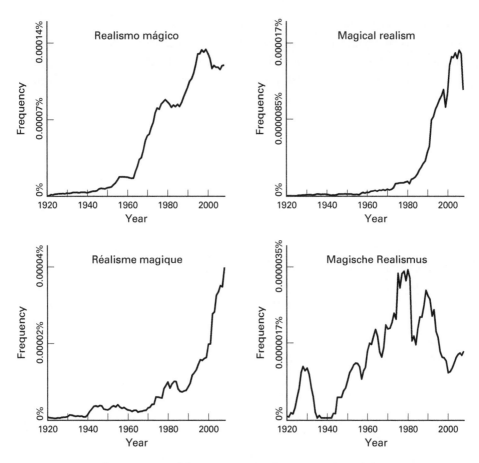

6.1 Frequency of the term *magical realism* in Spanish, English, French, and German publications (1920–2008).

Source: Google Ngram Viewer.

pervasive that scholars worldwide grew tired of its use and abuse. For some of them, it was even "ideologically dangerous." Cultural brokers developed two strategies to deal with this controversial usage. One strategy was to make magical realism more local, that is, to refer to it as something specific to the Latin American writers Carpentier, Asturias, Juan Rulfo, and García Márquez and just some of their works—*The Kingdom of this World* (1949), *Men of Maize* (1949), *Pedro Páramo* (1955), and *One Hundred Years of Solitude*, respectively. The other (and more common) strategy was to globalize magical realism. For the brokers that followed this strategy, magical realism was not a genre specific to Latin America literature in the mid-twentieth century; it was an older transnational genre. So, according to this strategy, Horacio Quiroga's "The Dead Man" (1920) could be the region's first magical realist story and Jorge Luis Borges could be as magical realist of a writer as García Márquez. Some scholars expanded the term beyond the region and called Thomas Mann's *The Magic Mountain* (1924) and Dino Buzzati's *The Tartar Steppe* (1940) works of magical realism. In North America, Latin America, and Europe, college textbooks associated magical realism with non-Latin American writers whose works are considered classics: François Rabelais, Walter Scott, Benito Pérez Galdós, Franz Kafka, Virginia Woolf, Italo Calvino, Tolstoy, Bulgakov, and Faulkner, among others. The global success of magical realism led to the creation of alternative labels, such as "dirty realism," coined in 1983 by a contributor to *Granta*, one of the world's leading literary magazines. Three decades later, in 2012, the committee of the Nobel Prize in Literature gave the award to Mo Yan for his "hallucinatory realism." For the committee, this realism "merges folk tales, history and the contemporary," which is a mixture that the writer himself claimed to have taken from García Márquez's magical realism.[18]

Other brokers keep denying that *One Hundred Years of Solitude* is a work of magical realism. Four decades after its publication, Colombian journalist and poet Ana Mercedes Vivas insisted that it was a Colombian work of "social realism." Others, on the contrary, have argued that it did not mark the beginning of magical realism but was rather its culmination: "probably, the most illustrative example of the so-called 'magic realism,'" as Swiss scholar Gustav Siebenmann put it. Anthologies and guides reproduce the view that this novel is "the highpoint of magical realism" and underline that "its magical realism spawned an enormous number of imitators." And other brokers, five decades later, continue to criticize the use and abuse of the term. As U.S. literary critic Fredric Jameson wrote, "Let's stop using this generic term for everything unconventional and consign it to the bin in which we keep such worn-out epithets as 'surrealistic' and 'Kafkaesque.'"[19]

The global (and controversial) success of magical realism prompted revisions of the literary history of Latin America. A dominant interpretation transformed Carpentier into the major figure of magical realism, while others, such as Mexicans Juan José Arreola and Elena Garro, were left out. Yet Arreola was among the first writers to abandon realism in the 1950s (when Carpentier also envisioned the marvelous real) and to write about themes later labeled as typical of magical realism. And Garro, a member of García Márquez's circle in Mexico City, published *Recollections of Things to Come* three years before *One Hundred Years of Solitude*. Some researchers now see her novel as a foundational work of magical realism. But, unlike García Márquez's fiction, Garro's work did not attract attention at the time mainly because she was a woman and men dominated the movement of the New Latin American Novel.[20]

Other authors were excluded because they wrote in small countries with little influence on the region's literature. For example, in 1933, Ecuadorian writer Demetrio Aguilera-Malta published *Don Goyo*, a novella with a 150-year-old protagonist who strives to preserve his cultural and natural environment. Only eight decades later did readers start to praise it as a pioneering example of magical realism. Yet some critics do so by comparing this novella to García Márquez's work and then judge it as inferior: "[Aguilera-Malta] lags only a little behind [García Márquez] in his lyrical evocation of the slightly unreal." A similar judgment applies to José de la Cuadra, whose novella *Los Sangurimas* (1934) is considered by fewer people as a forerunner of *One Hundred Years of Solitude*'s magical realism (see chapter 8). Exclusion also applies to Latin American writers working after García Márquez's novel came out. Paulo Coelho, Laura Esquivel, and Isabel Allende followed magical realism. But numerous scholars, critics, and other cultural brokers dismiss their works as too popular and commercial. Other works, on the contrary, are not excluded but occupy a secondary position. Rulfo's *Pedro Páramo* (1955) is customarily presented in anthologies and textbooks as a "precursor to magical realism."[21] This labeling has happened despite efforts of powerful members of the global intelligentsia, such as U.S. critic Susan Sontag, who tried to attract the attention of English-language readers to *Pedro Páramo*. Counterfactually, had Rulfo published his novella in 1964, when *The Time of the Hero*, *The Death of Artemio Cruz*, *Hopscotch*, *Bomarzo*, and *Explosion in a Cathedral* were best sellers, its global trajectory would have been quite different.

Writers themselves are important cultural brokers in the globalization of magical realism. "I was sitting in my office at Random House," said African American writer Toni Morrison, then an editor with two of her novels published,

> just turning the pages of *One Hundred Years of Solitude*. There was something so familiar about the novel, so recognizable to me. It was a certain kind of freedom, a structural freedom, a [different] notion of a beginning, middle, and end. Culturally, I felt intimate with him because he was happy to mix the living and the dead. His characters were on intimate terms with the supernatural world, and that's the way stories were told in my house.

Morrison, who shared a similar literary imagination with García Márquez, published her breakthrough novel *Song of Solomon* in 1977. It tells the story of Macon

Dead III. (Notice the similarity in the spelling and sound with Macondo.) After *Song of Solomon*, which won the National Book Critics Circle Award, Morrison quit her job in publishing, became a best-selling author, and won the 1993 Nobel Prize in Literature. As a professor at Princeton University, she taught García Márquez and *One Hundred Years of Solitude* to new generations of college students. Like Morrison, British Indian Salman Rushdie was another budding writer who appropriated *One Hundred Years of Solitude*: "I knew García Márquez's colonels and generals, or at least their Indian and Pakistani counterparts; his bishops were my mullahs; his market streets were my bazaars. His world was mine, translated into Spanish. It's little wonder I fell in love with it—not for its magic . . . but for its realism." Then, Rushdie turned into English his own world as seen through the lens of García Márquez's magical realism. The outcome was his breakthrough novel, *Midnight's Children* (1981). It won the prestigious Booker Prize in 1981, the Booker of Bookers in 1993, and enjoys long-selling status.[22]

The influence of the magical realism in *One Hundred Years of Solitude* has extended beyond the generation of writers that, like Morrison and Rushdie, came of age in the novel's first decade. This novel influenced older writers, like U.S. author Norman Mailer, who praised it as a technical tour de force: "At the moment the only great writer who can handle forty or fifty characters and three or four decades is García Marquez. *One Hundred Years of Solitude* is an amazing work. He succeeds in doing it, but how, I don't know. In my Egyptian novel [*Ancient Evenings*], it took me ten pages to go around a bend in the Nile." As it once did among older writers, *One Hundred Years of Solitude* now touches younger generations of authors in and beyond Latin America. Indian novelist Amitav Ghosh acknowledged that "García Márquez was much more important to [his] writing" than Rushdie's *Midnight's Children*. Dominican American writer and MIT professor Junot Díaz appropriated *One Hundred Years of Solitude* to the point that, he claimed, "We are the eighth generation. We are the children of Macondo." (García Márquez's novel tells the story of seven generations of the Buendía family.) Díaz, who went on to win the Pulitzer Prize for his international best seller *The Brief Wondrous Life of Oscar Wao* (2007), recalled reading *One Hundred Years of Solitude* in 1988: "The world went from black-and-white to Technicolor." And he added, "I was a young Latino-American-Caribbean writer desperately looking for models. This novel went through me like a lightning bolt: it entered through the crown of my head and went right down to my toes, redounding through me for the next several decades—up to right now." Indeed, the works not only of Díaz but also of Chilean Roberto Bolaño, who in fact despised magical realism, have been read and studied through the lens of this novel and its global style.[23]

Briefly, the global reach of magical realism is also present in the best-selling and award-winning works of the following writers, several of whom are Nobel laureates: in Mozambique, Mia Couto's *Sleepwalking Land* (1992); in Japan, Haruki Murakami's *The Wind-Up Bird Chronicle* (1994); in Martinique, Patrick Chamoiseau's *Texaco* (1992); in Canada, Jack Hodgins's *The Invention of the World* (1977); in Egypt, Naguib Mahfouz's *The Harafish* (1977); in former Yugoslavia, Danilo Kiš's *The Encyclopedia of the Dead* (1983); in Turkey, Latife Tekin's *Dear Shameless Death* (1983); in England, Angela Carter's *Nights at the Circus* (1984); in Algeria, Rachid Boudjedra's *1001 Years of Nostalgia*; in Germany, Patrick Süskind's *Perfume* (1985); in Hungary, Ádám Bodor's *Sinistra Zone* (1991); in Nigeria, Ben Okri's *The Famished Road* (1991); in France, Marie Darrieussecq's *Pig Tales* (1996); in Australia, Peter Carey's *Illywhacker* (1985); in India, Arundhati Roy's *The God of Small Things* (1997); and in China, Mo Yan's *Big Breasts and Wide Hips* (1996).

Cultural brokers with no connection to the literary establishment have also appropriated the novel as an example of magical realism. As mentioned earlier, after the Macondo explosion in 2010, an environmental-policy advocate referred to the blowout as "tragic realism." In 2017, a contributor for the *Guardian* referred to this novel as "dark magic realism" for its violent description of gender relations.[24] Furthermore, the language of magical realism has entered cinema via successful blockbusters, indie movies, and Oscar-winning films such as *The Purple Rose of Cairo* (1985), *Pan's Labyrinth* (2006), *Amen* (2010), *Beasts of the Southern Wild* (2012), *Life of Pi* (2012; a movie adaptation of the 2001 novel), *Birdman* (2014), and *A Fantastic Woman* (2017), among others.

According to Argentine scholar Mariano Siskind, "Magical realism goes global as a particularistic aesthetic that satisfies a demand for local color from marginal cultures in the global field of world literature."[25] One thing is certainly clear. Debates about the definition and boundaries of magical realism have strengthened the supposedly universal value of *One Hundred Years of Solitude* as the literary work that, for some cultural brokers (and most incorrectly for others), most purely exemplifies this genre.

A NOVEL APPROPRIATED BY ALL KINDS OF PEOPLE AND ORGANIZATIONS

One strategy cultural brokers use to appropriate a work of art is to compare it to other well-known works of art. Used in this way, the work of art finds similarities with other works and can then set the boundaries of literary traditions and give access to professional resources.[26] In that way, *One Hundred Years of Solitude* acts as a measure for the worth of other works and helps define the literary status quo. As this practice repeats across generations, works of art obtain a reputation. So, new generations of cultural brokers must position themselves in relation to an existing cultural good that has influenced older artists, publishers, critics, scholars, and common readers. Latin American writers certainly know this. They have found it difficult to publish their work abroad if it does not adapt to the image of Latin America promoted by *One Hundred Years of Solitude*, an image also perpetuated by the international success of the novels *The House of the Spirits* and *Like Water for Chocolate*. Readers, publishers, and critics expect Latin American writers to define their identity in relation to *One Hundred Years of Solitude* (especially its magical realism). Antonio Skármeta, Luis Sepúlveda, and Louis de Bernières did so in agreement with this novel, and Juan José Saer, Fernando Vallejo, Alberto Fuguet, and Bolaño did so in opposition.[27]

This tendency to measure the worth of literary works in relation to *One Hundred Years of Solitude* shows no signs of receding after six decades. Senior, mid-career, and new writers in Colombia, for example, Piedad Bonnett, Roberto Burgos, María Mercedes Carranza, Héctor Abad Faciolince, Daniel Ferreira, John Jairo Junieles, William Ospina, and Juan Gabriel Vásquez are still expected to position themselves in relation to García Márquez's legacy. Beyond Colombia, new generations of writers have branded themselves in ways that allude to *One Hundred Years of Solitude*, the New Latin American Novel, and the Boom. Some of these brands are McOndo, Mini-Boom, Crack, the Newest Ones, Baby-Boom, Post-Boom, Boomerang, and *los nietos del boom* (the grandchildren of the boom). Members of McOndo and Crack went as far as to write manifestos that criticized *One Hundred Years of Solitude* and rejected the exoticism of magical realism and García Márquez's followers. On the contrary, *los nietos del boom*, such as Peruvian Gustavo Rodríguez, claim to love their grandparents and their works, García Márquez and his classic novel included.

Critics are cultural brokers involved in the making of classics, too. If they consecrate a work of art, they can give it higher visibility. With *One Hundred Years of Solitude*, critics of different generations collaborated in its consecration. At the time of its publication, Ángel Rama, Emir Rodríguez Monegal, and Ernesto Volkening agreed that Macondo was a Latin American adaptation of Yoknapatawpha County in Faulkner's works. Thanks to this connection, readers and publishers of Faulkner in the United States and internationally became interested in *One Hundred Years of Solitude* and other works by García

Márquez. Decades later, new generations of critics (and readers) repeat that connection, not even aware of what Rama, Rodríguez Monegal, and Volkening wrote over half a century earlier.

Although new generations ignore what past critics wrote, researchers continue to overemphasize the role of critics in the consecration of a work of art. A "literary critic," as a writer put it, "is the one who is born and dies with the generation he judges."[28] Critics rarely transcend the times in which they are professionally active. However, the works of art a critic judges can transcend. This means that classics in particular outlive critics, but critics (and their judgments) do not outlive classics. Present-day critics themselves would have a hard time recalling the names of the first critics of *Frankenstein* or *War and Peace*. Yet, these critics would readily admit that these books continue to be regarded globally as classics, even if they do not agree with their classic status. Situations like this do not mean that critics' reviews are unimportant; the point is to stress that reviews are normally published after the book's release and just one time. Therefore, reviews (and critics' opinions) have a limited influence in compelling future readers to pick up the novel. (Republications of initial reviews are rare even for a new edition or new translation of the work under review.) The vast majority of present-day readers of *One Hundred Years of Solitude* in say, China or Zimbabwe, will not read it because of the criticism of Rama, Monegal, and Volkening, who, along with most of the novel's early reviewers, are dead. Critics can predict best-selling success but not success as a classic. Furthermore, critics who praised *One Hundred Years of Solitude* did the same for *Paradiso* and other literary works that are all but forgotten (see chapter 8). In reality, reviewers behave more like stockbrokers. They have an informed yet uneven understanding of tendencies in the literary market. Thus, they can calculate whether a book will become a hit in the short term, but they cannot predict how a literary work will perform in the long run. (For more on critics, see the appendix.)

The rise of the Internet and digital platforms for sharing information globally is making visible like never before the role of ordinary readers in the making of classics. The visibility of their actions also challenges the view of critics as sole fabricators of such status. New studies confirm that the judgments of other people and groups do not simply imitate that of critics. In fact, readers' choices can often contradict critics' taste. Eager to increase traffic on their websites, the comments section of mass media, online bookstores, and other outlets have become public spaces where readers post their opinions about the value of literary works. One of these spaces is Goodreads, the world's largest platform for book recommendations with over 90 million registered users and entries for 2.6 billion books. On this platform, readers have tagged *One Hundred Years of Solitude* as a classic. As of April 2020, this novel received 4.1 points out of 5 based on 706,016 ratings, plus 28,114 reviews in 47 languages. Amazon, the world's largest bookstore and e-commerce marketplace, tags *One Hundred Years of Solitude* as a #1 best seller with a ranking of 4.2 out of 5, and it sells the novel in online stores in seventeen countries. The novel (as well as some of its characters and the village of Macondo) has active profiles or hashtags in several languages on Twitter, Facebook, Pinterest, Instagram, YouTube, Reddit, and other social media platforms. Furthermore, these online platforms were invented in a context foreign to the niche that made *One Hundred Years of Solitude* in the 1960s. More than five decades later, they are (and will continue to be for some time) major cultural brokers in the global diffusion of this novel's classic status.

Arguably, celebrities influence readers' decisions more than critics. American TV celebrity Oprah Winfrey selected *One Hundred Years of Solitude* for her book club in 2004. The novel then rose to number one in sales in the United States as part of what experts call the Oprah Effect.[29] A related cultural broker is the politician. As the *New York Times* reported, U.S. President Barack Obama "gave his daughter Malia a Kindle filled with books he wanted to share with her (including *One Hundred Years of Solitude*, *The Golden Notebook*, and *The Woman Warrior*). Heads of state, such as Indira Gandhi, François Mitterrand, Mikhail Gorbachev Bill Clinton, and Fidel Castro, have praised the book in public. Several of them have even claimed that the novel helped them to understand Latin America politically and culturally. Their brokerage is important because it can affect the decisions of ordinary readers, who, now acting as cultural brokers, can select this novel for a book club, as it continues to be the case in multiple countries, where the book is still read this way.[30]

What about the brokerage of educational and research organizations? Before 1967, García Márquez's works attracted little academic interest, as figure 6.2 shows. But it skyrocketed after the publication of *One Hundred Years of Solitude* and picked up in 1982, after he received the Nobel Prize in Literature. The inclusion of a literary work in educational curricula and history of literature textbooks proves that cultural brokers think its value is long-lasting. In the case of this novel, organizations such as universities and secondary schools have made it available to new generations in different countries and cultural regions. Since the 1970s, the novel has entered high schools and universities programs in Latin America, Europe, the United States, and India, among other places.[31]

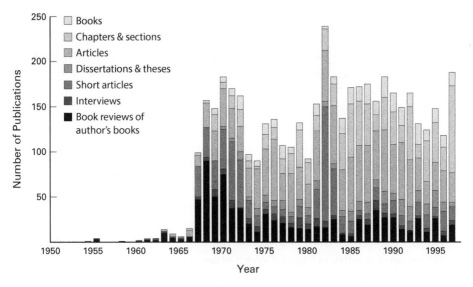

6.2 Number and type of publications on García Márquez and his works (1950–1997).

Source: Santana-Acuña 2014.

The academic consolidation of Latin American literature paralleled that of *One Hundred Years of Solitude*, as textbooks show. In Spain, scholar Ramón D. Perés published in 1964 the first edition of his popular eight-hundred-page survey *Historia universal de la literatura* (*History of Universal Literature*). Except for brief references to Rubén Darío and José Enrique Rodó, this textbook had no section on Latin American literature. Everything changed in the second edition of 1969. The region's literature boomed in between those years, and the new edition included a twenty-four-page chapter on "Latin American literature." Perés concluded his survey of the region's literature with *One Hundred Years of Solitude*: "an eagerly awaited book, because it is said that it will become one of the pillars of the new America." In 1971 and especially 1972, the first textbooks and comprehensive studies on the most recent Latin American literature were published in at least five countries.[32] In these publications, *One Hundred Years of Solitude* started to receive important, yet unequal, attention.

Leading literary scholars of the past half-century have expressed their opinions about *One Hundred Years of Solitude* and García Márquez. They became the subject of two refurbished editions of the two series by Harold Bloom: the influential *Bloom's Modern Critical Views* (1989 and 2007) and *Bloom's Modern Critical Interpretations* (2003 and 2009). Bloom also included *One Hundred Years of Solitude* in his controversial list of books that form the Western canon.

He was among the world's most influential literary scholars. He passed away in 2019. Yet his passing will not alter the value of *One Hundred Years of Solitude*, as the continuation of its value does not depend on the action of a single cultural broker or a group. Like Bloom, Italian literary scholar Franco Moretti used *One Hundred Years of Solitude* to advance his own agenda about world literature and distant reading. The Modern Language Association, the world's largest professional organization for the study of language and literature, with more than twenty-five thousand members in one hundred countries, published in 1990 a guide containing different teaching approaches to *One Hundred Years of Solitude*. New textbooks and anthologies include this novel in Great Books programs and in connection to world classics, and international conferences where this novel is mentioned take place regularly. Annotated and critical editions have ensured that there are multiple options to imagine this novel as an artwork of "universal" value. Furthermore, area studies and chairs of Latin American literature were created on all continents except for Antarctica, including countries with influential literary traditions: Germany, Spain, the United Kingdom, the United States, France, and Italy. In addition, new academic journals dedicated to the region appeared. Authors and their language became "classic," and their works were canonized and taught at universities internationally. At the same time, *One Hundred Years of Solitude* rose in academic circles as "the Boom [novel] par excellence." In addition, since research on certain topics and works is more prone to attract major funding resources, increase book sales, and bolster academic careers, from the 1970s to the present, scholars at different stages in their careers continue to find it profitable to work in their publications on *One Hundred Years of Solitude*, even indirectly. Working on this novel, in return, maintains its visibility and worth among new generations of scholars.[33]

Although educational and research organizations such as high schools, colleges, and universities have a profound influence on continued appreciation, new studies suggest that even their brokerage has been overemphasized and is shrinking since the rise of digital media platforms mentioned above.[34]

Other organizations have appropriated the legacy of major Latin American authors by acquiring their archives. In particular, Princeton, Iowa (with a top writing program in the United States), Stanford, and University of Texas at Austin have created collections to keep the papers of Latin American writers and critics, such as Asturias, Rodríguez Monegal, Emmanuel Carballo, Julio Cortázar, José Donoso, Carlos Fuentes, Guillermo Cabrera Infante, Pedro Lastra, and Mario Vargas Llosa. In 2015, the Harry Ransom Center in the United States purchased the Gabriel García Márquez Papers. The acquisition of his archives prompted an international controversy. The Latin American public lamented that the governments of Colombia and Mexico (the writer's home country and his life-long country of residence, respectively) did not buy the papers. But others celebrated the acquisition because the Ransom Center has also purchased papers by authors who shaped García Márquez's imagination, especially Borges, Faulkner, Woolf, James Joyce, Graham Greene, and Ernest Hemingway. This controversy once more brought *One Hundred Years of Solitude* to the forefront, as global media publicized that two copies of the final manuscript of the novel were among the treasures of his archives.[35] In terms of cultural brokerage, this purchase means that the world's largest collection of García Márquez's papers is not in Latin American but in the United States. (Likewise, as another example of how global appropriation helps create classic value, the largest Shakespeare collection, the Folger Shakespeare Library, is not in England but on U.S. soil.)

After 1967, García Márquez and *One Hundred Years of Solitude* became a regular theme in local, regional, and international newspapers. In these publications, the writer is customarily called "the author of *One Hundred Years of Solitude*."[36] And this keeps happening despite the fact that media organizations have been created, undergone changes, or disappeared. For example, in 1970, *Time*, the world's largest print magazine, listed *One Hundred Years of Solitude* as one of the best books of the year. Two decades later, under new management, the magazine called García Márquez one of "Time 100 Most Influential Writers" and said that *One Hundred Years of Solitude* is a phenomenon worldwide. In 2017, again under new management, *Time* partnered with the Ransom Center to celebrate the novel's fiftieth anniversary. In short, this magazine's coverage of the novel spans over four decades, and its commitment to publicize it persists beyond changes in staff, management, and ownership.[37]

On the other hand, magazines that first promoted the novel disappeared. The absence of *Primera Plana*, *Mundo Nuevo*, or *Siempre!* has not lessened its status because new publications stepped in. The *London Review of Books* did not exist when the novel came out in 1967. Since its creation in 1979, this journal has had a global reputation as a highbrow tastemaker. Its contributors have written reviews in which they cite *One Hundred Years of Solitude* regularly, and one wrote a special essay to mark the novel's fiftieth anniversary. One of the leading newspapers in the Spanish language, *El País*, promotes this novel, García Márquez's works, and news about the age of the Latin American Boom. In 2015, the newspaper launched *Biblioteca García Márquez*, the publication of all his fiction in twenty affordable volumes. Over the years, *El País* has become a global newspaper and part of Prisa, a powerful news media agency. Prisa has also ties with Grupo Santillana (publisher of school textbooks in Spain and Latin America), Alfaguara (publisher of works by Boom writers), and Cátedra, publisher of critical editions of international classics, including, for the moment, the only scholarly edition of *One Hundred Years of Solitude*. When this novel was published, *El País*, Prisa, and Cátedra did not exist, and Grupo Santillana and Alfaguara were barely eight and three years old, respectively. Yet by the 2010s, they had become active cultural brokers in the promotion of the novel, its author, and his legacy. Likewise, Mexican company Televisa did not exist in 1967. In the early twenty-first century, it became the largest multimedia mass media company in the Spanish-speaking world. Over time, it has produced short stories based on García Márquez's works, which are sold to Spanish-language TV stations in Latin America, the United States (via Univisión), and Spain. In 2003, the BBC, then the largest broadcaster in the world, launched the Big Read series. This initiative sought to select the hundred best-loved books. By the end of the series, viewers had cast three quarters of a million votes. *One Hundred Years of Solitude* appeared on the list on the thirty-second position. The only other work in the Spanish language on the list was García Márquez's novel *Love in the Time of Cholera*. With its high ranking, *One Hundred Years of Solitude* rubbed shoulders with all-time classics and contemporary best-selling books. The *Atlantic*, *Time*, *El País*, *Vanity Fair*, Russia Today, BBC News, the *Guardian* (which named it book of the month on May 2017), and other new and old mass media publicized the novel's fiftieth anniversary, unanimously presenting it as a literary work of long-lasting value. International media have kept promoting it beyond its anniversary. In 2019, France's most famous newspaper, *Le Monde*, listed it as one of "the 100 novels that have most excited 'Le Monde' [The World] since 1944."

Awards and translations are traditional indicators of a literary work's commercial success, worth, and consecration.[38] But they are also cultural brokers that can uproot a work of art. *One Hundred Years of Solitude* started to receive awards shortly after its publication.[39] Yet it did not win the most prestigious literary award that catapulted New Latin American Novels into popularity: the Biblioteca Breve, which was awarded by Seix Barral. Given the book's best-selling sales, its failure to win this prize led to a controversy that increased its visibility in the media. A decade later, in 1982, García Márquez received the Nobel Prize in Literature. The award reinforced the position of *One Hundred Years of Solitude* as the quintessential novel of the Boom and of Latin America literature. The Nobel also framed García Márquez's work as a place where fantasy and reality coexisted. According to the committee, he received it "for his novels and short stories, in which the fantastic and the realistic are combined in a richly composed world of imagination, reflecting a continent's life and conflicts."[40] This statement helped present all of García Márquez's fiction works to new and existing audiences as magical realism.

Artists and public figures are two important cultural brokers in the global appropriation of *One Hundred Years of Solitude*. The novel has inspired musicians, painters, opera composers, and many others (see chapter 8). Other brokers, while not directly under its influence, have expressed their admiration for the novel. Picasso allegedly stated that it moved him like no other literary work he had read recently.[41]

In 2010, the *New York Times* selected the opening of *One Hundred Years of Solitude* as the exemplar Spanish text in order to test the efficacy of the Google translator in different languages.[42] Briefly, the novel's village, Macondo, is the name of a public park in Mexico City, a Panamanian general cargo vessel constructed in 2005, a Haitian art gallery in Pittsburgh, a bookstore and a restaurant in Manhattan, and a star in the constellation of Antlia, among many other things. In sum, as this section has shown, cultural brokers involved in the uprooting of a work of art can be of any kind.

A NOVEL TURNED INTO OBJECTS AND MERCHANDISE

A Japanese wine. A Venezuelan rum. A Caribbean hotel. A FIFA soccer ball. A Mexican opera. A Peruvian cumbia song. An Italian folk song. A U.S. video game. These are some of the multiple forms that *One Hundred Years of Solitude* has taken over the years beyond its original book format. Classics are among the cultural objects that have this power. They can enter people's lives through different formats than those intended by their creators. Some of these objects can also be merchandise.

Since its publication, *One Hundred Years of Solitude* has never been out of print in Spanish, English, French, Italian, German, and other major literary languages. Being such a profitable long-selling novel, it is a cash cow for multiple organizations unrelated to its niche. Despite global policing by Balcells Agency, pirated copies of the novel have been sold in García Márquez's home country, First World countries such as Germany, satellite states behind the Iron Curtain, and nations with emerging economies such as China. Before the dissolution of the Soviet Union, *One Hundred Years of Solitude* circulated in clandestine recorded cassettes in Georgia, Armenia, Uzbekistan, and Kazakhstan.

In China, the novel was translated in 1972 but only in 2011, after the sale of hundreds of thousands of pirated copies, was the first legal edition available.[43]

Special editions of *One Hundred Years of Solitude* entered the market as early as 1967. That year Sudamericana released an LP record on which García Márquez read the first chapter of the novel. The same year, Universidad Nacional Autónoma of Mexico issued another audio recording. On it the author read a fragment of chapter 12, and the recording featured a preface written by leading Mexican critic Carballo. This recording has been reissued at least four times. Both recordings are also available free of charge on multiple websites. In 1970, the book club Círculo de Lectores in Spain issued its own edition of *One Hundred Years of Solitude* for subscribers, which at the time had almost one million members. Since then and until the closing of the company in 2019, this novel was a perennial best seller, having sold hundreds of thousands of copies. Yet neither the sale nor the worth of the novel were under the exclusive control of this cultural broker. Other commercial publishers in Spain have bought the rights to print their own editions. Along with mass-market editions, the 1980s and 1990s were another important moment in the consolidation of the novel: the publication of the first annotated and scholarly editions. Prestigious publishers Espasa Calpe in 1982 and Cátedra in 1984 released critical editions as affordable paperbacks. As previously mentioned, this novel and García Márquez were the subject of Bloom's two series. Other inexpensive paperback editions have remained on the market in several countries.[44] In 2007, a Colombian publisher issued an abridged edition of sixty-two pages for children and adolescents. All of these different editions have ensured the presence of this novel across generations and publics.

Likewise, to celebrate the fortieth anniversary of *One Hundred Years of Solitude*, the Spanish Royal Academy of Language produced an inexpensive edition (9.75 Euros). The Academy marketed it as the definitive edition, since the author himself revised the text. Grupo Santillana, part of the mass media conglomerate Grupo Prisa, was in charge of printing and distributing this edition worldwide. Its publication followed a marketing strategy implemented by the Bertelsmann Group, one of the world's largest mass media companies and with presence in the service sector and education. The Academy edition sold half a million copies in two months. Along with Spain, all Latin American Academies of language (a total of nineteen countries), plus affiliate organizations in the Philippines, the United States, and Canada, sponsored this edition. One of its targets was the growing market for programs in Spanish as a second language in the United States and all over the world. Thanks to this edition, *One Hundred Years of Solitude* became the most global of Latin American novels.[45]

Other special editions of García Márquez's novel had a different audience in mind: high-end buyers and collectors. In 2006, the Folio Society released a luxurious slipcase edition of this novel. This London-based publisher sells illustrated hardcover editions of classic fiction and nonfiction books, poetry, and children's titles. Other publishers have appropriated this novel for new business ventures. In 2011, bookseller Barnes & Noble, a Fortune 500 company with the largest number of retail outlets in the United States, entered the publishing business by releasing its own edition of the novel as part of its Leatherbound Classics collection. In 2017, to mark the novel's fiftieth anniversary, publisher Penguin Random House, then the largest general interest paperback publisher in the world, released an illustrated edition, conceived as a Beautiful Book gift. The publisher has also released in English-speaking countries a Spanish edition of the novel to cater to the needs of the growing market of Spanish learners. Editions from The Folio Society and Barnes & Noble are now out of print and have become a collector's item. The availability of this novel in multiple formats (from cheap, unassuming paperbacks to expensive, luxurious editions) has secured its visibility as a valuable investment. In the rare and collectible book market, copies of the first edition in Spanish start at US$3,000 and go up to US$20,000, according to AbeBooks, a leading global online marketplace. Rare editions of the novel, especially if signed by the author, can sell for higher prices. Thus, dealers who specialize in old books and manuscripts have become interested in this novel and other García Márquez works and papers. In 2001, the galley proofs of the novel were put on sale for US$1,000,000. UNESCO certified that these proofs were the only autographed copy of the manuscript.

As mentioned earlier, the commodification of this novel has happened beyond its book format. Thanks to the partnership with Audible, *One Hundred Years of Solitude* is also the audiobook that InterContinental Hotels Group, a British hospitality company with over one hundred and ninety locations worldwide, started to offer in 2018 to hotel visitors in Cartagena, Colombia. The goal is that selected titles reflect "the worldliness of InterContinental Hotels & Resorts." An executive producer of *The Paris Review* podcast helped to curate the selection. In this case, four cultural brokers unrelated to the novel's niche—three of them did not even exist in 1967—are marketing this novel to global visitors of an exclusive Colombian hotel.[46] *One Hundred Years of Solitude* is at the center of the Colombian graphic novel *Gabo: memorias de una vida mágica*, translated into seventeen languages and to be adapted into an animation film (see figure 7.1 in chapter 7). In Japan, Kuroki Honten Co. manufactures an exclusive barrel-aged barley shōchū (a national alcoholic drink similar to sake) named "One Hundred Years of Solitude" that sells for US$129.99 per bottle. This novel has also taken the form of a main course. To mark its fiftieth anniversary, a group of chefs met at Aquarelle Bistro in Mexico City and created a special dish based on flavors in the novel. Likewise, this book appears on T-shirts, coffee mugs, tote bags, posters, water bottles, and other kinds of merchandise. But the novel is not just something cultural brokers wear, eat, or carry; they can even tattoo it on their skin. An Internet search yields multiple results for images of people in different countries with tattoos that show Macondo, the four-year rain, the yellow butterflies, and of course García Márquez's face.

Key components of the novel have made it into film scripts. For example, in Roman Polanski's movie *Chinatown*, a scene takes place at El Macondo Apartments. More references of this kind appear in Hollywood productions, international blockbusters, Oscar winners, indie movies, and TV series: *Fitzcarraldo*, *The Mosquito Coast*, *Amélie*, *Sorcerer*, *Interstellar*, and *Friends*, among others. This novel has also inspired the animated series *Hey Arnold!* However, an important form of appropriation, a movie adaptation, did not happen for more than five decades. In particular, Hollywood has tried since the 1980s to adapt *One Hundred Years of Solitude* to the big screen. Although an adaptation would boost its sales globally, the lack of it did not stop this novel from becoming a classic, which is why Netflix's announcement caused a global controversy. In 2019, this company, a leading Internet entertainment service with over one hundred and fifty million memberships in more than two hundred countries, announced it would create the first adaptation for the screen. The news started a global debate in mainstream and social media on whether the adaptation should be done at all, since its author had strong reservations about it. The debate reappeared after the global release of the series.

Cultural brokers have merged *One Hundred Years of Solitude* with new technologies. Sparky Sweets is the nickname of an African American social media influencer. He dresses up as a hip-hop hooded gangsta and uses slang and jokes to conduct "Thug Notes," a video series that breaks down the classics in about five minutes each. The videos are available on popular social media platforms and are for sale on Amazon. Just on YouTube, his "Thug Notes" on *One Hundred Years of Solitude* has over four hundred thousand views. In the video, Sparky Sweets offers his interpretation of the novel in universal terms: "On the real, life is a cycle where the same mess happens over and over. You can peep that theme reflected in the dankest symbol of this book: mirrors." In contrast, John and Hank Green, middle-class white U.S. brothers, offer a video on this novel as part of their online teaching platform, "Crash Course," which has over nine million subscribers on YouTube. Their two-part series on the novel has over half a million views on YouTube alone. These two cultural brokers, Sparky Sweets and the Green brothers, come across differently in their self-presentation, style, and language. Yet they, like other cultural brokers online, agree to promote this novel to viewers worldwide.[47] And they promote it in a way that creates new generations of readers and, of course, nonreaders, people who, after watching their video summaries, will be able to talk about *One Hundred Years of Solitude* without having read it. In so doing, nonreaders also help this novel live longer beyond its pages, making it more meaningful, more classic.

Other uses of news technologies that can target readers and nonreaders alike include art installations and electronic games. *Imagining Macondo* was a traveling, public art installation first displayed in Colombia in 2015. It invited viewers "to submit photographs that represent 'their own Macondo.'"[48] People did so, for example, by taking selfies dressed up as one of the twelve characters in *One Hundred Years of Solitude*. The novel has inspired video games such as *What Remains of Edith Finch* (2016), which tells the story of a cursed family in the state of Washington. The video game does not openly acknowledge this novel as a source of inspiration, which is another frequent form of appropriation that helps extend the life of a work of art.

THE WRITER AS A CLASSIC

The success of *One Hundred Years of Solitude* marked a before and after in the life of García Márquez. He became a popular global writer during his lifetime and remains one after his death. According to UNESCO's Index Translationum, he is the most translated Spanish-language literary writer (1,396 translations as of 2020) and the forty-ninth most translated author in the world. As shown by the twenty-one voluminous scrapbooks in the Gabriel García Márquez Papers at the Ransom Center, every new work by him generated a lot of attention among general interest and mass media and premiered in major outlets such as *Vanity Fair*, the *New Yorker*, *Le Monde*, and *El País*, as well as local media. In particular, each new work of fiction was compared to *One Hundred Years of Solitude*. Reviewers and readers compared every new book to that novel and often asked whether one could find the "magical realism" of *One Hundred Years of Solitude* and Macondo again or whether his latest book was better or worse. These comparisons served to discuss the uniqueness of the novel and attract new readers. His first novel after *One Hundred Years of Solitude*, *The Autumn of the Patriarch*, was hugely anticipated and was considered disappointing; most readers expected a continuation of *One Hundred Years of Solitude*. But instead the novelist wrote a highly sophisticated and complex book: a long poem in prose in which multiple, unidentified voices tell the story of a dictator. His next work of fiction was quite different: *Chronicle of a Death Foretold*. Published in 1981, it is a short novel, written in the clear and concise language of a journalistic reportage. It had an initial print run of one million copies in Spanish. To this day, it remains the largest single printing of any Latin American novel in history. *The General in His Labyrinth*, *News of a Kidnapping*, and especially *Love in the Time of Cholera* had first editions that sold millions, were published in all major literary languages, and reviewed worldwide instantly. In the 2000s, he released his best-selling autobiography, *Living to Tell the Tale*. Readers around the world expected that a second volume of his autobiography would deal with the making of *One Hundred Years of Solitude*. Instead, he published his last novel, *Memories of My Melancholy Whores* (2004).[49]

To the author's bitterness, none of his literary works received as many distinctions, honors, and international prizes as *One Hundred Years of Solitude*. Yet this novel's success permitted him to extend his influence beyond literature. In 1973, he said that he wanted to use the novel's fame "for political purposes" and hence returned to political journalism. He wrote or commented on current political affairs such as the Nicaraguan Revolution, Cuba's Operation Carlota in Angola in 1977, the campaigns against Ronald Reagan, the death of Panama's President Omar Torrijos, the Falklands War, and the Arab-Israeli conflict. He also interviewed major political actors such as a CIA agent, French philosopher Régis Debray, and politicians Torrijos, Felipe González, and Hugo Chávez, among others. (Likewise, he interviewed cultural icons such as pop star Shakira.) The mainstream international media that published his political pieces often presented him as "the author of *One Hundred Years of Solitude*."[50]

His political journalism was a magnet for awards. The image of the engaged writer was also attractive to committee members of the Nobel Prize. In public, he claimed that he would never receive the Nobel. In private, he lobbied the committee, cashing in on the international popularity of *One Hundred Years of Solitude*. In the 1970s, he visited Stockholm several times. He befriended Swedish writer and communist supporter Artur Lundkvist, who previously influenced the committee to award the Nobel to Latin American writers Asturias and Neruda. As the gatekeeper of the committee's decisions on Spanish-language candidates, Lundkvist might have prevented Borges from receiving the award because of his growing conservatism and controversial support of Augusto Pinochet's dictatorship. García Márquez, on the contrary, criticized Borges's politics and attacked Pinochet relentlessly. He even famously proclaimed that he would never publish fiction again until Pinochet was removed from power. At the same time, he sided with the Cuban Revolution and Castro's communism. Lundkvist liked these political activities and their friendship grew. Years later, García Márquez received the 1982 Nobel Prize in Literature. His acceptance discourse, "The Solitude of Latin America," revisited the theme of his best-selling novel: solitude. Its content combined historical and political analysis with references to the region's magical realism.[51]

Despite growing criticism, before and after the Nobel, García Márquez received a deluge of correspondence and invitations. In his interview with The Paris Review, he stated that fame was a tragedy and added that he would have preferred One Hundred Years of Solitude to be published after his death. Instead, he gained more free publicity in the news for rejecting awards than for receiving them. For example, he turned down twice Spain's equivalent to the Nobel Prize, the Cervantes, and an honoris causa degree from the Sorbonne, one of the world's oldest and most prestigious universities. After the Nobel, his public life became a "carefully organized spectacle" and, as a scholar put it, a "one-person literary theme park." As a global literary celebrity, he would charge up to US$50,000 for a thirty-minute interview. He started to receive millions of dollars for book advances, a fact carefully filtered to the media as part of book marketing campaigns. His lifestyle attracted attention, too. It was featured on magazine covers and regular interviews with high-profile media: BBC, Playboy, Atlantic Monthly, Newsweek, the New York Times Book Review, the New Yorker, Los Angeles Times, Clarín, Cambio 16, the Washington Post, and El País, among others. The French-language weekly news magazine, Paris Match, which follows the lifestyle of celebrities, covered the inauguration of his new home in the tourist city of Cartagena. The media reported that he owned another five properties in five countries.[52]

The popularity of One Hundred Years of Solitude and the Nobel Prize helped him be a controversial broker in international political conflicts in the 1970s and 1980s, including his participation in the International War Crimes Tribunal, UNESCO fori, and summits of world leaders. His fame facilitated friendships with several presidents: Carlos Andres Pérez (Venezuela, installed in 1974), Colombians Alfonso López Michelsen (1974) and Belisario Betancur (1982), Mexicans López Portillo (1976) and Miguel de la Madrid (1982), François Mitterrand (France, 1981), Felipe González (Spain, 1982), and Olaf Palme (Sweden, 1982). The most controversial of his friendships involved

Fidel Castro. In 1971, during the Padilla affair (the political repression of poet Heberto Padilla), García Márquez rallied with Castro and proclaimed he was a loyal communist. His support of Castro got him life-long admiration by many as well as enmities and denunciations, especially from early promoters of his work, such as Emmanuel Carballo, Mario Vargas Llosa, and Reinaldo Arenas. Castro, on the contrary, appreciated García Márquez's support as proof of political commitment. As he put it, "his literature is the unfailing proof of his sensitivity and irrevocable attachment to his origins, of his Latin American inspiration and loyalty to the truth, of his progressive thinking."[53]

With Castro's support, García Márquez backed the Foundation for New Latin American Cinema in Havana and the International Film School of San Antonio de los Baños. The school began by shooting García Márquez's screenplays. These organizations allowed him to instill his ideas into the imaginations of budding scriptwriters and filmmakers. In 1994, he also created the Fundación para el Nuevo Periodismo Iberoamericano to promote ethical and state-of-the-art journalism among professionals from Latin America and beyond. After his passing, it was renamed Fundación Gabo (a popular nickname for the writer). Among its many activities to disseminate the author's legacy, the foundation organizes the Gabo Festival and awards the Premios Gabo, which media in the region have labeled Latin America's Pulitzer Prize in Journalism.[54]

In the years prior to his death, references to García Márquez shifted from biography to hagiography, as he was turned into a living monument.[55] In 2009, his agent's announcement that he would never write again due to illness caused international consternation. Global media dutifully reported his last visit to his hometown of Aracataca as part of the fortieth anniversary of *One Hundred Years of Solitude*. By then, although contested, equating García Márquez with Cervantes had become quite common in the media, scholarly books, the Internet, and so on. In 2014, the Museo del Caribe in the city of Barranquilla inaugurated a permanent gallery dedicated to him; on display are several personal objects including one of his first typewriters. Near the museum there has been a statue of him since 2016. His childhood home (which inspired the one in *One Hundred Years of Solitude*) is now a national monument and museum, and the town of Aracataca has become a tourist destination for global visitors, like Gustave Flaubert's home in Rouen, Marcel Proust's Illiers-Combray, the Robinson Crusoe Island owned by Chile, or Charles Dickens's Manette Street in London. A grassroots initiative even attempted to rename Aracataca after Macondo. In 2012, Russia announced the Year of Gabriel García Márquez, which President Dmitry Medvedev inaugurated by awarding the writer the

Order of Honor. The year continued with cultural events, such as decorating subway cars in Moscow with images of the writer, and quotes from *One Hundred Years of Solitude*, among other works.[56]

Two years later, in 2014, García Márquez passed away at the age of eighty-seven. His death was reported on the cover of *El País*, the *Times of London*, *Le Monde*, the *New York Times*, *Frankfurter Allgemeine Zeitung*, the *Guardian*, *Clarín*, and many other mainstream and local media worldwide. There was a cascade of praise from numerous people and organizations, U.S. President Obama, former U.S. President Bill Clinton, past and current presidents of most Latin American countries and Spain, singer Shakira, the Revolutionary Armed Forces of Colombia (FARC), the Nobel Foundation, UNESCO, Penguin Random House, Hollywood actors, and writers on all continents, including his former friend Vargas Llosa. One reader lamented the fact that future generations of readers will be born in a world in which there is no longer the expectation of reading the newest book written by García Márquez. Of course, his death prompted the usual increase in sales following the passing of a famous writer. In his case, this surge was global. For example, in Kolkata's historic College Street, India's largest book market, a bookseller said to a *Times of India* reporter two days after the writer's death: "We are sending away customers as there is not supply . . . we sold out." The book that customers demanded the most, he said, was *One Hundred Years of Solitude*.[57]

García Márquez's stature has not diminished since his death, even if he remains a controversial figure. In 2016, Colombia's national bank released a new fifty-thousand-peso bill featuring him. The following year, the city of Paris named a square after him, located near the Boulevard Saint-Germain, home of historic coffeeshops for many writers and artists. In 2018, Google designed a Doodle to commemorate what would have been the writer's ninety-first birthday. The Doodle, which appeared on Google's main page, was seen by millions of daily users. The same year, in connection with the #MeToo movement, criticism surfaced when some people were concerned that García Márquez may have promoted reprehensible behavior, at least as shown in *Memories of My Melancholy Whores*, a story about a nonagenarian who wants to have sex with a young virgin. The same year, in an interview with U.S. National Public Radio, writer James Patterson, one of the top best-selling authors of all time, with over three hundred million books sold worldwide, said, "[*One Hundred Years of Solitude*] is probably my favorite book." A year later, leading African American scholar Henry Louis Gates declared to the *New York Times* that the book he wished he had written is *One Hundred Years of Solitude*. In 2020, the Ransom Center opened the first international exhibition drawing on the author's papers and was dedicated to his transformation into a global writer. Finally, according to Google Alerts (a content change detection and notification service offered by this company), there is an average of ten new pieces of content created weekly on García Márquez alone, not to count *One Hundred Years of Solitude*. This global conversation about him has ensured that he is remembered as a "universally beloved Latin American writer" and especially as the author of *One Hundred Years of Solitude*.[58] So beloved that, for example, a Brooklyn-based company, The Unemployed Philosophers Guild, designed a finger puppet of García Márquez that also works as a fridge magnet and is for sale in more than thirty states around the world, including Andorra, Liechtenstein, and the Isle of Man. Taken together, these and other examples create memories, and these memories ensure that new generations of readers and nonreaders need to position themselves in relation to the author and his most famous novel. In so doing, many of them would act as cultural brokers and contribute to reproducing the classic status of *One Hundred Years of Solitude*.

CONCLUSION

There is no single recipe to turn a work of art into a classic. But any recipe needs one basic ingredient: the participation of cultural brokers. They appropriate the work of art generation after generation, giving it the visibility that it needs to attain and maintain its classic status. In the case of *One Hundred Years of Solitude*, cultural brokers keep helping new generations of brokers build the reputation of this novel as a classic—a reputation that is not under the full control of one organization or individual. Some of the strategies that the cultural brokers of *One Hundred Years of Solitude* have used over the decades and across national boundaries include repetition (or reinvention) of myths associated with the novel's conception, writing, and publication; comparison of this novel with other classic works; its transformation into objects that are different from the original book format; and the global consecration of García Márquez as the author of *One Hundred Years of Solitude*.

7

INDEXING A CLASSIC

One Hundred Years of Solitude . . . a work, that if a painting, would
certainly be displayed alongside the *Mona Lisa* at the Louvre.

—Anonymous Barnes & Noble reviewer [2000][1]

"To be, or not to be, that is the question." "Those over there are not giants but windmills." "Happy families are all alike; every unhappy family is unhappy in its own way." "Bah! Humbug!" Sirens whose hypnotic singing lures sailors to death. The taste of that little piece of madeleine. Big Brother . . . If there is one thing that permits us to quickly recognize classics as such is that they create small units of significance, such as the ones mentioned above, that different kinds of people are familiar with. And some of these people use or come across these units in all sorts of situations. They can find them in advertisements, movies, and jokes. They can encounter them in conversations on public transportation, at shops, bars, and airports. People can use them to say that someone behaves like a Don Juan, is as ugly as Frankenstein, as innocent as the Little Prince, or as temperamental as Madame Bovary. People can suffer from Peter Pan syndrome or Cinderella complex. A wildfire in a forest can be of Dantesque proportions. One's endeavor can be Quixotic. A situation can become Kafkaesque. What is remarkable is the fact that people use these small units of significance even if they do not know where they actually originated. (Ask around you from what classic the expression "apple of discord" comes.) People can also use them without having had any contact with the classic (for example, they have never seen a performance of *Hamlet*). And even if they know the classic, people may not agree on what this unit means. More than four hundred years later, people still disagree about the real meaning of "To be, or not to be, that is the question."

Deep knowledge of classics (or their meanings) is not necessary for people to participate in situations in which these small units of significance appear.

Classics are classics because they create these units that even people who have not read the classic can share across generations, cultures, and nations. In its path to becoming a classic, *One Hundred Years of Solitude* has developed these units of significance that I call indexicals.[2] Cultural brokers do not use them randomly. They follow a social pattern, and these patterns help the work of art transcend the niche in which it was made. One such pattern is lived experience, which means using these units to refer to situations of everyday life, current affairs, and so on. People, for example, have indexed Macondo or Remedios's ascent to heaven to talk about real places or women. People can also use indexicals from *One Hundred Years of Solitude* to make statements that are supposed to have universal resonance. This is the pattern of universalization. Another pattern, commensuration, consists of using the novel to compare it to other works of art and cultural goods. For instance, people have indexed the opening sentence of *One Hundred Years of Solitude* to compare it to the opening of *Anna Karenina*. Finally, people can index events, characters, or situations from a work of art to criticize it. This last pattern, which I call entrenched criticism, is one of the most understudied characteristics of classics. Yet it is crucial: people can use these units of significance to express their negative opinions about the work of art (even if they have not seen or read it). As it is often said, bad press is better than no press. Indeed, researchers have shown that sustained "negative attention can be reputation-building," suggesting that praise alone cannot ensure that a work of art will become a classic in the long run.[3] And few works of art can benefit so much from entrenched criticism than classics. The plays of Shakespeare, for example, have in Voltaire, T. S. Elliot, Virginia Woolf, J. R. R. Tolkien, and Leo Tolstoy some of their most distinguished (and classic) detractors. By now, *One Hundred Years of Solitude* has generations of people who despise it, too. Taken together, the patterns of entrenched criticism, commensuration, universalization, and lived experience show that the actions of cultural brokers are not random. They need to follow a certain path to keep visible a work of art decades and centuries after its making.

INDEXING *ONE HUNDRED YEARS OF SOLITUDE*

Which parts of the novel, and how, have cultural brokers in six continents indexed over the decades? The six elements under analysis here are the novel as a whole, its opening sentence, the town of Macondo, magical realism,

Remedios's ascent to heaven (this serves to analyze at the same time a character and an event), and García Márquez.[4]

One Hundred Years of Solitude: The Making of a Classic

Indexing this novel now is a meaningful way of saying something about current affairs, discussing "universal" human nature, expressing opinions about the history of literature, and critically assessing the novel's contribution to the arts. These ways of indexing of *One Hundred Years of Solitude* have contributed to its long-lasting reputation.

To make sense of their own lived experiences, new audiences have embraced the belief that *One Hundred Years of Solitude* reveals self-evident truths about life or that it can influence people's actions. For an anonymous Amazon U.S. reader, this novel is "a necessary journey for any reader engaged in the human struggle and the cycle of life" [1996]. For an anonymous Amazon UK reader, "it is a mirror of the human soul and of our society" [1998]. For writer Milan Kundera, Czechoslovakian-born, his afterword for *One Hundred Years of Solitude* in 1968 was his first text prohibited in communist Czechoslovakia, and "that prohibition started the second half of my life, which is that of an outlaw writer in his own country" [2002]. Saudi Arabian reader Amr Ahmad Alghamdi "was dreaming through the pages of this epic story" [2011]. U.S. writer Francine Prose declared that *One Hundred Years of Solitude* "convinced me to drop out of Harvard graduate school" [2013]. And a Filipino collector [2020], thinking about his retirement library, trimmed down hundreds of books and kept his copy of *One Hundred Years of Solitude* as one of the "things I would actually live with in my old age." Other brokers prefer to recall the moment when they first read the novel. In early 1970, Richard Locke, editor at Simon & Schuster and *Vanity Fair*, was the assigning editor at the *New York Times Book Review*. "When the novel came in," he said, "I realized it was a very important book by a very different kind of writer—and in a new form that we had never seen before. And I gave it an enthusiastic report" [2015]. "After fifty pages," Portuguese writer and Nobel laureate José Saramago had to stop reading it because of "the shock it caused [him]" [2009].

Other cultural brokers keep using a novel written more than half a century ago to make sense of current affairs. *Literary Hub*, a daily literary website, posted an essay by U.S. writer Scott Esposito months after the presidential election of Donald Trump. Esposito denounced that "the likes of Fox News and Breitbart" have crafted narratives that "have convinced millions of people that certain minorities abuse social aid programs, or that the deficit always requires cutting government spending (except when it comes to the military), and that radical Islamists are perpetually on the verge of overrunning our nation" [2017]. Novels like *One Hundred Years of Solitude*, he believed, are an antidote against this type of alt-right narratives. A year later, Kuwaiti activists called for demonstrations against book censorship by authorities. They took their protest online, where the hashtags #Banned_In_Kuwait and #Dont_Decide_For_Me trended on Twitter and other social media platforms. *One Hundred Years of Solitude* was among the forty-four hundred books banned from Kuwaiti bookshops and libraries for the past five years [2018].

When it was published, *One Hundred Years of Solitude* sought to offer an alternative to the literary styles that dominated literature in the 1960s. For this reason, Spanish-speaking audiences celebrated this novel for its "return to narrative imagination," as writer Pere Gimferrer put it [1967]; for representing "a narrative feat," as journalist Pascual Maisterra wrote [1968]; and for being an "atmospheric purifier," according to writer Luis Izquierdo [1969]. But this kind of interpretation changed over time and it gave way to a pattern of universalization. According to U.S. writer William Kennedy, this novel is "the first piece of literature since the Book of Genesis that should be required reading for the entire human race" [1970] and John Updike wrote "[it] has a texture all its own" [1972]. For Colombian critic Samuel García, the novel is a "synthesis of three thousand years of literature" [1977]. For Jorge Luis Borges, it is "one of the great books not only of our time but of all time" [1980]. This tendency to universalize the novel appears also among common readers. Amazon Canada reader Mark E. Baxter wrote that the book "applies to everyone and its themes and characters are universal" [2004] and Seadet Kerimova, a BBC News reader from Azerbaijan, posted that it is "a hymn to the solitude of each of us" [2007].

Scholars have universalized *One Hundred Years of Solitude* by using it to index many (and often incompatible) approaches to understanding major social issues. For U.S. scholar Gregory Lawrence, this novel "illustrates the Marxian conception of alienation" [1974]. Writing in the aftermath of the 1973 oil crisis, for U.S. scholar Seymour Menton, this novel "marks the end of capitalist society" [1976]. Drawing on postmodernist theory, Peruvian scholar Julio Ortega argued that *One Hundred Years of Solitude* "constructs the world as an act of multiple reading" [1995] and U.S. journalist Martin Kaplan called it "a postmodernist jungle" [1978]. For U.S. scholar Robert Sims, the novel "reads like Lévi-Strauss's structural analysis of myth" [1986]. Similarly, scholars Iddo Landau from Israel and Arnold M. Penuel from the United States pointed out connections between the novel and Hegelian philosophy or pragmatism, respectively [1992 and 1994]. In the 2010s, as climate change became global news, brokers connected this novel to environmentalism. For example, scholar Raymond L. Williams has indexed it as "a work of ecological wisdom" [2010], that is, humanity can draw lessons about environmental protection from this literary work.

Another way in which cultural brokers contribute to the classic value of *One Hundred Years of Solitude* is the pattern of artistic commensuration, which consists in comparing this novel to other cultural objects of long-lasting value. Scottish scholar P. E. Bentley compared this novel to Velázquez's classic seventeenth-century painting *Las Meninas* [1975]. Soviet translator Valeri Stolbov [1979], Argentine scholar Jorge Rogachevsky [1981], and Cuban writer César Leante [1984] agreed on comparing *One Hundred Years of Solitude* to *War and Peace*. Puerto Rican writer A. Villanueva-Collado [1990] and Greek theologian Jonas Barciauskas [1993] preferred to compare it to the *Divine Comedy*. For Colombian scholar C. R. Figueroa Sánchez, in *One Hundred Years of Solitude*, the Bible "functions as [a] kind of intertext" [1997]. For U.S. literary scholar Harold Bloom, this novel is "the new *Don Quixote*" [1989]. And for Katie, a customer of the Russian online bookstore Ozun, it is like Mikhail Bulgakov's "*The Master and Margarita* in its own way" [2001]. Artistic commensuration can also mean connecting the novel to something that is more familiar to the culture of the reader (as the Ozun customer did when she compared *One Hundred Years of Solitude* to a twentieth-century Russian classic). But this is not always the case. Writer Leante, mentioned above, did not compare *One Hundred Years of Solitude* to Cuban classics (for example, José Martí's poetry) but to foreign classics such as "*War and Peace, Madame Bovary, Moby Dick*" [1984]. Likewise, U.S. scholar Mary E. Davis compared *One Hundred Years of Solitude* to a "Sophoclean tragedy" [1985], an art form dating from the first millennium BC, rather than the novels of William Faulkner, who inspired García Márquez's novel.

Since its publication, *One Hundred Years of Solitude* has been a topic of entrenched criticism. In 1971, Mexican writer José Emilio Pacheco had to defend the novel against accusations of plagiarism by Guatemalan writer and Nobel laureate Asturias; Pacheco stated "how absurd and unfounded is the accusation of plagiarism" [1971]. For Mexican poet and Nobel laureate Octavio Paz, this novel is "watery poetry" [1973]. While recognizing its "undoubted power," the best-selling English writer Anthony Burgess, author of *A Clockwork Orange*, wrote that *One Hundred Years of Solitude* cannot be "compared with the genuinely literary explorations of Borges and Nabokov" [1983]. And Carlos Barral, the influential Spanish publisher and promoter of Boom novels in the 1960s, said that this novel "is not the best novel of its time" [1988].

Important celebrations are also a perfect occasion to voice criticism against the novel. In 1982, García Márquez won the Nobel Prize in Literature, thanks greatly to the success of *One Hundred Years of Solitude*, and on this occasion Chilean novelist Jorge Edwards wrote a piece to criticize it, saying "I couldn't read beyond page 155." At the end of the millennium, English scholar Jonathan Bate wrote for the *Telegraph* about the most overrated books of the past thousand years: "Let us hope that [*One Hundred Years of Solitude*] will not generate one hundred years of overwritten, overlong, overrated novels" [1999]. In 2014, when many around the globe mourned the death of García Márquez, members of the Economics Job Market Rumors, a global forum for economists to discuss economics, economics jobs, conferences, and journals, opened a thread on a non-economics topic: "Gabriel García Márquez's novels are rubbish." One of the participants, user 5c52, scorned *One Hundred Years of Solitude* for being "just standard plotlines, enough to read through" [2014].

Criticism reappeared in 2017, on the occasion of the novel's fiftieth anniversary, and in 2019, when Netflix announced the novel's adaptation for the screen. The announcement caused mixed reactions, many of which were compiled by media platforms such as *Oprah Magazine*. Entrenched criticism, of course, is rampant on online bookstores and social media. M. H. cawdor83, an Amazon Germany reader, confessed that "I had to force myself not to throw the book out the window" [2005]. For Vasily Yakovlev, an Ozun Russia reader, it is "a nasty book about a family of freaks and perverts" [2008]. Ahmad Ashkaibi in Jordan, author of one of most liked negative reviews of the novel on Goodreads, a platform for book recommendations with over eleven million registered users at the time, wrote, "Life is [too] short to waste it reading such a bad book" [2012]. Four years later, Goodreads surpassed the fifty million mark and feminist reviewer "V. A Court of Wings" attacked the novel for being full of "* Pedophilia/rape * Incest/child abuse * Non sensical Violence," among other "disgusting" contents [2016]. Even García Márquez himself admitted years later his strong negative feelings toward it: "I do not deny *One Hundred Years of Solitude*. Something worse happens to me: I hate it" [1991]. This kind of entrenched critique, and not only praise, helps a work of art build a long-lasting and controversial reputation as a classic.

An Imitated Opening: "Many years later, as he faced the firing squad"

When *One Hundred Years of Solitude* came out, the public did not refer in particular to its now globally famous opening. But as time went by, the creation

7.1 Korean version of comic showing the moment when the first sentence of the
novel came to García Márquez.

Source: Gabo: Memorias de una vida mágica (2015). Image courtesy of John Naranjo.

of the opening has become one of the myths associated with the genius of
García Márquez; a myth that continues to take multiple forms as in a graphic
novel based on the author's biography translated into more than fifteen languages [2015; see figure 7.1]. Rephrasing the opening sentence is for many cultural brokers the best way of sharing memorable life experiences with other
people. For example, Canadian critic Geoff Hancock compared his discovery
of the totem poles in Stanley Park in Vancouver, British Columbia, to Colonel
Buendía's discovery of ice [1986].

Other cultural brokers prefer to index the opening by recalling when
they first read it. For Rob Crawford, an Amazon UK customer from France,
it "became a touchstone in my memory thirty-six years ago" [2011]. So felt
U.S. writer Stephen Koch after an editor said to him, "Read the first sentence. Just the first sentence." He did and wrote, "I remember it still" [1976].

Some brokers summarized their amazement in one or two words: "superb" for the anonymous *Time* magazine reviewer [1970], "arresting," for U.S. scholar Brian Conniff [1990], or "immortal," for English journalist Ed King [2008]. Others recall that the opening is written to "trick readers" in the opinion of U.S. scholar E. Waters Hood [1993], to disorient them, according to Irish scholar Patrick O'Neill [1994], or to catch them: "I was absolutely hooked," wrote P. Sadler, an Amazon UK reader. Other brokers, in trying to recall the opening, make mistakes, such as Philippine businessman Antonio R. Samson, for whom the discovery was not about ice: "I look forward already to . . . relive the trip to that mythical village of Macondo and the first experience of ice cream" [1999]. And in 2016, the *New York Times* turned its obituary of translator Gregory Rabassa into a lengthy explanation of his craftsmanship when translating the novel's opening and why he preferred "firing squad" over "firing party," "remember" over "recall," "discover ice" over "know ice" or "experience ice," and "distant" over "remote."[5]

As part of the pattern of artistic commensuration, writers seeking a professional reputation and critics have emulated the novel's opening sentence. Allie Fox, the main character in Paul Theroux's novel *The Mosquito Coast* (1981), is a brilliant inventor, like José Arcadio Buendía in *One Hundred Years of Solitude*. He decides to move with his family from the United States to the jungle in Central America. During a key scene about the fabrication of ice in the jungle, Fox famously states, "Ice is civilization." *The Mosquito Coast* became a best seller, won multiple awards, and was a Hollywood blockbuster in 1986, with Harrison Ford in the leading role and Paul Schrader (*Taxi Driver*) as the scriptwriter. In his review for the *New York Times*, critic John Leonard wrote that the main character reminded him of "Lord Jim, John Galt, Henderson the Rain-King, Ahab, and one of the crazier Buendías in *One Hundred Years of Solitude* (García Márquez, remember, had ice in his tropics)."[6] The similarities between this novel and *The Mosquito Coast* remain a subject of discussion on social media on whether Theroux plagiarized García Márquez's text. In another contemporary film, Werner Herzog's *Fitzcarraldo* (1982), the main character presented a block of ice to the leader of the Jivaros tribe. Its members took the ice as a sign of the white's man magic. In his movie review for the local newspaper, the *Stanford Daily*, reviewer Steve Vineberg criticized the "scene (perhaps inspired by a marvelous incident in García Márquez's novel *One Hundred Years of Solitude*) [because it] has no climax" [1982].[7]

Imitation, of course, occurs in numerous literary works. Salman Rushdie wrote a sentence similar to the opening of *One Hundred Years of Solitude* in the first chapter of *Midnight's Children*, the novel that brought him commercial success and professional recognition [1981]: "Many years later, when the hole inside him had been clogged up with hate, and he came to sacrifice himself at the shrine of the black stone god in the temple of the hill, he would try to recall his childhood springs in Paradise." So did Isabel Allende in the last pages of her breakthrough novel *The House of the Spirits* [1982]: "At the end of his life, when his ninety years had turned him into a twisted fragile tree, Esteban Trueba would recall those moments with his granddaughter as the happiest of his whole existence." The opening has also motivated aspiring artists. Maryam Pajotan, an Iranian BBC News reader, confessed that, if she ever writes a book, "it will start by saying: 'And a hundred years later' " [2007].

Brokers across cultural regions have compared this opening to ones of literary and nonliterary classics. For U.S. writer John Barth, it is comparable to the opening sentences of *Anna Karenina* and *Finnegans Wake* [1980]. The oldest operating bookstore in the world, Livraria Bertrand in Lisbon, Portugal, founded in 1732, compares it to "the celebrated . . . opening words of *Don Quixote* or *In Search of Lost Time*" [2013]. For an anonymous Amazon UK reader, the opening "is almost a 'Ben Hur' effect" [1997]. For U.S. scholar Michael G. Cooke, it is a "Virgilian scene" [1987], and his colleague Matthew J. McDonough compares it to *Don Quixote* [1991]. For Italian scholar Franco Moretti, the opening functions as a Wagnerian leitmotif in *The Ring of the Nibelung* or in Joyce's *Ulysses* [1996]. And English scholar Robin W. Fiddian stressed the opening's biblical connotations: "intended to mimic the idea of Creation" [1995].

In terms of universalization, the opening remains a meaningful reference. But understanding its meaning has prompted different interpretations, using approaches that have little in common with the novel's niche. Some of these interpretations are Freudian according to Argentine scholar Josefina Ludmer [1972], semiotic according to Bulgarian critic Tzvetan Todorov [1978], religious for Romanian scholar C.-A. Mihailescu [2003], postmodern for Canadian scholar John Moss [1985], and cinematic according to Italian writer Elena Clementelli [1974]. Furthermore, German writer U. M. Saine [1984] and South African writer André Brink [1998], respectively, found similarities between the opening and the theory of relativity. Saine wrote that "the inability to tell . . . space from time, which is characteristic of relativity, [shows] on the first page of the novel," and Brink wrote, "Just as Einstein invented, from the old Newtonian categories of time and space, the new concept of spacetime, Márquez here establishes his own distinctive language-time." Contrary to such interpretations, scholars, critics, and writers in Uruguay, Colombia, United States, Trinidad and Tobago, England, Belgium, Hungary, and former Czechoslovakia [1969, 1973, 1975, 1977, 1983, 1988, 1989, and 2009] have preferred to stick to more descriptive meanings of the opening. For example, "the narrator involves us in three aspects of time" or "performs the simultaneity of three time levels."

Celebrities are important brokers in the universalization of the opening, too. Oprah Winfrey presented it to the hundreds of thousands of readers of her book club as "one of the most fabulous openers in the history of literature" [2004]. An anonymous Amazon UK reader had a similar opinion four years earlier: "One of the best and most memorable opening sentences in literature" [2000]. And U.S. writer Eric Ormsby concluded, "It seems always to have existed, in precisely those words, in our own English tongue" [2005]. Cultural brokers also take advantage of special occasions to promote the opening. A month after García Márquez's passing in 2014, *20 Minutes*, a daily newspaper distributed for free among commuters in at least ten of France's biggest cities, published a piece on the extraordinary success of *One Hundred Years of Solitude* that informed its over one million readers that "in Latin America, readers know the sentence by heart." Sometimes the audience is smaller and more limited. 65ymás.com, a Spanish digital newspaper for those sixty-five years old and over, started the article "García Márquez: el hombre que reinventó la literatura" by citing the opening as capital to his reinvention of literature [2019].

Along with unconditional admirers, the opening has also had its share of detractors over the years. Colombian writer Fernando Vallejo asked, "Where is the originality?" For him, the novel simply begins by saying, "One hundred years later, Colonel Aureliano Buendía was to remember that time" [2002]. And Goodreads reviewer Nathan "N.R." Gaddis wrote, "One hundred years of reading the opening paragraph over and over," in reference to how boring the novel was, and he wondered why the author received the Nobel Prize in Literature [2017].

Macondo: A Fictional Colombian Village Becomes Universal

Cultural brokers have referred to Macondo in multiple and conflicting ways. Yet their actions have made the village at the center of novel more meaningful over the decades. Regarding the pattern of lived experience, different audiences have used Macondo to index past and current events. Orhan Miroğlu, a Turkish politician of Kurdish descent, wrote a column for the newspaper *Star* entitled "Armenians, Macondo village, and centuries of solitude." He claimed that the plague of insomnia that affected the inhabitants of Macondo affects the Turkish government. He criticized Prime Minister Erdoğan for forgetting the sufferings of the Armenian people in 1915, regarded as one of the first modern genocides [2014]. U.S. scholar Peter Earle [1981] indexed Macondo to express his views on the fate of Latin America in the 1980s; back then, dictatorships and rising violence spread across the region. Similarly, Nicaraguan writer Sergio Ramírez reported that a Sandinista guerrilla leader used Macondo as his war name in the 1980s when clashes between the Sandinistas and the Contras surged [1992]. For Japanese writer Kōbō Abe, Macondo "is no longer a [Latin American] region but has become a contemporary question" [1983]. In the 1990s, Jo Durden-Smith, an English filmmaker living in Russia after the fall of communism, renamed Moscow as "Moscow-Macondo." For him, the capital of the recently created Russian Federation was "the theater of the absurd on the Moscow river" [1994].

This pattern—linking Macondo to events with global resonance—has continued in recent decades. In 2020, as the Covid-19 began to quickly spread worldwide, people on social media found similarities between the coronavirus pandemic and the insomnia plague that infected Macondo. Ten years earlier, global media reported that the BP oil spill in the Gulf of Mexico occurred in a well named Macondo [2010 and 2013; see figure 7.2].

Other cultural brokers indexed Macondo as a real place as well. So did Spanish writer Juan Benet [1969], French politician François Mitterrand

7.2 Explosion of the Deepwater Horizon in the Macondo Prospect, Gulf of Mexico, 2010.

Source: Wikimedia.

[1975], an anonymous Amazon Canada reader [2002], and Mexican writer Carlos Fuentes [1976]. The last asked, "Who has not found in the genealogy of Macondo, his grandmother, his girlfriend, his brother, his nanny?"[8] For others, the fictional village is a space to escape from reality, with one's imagination, as Natalia, a Ukrainian reader, put it [2001] or as travel destination; Waldo's, a travel agency in Suriname, advertised Colombia as the location of Macondo, at the center of the "magical universe of García Márquez," and said that "coming to Colombia is discovering a whole new world" [2015]. In 2020, "macondistas," the so-called members of the Macondo Writers Workshop (founded in 1995 by Mexican-American writer Sandra Cisneros), met for their annual meeting in San Antonio, Texas, to continue to foster "a global sense of community" through creative writing. In addition, Macondo is the name of a Venezuelan liquor made since the 1970s,[9] a Spanish tarot [1999], a Latin American literary movement, McOndo [1996], a U.S. foundation [1998], and a soccer ball used by the Colombian National Football Team during the 2014 FIFA World Cup qualifying matches. Since 2019, Macondo is something outside the Earth. The International Astronomical Union named star HD 93083 after Macondo and its satellite HD 93083 b is named Melquíades, the character who in the novel "orbits" the village.

Macondo is also the name of a song and a telling example of how brokers appropriate cultural goods. Composed in 1969 by Peruvian Daniel Camino Diez-Canseco as a cumbia song (a popular music and dance in Latin America), "Macondo" retells the story of the village and its main characters: José Arcadio, Aureliano, Remedios, Amaranta, Melquíades, and Mauricio Babilonia and his yellow butterflies. Famous interpreters across the region have sung it: Johnny Arce (Peru), Óscar Chávez, Rigo Tovar and Costa Azul, and Celso Piña (Mexico), Los Hispanos orchestra (Colombia), and the salsa orchestra Billo's Caracas Boys (Venezuela). The latter orchestra made a popular version thanks to which the events of Macondo and its main characters "entered through the ears, at parties and dances in the 1970s, to Venezuelans and Colombians who had not yet read *One Hundred Years of Solitude*."[10] Billo's Caracas Boys toured other countries of Latin America and Spain in the 1970s and 1980s, with "Macondo" in its repertoire.

As part of the pattern of universalization, Macondo has been used as a (contentious) indexical of the history of mankind. In the early 1970s, rather than a fictional Colombian village, for U.S. critic Alfred Kazin, Macondo is the place "through which all history will pass" [1972]. For English scholar James Higgins, it is "a microcosm of a larger world" [1990]. For Vera Székács, a Hungarian translator, Macondo "is eternal" [1997]. Not only critics but also ordinary readers have said that Macondo is a "microcosm of human history," as Amazon Japan reader Kotaro Minami wrote [2008].[11] Scholars have used the fictional Macondo as if it were true historical evidence. In *Imagined Communities* (published in 1983 and reissued in 1991 and 2006), an influential book on nationalism that has sold over a quarter of a million copies worldwide, China-born, Irish historian Benedict Anderson cited Macondo to indicate how the village's fictional story exemplified the actual geographical isolation of many parts of the region. Finally, a particular example of universalization is the adjective "macondiano" ("Macondian") which has entered into language and is spreading.[12] For Colombian politician G. Bell Lemus, macondiano is "a universal adjective, such as Quixotic and Kafkaesque" [2000].

However, other cultural brokers oppose universalization and claim that Macondo is just "a tiny, fictional Colombian town" as pointed out by Canadian editor Caitlin Kelly [1980], English writer Angela Carter [1982], and German scholar Vera Kutzinski [1985]. So did the *Herald*, Zimbabwe's largest newspaper with a circulation of five million, in a story about the greatest books ever written, which used as its source not an African publication but the *Encyclopedia Britannica* [2018], an indication of how not one but several cultural brokers can mediate readers' access to information about *One Hundred Years of Solitude*. For Taiwanese news media site *The Storm*, "Márquez fictionalized his hometown of Aracataca in the town of Macondo" [2019].

Regarding the pattern of artistic commensuration, the uniqueness of Macondo in literature has been a meaningful subject of debate. For U.S. scholar José Saldívar, "nothing like Macondo appears in world literature" [1991]. For others, on the contrary, Macondo shows clear similarities to modernist classics *Ulysses*, *The Waves*, or *Absalom, Absalom!* according to U.S. scholar Morton Levitt [1986] and to the story of Ancient Greek heroes "the Argonauts" according to Swiss scholar Gustav Siebenmann [1988]. Furthermore, as early as 1968, cultural brokers started to debate Macondo's links to other classic literary settings, such as Proust's Combray, according to French journalist Philippe Lançon [2003]; the Megalokastro of Greek writer Kazantzakis and the Kfaryabda of Lebanese writer Maalouf, according to Australian writer Renee Bittoun [1995]; and especially Faulkner's Yoknapatawpha County. On this Faulknerian connection, for Juan Bosch, a Dominican politician, Macondo "has nothing to do with Yoknapatawpha" [1968]; for Italian scholar Darío Puccini, Macondo "might suggest Faulkner's 'nearby' Yoknapatawpha County" [1989]; and for U.S. writer David Young and scholar Keith Hollaman, "the relations between Faulkner's Yoknapatawpha and García Márquez's Macondo are fascinating to contemplate" [1984]. Thirty-three years later, these relations still attracted the attention of Catholic writer Juan Manuel de Prada, who wrote for *L'Osservatore Romano*, the newspaper of the Pope's Vatican City State: "The creation of Macondo itself could not be understood without the antecedent of Yoknapatawpha" [2017]. Despite being a catholic newspaper, de Prada's piece on the novel was not about its link to a religious text. The year before, on the contrary, the Icelandic National Broadcasting Service (Ríkisút-varpiÐ) selected *One Hundred Years of Solitude* as book of the week, and this national media company in a majority Lutheran country stressed the connection between Macondo and the Book of Genesis [2016].

As part of the entrenched criticism pattern, since the 1970s, by challenging Macondo's "reality," "universal" reach, or literary value, detractors keep contributing to this novel's visibility. For example, Colombian critic J. Mejía Duque referred to "the plague of Macondism" [1973]. And four decades later, an anonymous Barnes & Noble reader concluded that Macondo "is clearly a world [that] readers fail to directly relate to" [2005].

Magical Realism: Universalizing a Genre

The globalization of magical realism has been fundamental to uproot *One Hundred Years of Solitude*. Across national and cultural boundaries (and at least since the early 1980s), literary critics and common readers started to refer to magical realism as a genre that gives access to a deeper understanding of reality and universal human nature. For Soviet Union critic V. Andreev, the magical realism of this novel "reflect[s] exactly the magic of real life" [1983]. For an anonymous Amazon UK reader, the style of this novel is "a magic way to summarize the story of humanity" [1999]. For an anonymous client of French bookseller FNAC, it captures "a world very similar to ours" [2004]. Martin Elfert, a Canadian priest in Vancouver, British Columbia, reacted the same way. He found in the magical realism of García Márquez (not in a religious sacred text), the words he was looking for to make sense of the fact that in the morning "a man took a dump in the church garden." And he *preached* these words to his online community on Facebook: when he saw the man, "I remembered immediately . . . the ambiguous or blurred relationship between the real and the metaphorical" [2016]. In 2020, as fires were spreading out of control throughout Australia during the bushfire season, local volunteer firefighter and novelist Jennifer Mills wrote that, for writers interested in "climate fiction," magical realism gives them narrative tools but "the Anthropocene brings its own challenges."

In the novel's early years, critics, scholars, peer writers, and journalists only referred to this fusion of magic and reality in *One Hundred Years of Solitude* [critic Dámaso Santos, Spain, 1968] and the genre's precise geographical location: Latin America [journalist, Francisco Cervantes, Mexico, 1970]. This usage remains stable as shown by the way journalists, scholars, and readers in Scotland, the Netherlands, United States, Argentina, Paraguay, and Spain index magical realism [1976, 1982, 1988, 1994, 1996, and 1997]. Transnational audiences in countries outside Latin America, such as Austria, Germany, and China continue to refer to *One Hundred Years of Solitude* as the best example of magical realism more than five decades after its publication [2008, 2011, and 2013]. Others do so by explicitly (and incorrectly) indexing him as its "creator" or "father," respectively, according to Argentine journalist F. J. Caeiro [2006] and the *National* [2014], the main newspaper in Papua New Guinea. And others do so by asserting, like Egyptian writer Alaa el Aswany, that García Márquez's style "has given us a model" [2007]. This is the model followed by Puerto Rican screenwriter José Rivera in his off-Broadway play *Cloud Tectonics*, as the newspaper *Indian Express* reported in 2015, when an all-Indian cast performed his play at Akshara Theatre in New Delhi. Three years later, Iraqi Shahad Al Rawi became the youngest female author to be shortlisted for the International Prize for Arabic Fiction. This award, also known as the Arabic Booker Prize, is given to the best novel published in Arabic each year and is supported by the Emirates Foundation in Abu Dhabi. The nineteen-year-old Al Rawi, who admires *One Hundred Years of Solitude*, was nominated for *The Baghdad Clock*, which eventually won the First Book Award at the Edinburgh International Book Festival in Scotland. In his review for the *National* in the United Arab Emirates, Malcolm Forbes said that the writer's "attempts at magic realism (a dog whose actions predict future events; a woman who finds a whale in her kitchen) lack purpose and fail to charm" [2018]. These are telling examples of how multiple cultural brokers can participate in the global circulation of magical realism.

Since the mid-1980s, there has also been a tendency to universalize García Márquez's writing style. For instance, theologian T. Aparicio López connected magical realism to previous Latin American writers such as Carpentier [1980], while Spanish critic José Antonio de Castro found elements of magical realism in modernist European writers Kafka and Virginia Woolf [1972]. Among scholars and writers from Canada, England, Nigeria, India, and Taiwan, magical realism emerged as the style that best defined new literature in Canada [Peter Hinchcliffe and Ed Jewinski, scholars, 1986], Africa [Chinua Achebe, writer, Nigeria, and C. L. Innes, scholar, England, 1992], the postcolonial world [Homi Bhabha, scholar, India, 1990], and globally [Stephen Hart and Wen-Chin Ouyang, scholars, England and Taiwan, 2005].

Whereas the meaning of the genre magical realism remains contested, its meaningfulness has increased over time, making *One Hundred Years of Solitude* more visible as an object of commensuration. For French journalist Régis Debray, magical realism "coincides with socialist realism" [1977]. For English critic, S. Meckled-Morkos, "anti-rationalism [is] one of the essential contents" [1985]. For U.S. scholar Irvine D. S. Winsboro, it "oscillates between super-realism and super-fantasy" [1993]. For Canadian scholar Dean J. Irvine, it contains "strains of postcolonialism and postmodernism" [1998]. For Polish critic, M. Szewczyk, it actually "represents a kind of reversal of the literature understood as magic realist" [2000]. For Amazon Japan reader Bunocio, it consists of an "exquisite blend of realism and the indigenous" [2009]. And for Amazon France reader Marine, its style is "science fiction" [2012].

The entrenched criticism of *One Hundred Years of Solitude* as the best example of magical realism has strengthened the connection between this novel and the genre among new generations of cultural brokers. For Costa Rican reader Gregory Bascom, its style resembles a more pedestrian one, that of "grandmothers, when telling a story to youngsters" [2003]. An anonymous Amazon Germany reader commented that there is no "consolation" in García Márquez's magical realism, but there is in the magical realism of other non-Latin American authors, such as Salman Rushdie and Toni Morrison [2001]. (Notice how, in indexing García Márquez's style, this reader has expanded magical realism beyond its Latin American origins to India and the United States.) A decade earlier [1991], U.S. scholar Regina Janes denounced that the genre had progressively "colonized Latin American reality." From a different angle, to react against this, scholars Louis Parkinson Zamora and Wendy B. Faris argued, "Readers know that magical realism is not a Latin American monopoly" [1995]. A decade later, English editor Robert McCrum proclaimed magical realism "dead or at least ready to receive the last rites" [2002]. In 2010, Argentine critic Martín Schifino reacted against Macondism by denying that magical realism has affinities with the reality of Latin America. For Todung R., a Goodreads reviewer in Indonesia, his "magical realism is sometimes so outrageous that it's hard to understand" [2019]. Even more critical was Sam Jordison in an article for the English newspaper the *Guardian* [2017]. He called it "dark magic realism [of] raped women, abandoned mothers and abused children . . . contented, warm-hearted, well-treated prostitutes."

Remedios's Ascent to Heaven: Indexing a Literary Event

Literary events in *One Hundred Years of Solitude*, such as the ascension of Remedios the Beauty to heaven in chapter 12, show that a cultural good can have meanings that go beyond the ones originally present in its niche. The ascent occurred when Remedios and two other women were folding sheets in the garden of the Buendías's house and suddenly Remedios rose to the sky and disappeared forever. Despite disagreements among fans and scholars about the origins of this event and what it really means, it has become one of the novel's most stable indexicals over time and transnationally.

As García Márquez did with other events in the novel, Remedios's ascent allowed him to offer a solution to a technical literary problem in the 1960s. Back then, many critics, writers, and readers accused the novel of excessive realism, as in Spanish social realism, and of excessive formal experimentalism, as in the French *nouveau roman*. So they welcomed the publication of *One Hundred Years of Solitude* for overpowering the shortcomings of both styles. Along with usage of adjectivized and poetic language (contra social realism) and a return to narrative and reader-friendly storytelling (contra *nouveau roman*), García Márquez's additional technical solution, in agreement with aesthetic options available at the time, was to punctuate the novel from beginning to end with supernatural or fantastic events. And what he did, decisively, was to present such events as real or pedestrian facts that required empirical demonstration. He did so with the appearance of the ghost of Prudencio Aguilar (see chapter 4) and other events.[13] In Remedios's case, he wrote that the "determined wind" (that is, a real force) caused the sheets (a material object) to open up wide, surround Remedios, and take her to heaven.

Different cultural brokers have confirmed the material and realist foundations of this event from the early 1970s onward. For example, as Spanish scholar Carmen Arnau put it, she "soars through the air but clinging to a bed sheet" [1971]. Furthermore, since 1967 García Márquez himself has insisted that the event was not pure fiction, it was based upon a real local story: a girl eloped with her lover.[14] The novel itself clearly mentions it a few sentences later: "The outsiders, of course, thought that Remedios the Beauty had finally succumbed to her irrevocable fate of a queen bee and that her family was trying to save her honor with that tale of levitation." To avoid mockery from the community, Remedios's family said that she went up to heaven. For a reader sharing the cultural code of García Márquez's Caribbean region in Colombia, that is the meaning of Remedios's ascent: she ran away with a lover.

This is the meaning that historian Germán Arciniegas found by interviewing a neighbor from García Márquez's hometown in Aracataca [1992]. The historian asked her: "You believed that Remedios ascended, right?" But the neighbor replied that García Márquez was a "liar," denying that the ascension was the real story.[15]

The vernacular meaning of this literary event has not escaped locals and some experts such as English scholar Michael Wood [1990] and German translator Dagmar Ploetz [2000]. But it has escaped most readers outside Caribbean Colombia, that is, outside the cultural region of *One Hundred Years of Solitude*. Since the early 1970s, foreign audiences have indexed Remedios's ascent differently. For Spanish scholar María E. Montaner, she does not go up but "stays on earth" [1987]. For Mexican writer Guillermo Samperio, her ascension was necessary "for the salvation of the family" [1997]. For Cuban scholar E. Camayd-Freixas, "the loss of virginity is represented by the opposite" [1998]. And for U.S. scholar Shannin Schroeder, aware of the importance of alchemy in the novel, her ascension "coincides with the stage of alchemy where metals and the soul begin their ascent toward gold" [2004]. For writers, scholars, and common readers in Catholic countries, such as Spain, Peru, and Italy, Remedios's ascent indexes a clear religious scene: the Virgin's ascent [1978, 1984, and 2008]. And even in this case, there is no agreement about the meaning of the event. The reference to the Virgin's ascent is "ironic" according to Belgian scholar Jacques Joset [1980]; it is "parody" as claimed by the Director of the Spanish Royal Academy of Language V. de la Concha [2007]; or a literary version "of popular depictions of the event in religious prints" for a Cuban scholar [1982]. Despite being so rooted in the Catholic tradition, this event can also appeal to non-Christian readers. In the eighteenth-century Chinese classic *Dream of the Red Chamber*, the character 秦可卿 (Qin Keqing) is a beautiful woman who also exits the novel mysteriously.[16] Unlike the previous cultural brokers, Argentine writer Rodrigo Fresán took a different position. For him, the real question is not why Remedios ascends to the sky but rather "where she goes after reaching cruising altitude" [2014]. He asked this in a piece published in *O Globo*, one of Brazil's leading print and digital newspapers, which selected seven writers to recreate the stories of García Márquez for Brazilian readers.

For these and other readers, Remedios is meaningful because she brings back the memories of a lived experience: "I always tell my twelve-year-old daughter that she reminds me of Remedios the Beauty," commented Giselle Díaz, a customer of Casa del libro bookstore in Spain [2002]. Colombian writer, Santiago Gamboa claims that tourists will feel Remedios's presence when visiting Aracataca: "the literary ghosts of Úrsula Iguarán or Remedios the Beauty arise" [2013]. In recalling the event, U.S. knitting pattern designer Nikol Lohr had to admit her failing memory: "I very distinctly remembered Remedios the Beauty ascending through a hole in the bathroom roof after her bath, surrounded and carried off by a cloud of yellow butterflies. I was a little surprised to read it again and discover how wrong I'd gotten it" [2012]. In the months leading up to the global outbreak of the #MeToo movement, Nadia Celis, a Colombian scholar based in the United States, declared that the ascent is not "the climax of her purity, but her flight from a world that could not accept her being free" [2017]. Remedios had to leave to avoid being the victim of sexual violence. Finally, other brokers used her ascent to make sense of García Márquez's lived experience. Argentine critic Tomás Eloy Martínez referred to her in recalling García Márquez's success in 1967 after the novel's publication: "[He and his wife] were about to sit down when someone shouted 'Bravo!' and broke into applause. A woman echoed the shout. 'For your novel!' she said. The entire theater stood up. At that precise moment I saw fame come down from the sky, wrapped in a dazzling flapping of sheets, like Remedios the Beauty, and bathe García Márquez in one of those winds of light that are immune to the ravages of time."[17]

Regarding the universalization of Remedios's ascent, references appear across audiences and national boundaries. For U.S. writer Paul Hedeen, her ascension symbolizes the "revolt against the day to day relinquishing of individuality to the drab commonality of solitude" [1983]. For an Ecuadorian scholar, the event can be understood as part of a longer literary tradition that acknowledges people's understanding of such kind of events as supposedly having a pseudo-providential foundation: "[García Márquez] is rendering one more version of a myth intelligible only through faith" [1985]. For Peruvian critic G. Faberón-Patriau, her ascent represents "the fatality of beauty" as if the event functioned as a universal principle [2003]. *Corriere della Sera*, one of Italy's most read newspapers, shared a similar idea with its half a million readers. The author of the piece, writer Romana Petri, said that Remedios was a "cruel beauty" [2015].

The pattern of artistic commensuration yielded numerous results, ranging from Ancient and modern literary classics to contemporary painting. For U.S. critic William Plummer, Remedios's ascent refers to Eula's abduction in Faulkner's *The Hamlet* [1976]. For Canadian scholar Amaryll Chanady, it is a transformation comparable to that of Samsa in Kafka's *The Metamorphosis* [1986]. For Korean scholar Byung-Joo Park, the sheets that surround Remedios as she ascended "remind us of the flying carpets in *One Thousand and One Nights*" [1989]. For Mexican scholar Ignacio Sánchez Prado, "a similar scene

7.3 Remedios's ascent to heaven depicted on a tarot card, 1999.

Source: Un tarot para Macondo. Image courtesy of artist Andrés Marquínez Casas.

happens in *Recollections of Things to Come*" by Mexican writer Elena Garro [2019]. Beyond literature, a Venezuelan journalist claimed that Remedios is similar to the *Mona Lisa*,[18] and for Uruguayan critic C. Martínez Moreno, the event is described "as if we have in front of our eyes a Chagall canvas" [1969].

Remedios's fate has become a meaningful artistic theme that continues to inspire visual artists and musicians globally: for example, graphic designer Andrés Marquínez Casas's *La ascensión* (Colombia, 1999; see figure 7.3), graphic designer Claire Niebergall's *Remedy V* (United States, 2011), illustrator David Merta's *Remedios the Beauty* (Slovakia, 2012), guitarist Bill Frisell's song "Remedios the Beauty" (United States, 1988), and Modena City Rambler's song "Remedios la bella" (Italy, 1997). Finally, efforts to make Remedios real on the screen have been criticized. For instance, in 2018, user Giuliana HMA posted on YouTube a comment about a short film adaptation of Remedios's story done by a group of Colombian students: "The girl is attractive but she does not fit my image of Remedios the Beauty" and for that reason, she thought, the screen adaptation fails to convince viewers that eventually she could fly to the sky. Other brokers have tried to simulate Remedios's experience by other means; "Rumedios" was the name of a tropical alcoholic drink offered to guests during the opening of the Harry Ransom Center's international exhibition on García Márquez [2020].

Whereas for Spanish scholar and writer Juan Manuel García Ramos, the ascent of Remedios "is the most poetic episode of the entire work of García Márquez" [2016], entrenched criticism of this event is common among cultural brokers. For multiple critics, her ascension is clearly an example of Macondism, which distorts the image of the real Latin America. Indeed, non-Latin American audiences have produced distorted views about this novel by transforming a specific event into widespread behavior. According to writer Thomas Pynchon, "folks routinely sail through the air" in One Hundred Years of Solitude [1988]. So claims U.S. scholar A. Kim Robertson: "Virgin beauties [ascend] to heaven with the sheets of the house" [1996]. The next step is to generalize from this novel to "colonize" the reality of Latin America, as critics of magical realism continue to denounce [cf. 1981]. Entrenched criticism is equally present in the debate about whether Remedios's ascent represents "the best of the book" [anonymous Casa del Libro reader, Spain, 2006] or the worst: it "is not acceptable" [Spanish scholar O. Carreras González, 1974], "the weakest aspects of his technique—the flying carpets, the sudden ascents to heaven" [U.S. writer Michael Greenberg, 2009], "totally out of place" [Jamrock, Amazon reader, England, 2010], and "it would not occur to me to ascend a character [to heaven]" [Argentine writer Andrés Neuman, 2011]. Furthermore, critics have disapproved of the event for not being a literary novelty [Argentine critic Agustín F. Seguí 1994]. Even those who share García Márquez's Caribbean cultural background have criticized the ascent, including his mother. She questioned the most basic fact: the real Remedios the Beauty was, she said, "very ugly."[19]

The Author: In Everybody's Mouth

Since the mid-1970s, some cultural brokers have preferred to index García Márquez for his political actions, acknowledging that the writer is also an influential public figure. During the Pinochet dictatorship in Chile in the 1970s and 1980s, U.S. scholar Anne Taylor hailed García Márquez's "leadership in the campaign against the Chilean fascists" [1975]. The Nobel committee in literature praised García Márquez's works for "reflec[ting] a continent's life and conflicts" [1982]. In reaction to widespread violence in Colombia associated with the activities of FARC guerrillas and drug cartels, Dutch journalist Peter van Vlerken wrote that he is "the personification of a national conscience in an almost unconscionable country" [1996]. Of a radically different opinion was Reinaldo Arenas, Cuban dissident, icon of the LGBT movement, and poet. He called for a campaign against García Márquez for supporting dictatorships in Cuba and Vietnam. "How much," asked Arenas, "directly or indirectly, does the author of *One Hundred Years of Solitude* charge for the dead body of each Vietnamese or Cuban lost at sea, while desperately trying to reach his freedom?" [1980]. A decade later, Chilean writer Roberto Bolaño marveled at the fact that García Márquez received Pope John II in his historic visit to communist Cuba in 1998 "wearing patent leather boots" [2004]. In Botswana, Duma Gideon Boko, leader of the opposition, stated in his concluding remarks during the state of the nation address that his party, the Umbrella for Democratic Change (UDC), offered "what that literary genius, Gabriel García Márquez, described so beautifully as an energy and novelty that belongs to us in its entirety and with which we ourselves are sufficient" [2015]. In 2019, National Public Radio in the United States published a story by Indian journalist Nina Martyris about García Márquez after President Trump offered to buy Greenland, and she claimed, "In the midst of it all, one could hear the ghost of Gabriel García Márquez chuckle." Here, the journalist was referring to the fact that in his novel *The Autumn of the Patriarch*, the U.S. government bought the Caribbean Sea and shipped it off to Arizona! For a similar reason, Tony Wood [2020] in a piece for the U.S. magazine the *Nation* vindicated the nonfiction writing of García Márquez, especially his journalism, as an antidote to political manipulation.

Other cultural brokers have preferred to index García Márquez's presence in their lives. Trapped at home during the siege of Sarajevo during the Yugoslav Wars, refugee Irena Marijanovic read his works, along with those of "Dostoyevsky, several novels by Balzac, Tolstoy, some Hesse, Victor Hugo" [1993]. Similarly, his complete works were at the disposal of members of an international spaceship crew "living in isolation in a . . . 'spaceship' outside Moscow [while] conducting experiments" [2011]. Chinese writer Mo Yan, recipient of the Nobel Prize in Literature, acknowledged, in his Nobel Lecture, García Márquez's presence in his own work [2012]. This acknowledgement was quite common during the avalanche of pieces written to honor him upon his death and to explain how he had influenced people. Convicted Hollywood producer Harvey Weinstein wrote in the *New York Times*, "Every time I saw him he always said something that had an impact on my life and work" [2014].

A widespread pattern of universalization is to index García Márquez as "the author of *One Hundred Years of Solitude*," giving preference to this novel over the rest of his works [1970, 1972, and 1988]. Statements can also include qualifying words: for example, "universally consecrated author of [*One Hundred Years of Solitude*]" [1981]. More importantly, such statements are associated with opinions about García Márquez and his literary contribution. In relation to *One Hundred Years of Solitude*, he was considered a "young master" by Spanish scholar Joaquín Marco [1967] and a great writer by peer writers in Spain [Miguel Delibes, 1971] and Argentina [H. Jofre Barroso, 1974], Romanian translator Darie Novaceanu [1978] and U.S. President Bill Clinton [2003]. At the same time, since the early 1980s, other audiences started to index García Márquez in more hagiographic, universalizing terms.[20] He is the "absolute master" for Spanish critic García Posada [1994] and "the Master" for an anonymous Amazon.com reader [2010]. "Each book by [him] is a major literary event," wrote Canadian writer Margaret Atwood [1990]. He "must live forever," commented an anonymous Amazon U.S. reader [1997]. For an anonymous Barnes & Noble reader, he is "a true literary genius" [2001]. "His perception into the human condition is amazing," wrote another Barnes & Noble reader [2002]. Diana, a Turkish reader, said that "Márquez cannot be described, he must be experienced" [2007]. And Bulgarian blogger Venezia posted on the cultural online magazine *Magnifisonz*, "I love you not because of who you are, but because of who I am when I am with you" [2016].

In 2016, too, Colombia's Banco de la República issued a new bill of 50,000 pesos showing García Márquez and another of the novel's most famous indexicals: the yellow butterflies (see figure 7.4). As mentioned in chapter 6, in 2018

7.4 Bill of 50,000 Colombian pesos showing García Márquez.

Google—a cultural broker that did not exist when *One Hundred Years of Solitude* was published—dedicated the Doodle on its main page to García Márquez on what would have been his ninety-first birthday. With this Doodle, the company associated its logo with the writer and, in return, helped make him more visible globally to new generations, along with his most famous work, as millions of Google users discovered after clicking on the Doodle. (That year the company's main page averaged 3.5 billion searches daily.)

In terms of artistic commensuration, cultural brokers have equated García Márquez to literary characters such as Madame Bovary [1984] and classic writers and artists.[21] For Greek translator K. Sotiriadou-Barajas, García Márquez is comparable to "Cervantes, Chaucer, Faulkner, Borges, Camus, Joyce and [classic Greek writer] Kazantzakis" [1992]. For Cavafis, an Amazon Japan reader, he represents "the second coming of Cervantes" [2008]. U.S. writer Selden Rodman compared him to English writer Chaucer and French writer Rabelais [1969]. Italian scholar Francesco Bausi compared him to Boccaccio [2000]. And for an anonymous Amazon Germany reader, he "does not write books, he paints books. His 'paintings' are reminiscent of Picasso" [2005]. As the Boccaccio and Kazantzakis comparisons showed, Italian and Greek brokers can refer to García Márquez as part of their own culture by equating him with recognizable authors of their own national tradition. But this is not always the case. Rather than comparing him to a French poet, French scholar Michèle Sarrailh asked whether García Márquez (a Colombian) would be the successor of Nicaraguan poet Rubén Darío [1979]. Whereas this French scholar opted for a Latin American comparison, a couple of French scholars, Florence Delay and Jacqueline de Labriolle, referred to how García Márquez departed from "Faulknerian tragedy" [1995], that is, a U.S. comparison, neither Latin American nor French.[22]

Commensuration can also take a narrow local form. In a review of the fourth installment of the autobiography of Norwegian novelist Karl Ove Knausgaard, Abdullah Shibli wrote in the *Daily Star*, among the largest circulating daily newspapers in Bangladesh: "like many great writers of the world, including Gabriel García Márquez and Syed Mujtaba Ali, [Knausgaard] knew from his teenage years that he wanted to be a writer" [2017]. Here, the reviewer equated García Márquez to Ali, a local Bengali author, most of whose works continue to be untranslated but are taught in Bengali schools.

As already described, to transform an artist into a meaningful figure requires sustained praise across generations as well as negative attention. García Márquez remains controversial due also to hostile and continued criticism from past and new generations of writers, critics, and readers. Although leading Italian publisher Feltrinelli promoted *One Hundred Years of Solitude* as the new *Don Quixote*, influential Italian filmmaker Pier Paolo Pasolini, one of Feltrinelli's best-selling authors, argued that García Márquez was "a worthless writer" [1973]. Pasolini wrote his review of *One Hundred Years of Solitude* when critics ranked him one of the most influential European filmmakers. In the 1980s, Cuban writer Cabrera Infante derided García Márquez's growing fame as that of "the *nouveau riche* that rubs elbows with high-society" [1983] and kept lambasting him for his friendship with Castro over the years. So did Peruvian writer Vargas Llosa, who called his former friend García Márquez "Castro's lackey" [1986]. This kind of political criticism is rampant on the Internet, including newspapers' comments sections and on social media. Less concerned about politics, Amazon China reader Horseshoe, commenting on a novel published forty-seven years before, brazenly stated that its author is "a madman who wrote about a bunch of lunatics" in reference to *One Hundred Years of Solitude* [2013]. Criticism of him has gone as far as to involve the public burning in Colombia of *One Hundred Years of Solitude* in 1978 along with classic works by Jean-Jacques Rousseau and Karl Marx. Forty years later, Alejandro Ordóñez, one of those involved in the burning, ran for president. Finally, even after his death, criticizing García Márquez remains a meaningful practice. Mexican historian Enrique Krauze wrote for the *New York Times* an opinion column, reprinted in Spanish by Latin American media, in which he claimed that the writer's "undeniable literary achievement has been overshadowed by a moral failing: his long, intimate friendship with Fidel Castro" [2014].

CONCLUSION

Macondo, Colonel Buendía's discovery of ice, Remedios's ascent to the sky, and other parts of *One Hundred Years of Solitude* have turned into small units of significance (or indexicals). Cultural brokers use these units taken from the novel in at least four ways: to interpret past and current events, to make comparisons with other works of art or cultural goods, to formulate universal statements about human nature, and to criticize the work of art in question (or its creator). Multiple cultural brokers from almost a hundred countries on six continents have used *One Hundred Years of Solitude* in ways that make it visible and meaningful generation and generation, and thus they contribute to its status as a global literary classic.

8

ASCENT TO GLORY FOR FEW, DESCENT TO OBLIVION FOR MOST

I had already learned that many a book—many a good book—"is born to
blush unseen and waste its sweetness on the desert air."

—Anthony Trollope[1]

nglish playwright Christopher Marlowe was stabbed to death at age twenty-nine, at the peak of his creative power and influence after writing five plays. What if the one stabbed were not Marlowe but William Shakespeare, who died a natural death at age fifty-two after writing at least thirty-eight plays? Would then Marlowe's *Doctor Faustus* be among the top Western classics rather than Shakespeare's *Hamlet*? If all eight poems of the Epic Cycle about the Trojan War had survived, would the *Iliad* and the *Odyssey* continue to be classics? What if one of today's classic were the blessed Jacobus da Varagine's *Golden Legend*, a collection of hagiographies that was one of the most widely read works in Europe after the Bible during the Middle Ages? What if the chivalry novel praised as a global classic were *Tirant Lo Blanc* and not *Don Quixote*? Would *One Hundred Years of Solitude* have become a classic if had been published in 1950, when García Márquez first imagined it, instead of 1967? These questions seek to answer how a work of art becomes a global classic from an alternative angle: art counterfactuals.[2] Until now, this book has been about a novel that attained success first as a best seller and then as a global classic. But what about works of art that did not succeed, even if they met the conditions to do so? And how can counterfactuals in literature improve our understanding of how works of art become classics?

This chapter studies five literary works published before, during, and after *One Hundred Years of Solitude*: *Los Sangurimas*, *La casa grande*, *Paradiso*, *The Obscene Bird of Night*, and *The Fox from Up Above and the Fox from Down Below*.[3] In their own countries of origin (and in Latin America at large in some cases), these works are considered classics and not just canonical texts.

(On the distinction between classic and canonical works, see the appendix.) But new generations of readers, scholars, and other cultural brokers have not appropriated these five literary works as global classics. Yet, in all five of them, there are crucial similarities with *One Hundred Years of Solitude*: story, format, narrative, style, place or year of publication, agent, publisher, author's biography, literary imagination, and so on. No work of art is consecrated because of a single factor, not even just because of its aesthetics. Libraries across the globe are full of beautiful but forgotten literary works, as Trollope's words remind us. For these five books, lacking a certain factor might have prevented them from attaining classic status globally. But what seems more decisive to reach this status is a particular alignment of these factors across time and space. And again, the text of the literary work, as central a factor as it may be, is only one of these factors.

NOT EVEN A FORERUNNER: *LOS SANGURIMAS*

José de la Cuadra's novella *Los Sangurimas* (1934, *The Sangurimas*) has key themes, characters, motives, and situations, plus writing techniques, that appeared thirty-three years later in *One Hundred Years of Solitude*.[4] Despite similarities between the two works, the case of *Los Sangurimas* suggests that what happens in the stages of imagination and production can influence how readers receive the literary work many years after its publication.

This novella narrates the life of the Sangurimas family, and the following details are the most important similarities with *One Hundred Years of Solitude*. The Sangurimas live in a village founded near a river, in a hostile environment, and separated from civilization; this small rural community becomes "a world unto itself"; it is located, like Macondo, in a tropical coastal region, the Montubio in Ecuador, where tradition drives the actions of superstitious characters; the story centers on the family household, whose patriarch witnesses the decline of the family as his two sons take over it, just like the characters of Aureliano and Arcadio in *One Hundred Years of Solitude*; the patriarch can talk to dead people and ends up tied to a tree and insane, as the Buendía patriarch was; men impose their *macho* world over the feminine (especially through sexual abuse and infidelity by males); the family saga starts with a homicide and ensuing escape into the jungle; incest is the origin and cause of the family's decline; the villagers' resistance to state power and institutions as well as uneasiness toward formalized religion are both recurring themes;

the stories have a cyclical structure (from genesis to apocalypse of the family and its village); key characters feel solitude; fantastic situations and events punctuate the plot; and both stories cover more than five generations "without ever citing a single date that allows for absolute fixity of time for the narrated events." Technically, like García Márquez's novel, it is unclear who the narrator is in *Los Sangurimas*. De la Cuadra used multiple narrative voices to tell the story, a writing technique that Faulkner, a contemporary of de la Cuadra, started practicing in 1929 in *The Sound and the Fury*, and which García Márquez followed as a model for his first novella, *Leaf Storm*.[5]

Since some of these thematic, stylistic, and narrative similarities have been key to the global success of *One Hundred Years of Solitude*, why is *Los Sangurimas* not a classic, too? First of all, this novella faced a big obstacle in the stage of imagination: the rise of Latin American literature. Although this novella and *One Hundred Years of Solitude* are works of *costumbrista* literature (a style that emphasized events of everyday life and traditions), de la Cuadra did not imagine *Los Sangurimas* as a New Latin American Novel. Yet had he conceived his work as Latin American, it would have also faced another problem in the stage of production. There was no regional audience for it and no publishers to pitch it to.[6]

Compared to García Márquez, who had to move to Mexico, de la Cuadra produced all his works in Ecuador, a country that, unlike Mexico, Argentina, or Brazil, occupied a secondary position within the region's literature. And it had an almost nonexistent commercial publishing industry in the 1930s. Yet de la Cuadra did not write in isolation. He belonged to an avant-garde literary circle, the Guayaquil Group, which embraced the style of social realism. Like García Márquez, de la Cuadra wrote fiction at the same time that he made a living as a journalist. He also benefited from growing contacts between Latin American writers and the publishing industry in Spain in the years prior to the Civil War. But *Los Sangurimas* only found a small publisher in Spain. Then, the outbreak of the war severed any ties de la Cuadra had with its publishing industry. The break could have been positive for him because, with Spain at war, publishers in Latin America started to pay more attention to regional writers. This attention was crucial to launch the careers of Jorge Luis Borges, Julio Cortázar, and others. But de la Cuadra died in 1941, leaving as his legacy one novella, five books of short stories, a book essay, a handful of journalistic pieces, and an incomplete novella.[7] Two decades later, when publishers and critics were searching for forerunners of Latin American literature, the output of de la Cuadra did not persuade them. They saw him as an Ecuadorian *costumbrista*, not as a cosmopolitan Latin American writer.[8]

In the 1970s, there were efforts to consecrate *Los Sangurimas* retrospectively. Ecuadorian writer Jorge Icaza, Mexican critic Emmanuel Carballo, and Fernando Alegría agreed that the novella was an antecedent of *One Hundred Years of Solitude*. The influential cultural center Casa de las Américas even published an edition of the novella in 1970. Other contributions presented de la Cuadra as a "first-class universal novelist" and *Los Sangurimas* as a "masterpiece" that preceded the achievements of the New Latin American Novel. In the 1990s, other efforts included an adaptation into a miniseries, PhD theses, and academic articles, including one by a García Márquez scholar who called *Los Sangurimas* a foundational work of magical realism, by then a popular genre thanks to the success of *One Hundred Years of Solitude*. The government of the city of Guayaquil even published de la Cuadra's complete works in one volume. But despite these efforts, *Los Sangurimas* remains unknown to common readers and most scholars of Latin American literature. Even in textbooks of Ecuadorian and Latin American literature, this novella and his author are mentioned in passing when not simply disregarded. The unsuccessful efforts to turn this novella into a classic remind us that the actions of cultural brokers in the present cannot always transform an old literary work into a global classic. Rather, the literary imagination that made this work possible is a critical factor to help with its retrospective consecration. Counterfactually, if *Los Sangurimas* had been published in the mid-1950s, at the onset of the New Latin American Novel, it would have been a contemporary of Alejo Carpentier's *The Lost Steps* (Cuba, 1953) and Juan Rulfo's *Pedro Páramo* (Mexico, 1955), both regarded as foundational works of magical realism. So could have happened to *Los Sangurimas*.[9]

Ultimately, the case of this novella reveals what García Márquez's fate would have been if he had stayed in Colombia. He would have worked as a journalist during the day to make a living, writing *costumbrista* literature infused with modernist techniques at night, and hanging out with the local literary groups in Barranquilla and Cartagena. He would have obtained a local reputation and faced global oblivion. García Márquez in Barranquilla and Cartagena and de la Cuadra in Guayaquil shared a literary imagination with other members, but their groups were not at the center of a network of producers of mainstream literature. They simply were informed consumers of such literature and amateur writers. If García Márquez had not left these Caribbean groups and joined the Mafia Group in Mexico City, which connected him to the international literary mainstream, he could have not imagined *One Hundred Years of Solitude* as a best-selling work of the New Latin American Novel. It is also worth pointing out that, if he had died at the age of de la Cuadra (thirty-eight years old), García Márquez would have passed away in 1965, that is, exactly when he started writing *One Hundred Years of Solitude*. Had this been the case, he would have left a literary output similar to de la Cuadra's: numerous journalistic pieces, three novellas, and a book of short stories—and all of them as influenced by the styles of *costumbrismo* and social realism as de la Cuadra's works were. García Márquez, like Shakespeare, lived long enough to write his masterpiece and several others. De la Cuadra, like Marlowe, did not.

THE LOCAL FORERUNNER: *LA CASA GRANDE*

According to several members of the Barranquilla Group, its most talented author, capable of writing a major literary work, was not García Márquez but Álvaro Cepeda Samudio. "We were certain, beyond doubt," as group member Germán Vargas put it, "of [his] ability to write, of his firm pulse as a narrator." In 1950, the year García Márquez had the idea for *One Hundred Years of Solitude*, he praised in a newspaper column his friend's "extraordinary conditions for writing." Until the 1960s, their biographies were similar on many fronts. (García Márquez was a year younger.) They shared a literary imagination, professional training, readings, a group of friends, and access to gatekeepers of the publishing industry. Their friendship was so close that they even exchanged ideas for their literary works and read each other's drafts (Cepeda Samudio commented on the final manuscript of *One Hundred Years of Solitude*). Thus, these strong similarities can explain the influence that Cepeda Samudio's *La casa grande* (*The Big House*) had on *One Hundred Years of Solitude*.[10]

Both writers were born in the Caribbean coastal region of Colombia. As *costeños*—the traditional name for those born there—they shared a cultural background. Cepeda Samudio was born in Ciénaga, literally translated as Swamp. This town sits next to the Ciénaga Grande de Santa Marta. With its seven hundred and thirty square kilometers, it is the country's largest area of marshland. Ciénaga and García Márquez's birthplace, Aracataca, are sixty kilometers apart. This large territory and its neighboring towns were central to the writers' imagination. When they met in the late 1940s, they both wanted to write a novel about the area. In their correspondence over the years, they referred to this idea as "the story of the swamp." Eventually, this swamp appears in Cepeda Samudio's work, and García Márquez's Macondo is located in it.[11]

Cepeda Samudio had read classic writers from Spain's Golden Age, as García Márquez did in high school. From the well-off Cepeda Samudio, a fan of Anglo-American modernist fiction, the penniless García Márquez borrowed his copies of books. Cepeda Samudio joined the Barranquilla Group in 1945, three years before García Márquez. As members, they learned how to apply the techniques of modernist authors to their own writing. Spanish exile and group leader Ramón Vinyes commented on the drafts of Cepeda Samudio and García Márquez. Thanks to this group, they knew about current literary works published in other parts of Latin America. Cepeda Samudio, for example, was among the first people in the region to write a review praising *Bestiary*, the first book by Cortázar, published only five months earlier in Buenos Aires. Cepeda Samudio foresaw the quality of this book, while most writers, critics, and readers did not notice it until the Boom of Latin American literature ten years later. Regarding professional training, Cepeda Samudio and García Márquez started their careers as journalists, including daily news coverage, columns, and reportage. In 1949, Cepeda Samudio moved to the United States on a fellowship and decided to pursue a college degree in journalism and literature at Columbia University in New York. He took courses in printing, production, magazine design, and contemporary fiction. More attracted to the city's nightlife than to college work, he did not finish his degree and went back to Barranquilla. After his return, the two writers shared another recent life experience: they were college dropouts.[12]

Early in their careers, they shared a passion for innovative journalism and mainstream modernist literature. So, along with other members of the Barranquilla Group, they launched the literary and sports weekly *Crónica*, which also featured their short stories. García Márquez published his first known attempt at writing *One Hundred Years of Solitude*, and Cepeda Samudio published short pieces, later included in his first book, the compilation of short stories *Todos estábamos a la espera* (*We Were All Waiting*). The group's tiny press, Librería Mundo, released his book. (It came out in 1954, a year earlier than García Márquez's debut book.) Cepeda Samudio's book imported narrative techniques, among other writers, from Ernest Hemingway, especially the usage of first-person narrative. At the same time, García Márquez was also writing short stories following Hemingway's style. He did this in his 1955 reportage on the shipwrecked sailor, which he modeled after *The Old Man and the Sea*. García Márquez read his friend's debut book while it was in progress. And once it came out, he published a laudatory review in his column for the national newspaper *El Espectador*. It is, he wrote, "the best book of short stories that has been published in Colombia."[13] The themes of waiting and solitude are at the center of the leading story that gave title to his friend's book. The theme of waiting would be key in García Márquez's next novella, *No One Writes to the Colonel*, which he started two years later. And the theme of solitude was central to *One Hundred Years of Solitude* a decade later.

Along with literature, the two writers shared another passion: cinema. They envisioned a career in filmmaking. In 1954, they collaborated on the script of *The Blue Lobster*, a surrealist movie. Five years later, they drafted a proposal to open a film school in Barranquilla. Even though this project fell through, two years later, they were still working together on films, such as a documentary on the Carnival of Barranquilla. They also shared connections with two of the most powerful gatekeepers during the heyday of the New Latin American Novel. In the 1960s, Carmen Balcells traveled to Latin America to meet with potential clients including Cepeda Samudio and other members of the Barranquilla Group. (García Márquez met her in Mexico City.) And influential critic Ángel Rama corresponded with Cepeda Samudio about how to best promote his works as examples of the New Latin American Novel, as he did with García Márquez.[14]

As these opportunities came to them, their correspondence confirms that they exchanged ideas about potential stories and the nuts and bolts of writing. "Don't steal it! God damn it!" García Márquez wrote comically in a letter to his friend in which he described to him a new idea for a story. His friend returned the joke by wittily accusing García Márquez of stealing from him the idea for the short story "The Handsomest Drowned Man in the World." It is no coincidence either that García Márquez's working title for his first draft of *One Hundred Years of Solitude* was "The House" and Cepeda Samudio ended up entitling his novella *The Big House*. Their exchanges continued by mail and in person when García Márquez was writing *One Hundred Years of Solitude* and he asked for his friends' feedback.[15] In March 1966, Cepeda Samudio joined him during a trip to the swampy, savanna, and tropical areas around Aracataca (the fictional location of Macondo). At this time, García Márquez was completing the last part of his novel, in which a key event occurs: the banana massacre. García Márquez likely received from his friend precise historical information on the story, which was fresh on his imagination because he had already published *La casa grande*. (García Márquez also sent him the final version of *One Hundred Years of Solitude* for feedback.)[16]

La casa grande tells the story of the strike of 1928 against the foreign banana company in the town of Ciénaga. The strike led to the massacre of hundreds of banana workers. Not only is the strike central to *One Hundred Years of Solitude* but the descriptions of the massacre are factually similar in both literary works. In his novella, Cepeda Samudio modeled his writing technique and style after Faulkner's *The Sound and the Fury*, as García Márquez did in *Leaf Storm*. Cepeda Samudio described events from multiple viewpoints, added changes in the temporal and spatial planes, and called characters not by their names but by their pronouns and roles: sister, brother, father, soldiers. There are also similarities between the plots of *La casa grande* and *One Hundred Years of Solitude*; the story centers on a family and its house, where an atmosphere of family decay grows, as told by testimonies of several of its generations. As the narrative evolves, the stories of the family and the village intertwine. As in *One Hundred Years of Solitude*, termites participate in the destruction of the house. Purple (not yellow) butterflies appear. Incest and solitude are present, too.[17]

Given their shared literary imagination, education, professional interests, and privileged access to gatekeepers in publishing, why did not *La casa grande* attain classic status? Three factors are crucial: Cepeda Samudio's personal and professional choices, the format of *La casa grande*, and the writer's peripheral position vis-à-vis the New Latin American Novel.

1. Personal and professional choices. Cepeda Samudio is a telling example of a talented writer whose bohemian lifestyle hindered a successful career. (On the contrary, García Márquez's bohemian behavior subsided over time). As Germán Vargas put it, "He never had the vocation and craftsmanship for the job of writer as García Márquez did[;] he got involved in what some people call the whirl of life and decided to live the good life." Another Barranquilla Group member, Enrique Scopell, believed that Cepeda Samudio was a superior writer and that García Márquez was simply more "tenacious." (Scopell knew García Márquez's writing ethic as he had helped him research cockfighting for *No One Writes to the Colonel*.) Only when Cepeda Samudio's life was (wrongly) in danger did he write *La casa grande*. "It was necessary," as Vargas explained, "that, due to a diagnostic error, a doctor would dare to say that Álvaro Cepeda was suffering from tuberculosis, so that he locked himself up, drinking milk and putting on paper, in front of his typewriter, this excellent novel."[18]

This lack of writing discipline also reduced the support that critics and agents were willing to offer Cepeda Samudio. Critic Rama wanted to publicize his work as part of the New Latin American Novel. So he published the opening of *La casa grande*, of which he was "an enthusiastic reader," in 1964 in *Marcha*, a leading Uruguayan magazine with regional circulation. Two years later, Rama sent a letter to Cepeda Samudio to inform him that he was writing an essay about contemporary literature, in which he wanted to cite Cepeda Samudio's works. The critic also asked the writer for permission to publish with Arca his hard-to-find first book of short stories. By then, Arca was actively promoting new Latin American literature, including works by García Márquez and Carpentier. Rama also knew, thanks to García Márquez and Germán Vargas, that Cepeda Samudio had written new short stories, and he invited him to submit one to *Marcha*. But Cepeda Samudio repeatedly delayed submissions of new work. Likewise, when his agent Balcells asked for new ideas and works that she could pitch to publishers eager to cash in on the international success of the New Latin American Novel, Cepeda Samudio requested one extension after another. Then, in 1970, he wrote to her, "I have not been able to keep any of the [literary] promises I made to you." Under these circumstances, there was little the powerful critic and literary agent could do to promote his unwritten works. His friend García Márquez, on the other hand, delivered new work at a crucial moment. In 1965, he understood that the time had come to write his first novel. He quit his job and asked for the help (and feedback) from his family, friends, and peers (Cepeda Samudio included) to commit all his energy to writing *One Hundred Years of Solitude*.[19]

Cepeda Samudio also knew it was a crucial time to publish; he was as aware as García Márquez of the momentum of the New Latin American Novel. But he missed the opportunity due to another personal choice: journalism. It is precisely in their different responses to journalism that the two writers' professional biographies started to separate. In 1961, when García Márquez renounced daily journalism, Cepeda Samudio embraced it fully. In October, he became the editor-in-chief of *Diario del Caribe* in Barranquilla. He worked eleven years for this local newspaper and led its modernization. Daily journalism fit his writing work ethic better—rapid conception, production, and circulation—as opposed to committing months and years to a literary work as a professional writer, which was García Márquez's dream.[20]

2. *Format of* La casa grande. With the exception of Juan Carlos Onetti's work, none of the classic works of the new Latin American literature published in the 1960s was a novella. Novels were what mass readers consumed and what commercial publishers more willingly promoted. In other words, what Cepeda Samudio, an unknown writer beyond the literary circles in Bogotá and Barranquilla published in 1962 with the small Colombian press Ediciones Mito was not the standard novel of over three hundred pages: it was a novella of just over one hundred pages. Yet 1962 turned out to be a watershed year for the Spanish-language literary market, when *The Time of the Hero*, a 343-page novel, won the prestigious Biblioteca Breve award. Until then, García Márquez had only written novellas and short stories, just like

Cepeda Samudio. But three years later, he undertook the writing of a novel, fully aware that the market wanted longer works. By choosing the novel format, García Márquez put *One Hundred Years of Solitude* in a more advantageous market position to reach mass readers than the novella *La casa grande*.

3. *An informed writer on the literary periphery.* Thanks to his correspondence with friends such as García Márquez, his job at *Diario del Caribe*, and connections with the publishing industry, Cepeda Samudio knew about the commercial success of New Latin American Novels. But he was not at the center of any mainstream group. His peripheral position as a creator (combined with his lifestyle and journalistic job) affected the imagination, production, and circulation of his work, which remained national rather than Latin American and cosmopolitan. He rarely left the Caribbean region. As with García Márquez, the Barranquilla Group educated Cepeda Samudio and helped him secure a local and national reputation as a writer. But the group could not help him connect with mainstream publishers. (As Germán Vargas did for García Márquez, he helped Cepeda Samudio find national publishers.) Like the early works of García Márquez, *La casa grande* had little circulation in 1962, with a print run of one thousand copies. At this time, the New Latin American Novel was emerging in Buenos Aires, Barcelona, and Mexico City (where García Márquez lived), not in the peripheral Barranquilla. Yet five years later, this novella had a rare second chance, as the market for the New Latin American Novel was booming. A second edition was published in Buenos Aires in 1967, the same year and city where *One Hundred Years of Solitude* came out. García Márquez wrote a strong blurb for *La casa grande* on the back cover: "It represents a new and formidable contribution to the most important literary phenomenon in today's world: the Latin American novel." His endorsement did not help the book become a best seller among consumers. And yet, two years later, García Márquez was now lobbying Luis Alcoriza, an influential player in the Mexican film industry, to adapt *La casa grande* for the big screen. The project fell through.[21]

Unlike the case of de la Cuadra's work, scholars and critics have tried to turn Cepeda Samudio into one of the real Boom writers and add *La casa grande* to the canon of Latin America literature. As the French translator said in 1984, this novella "has not yet become what it actually is: a Latin American classic." In 2015, it was included in the volume *Obra literaria* (*Literary Works*) in the *Archivos* collection—a multinational publishing initiative backed by UNESCO that seeks to canonize works of Latin American writers. This volume presented Cepeda Samudio as an innovator of Latin America literature, who built on narrative techniques from Anglo-American, French, and Russian literatures. To do so, he introduced fragmentary narrative at the same time as major works by Cortázar's *Hopscotch*, Carlos Fuentes's *The Death of Artemio Cruz*, Mario Vargas Llosa's *The Time of the Hero*, published in 1962 and 1963. According to this volume, Cepeda Samudio innovated because he did away with "expired Hispanic *costumbrismo*[,] social realism [and] pure official nationalism." Another edition of the novella was published in 2017. Although these efforts have been more successful than those regarding de la Cuadra's works, the actions of cultural brokers have not turned *La casa grande* into a classic. As is the case for *Los Sangurimas*, the trajectory of Cepeda Samudio's novella shows that the actions of powerful cultural brokers such as UNESCO cannot by default increase the value of a work of art. Counterfactually, had Cepeda Samudio been a more disciplined writer, had he published in 1962 a novel instead of a novella, and had he lived in a more central location with access to mainstream publishers, *La casa grande* might enjoy a higher literary status.[22]

THE CANONICAL BUT NOT CLASSIC NOVEL: *PARADISO*

The novel that the publishing and cultural establishments welcomed as the greatest achievement of Latin American literature was not *One Hundred Years of Solitude* but *Paradiso* (1966). After two decades of publishing, its author, José Lezama Lima, was a major figure of Cuban literature and a consecrated poet in the rest of Latin America among peers and the cultural intelligentsia. In previous years, he had created magazines and hosted groups with the goal of promoting cosmopolitanism: "an artistic tradition was created in Cuba, and the first thing that surprises us, after twenty years, is to realize that we are working at the universal level, without provincialism." Like *One Hundred Years of Solitude*, *Paradiso* was Lezama Lima's first novel. With chapters premiered in several periodicals, this 617-page novel was greatly awaited at a moment when the industry marketed (and the reading public consumed) long cosmopolitan and Latin American novels. France's leading press Gallimard contacted Lezama Lima a year before he finished the novel to buy the publication rights in French. Aware of Gallimard's interest, Le Seuil (which published *One Hundred Years of Solitude* in France) offered Lezama Lima a better deal and eventually published it. Given this and other pre-publication news, influential media did for *Paradiso* what they did not for other contemporary literary works.[23]

The region-spanning magazine *Primera Plana* in Argentina premiered not just one chapter of his novel (as it did with García Márquez, Cortázar, Guillermo Cabrera Infante, and others) but two chapters. One issue also dedicated the cover to Lezama Lima. But instead of the standard photo of the writer, it featured a full-size portrait painting of him. And the main cover line read "America and his new genius." On page one, in the box that highlighted the leading event of the week, the magazine noted, "Argentine readers have begun to devour [*Paradiso* as] one of the canonical texts of Latin American narrative," as readers were already doing in Cuba. The magazine's main literary critic, Tomás Eloy Martínez (who wrote a favorable review of *One Hundred Years of Solitude*), traveled expressly to Havana to interview the "ignored maestro." Martínez wrote a four-page reportage on the writer, his works, and *Paradiso*. Cortázar's enthusiasm for this novel appeared prominently in this *Primera Plana* issue. Given Cortázar's success as a writer, his support ensured that readers in Latin America would take an interest in the novel. (Cortázar also supervised the translations into French and English.) In Mexico, too, the popular supplement *La Cultura en México* featured Lezama Lima on its cover and included enthusiastic endorsements about the book by Cortázar, Manuel Díaz Martínez, and Mario Vargas Llosa. As with *One Hundred Years of Solitude*, members of different generations supported *Paradiso* publicly. Octavio Paz praised Lezama Lima for his masterful use of language and his capacity to write a cosmopolitan Latin American novel.[24]

Across the Atlantic, the Paris-based literary magazine *Mundo Nuevo*, distributed in over twenty countries, presented *Paradiso* as a pathbreaking work of Latin American literature. The person in charge of doing so was again Vargas Llosa, who praised it as an extraordinary achievement of "creative imagination." In Spain, *Paradiso* was well received by writers and critics. One of its most influential and best-selling writers back then, the social realist Camilo José Cela, stated that he liked it. For Catalan poet Pere Gimferrer, *Paradiso* proved the vitality of Latin American literature, along with *One Hundred Years of Solitude* and other novels. Additional promoters of *Paradiso* included writers José Manuel Caballero Bonald, Juan García Hortelano, and critic Rafael Conte, who called it the "true phenomenon of literature of all time." Furthermore, Lezama Lima had on his side the detractors of Latin American Boom literature. José Blanco Amor, who accused writers such as García Márquez to be part of a self-promoting mafia, wrote about Lezama Lima: "This man's talent is so superior to that of today's man."[25]

Yet not even the full support of the media and literary establishment at its peak of influence on the international book market helped *Paradiso* become a best seller. Low sales over the years did not discourage influential critics and scholars, who continued to praise it as a high-quality work. *Paradiso* has several critical editions, including a volume in the canonical collection *Archivos* (1988), and a film adaptation. Also, leading literary scholar Harold Bloom argued that Lezama Lima's treatment of language justified the inclusion of *Paradiso* in the Western canon, rubbing shoulders with the works of Homer, Virgil, Dante, and Shakespeare, among others. Taken together, this evidence shows that *Paradiso* is a great example of how the canonization of a literary work and its consecration as a classic are not exactly the same thing. The endorsement of an influential academic scholar or organization—no matter how powerful they are—does not guarantee that a literary work will be imagined as a classic by other publics. Other cultural brokers need to intervene, as is the case with *One Hundred Years of Solitude*.[26]

Paradiso is what experts call a *Bildungsroman*, a novel that follows the main character during his formative years. In this book, the main character is José Cemí (modeled in part on Lezama Lima). The story tells of his childhood, adolescence, and university years as he follows his path to artistic creation of poetry. Cemí's story is set in Cuba years before the revolution of 1959, and it is also the story of his upper-middle-class family for several decades. But the reputation of this novel does not reside so much in the story itself as much as in how Lezama Lima wrote it, with a sophisticated (and erotic) use of language and constant references to ancient, medieval, and contemporary classic literature, including non-Western literary works.

Yet language is also at the heart of *Paradiso*'s obstacles to become a global classic. This language is neo-baroque, the same one that important writers, critics, and scholars praised as the most adequate tool to write the region's true literature.[27] The reality is that Lezama Lima's demanding language and interwoven narrative has made it a difficult book for most readers. Just a few pages in, readers face sentences that need to be read several times to understand them because they seem to lack words or are labyrinthine: "The Colonel's worktables: he was also an engineer, a fact which bred in his soldiers—as they raptly watched him cover blackboards with coastal-artillery problems—the same devotion that might have been shown a Coptic priest or an Assyrian huntsman-king."[28]

This innovative language and narrative style prevented *Paradiso* from being consumed by mass readers. The novel then fell outside the transnational market of best-selling New Latin American Novels that celebrated *One Hundred Years of Solitude*, despite enthusiastic reviews of *Paradiso*'s translation into English by leading critics and media such as the *New York Times*. Not surprisingly, the novel did well among academics and in a market characterized for its complex, analytical writing: France. There, the first edition of five thousand copies sold out in less than two months and French critics praised Lezama Lima as a "Caribbean Proust." Regarding academics, along with Bloom's endorsement, this novel received praise from Roberto González Echevarría, a leading scholar of Latin American literature. He wrote, *Paradiso* "is a profound work that invents its own discourse and responds to the deepest issues in the human condition," the same kind of appeal to universality that one finds in literary criticism on *One Hundred Years of Solitude*. But this kind of appeal has not elevated *Paradiso* to classic status. It has only secured its reputation as "one of the great novels of Cuba."[29]

THE BELATED NEW LATIN AMERICAN NOVEL:
THE OBSCENE BIRD OF NIGHT

If a writer was ever expected to publish a watershed novel and a major Latin American best seller, that writer was Chilean José Donoso. He was "the most literary novelist of his generation" and the one called to enjoy the position of literary success that García Márquez ended up occupying. He was the rising Latin American star in international literary circles, not García Márquez. Unlike the latter, Donoso came from an upper-middle-class family and was a Princeton University graduate, where he majored in literature. His class background, prestigious education, and fluency in English ensured his rapid admission to the cultural intelligentsia in Latin America and the United States. Early on, he also acted as a gatekeeper and shared his agenda with budding writers. He started to do so when the New Latin American Novel was growing as an international movement. Between 1960 and 1965, he was a critic for Chile's leading weekly magazine, *Ercilla*. He wrote eighty pieces that showed his familiarity with classic and new literary works published in the region and abroad. He also wrote several chronicles of symposia of Latin American writers, most of which he attended. And between 1965 and 1967, he spread his vision of the region's literature as a visiting professor at the prestigious Iowa Writers' Workshop. By then, he was a fully integrated professional with personal, network, and market conditions in his favor.[30]

Critics, writers, the media, publishers, and mass readers were on Donoso's side. In 1958, Chilean critic Ricardo Latcham wrote about him in *Antología del cuento hispanoamericano contemporáneo* (*Anthology of the Contemporary Spanish*

American Short Story) "He contributes, like few members of his generation, to rectify the directions of the short story. . . . He has clear technical mastery and creates interest with small elements, like the classic writers of the genre." Critic Rama praised Donoso as the best writer of "urban critical realism" of his generation; this was a key endorsement when best-selling New Latin American Novels were preferably urban stories. Critic Rodríguez Monegal added Donoso to the New Latin American Novel movement in the early 1960s. Donoso sent him drafts of work in progress for feedback. (García Márquez did the same with critic Carballo during the writing of *One Hundred Years of Solitude*.) Rodríguez Monegal was then editor-in-chief of *Mundo Nuevo*, the flagship magazine of new Latin American literature, and he helped Donoso to position his work as Latin American. International critics were on his side, too. His early works were quickly translated and well received at a time when few New Latin American Novels were reaching audiences worldwide. His books reached them sooner, and Donoso became a Latin American star. English newspaper the *Guardian*, for example, praised him as "a writer of versatility and macabre power."[31]

Along with critics' support, Donoso had that of major gatekeepers of the international publishing industry. At a moment when most Latin American writers could not even imagine hiring a literary agent, Donoso was in the hands of literary agents Carl Brandt in New York and Balcells in Barcelona—centers of the publishing industry in English and Spanish, respectively. The top Latin American publisher, Sudamericana, put out his work, which also received laudatory reviews and awards. His book *Coronation* won the 1962 William Faulkner Foundation Award for notable debut novel and was published in English three years later. Publisher Alfred A. Knopf, donors Barbara and Rodman Rockefeller, and writer John Hersey, author of the famous reportage *Hiroshima* and leading member of New Journalism, were among another twenty guests at the author's book launch party in New York. About *Coronation*, the *Daily Telegraph* in England stated, "A startlingly lively novel . . . the writing of the book has great vigour."[32]

Peers were also on Donoso's side. All the positive things that Fuentes, the leader of the Mafia Group, did for García Márquez, he did even more for his childhood friend Donoso. In person and by mail, Fuentes recommended his friend's work to international publishers, literary agents, and critics. Fuentes encouraged Donoso to send *Coronation* to Brandt for publication in English.[33] Years later, not only did Fuentes invite his friend to join the Mafia, but Donoso also lived in Fuentes's house in Mexico while writing the novel *Hell Has No Limits*. (At the same time, García Márquez had to retreat from work for a year, fell behind on rent payments, and lived on credit to write *One Hundred Years of Solitude*.)

In terms of literary imagination, Donoso and García Márquez shared an interest in houses. Donoso acknowledged that most of his novels—*The Obscene Bird of Night* included—happen in houses, as *One Hundred Years of Solitude* does. In Mexico, not only their imaginations but also their biographies started to converge. (At this time, the biographies of Cepeda Samudio and García Márquez started to diverge.) Donoso and García Márquez had moved repeatedly, and their moves strengthened their professional networks. Both emigrated to Mexico because they could not make it as professional writers in their own countries. In Donoso's case, the publishing industry in Chile was underdeveloped and new literary trends were poorly received. Like García Márquez, Donoso had to distribute and sell his own books. They probably met in 1965 at a professional conference in Mexico and confessed to each other they were suffering from paralyzing writer's block. What added to their anxiety was that they knew that the New Latin American Novel was one of the most commercially successful literary trends at the time. Donoso knew this even better than García Márquez because he was at the center of the trend. United by literary and professional anxieties, they became friends and members of the Mafia. They both had great literary expectations for their work.[34]

García Márquez imagined *One Hundred Years of Solitude* as his watershed novel. Donoso imagined *The Obscene Bird of Night* as his. With its 543 pages and cosmopolitan title taken from Henry James, Donoso wanted his book to be his best-selling New Latin American Novel. His peers, agent, critics, and readers had been waiting for it since the mid-1960s. To promote it, he followed the same marketing strategy his peers had used. Between 1964 and 1967, he premiered chapters of his book in progress in the same mainstream, region-spanning outlets in which chapters of *One Hundred Years of Solitude* also appeared; *Marcha*, *Diálogos*, *Primera Plana*, and *Mundo Nuevo*. As they did for García Márquez, critics praised Donoso's advance chapters.[35]

But despite ample support, visibility, and the author's prestige, *The Obscene Bird of Night* was not a best seller. Briefly, this nonlinear novel tells the story of a house, its multiple occupants, and successive generations of the declining Azcoitia family. It contains gothic events such as a deformed boy and his court of servants. This novel's thematic similarities with *One Hundred Years of Solitude* are abundant. Over the years, Donoso's novel has received the endorsement of influential critics. Like *Paradiso*, critic Bloom considers it to be a part of the Western canon.[36] So, why did not a literary work (and a writer) expected to be as important as *One Hundred Years of Solitude* (and García Márquez) attain global classic status? Considering the novel's text and its themes, the writing, language, and topic of *The Obscene Bird of Night* were not much different from those novels that garnered him success a few years before. Then, why did not the novel succeed? Other factors beyond the text ended up being more important for the novel's fate, especially the writer's personality and censorship.

Artists' personalities can influence the trajectory of their work, because they can affect the support of their peers. In that way, Donoso was a confrontational figure. After joining the Mafia, he had arguments with writers and members Juan García Ponce, Juan Vicente Melo, José Emilio Pacheco, Salvador Elizondo, and even Fuentes. The turning point was, arguably, his review of the novel *Beber un caliz* (*Drinking a Chalice*) by Ricardo Garibay. It was published in the July 14, 1965 issue of the cultural supplement *La Cultura en México* (the publishing outlet for most members of the Mafia). His review made several contentious generalizations about the past and present of Mexican literature (a tradition to which Fuentes and most Mafia members belonged): "In the dryness of Mexican prose today, finally, a book written with emotion." His intention was to praise Garibay's novel. But his review had more controversial and patronizing statements: "It will be said: an unpleasant book. But it is not. On the contrary, there are times when it has great nobility." He went on to use stronger language in reference to the novel's style: "This mannerism is regrettable." Mixing patronizing praise with open criticism, he even wondered about Garibay's capabilities: "Will this author so extraordinarily gifted be able to write a book that is more than a piece of himself?" Donoso's statements were so offensive that a staff member at *La Cultura en México* printed a line in bold at the end of the review: "Very good at criticizing but he is a poor beast. . . ." This insulting line reached the supplement's hundreds of thousands weekly readers and provoked a furious letter from Donoso to the editors. They publicly apologized to him in an open letter, claimed that he was a "friend," called that line an inexplicable typographic error, and opened an investigation. A few weeks later, the editors found a scapegoat. They accused a linotypist of inserting the offending line, and he was fired. But this episode was not the end of the Mafia's growing animosity toward Donoso.[37]

Barely two months later, the September 29 issue of *La Cultura en México* featured Fuentes on its cover and included an eleven-page reportage. The reason for this coverage was Fuentes's momentous public talk about his career a few weeks earlier. The reportage contained a photomontage of a party of Mafia members that was humorously named after the classic movie: "Gone with the Mafia" ("Lo que la Mafia se llevó"). Photos of party participants had speech bubbles over their heads to parody their conversations. Donoso appeared in only one picture. He was seated and, unlike most guests, wore a formal suit. His speech bubble included no words, only typical symbols of angry cartoon talk: ☆◉! In front of him, a smiling Fuentes was looking away and saying, "This bearded man is very good at criticizing" in clear reference to the insulting line in his review. The photomontage included three photos of García Márquez that showed him in a really different light. In one photo, he had a drink in his hand and a comic expression on his face. In another, he was dancing with writer Elena Garro. And in the third, he was putting a jacket on a woman and saying kindly, "Wrap up well, golden bones, it is raining in Macondo." These photos highlighted two important facts about the different status of Donoso and García Márquez within the Mafia. First, García Márquez was blending in and strengthening ties with members of the cultural intelligentsia. And second, they heard him talk about Macondo. Not coincidentally, at this precise moment, September 1965, he was starting to work on *One Hundred Years of Solitude* and several Mafia members were about to help him do that. Contrary to Donoso, who had arguments with Melo and Pacheco, these peers collaborated with García Márquez as his research assistants for *One Hundred Years of Solitude*. (Later on, García Márquez's older son married the daughter of Elizondo, with whom Donoso also had arguments.) In sum, García Márquez, rather than being confrontational, followed the status quo, was cooperative, and in return received the group's professional support during the writing, production, and early circulation of his novel. Donoso did not.

Donoso continued to antagonize peers as well as publishers and critics. His masterpiece, *The Obscene Bird of Night*, was all set to win the 1970 Biblioteca Breve from Seix Barral. The award would have greatly increased sales and attracted offers for foreign translations, as it did for other books over the last decade. But the novel did not win due to a growing internal conflict within the company. It was partly prompted by the unsuccessful attempt to give the 1969 award to *One Hundred Years of Solitude*. But Donoso himself recognized years later that he had an argument with Barral, which may have prevented the reception of the award. His personality also got in the way of his inclusion in *Into the Mainstream*, a best-selling book about major Latin American writers. Its editor, Chilean Luis Harss, received recommendations from Cortázar and Fuentes to include Donoso, a fellow Chilean. Harss had read his award-winning novel *Coronation* and did not like the language: "I could not understand well what he said, his sentences were difficult." His negative opinion extended to the writer himself after meeting him. "I found him ambitious and mediocre," Harss said.[38] He did not include Donoso, but he followed Fuentes's recommendation regarding the inclusion of a writer who, unlike Donoso, was unknown to most readers and publishers: García Márquez. *Into the Mainstream* also publicized his next novel, *One Hundred Years of Solitude*. His inclusion in this volume attracted the attention of major commercial publishers, which offered him a contract to publish his next novel in Spanish and in English when he had just barely started writing it.

The Spanish censor was another gatekeeper that Donoso antagonized. Before the early 1960s, none of his work had been censored in Spain. Quite the opposite; censors praised his "Hispanic" style. They thought it was reminiscent of the style of Pío Baroja, one of the major figures of twentieth-century Spanish literature. (Curiously, Donoso belittled Baroja in his personal diaries: "First of all, I think he's just a silly writer.") Spanish censorship subsided in the mid-1960s to help its booming publishing sector. But paradoxically, it was then when Donoso's works started to run into problems with censors. In 1967, *Hell Has No Limits*, published months before in Mexico, did not clear censorship in Spain until the following decade. Two years later, censors accused *The Obscene Bird of Night* of pornography and complained that no line in the text condemned the characters' attitude; by now, this stipulation was a censor's minimum condition to grant approval. It meant that Donoso faced censorship at the worst moment of his writing career, just when New Latin American Novels were trendy products in the literary market. Censors delayed the publication of his most important novel for at least a year, while *One Hundred Years of Solitude* cleared censorship in less than three weeks.[39]

The case of Donoso is a reminder of the importance of censors as gatekeepers in publishing. (They got in the way of another unsuccessful New Latin American Novel, Cabrera Infante's *Three Trapped Tigers*, released the same year as *One Hundred Years of Solitude*.) After several delays, *The Obscene Bird of Night* came out in 1970. Its rapidly decreasing sales (a first edition of fifteen thousand copies and a second edition of five thousand a year later) and awareness that his time had passed made Donoso increasingly pessimistic and bitter. His daughter's memoirs show, he grew resentful toward García Márquez's fame. He believed that his novel should have been the one in the spotlight, not *One Hundred Years of Solitude*. Although Donoso joined the group of genuine Boom writers who gathered in Barcelona from 1968 onward, he decided to live far from the city. Vargas Llosa and García Márquez, meanwhile, lived only blocks away from each other in the city, offered mutual feedback on their work in progress, and visited their agent Balcells weekly, which led to an intimate, lifelong professional relationship. In comparison, Donoso soon had problems with Balcells. He portrayed her as an abusive person in his 1972 book, *The Boom in Spanish American Literature*. The fact that he slowly became the antagonist of the group of Boom writers was confirmed by editor Carlos Barral himself (who released most of Donoso's novels in Spain): "I didn't know [him] well."[40] His pessimism turned into literary hatred. In 1981, he published the novel *The Garden Next Door*, in which he attacked Balcells, García Márquez, and the Latin American Boom.

In sum, early in his career, Donoso was more stable in his literary output than García Márquez. His productivity secured him quicker international visibility, higher sales, and stronger ties to the publishing establishment and mass readers. But he published his breakthrough work when the New Latin American Novel was facing increasing competition and right when *One Hundred Years of Solitude* topped the market. His never-ending confrontations with peers, agents, publishers, and censors played against the expected success of *The Obscene Bird of Night*. These clashes isolated him when he most needed collaborators on his side to publicize his novel, and this separation jeopardized the novel's success among his once-loyal mass readers.

A PERIPHERAL VIEWPOINT: *THE FOX FROM UP ABOVE AND THE FOX FROM DOWN BELOW*

"Maybe Latin American literature is a journey from the depression of Arguedas to the enthusiasm of García Márquez," University of Iowa professor and Spanish writer Manuel Vilas wrote. More than five decades after his suicide, Peruvian writer José María Arguedas occupies a secondary position in standard histories of Latin American literature. But in the 1950s and 1960s, his professional standing was quite different. He was an avid participant in the meetings of international intellectuals and authors who sought to create a regional community of writers. These meetings contributed to the aesthetic liberation of Latin American literature in the region and internationally. Back then, Arguedas fitted well. He had a Latin American outlook. In 1964, his vision of the region was featured in the special issue on Latin American literature of the mainstream journal *Casa de las Américas*. It included the work of three generations of Latin American writers, plus several articles about them. (The person in charge of praising Arguedas was Vargas Llosa, who four years later became his fierce critic; see chapter 5.) Arguedas was also engaged in what peers regarded as a key component to achieving the region's cultural autonomy: language. His strategy on that front was to favor the "*quechuización*" of Spanish. This meant incorporating in his literary writing words, grammar, and syntax taken from Quechua, an indigenous language spoken by the

Quechua peoples in the Andes and highlands of South America. Influential critics in favor of Latin Americanism supported this linguistic strategy. In 1962, Chilean Latcham wrote in his best-selling *Antología del cuento hispano-americano contemporáneo*, "Arguedas's stories offer us the most refined version of the true Indian." Two years later, critic Rama referred to him as the "admirable narrator of Peruvian indigenism." A decade later, the critic continued to praise Arguedas for using indigenous language in his prose. His name was also known to common readers in the region.[41]

The problem, however, was that Arguedas had a different understanding of Latin America. His style was not cosmopolitan Latin Americanism. For him, the indigenous legacy defined the region, so his viewpoint was different from the one embraced by Cortázar, Carpentier, Fuentes, and Vargas Llosa, leading partisans of the New Latin American Novel. Rather than using Quechua (or other indigenous languages), these writers favored Latin American Spanish influenced by the baroque language of the Golden Age of Spanish literature in the seventeenth century and by mid-twentieth century Anglo-American modernism. These influences evolved into neo-baroque language, which writers such as García Márquez used to imagine literary works like *One Hundred Years of Solitude*. In 1964, Arguedas published his longest and most ambitious novel, *Todas las sangres* (*All the Bloods*). It came out the same year García Márquez was reporting from Mexico City to his friend in Colombia that *Hopscotch*, *The Death of Artemio Cruz*, *The Time of the Hero*, and *Explosion in a Cathedral* were selling really well internationally. These Latin American novels embraced a cosmopolitan view of the region. Arguedas's novel, on the contrary, presented, "an archaic and utopian world," as Vargas Llosa later described it.[42] Paradoxically, these are also the characteristics of Macondo in *One Hundred Years of Solitude*: an archaic and utopian world. But in this case, they were imagined as cosmopolitan by García Márquez and framed as such by his peers (including Vargas Llosa), critics, and common readers.

By the late 1960s, Arguedas's indigenist Latin Americanism started to clash with leading ideologues of the New Latin American Novel, when this movement started attracting international attention, growing sales, and prestigious awards. Arguedas criticized Fuentes for his trivial universalism and exchanged insults with Cortázar, accusing him of being a snobbish cosmopolitan. Cortázar then accused Arguedas for being a folkloric provincial. Their confrontation forced Vargas Llosa, a fellow Peruvian, to attack his compatriot and defend his friend Cortázar. (Vargas Llosa continued to criticize Arguedas even after his death.)[43]

Scholars and critics have noticed that adversaries treated Arguedas very harshly. "Vargas Llosa," Harss explained, "was against any indigenism, but Arguedas was more than that." Harss liked Arguedas's work (unlike Donoso's) and thought about selecting it for *Into the Mainstream*. Counterfactually, if Harss had chosen his work, the fate of Arguedas and that of indigenist Latin Americanism would have been quite different. But Harss did not include him because, as he explained four decades later, "Even today, I don't know what to do with a writer like him." Indeed, Arguedas is a difficult writer to classify. Whereas critics and scholars regarded him as an indigenist writer, he rejected the label as early as 1950: "It has been said of my novels *Agua* (*Water*) and *Yawar Fiesta* that they are indigenist or Indian. And it is not true." He declined aesthetic labeling at a time when contemporaries such as Carpentier were doing the opposite: imagining labels such as "the marvelous real" with the goal of finding a common aesthetic ground for a region-spanning Latin American literature. His rejection of labels was the opposite of what García Márquez did. With the help of collaborators, he worked his way up to position *One Hundred Years of Solitude* as part of the New Latin American Novel and himself as a professional Latin American writer. Furthermore, not only did Arguedas avoid stylistic labels, but he also declared himself an "anti-professionalist." This additional rejection turned him into an adversary of Latin American authors seeking full-time professional writing. So, Arguedas's aesthetic homelessness and anti-professionalism ended up puzzling critics who, like Harss, wanted to publicize his Latin American viewpoint in the region and beyond.[44]

The literary nonagenda of Arguedas is present in *The Fox from Up Above and the Fox from Down Below*, published posthumously in 1971 by leading Argentine press Losada.[45] At the heart of this 325-page novel—the perfect length for what many readers consumed and publishers marketed—is the same narrative that drives the plot of *One Hundred Years of Solitude*: the destructive consequences of rapid modernization in a small town. The port of Chimbote—a real place located in northern Peru—experienced a fishing boom, which turned it into a rapidly industrialized town. This fast development was bad for Chimbote, which suffered from the vices of modern life: crime, brothels, and unruly bars. The same vices that led to the decline of Macondo, which modernized quickly during its banana plantation fever. Not only are the master plots of *One Hundred Years of Solitude* and *The Fox from Up Above and the Fox from Down Below* essentially the same, but Arguedas also stated that he liked García Márquez's book (while criticizing other New Latin American Novels). Another remarkable similarity between the two novels has to do with indigenism and *costumbrismo*. Critic Rama noticed elements of indigenism in *One Hundred Years of*

Solitude.[46] García Márquez declared to have a *costumbrista* background in an interview published the fall of 1965, when he had just started *One Hundred Years of Solitude.* Arguedas was also perceived as part of the branch of *costumbrismo* that dealt with indigenous people. But as seen above, he was criticized for it. His descriptions of archaic and rural communities, which were so central to the initial success of *One Hundred Years of Solitude,* were framed as idealistic, romantic, and out of touch in *The Fox from Up Above and the Fox from Down Below.*[47] Underlying their different descriptions of rural life was a critical factor: their imagination. In *The Fox from Up Above and the Fox from Down Below,* Arguedas expressed his "anti-universalist" view of Latin America.[48] *One Hundred Years of Solitude,* on the contrary, was imagined by his author and collaborators as a cosmopolitan work, and it was marketed as such to consumers who had already developed a taste for New Latin American Novels.

The fate of Arguedas was depression and ultimately suicide. The fate of García Márquez was success and eventually consecration as a literary icon. Only in the 1990s, due to criticism of the idea of Latin America as the product of elite, white Creole writers, did *The Fox from Up Above and the Fox from Down Below* and Arguedas attract some renewed attention, but mainly in scholarly circles.[49] Despite the efforts of academic cultural brokers ever since, Arguedas's novel remains unknown to other cultural brokers that could raise its global literary value, reminding us that no single group of brokers has the power to shape all public opinions on the value of a work of art.

CODA

By now, readers will have noticed two important absences in the selection of literary counterfactuals: female and nonwhite authors. As I discussed in chapter 5, their absence explains an important feature of Latin American literature in the 1960s: the New Latin American Novel was mainly the "creation" of males and, for the most part, whites. This exclusion prevented works by female writers from three generations, such as Silvina Ocampo, Clarice Lispector, and Rosario Castellanos, to become global classics. In the case of Brazilian Lispector in the 1970s, even with the support of the Balcells Agency and Sudamericana Press, which published four of her books, did not help circulate her work as widely in the region as it did for male writers. Although Sudamericana and Balcells tried to add her to the Latin American Boom, other factors, not simply the support of powerful gatekeepers, are necessary for a cultural good to attain best-selling success and classic status. The same can be said about the lack of nonwhite authors during the Boom. Its members were whites of Creole descent, including the indigenist Arguedas.

CONCLUSION

A literary work does not become a classic because its contents speak to all people across centuries and because it reveals universal truths about human nature. The universal is no more than a set of long-lasting beliefs shared by cultural brokers, who use these beliefs to define what they recognize as universal. And this recognition, which often takes the form of the aesthetics of the work of art, is culturally and historically specific. The five literary counterfactuals analyzed here (and another twenty-five mentioned in the endnotes) shared crucial similarities, some of which explain the success of *One Hundred Years of Solitude*: scope, language, style, theme, and so on. But comparing this novel to literary works that have not become global classics further demonstrates that no single factor underlies the classic status of *One Hundred Years of Solitude*. Instead, explanations of how literary works attain classic value must rely on the elective affinities (or long-term interactions) among these factors and not just in the uniqueness and strength of each factor.

CONCLUSION

Perhaps the future of [*One Hundred Years of Solitude*] is like that of
Don Quixote, a classic book that is bought, put on the shelf of the house,
but nobody ever reads it.

—Alejandro Herrero-Olaizola[1]

In 2009, during a talk on arts and politics at Harvard University, I asked Latin American writer Carlos Fuentes how a literary work becomes a classic. "A literary work," he answered, "stands because of its literary value . . . let me be clear about this, I think in literature what counts basically is the quality of the imagination and of the language . . . what counts and remains is the quality of the work, the quality of the imagination and the language." In his response, Fuentes, like me, referred to a factor that most studies about the consecration of cultural objects overlook: imagination.

No work of art is produced without first being imagined, no matter whether it is Homer's *Iliad*, Michelangelo's *The Creation of Adam*, or The Beatles's *Yesterday*. Before the work of art is produced and circulates, the creator (often with the help of collaborators) has to overcome multiple obstacles to imagine it. Once it is made, the work of art can quickly or gradually disappear from view. It can also be rediscovered, make a splash, and vanish again. But only a handful of works of art achieve the long-term visibility associated with classics. In the case of *One Hundred Years of Solitude*, García Márquez and his collaborators imagined this novel in the 1960s in the niche of the New Latin American Novel. And then, from the 1970s onward, cultural brokers have intervened, using the novel in ways that its creator both intended and did not intend. And in so doing, they have helped expand the novel's reach and global value. Among these brokers are common readers, non-readers, artists, publishers, booksellers, teachers, celebrities, politicians, universities, book clubs, private companies, non-profit organizations, national governments, mass media, and social media. Sometimes the names we give to these brokers change throughout history. Monks in European convents during the Middle Ages and translators in Abbasid Baghdad brokered the classic status of literary texts from Ancient Greece. They handwrote copies of these texts that are the basis for modern editions. Many brokers will never see their names in history books, such as the thousands of people who have turned the *Mona Lisa* into one of the most reproduced paintings of all time. Distant and anonymous as they might be, these brokers contribute in different degrees to the making and visibility of a classic. They do so for *One Hundred Years of Solitude*.

Those participating in the imagination, production, and early circulation of the work of art lose control over it as years pass. They are replaced by cultural brokers and their influence over the work's long-term circulation. Brokers' involvement is what makes the classic possible as a public good with durable value that transcends cultural boundaries. The classic's trajectory is independent from the actions of the people and organizations that brought it into being and, at the same time, its status depends on the aggregate result of the actions of multiple brokers over time. For this reason, being a classic has little to do with the deep-seated belief that the classic work of art is more "universal" than others. Instead, being a classic has everything to do with the continuous support of cultural brokers.

This book also argued that if we want to explain the making of a work of art (especially the classic) we must understand how the stages of imagination, production, and circulation intersect. Until recently, most researchers studied these stages individually and focused on the last two. In reality, the boundaries between these three stages are more porous than previously believed. And it is their joint intervention that turns a cultural object into a classic, as it has happened to *One Hundred Years of Solitude*. Critics, for example, can help the creator to imagine the work of art as it is being made. García Márquez received feedback on his novel from leading critics while he was writing it. Obviously, the case of this novel is not unique, and more research is necessary to show how critics influence the making of works of art and hence how they sometimes act before the stage of circulation (where most research sees them as influencers in the creation of the value of the work of art).

Artists, who are often seen as participants only in the stages of imagination and production, can also influence the stage of circulation by acting as critics of their peers' works. In so doing, these artist-critics can shape the taste of professional critics and mass readers before they come in contact with the work of art. Fuentes, Mario Vargas Llosa, and other writers published reviews in international media praising *One Hundred Years of Solitude*. And they started to do so one year before the novel's release and when García Márquez was still writing it. Their reviews, based on an unfinished manuscript, molded how thousands of general readers and influential critics first received the novel in Latin America and beyond.

Readers can also influence the making of a work of art when an artist shares with them the work in progress to test their reactions. This allows the artist to benefit from readers' feedback and, if necessary, change the work before its completion. García Márquez, imitating what his peers did, started to premiere chapters of *One Hundred Years of Solitude* when he was five months away from completing it and more than a year before its publication. He premiered one-third of the novel to receive feedback about his work from readers, peers, and critics present in the stages of production and circulation. And in so doing, two things happened. First, the artist, who was still imagining the work of art, left his mark in the stage of circulation by sharing work in progress with advance readers. And second, the feedback he received from these readers entered the stage of imagination and shaped the artistic choices that the writer and his collaborators were making about the novel still unfinished.

Present in the stages of imagination, production, and circulation, there are three strategies of making art that researchers have also studied independently: adaptation, collaboration, and competition. Briefly put, some researchers argue that a work of art only gets produced and circulated when it meets the conditions of the art market. Others claim that the work of art results from the collaboration between creators and gatekeepers. And others contend that, to be produced and circulated, the work of art has to win over competing works. These three explanations get several things right. But they also overlook the importance of imagination and how it helps certain literary works resonate more than others. To be successfully imagined, *One Hundred Years of Solitude* had to adapt to the creative conditions set by the New Latin American Novel. To be successfully written, the author and his collaborators engaged in networked creativity. And to be successfully released, this novel had to comply with the market conditions of the Spanish-language publishing industry and, at the same time, compete against other literary works on the market. Then, as years passed, the novel's consecration as a classic also required collaboration, adaptation, and competition among cultural brokers that appropriated this novel to praise it, conform to the status quo, or criticize it. Unlike praise and conformity, entrenched criticism is an understudied factor that contributes to classic status and calls for further research. In the case of *One Hundred Years of Solitude*, over half a century after its publication, its haters are as bellicose an army as its lovers.

The classic status of *One Hundred Years of Solitude* is ensured for the years to come, as it continues to enter the lives of new generations of readers (and non-readers) globally. In 2020, the Harry Ransom Center at the University of Texas at Austin, which owns the Gabriel García Márquez Papers, opened a blockbuster exhibition dedicated to his life and works. Among the items on display was the manuscript of *One Hundred Years of Solitude*. Netflix, too, is finalizing the production of the first adaptation of this novel for the screen. News about the adaptation provoked a global controversy since García Márquez, who died in 2014, rejected several offers to adapt it. Many predicted a catastrophic adaptation. But the truth is that no classic has lost that distinction because of a bad version. On the contrary, controversy about the quality of the adaptation reinforces the novel's global visibility and standing as a classic.

Both the Ransom Center and Netflix are cultural brokers with no links to the niche in which *One Hundred Years of Solitude* was made. The Ransom Center opened its doors seven years after García Márquez conceived the idea for his novel. And Netflix was founded in 1997, thirty years after the novel's publication. One cultural broker is a research and public institution, whose mission is to preserve for future generations the papers of writers such as Virginia Woolf, Lewis Carroll, and James Joyce and works such as Geoffrey Chaucer's *The Canterbury Tales*, Luís de Camões's *The Lusiads*, and William Shakespeare's first folio. The other cultural broker, Netflix, is a private entertainment company. With more than one hundred and fifty million subscribers in over two hundred countries, it competes against Hollywood over the global production of popular media culture. The Ransom Center and Netflix are new additions to the list of thousands of cultural brokers on seven continents that keep reinforcing the status of this novel as a global classic more than half a century after its publication. And until new cultural winds do away with the support of these and other brokers, *One Hundred Years of Solitude* will continue to stand as the peculiar kind of social institution known as the classic.

APPENDIX

WHY AND HOW TO STUDY CLASSICS?

A common social situation inspired me to write this book: people can admit something has high value without firsthand knowledge of it. Someone will say, for example, that a literary work is a classic without having read it. Or people might have a conversation about a book while hiding the fact they have not read it. This kind of situation poses an intriguing sociological problem. Do even nonreaders of a literary work, let's say *Hamlet*, pass on from generation to generation the belief that the book is a classic? If so, how? And more broadly, can the actions of people without firsthand knowledge of something be necessary to keep a situation or even social life going? The study of classic works of art is relevant to answer these questions because from generation to generation people with little or no knowledge of those works help to retain their high value. And in doing so, the classic enters the lives of new generations as a social institution. This is the way most nonreaders of *Hamlet* encounter it throughout their lives, not simply as a literary work but as a social institution. Thus, it should come as no surprise that, over time, the classic grows into an object whose influence branches out into multiple social arenas, such as symbolic boundaries, cultural differences, emotions, aesthetics, and history. Given their ramified quality, classics are especially useful for interdisciplinary research in the fields of cultural sociology, literary studies, and history of the book.[1] For practitioners in these fields, the findings of this book have implications in four areas: value, cultural brokers, and collective representations; myths, inevitability, genius, and the universal; power, circulation, and world literature; and materiality and social relations.

CULTURAL MAKING

To understand how a work of art becomes a classic, one has to study how it was conceived in the first place. Conception happens in what I call the stage of imagination, which refers to the aesthetic ideas, creative techniques, intellectual principles, professional values, and social expectations that make it possible for an artist to imagine a work of art at a given moment. In this stage, artists encounter the first barriers that they have to overcome, often with the help of collaborators, in order to make the work of art. They need to have a place to work and time to think and develop their ideas. And certainly they are better off if they have peers and mentors to talk to about their ideas. These are some of the barriers that exist before the other barriers that artists face during the production and circulation of a work of art. By the time the work of art enters production and circulation, artists are already committed to making it. The barriers that they encounter then are different and better studied. In the case of a literary work, these barriers include finding a publisher, negotiating a favorable publishing contract, and receiving positive reviews. So, before a work of art is made, the people and conditions present in the stage of imagination filter which works an artist can imagine now, which ones will need to wait longer, and which ones will never be imagined. Because of the filter of imagination, Leonardo da Vinci could conceive the *Mona Lisa* but not *The Starry Night*. The ideas, techniques, principles, values, and expectations necessary to imagine the latter painting and similar others were only accessible to artists like Vincent van Gogh but not to da Vinci or his contemporaries.

Although social forces shape how an artist imagines a work of art, researchers have preferred to focus on the stages of production and circulation, as if one could readily and solely find in these two stages all the answers to the making of a work of art.[2] But the reality is that no work can ever be produced and marketed without overcoming the obstacles present in the stage of imagination. The influence of this stage is more evident for classics. Explaining their consecration requires studying more than just their production and circulation. Classic works of art capture in complex ways the imagination of a historical and cultural moment and at the same time they transcend that moment by entering into the lives of future generations that will consume them. This book analyzes what the stage of imagination does along with the stages of production and circulation—I call this the study of *cultural making*—in order to offer an all-encompassing explanation of how a work of art becomes a classic.

THE CLASSIC AS A SOCIAL INSTITUTION

A classic work of art is more than a memorable set of images, notes, or words. Mixed together with these aesthetic ingredients, the classic carries with it norms, values, beliefs, and emotions that are integral to the societies in which the classic is revered and also, let us not forget, criticized. This is why the study of classics matters sociologically. The classics are cultural units that transmit ideas and feelings that serve to educate, inspire, and antagonize us; make us happy or sad; and, of course, entertain or bore us. Think about the *Epic of Gilgamesh*, the *Story of Sinuhe*, the *Odyssey*, and the *Mahābhārata*. They are among humanity's oldest cultural objects and have survived to this day for a reason. And this reason has something to do with their capacity to transmit (not always in perfect condition) a blueprint of norms, values, beliefs, and emotions in ways that other works of art or cultural objects cannot. Classics, in this sense, behave as social institutions that safeguard such a blueprint. Given their power, it is difficult to imagine social life without classics. Imagine for just a moment a world in which a melancholic prince never said "To be, or not to be, that is the question," a lunatic knight did not fight against windmills, or a big bad wolf did not trick a girl on her way to her grandmother's house.

The power of classics is such that all kinds of people and organizations willingly protect them as part of the world's heritage. In anticipation of a major catastrophe on Earth, the Doomsday Vault preserves digitized copies of several classics. They are buried in a mine in the Arctic. There, too, the Global Seed Vault safeguards the world's largest collection of crop diversity. The preservation of seeds tries to ensure the survival of the human species after a planetary disaster, and the protection of classics seeks to guarantee the continuation of humanity's culture. Beyond planet Earth, classics designate places in the universe. To date, twenty-five of Uranus's twenty-seven moons are named after characters in Shakespeare's plays, while Beethoven, Rembrandt, and Dickens are the names of craters on Mercury. Likewise, classics are part of humanity's efforts to contact intelligent extraterrestrial life. The *Voyager 1* and *Voyager 2* spacecrafts have been exploring outer space for decades. They have attached to their outside a golden record with information about life on our planet. This record can play natural sounds like thunder, wind, songs of birds as well as musical selections from classics by Mozart and Beethoven. These compositions are now part of nature that humans have created and are also telling examples of why it is so difficult to imagine social life without classics.

Before the Doomsday Vault was built and the *Voyager* spacecrafts were launched, researchers already knew about the normative power of the arts over social relations in general and about the strong relation between social institutions and literary texts in particular. And they knew about these connections because research on the arts has been at the forefront of key advances in the study of society over the past two centuries.[3] Karl Marx was an avid reader of Honoré de Balzac. He hoped to finish *Das Kapital* quickly so he could write a study of Balzac's novels to further understand the ills of capitalism. Although he never wrote that study, in his introduction to *A Contribution to the Critique of Political Economy*, he noticed that classic art lives beyond its conditions of production. Émile Durkheim found in objects of so-called primitive art, such as the totem, an answer to the origins of society. Max Weber's analysis of music systems in the West and beyond helped him develop his famous ideas on rationalization in modern societies. Georg Simmel insisted on the autonomy of the aesthetic sphere in his book on the Dutch painter Rembrandt. In his study of Mozart, Norbert Elias proposed a pioneering sociological explanation of the concept of genius. And at the center of Pierre Bourdieu's field theory was his book on Gustave Flaubert's classic novel *Sentimental Education*. Research on the arts from a humanities and social scientific viewpoint keeps developing innovative approaches to the study of society.[4]

Thanks to this research, there are several explanations for how works of art become classics. For some researchers, the classic is first and foremost the work of a genius. An argument along these lines would mean that Michelangelo alone changed the course of art history with his paintings in the Sistine Chapel. According to another explanation, what gives a work of art its classic status is its form, that is, its style, materials, technical achievements, and so on. This means that the *Mona Lisa* is a classic because of its formal attributes such as the stylistic conventions of a Renaissance portrait; mixtures of pigments like lead white, burnt umber, and red lac; and the use of aerial perspective, sfumato, and *verdaccio* underpainting. Almost at the opposite end is another explanation: the value of a classic does not reside in its formal characteristics but in its social context. A work of art is a classic because it is the best product of an important historical moment. Therefore, a work such as George Orwell's *1984* would be the offspring of the rise of totalitarianism in Europe and World War II. Finally, in their explanation, other researchers stress the role of gatekeepers—agents, producers, critics, and so on—whose actions create and maintain a work's classic status. A clear example of gatekeepers' influence is that of French publisher Gallimard. It famously rejected for publication the first volume of Marcel Proust's novel *In Search of Lost Time*.

But shortly after, Gallimard changed its mind, bought the publishing rights from the smaller Grasset, and gave the novel more international fame it could ever have obtained with Grasset. The story of this novel's transformation into a classic is now inseparable from this gatekeeper's support.

Each of these explanations gets something right, but there are also important pieces missing. Rather than presenting the classic as the work of a genius, this book defines the genius as a hypersocialized person. Simply put, the so-called genius is someone who masters the rules of the social game in which that person participates and hence can successfully bend and transform such rules, if necessary. In the case of the game of making art, first, the genius masters the conventions of a given domain of artistic practice (quickly or after decades of learning, but never completely alone). Second, the genius transforms these conventions via an innovative work (and in a seemingly effortless way). And third, the genius receives the support of the art establishment and the public for the resulting groundbreaking work. In the case of *One Hundred Years of Solitude*, it took García Márquez almost two decades to master the necessary skills to write that novel. And critics and ordinary readers have received it over the decades as the effortless work of a genius and praised it for changing many conventions in contemporary literature and the arts at large.

Regarding the explanation about formal attributes, this book shows that the form of the work of art matters in understanding its classic status. But one has to explain the form in relation to its creator and his collaborators. For *One Hundred Years of Solitude* to succeed, it made a difference that its author and other best-selling writers of his generation preferred one form: novels that were on average three hundred pages long, instead of writing more succinct works such as poetry and short stories, as previous generations did. The style of the work of art matters, too, because it is related to taste and taste is social. So, the consecration of *One Hundred Years of Solitude* hinges on the success of a global taste for the style known as magical realism.

The explanation that emphasizes the historical context of a work of art as a factor for its classic status is of course important, especially if we understand the context as a social space that presents the artist's imagination with a range of options about what kinds of works of art are imaginable in a given moment. Within that range, García Márquez could conceive *One Hundred Years of Solitude* but not *2666*. The conditions needed to imagine the latter as a novel that narrates, among other events, female homicides in a Mexican city near the U.S. border, were only available to writers like Roberto Bolaño four decades later.

Finally, regarding the explanation that underscores the role of gatekeepers, this book shows that they are important but not indispensable in explaining how a work of art becomes a classic. In Homer's time, for example, there were no literary agents, publishers, and book reviewers. Yet their absence did not stop the *Iliad* from attaining classic status. Like *One Hundred Years of Solitude*, what the *Iliad* needed for its consecration were cultural brokers—people, groups, objects, and organizations that facilitate the circulation of a work of art from one culture, country, and generation to another. By that means, their brokerage contributes to the work's ascent to glory.

To merge these explanations into a single argument, this book claims that the classic is, at first, one of many works of art shaped by the social world in which it was born and then, once it becomes a classic, the work of art shapes the world around it over the long term. Classics like *One Thousand and One Nights* (first compiled in 850 CE), *Don Quixote* (published in 1605), *The House of the Seven Gables* (1851), and *Explosion in a Cathedral* (1962) are a part of the social world that modeled how García Márquez wrote *One Hundred Years of Solitude*. And years later, that novel started to have an impact on the world, influencing the making of books such as Naguib Mahfouz's *The Harafish*, Angela Carter's *Nights at the Circus*, Patrick Süskind's *Perfume*, and Junot Díaz's *The Brief Wondrous Life of Oscar Wao*. The impact of *One Hundred Years of Solitude* on the world now transcends literature. One finds its presence in other works of art, branded products, printed and online publications, names of people and places, including a star and an extrasolar planet. The classic, indeed, has the power to enter and stay in our lives in formats that are different from the one its creator imagined. And in so doing, the classic shapes, with the help of cultural brokers, the social world it inhabits.

Although there is no one-size-fits-all formula to explain how a work of art turns into a classic, at least two basic processes need to happen: one, the creator and the collaborators lose control over the work of art as time passes and, two, cultural brokers appropriate the work as an object of classic value.

WHO TALKS ABOUT CLASSICS? VALUE, CULTURAL BROKERS, AND COLLECTIVE REPRESENTATIONS

Sociologist Erving Goffman stressed the importance of situations in which people participate without firsthand knowledge of something. For him, these situations help to maintain the daily rhythm of social life and are the basis of what he called a "surface of agreement," that is, a consensus that emerges when participants in a given situation "assert values to which everyone present feels obliged to give lip service."[5] These surface agreements are crucial for a coherent and lasting social life. The idea that agreement about a classic surfaces among participants with no direct knowledge of it was what made me formulate the hypothesis in this book: a work of art becomes a classic when it is part of what Émile Durkheim called "collective representations" and Charles Taylor and Gérard Bouchard call "social imaginaries"; that is, classics become symbols that embody ideas and values, beliefs and emotions, and norms and expectations that are meaningful to people.[6] By meaningful, I mean that they can use classics as a blueprint to make sense of their social worlds.[7] This book wants to understand how a cultural object, such as *One Hundred Years of Solitude*, becomes part of a collective imaginary, one inhabited by literary works such as *Crime and Punishment*, *Pride and Prejudice*, and *The Tale of Genji*, among others.

What is then the role of intermediaries in the making of a classic? Some cultural sociologists, literary scholars, and historians of the book argue that the creation and reproduction of a work's classic value mainly rests in the hands of critics, academics, readers, and organizations that can eloquently talk about it.[8] Yet the evidence in this book suggests that nonreaders are also central to create and reproduce a work's classic value. How so? Imagine, for example, a situation in which a person mentions the classic to another who has never heard about it. At this moment, social expectations step in, that is, the pressure of social conformity on us as channeled by other people and organizations. In certain situations, some people will conform by reading the classic. Most will not, which does not mean they refuse to conform socially; instead, they opt for nonreading. As this book shows, anybody with full Internet access (and no firewalls or censorship present) can read reviews or watch videos that summarize the classic. The Internet obviously did not create nonreaders. But it makes their actions more visible for researchers interested in how things become viral and how some things attain high value in the long run. Along with critics, academics, and common readers, nonreaders (and more broadly nonconsumers) are what I call cultural brokers. They are the ones who continue to find meaningful a work of art such as *One Hundred Years of Solitude*. Acting as this novel's cultural brokers, I found a constellation of individuals, objects, and organizations: nonreaders, teachers, reviewers, translators, artists, bloggers, journalists, priests, businesspeople, war refugees, celebrities, influencers, merchandising, works of art, buildings, statues, language academies, bookstores, awards, book clubs, private companies, nonprofit organizations, national governments, mass media, and social media platforms. Of course, there are many more, and their exact contribution to the making of classics deserves further research.[9]

To advance in this direction, this book offers two new ways of understanding the input of critics, scholars, and readers in forming the value of a work of art. First, the boundary between production and criticism is fuzzier than previously believed. Critics and scholars do not always engage in critiquing a work of art after it is publicly available. They can critique it earlier. In other words, they can be *sui generis* cocreators of the work of art. Latin American literary critic Emmanuel Carballo gave feedback *in private* to García Márquez on the entire manuscript of *One Hundred Years of Solitude*. Every weekend, the writer brought the critic the new pages he had drafted during the week. The critic's feedback influenced the writer's aesthetic and narrative choices during the writing of the novel. And then, after its release, the critic assumed his (public) role as a reviewer by writing a review of the novel for an influential magazine, whose readers bought similar novels. This collaboration among artists and critics was neither an exception for Latin American writers in the 1960s (for example, scholar Emir Rodríguez Monegal advised José Donoso on his works in progress) nor for other creators (for example, artists, gallerists, and politicians visited Picasso's studio when he was painting *Guernica*). So this book fills a gap in the literature on how critics and scholars get involved in the stages of imagination and how they influence the conception of the work of art before it is finished and starts to circulate in public.

Second, critics and scholars have in practice a limited influence in the reception and valuation of works of art, especially in the long run. The spread of digital social media platforms (for example, Goodreads had over ninety million users in 2020) makes plainly visible a practice that used to go mostly unexplained: common readers express their opinions about a work of art without necessarily agreeing with (or even knowing) the opinions of critics and scholars. New research shows that the taste of these gatekeepers does not neatly align with the taste of common readers.[10] Moreover, the capacity of critics and scholars to influence readers' taste weakens as the work of art acquires higher value over time. Reviews of most books—including classics— are published only once and after the book's release. So, it is unlikely that common readers will decide to read William Shakespeare's *Hamlet* because they found a critic's enthusiastic review in mainstream media. Other situations come to mind. Critics' lukewarm reception and scholars' disdain for, say, Kahlil Gibran's *The Prophet* may have prevented this book from being canonical in English literature but not from becoming a classic. Critics' continuous support secured the canonical status of Kate Chopin's *The Awakening*. But despite their support, this novel does not have classic status in the United States or abroad. To decide whether to read *One Hundred Years of Solitude*, consumers are not reading, for example, the review published in 1970 in the *New York Times* by Robert Kiely, a Harvard professor. In sum, more strategies and cultural brokers influence what becomes classic. For this reason, the opinions of partially informed consumers or nonreaders, which are the understudied majority, call for serious analysis if we want to better explain the reproduction of a work's classic value.[11]

REVISITING MYTHS, GENIUS, THE UNIVERSAL, AND INEVITABILITY

Studying a classic is key to examining whether myths, inevitability, genius, and the universal can influence the making of a cultural object. As the case of *One Hundred Years of Solitude* suggests, myths have the ability to efface evidence about the object's creation. And in doing so, myths help the object attain long-lasting value. One of the myths that hides facts about this novel's making involves the cow that crossed the road when García Márquez came up with the opening line of the novel. The author himself contributed to mythmaking by embellishing the story about the novel's origins and leaving no traces of his creative process. He burned all writing materials after receiving the first printed copy of the novel. This book seeks neither to deconstruct these myths nor to aggrandize them, only to ask how they increase the high value of a work of art by effacing, distorting, or reinventing the participation of ideas, people, organizations, and objects in its making.

As mentioned above, arguments in favor of genius and universality have been a popular line of reasoning to explain the making of classics. This book understands genius and universality as conventions that historically situated communities apply to a cultural object and its maker. Genius is an exaltation of the cherished Western idea about the free-acting, creative individual. This view of the genius is especially widespread in the arts. Currently, new technologies, such as genetic testing and neuroscience, strive to provide a biological answer to the argument that the genius is born, not made. But the reality is that all previous theories seeking to explain the genius as the result of innate biological traits have failed, including humor theory, craniometry, psychometry, physiognomy, and intelligence quotient (IQ), among others.

Meanwhile, theories that stress the social conditions underlying the activities of the so-called genius have been going strong since Norbert Elias's study on Mozart. In agreement with these theories, this book defines the genius as a hypersocialized person. Genius comes from someone who has fully mastered the conventions in a domain of artistic practice and, hence, can transform these conventions in an innovative way with the support of the art establishment and the public. The professional trajectory of García Márquez in the 1950s and 1960s turned him into a privileged observer of the New Latin American Novel and mainstream contemporary fiction in Europe and the United States. After two decades of observation, combined with learning and practice in a multi-lingual and multinational environment, he was a hypersocialized professional. Along with several of his peers, he had the tools to create a work of art that could transform conventions in literature. And he did not do it in isolation. He received support from friends, peers, and gatekeepers in Mexico City and in several other countries. García Márquez's collaborators gave him feedback on the manuscript in progress, and some of them worked for him as research assistants and influenced his creative decisions. His writing of *One Hundred Years of Solitude* is a telling case of what I call networked creativity.[12]

What about the universal? The universal is no more than a set of beliefs held by cultural brokers, which delimits what the brokers collectively recognize as widely shared, whether it is an object, a person, or an idea. And this recognition is culturally and historically specific. In our times, most people no longer read as a classic *The Imitation of Christ*, a fifteenth-century book by Thomas à Kempis. For centuries, artists, editors, and readers imagined, produced, and consumed copies of this popular Christian devotional work. Many generations of cultural brokers kept reading or mentioning this text because it was closer to the collectively shared understanding of what "universal" was, that is, a belief in spiritual life arising within oneself and in the closeness to God. A similar example is that of *Gesar*, the world's longest known epic, which tells the story of King Gesar. From the twelfth century to the present, this epic is widely known in Central and South Asia. There, people consider it a classic and King Gesar a hero—the same kind of hero as the King of Ithaca, the so-called universal character of the *Odyssey*, which like *Gesar* tells the epic story of a monarch. The fact that *Gesar* and the *Odyssey* are regarded as classics has more to do with the cultural construction of the universal and the classic than with the idea that one epic is aesthetically superior to another. Aesthetics, as this book shows, unfold in a cultural and historical context and never in a social vacuum. For this reason, raw universality tells us nothing about how a work of art becomes a classic. What matters is how universality is cooked, so to speak, that is, how cultural brokers imagine something as classic and how they create a collective understanding of what is long-lasting and meaningful. And again, this understanding is culturally and historically specific.

Was the success of *One Hundred Years of Solitude* inevitable? Of course not. The shelves of national libraries have scores of literary works that are written in astounding language, narrate masterful plots, and describe unforgettable characters. And yet these works did not become classics. The question of inevitability in the success of classics is connected to the issues of contingency, causality, and counterfactuals. By showing that there was nothing intrinsically unique in the success of *One Hundred Years of Solitude*, this book offers an anti-teleological narrative of consecration by using counterfactual reasoning: the "what if" question. This book analyzes five "forgotten" works or what I call, to be more precise, literary counterfactuals. Despite their multiple similarities with *One Hundred Years of Solitude*, they have not ascended to global classic status. Their cases remind us about the importance of factors that are outside a literary work itself and yet are critical to its consecration as a classic. These factors include the predominant norms and conventions in a particular culture or social context that enable the making of literary texts. Let me point out that this argument is not about rescuing the old mantra that a literary text simply reflects its social reality. Rather, it is about specifying how a work's connection to a certain organizational setting enables or prevents its production, early reception, and consumption in ways that are not exclusively dependent on the aesthetic quality of the text.

THE INVENTION OF TRADITION: POWER, CIRCULATION, AND WORLD LITERATURE

Historical and sociological studies that cover the ascent of a work of art to global classic status are scarce.[13] Like *Things Fall Apart* by Nigerian Chinua Achebe and *Ficciones* by Argentine Jorge Luis Borges, *One Hundred Years of Solitude* originated in the literary periphery, arrived in the center, and redefined the literary mainstream globally.[14] How can literary works written at the periphery move to a central position and stand next to literary works that belong to French, English, Russian, and other prestigious literary traditions? For this move to happen, the literary work first needs to belong to a literary tradition that houses it.

The world literature approach is useful to explain this move.[15] Yet scholars criticize this approach for focusing on histories of literary influence and circulation and for obviating questions about power in production and circulation, especially gatekeepers' decisions.[16] While partly on target, this critique also disregards the role of aesthetic labeling in upscaling the circulation of a literary work. Readers, critics, and book-industry organizations would judge the value of a new literary work by relating it to similar works in the tradition to which it belongs. Most writers, journalists, critics, and readers applied the label *Latin American literature* (rather than Colombian literature) to *One Hundred Years of Solitude* upon its publication. And by doing so, they enabled the immediate success in the region and abroad of a novel set in a remote Caribbean village. Then, over the years, *One Hundred Years of Solitude* has helped redefine the idea and boundaries of world literature and the contents of the Western canon.[17] Thus, the case of this novel can throw light on the question of how a cultural object can contribute to rescaling a literary tradition globally, as it did for Latin American literature.[18]

Unlike world literature, stylometry is an approach of little use for the issues analyzed in this book. Some stylometricians argue that the answers to all questions about a text can be found in the text itself. Equipped with the tools of big data, this new breed of formalists analyzes dozens of texts to, for example, crack the best-seller code, as if the answer to what makes a literary work a best seller is just sitting there in the text. But what is the point of discovering that the most prevalent word in Vladimir Nabokov's fiction is the color "mauve"? Without an understanding of how he imagined his works and how they were produced and received, this finding is meaningless; it is simply an example of an empty formal analysis.[19] Cultural sociologists and historians have long shown that a cultural good can acquire meanings that go beyond the original ones.[20] The world literature approach is also a mighty antidote to radical formalism in the age of big data.

MATERIALITY AND SOCIAL RELATIONS

People do not move freely in social space. They encounter others in positions they need to go through or occupy while moving around. People also create objects that can influence—long after their creators are gone—the positions that new generations of people occupy. For this reason, objects serve to reproduce norms, values, ideas, and social boundaries. And furthermore, these reproductions can become a part of durable social organizations thanks to objects. The new historicism approach has shown that texts can be a structural force, and research on fields of cultural production has explained that fields are systems of positions occupied by people who pass on norms and values.[21] My claim is that objects also occupy positions that enable or restrict people's positions and the social relations they create in the social field. Classics, in particular, are carriers of norms, values, and ideas. Classics police social boundaries, too.

Like da Vinci's *Mona Lisa*, classics are objects that their creators left behind, and they take on lives of their own as new generations of cultural brokers use them in traditional or unintended ways. No one in the fifteenth century expected that the *Mona Lisa* would be hanging in the Louvre today. No one thought when photography was invented that this painting would be among the most photographed works of art in the world. And no one anticipated that it would become a symbol of French culture. Whereas other approaches explain objects as outcomes of cultural production and reproduction, scholars increasingly skeptical of the secondary position of objects in research on cultural production acknowledge that the work of art is "involved in the drama of its own making."[22] As a renewed interest in materiality develops, cultural sociologists, literary scholars, and historians of the book claim that cultural objects such as literary works can influence organizational arrangements and human relations. The claim that unifies this scholarship is that objects can be coproducers of social orders.[23] This is certainly the case, as this book claims, of the social institution called the classic.

HOW TO STUDY A CLASSIC?

To address the issues above, I built on the interdisciplinary approach to literature advocated by historian Roger Chartier and sociologist Pierre Bourdieu.[24] I developed a series of concepts that, taken together, offer a new theoretical approach to the study of the classic in particular and cultural objects in general. These concepts are imagination, niche, the trio collaboration-adaptation-competition, disembedding, indexicals, and counterfactuals. To develop this approach, I first had to distinguish between the canonical and the classic.

THE CANONICAL AND THE CLASSIC

Defining these two terms can be confusing since consecration as a classic and canonization overlap and influence each other. This book distinguishes more clearly between them. To begin, classics are for the most part canonical works (*War and Peace*, for example). But not all canonical works are classics, such as *The Obscene Bird of Night*. Despite national and cultural boundaries and changes in lists of canonical works, classics (and artists) display remarkable stability over time.[25] Yet canonical and classic works diverge at a particular moment, which this book locates.[26] The key difference between canonization and consecration as a classic is the control that individuals and organizations exert over the cultural object. This control is substantial in the case of the canonical work and negligible in the case of the classic. The consecration of a cultural object as a classic requires uprooting it from its conditions of production and early circulation, especially from the influence of critics, scholars, and publishers. As a result of its uprooted autonomy, the classic outlives lists of canonical works that are born and perish like the critics, scholars, and organizations that promoted them. Canonical works, on the contrary, do not attain a comparable level of autonomy in the long run. They are only partially uprooted because they still depend on the support of interested organizations to reproduce their status.

Classics do not depend on the support of gatekeepers to preserve their status. For example, *Othello* and *As I Lay Dying* do not need the backing of the British Academy and publisher the Library of America, respectively, to reproduce their classic status. But *Anthology* by Gabriela Mistral and *Diary of a Country Priest* by Georges Bernanos depend on support from the Royal Spanish Academy and French publisher Gallimard, respectively, to maintain their canonical status. The autonomy of the classic is further proven when critics, scholars, or organizations can benefit more from associating their names with the classic than the classic benefits from its connection to a gatekeeper. For example, a publisher can attract international attention by releasing an artsy, annotated, or academic edition of *Ulysses* or *The Little Prince*. But it would not attract similar attention if it released such an edition of Ben Jonson's *Epicoene* or Champfleury's *Les Bourgeois de Molinchart*.

Based on these definitions of the canonical and the classic, I understand the literary canon to be a group of works that specific gatekeepers historically consider and promote as chief examples of the available literature falling under certain and sometimes overlapping parameters; nation, language, culture, professions, and historical period, among others.[27] Accordingly, the canonical work of art is subservient to gatekeepers that support it, while the classic is larger than and independent from gatekeepers that may have an interest in promoting it. Unlike the canonical work of art, the classic is a public cultural object of long-lasting value that can influence social relations and is impervious to exclusive control by an individual (writer, literary agent), organization (publisher, university, academy of language), or cultural conglomerate (literary tradition, national discourse).

IMAGINATION

Sociologist Pierre Bourdieu once criticized "the received idea" that sociology could only "give an account of cultural consumption but not of production."[28] Bourdieu and scores of researchers have disproved this idea over the past decades. Indeed, sociology is fully equipped to explain cultural production. But another received idea still lingers: the making of a work of art occurs only during its cultural production. And hence, it seems as if sociology does not have to give an account of cultural imagination to understand how works of art are made. Sociology also needs to disprove this idea. Imagination is a fundamental stage in the making of works of art, as this book argues by studying *One Hundred Years of Solitude*. Simply put, imagination refers to the coming into being of a work of art since it is a stroke of inspiration, an intuition worth pursuing, or a recurrent thought. Most studies of cultural production and consumption overlook the analysis of the plethora of ideas for works of art that do not move beyond the stage of imagination. And these ideas cannot move further because this stage is the first (and understudied) "gatekeeper." Imagination is the stage a work of art has to enter before reaching the stage of production. The foundational values and rules that enable or constrain what artists can make are present in the stage of imagination. For this reason, cultural production cannot happen without imagination. Of course, this imagination is not located only in the creator's mind. This book shows how imagination takes the form of specific ideas, creators, organizations, and objects that furnish an artist's creativity. Collaborators play an important creative role by helping the artist imagine the work and push it into the stage of production.[29] The case of *One Hundred Years of Solitude* also shows that imagination does not end when the works move into the stages of production and circulation; imagination is equally necessary to understand works' long-term success.

NICHE

The concept of niche refers to the people, organizations, and objects that participate in the imagination, production, and early circulation of a certain good. Scholars in the fields of literary studies, history of the book, and cultural sociology have rightly underscored the actions of people and organizations when studying the production and circulation of cultural objects. Particularly in sociology, art makers, gatekeepers, and consumers influence the shape taken by spaces of cultural production such as the field, art world, and culture-industry subsystem. To these approaches, the one in this book adds that objects are coparticipants in cultural making, along with art makers, gatekeepers, and consumers. Thus, the niche is a space of cultural making that is inhabited by people and organizations, and decisively also by objects. The latter can influence actions and positions of people and organizations in society. An approach anchored in the concept of niche is particularly suitable for the study of classics. *The Metamorphosis*, *Wuthering Heights*, and *Dream of the Red Chamber*, among others, inform the actions of new generations of art markers, organizations, consumers, and cultural objects. In the case of *One Hundred Years of Solitude*, its niche includes this novel, its relation to previous and current cultural objects (particularly Western and Latin American literary works, Colombian folk music, and Italian neorealist cinema), the dominant artistic conventions of cosmopolitanism and Latin Americanism, its author and collaborators, peer writers in North America, Latin America, and Europe, gatekeepers of the publishing industry (literary agent Balcells and publishers Sudamericana, Seix Barral, Era, and Harper & Row), and the first generation of common readers, contemporary critics, and scholars in Latin America, Spain, the United Kingdom, the United States, and France. They might be part of a field, an art world, and a culture-industry. But when they are analyzed as a whole, they are not just under the influence of a field, an art world, or a culture-industry; they come together in the more flexible and loosely bounded space of production that I call niche.

COLLABORATION, ADAPTATION, AND COMPETITION

The making of a cultural object, such as a literary work, requires collaboration, competition, and adaptation among producers.[30] The object cannot be conceived, produced, and marketed exclusively under conditions of competition, struggle, or conflict. In order for the work of art to come into being, an art maker has to collaborate with other producers at times and at other times adapt to the standards of others, especially gatekeepers.[31] The making of *One Hundred Years of Solitude* required two decades of multinational collaboration among three generations of writers, critics, and publishers to imagine it as a work of art. Then, during its writing, this novel had to adapt to the commercial standards set by gatekeepers in Spain, Latin America, France, and the United States. Finally, when this novel was published, it competed against other commodities in the literary market. As this book shows, collaboration, adaptation, and competition played a necessary and concrete role in the making of this literary work. And this is certainly the case with other cultural objects.[32]

DISEMBEDDING AS UPROOTING

The concept of disembedding underscores a key feature of the classic that distinguishes it from the best seller and canonical work of art: the classic becomes autonomous from its conditions of imagination, production, and circulation. In other words, no single person, organization, or culture can control the career of a classic. I mentioned above that a work of art is born (or embedded) in a niche. But this does not only happen to works of art. Researchers have shown that individuals and organizations are embedded in networks of social, economic, and cultural relations that explain their actions, as opposed to explanations based on abstract structural determination or the rational action of individuals.[33] But in its career to become a classic, a work of art has to separate from its niche. I refer to this separation as disembedding or uprooting. Consider Gustave Flaubert as an example. The aesthetic ideas of nineteenth-century French realism, the writer, his collaborators and publisher, controversial book reviews, contemporary novels on adultery, and even a trial contributed to the making of *Madame Bovary* (1856). None of the ideas, individuals, and organizations present in this novel's niche survive in their original form two centuries later. (Only objects from that era remain, such as the first edition of the novel.) Unlike Ernest-Aimé Feydeau's best-selling *Fanny* (1858) and similar contemporary French novels on adultery, *Madame Bovary* did not die within its niche; the novel escaped from it as cultural brokers (new generations of artists, gatekeepers, cultural objects, and readers) unrelated to the novel's niche appropriated it and helped it to transcend historical, aesthetic, national, and cultural borders to become a classic. Through them, the work attained resonance and immanence.[34] *One Hundred Years of Solitude* has the same trajectory: that of an uprooted cultural object. Its niche has basically vanished in the half century since its publication. The aesthetic ideas that permitted this novel to be imagined, the author, his collaborators, publishing-industry gatekeepers, most contemporary Latin American novels, and the first generation of readers, critics, and scholars stopped influencing the novel's career decades ago. As in the cases of *Madame Bovary* and *One Hundred Years of Solitude*, explaining the classic status of a literary work is about analyzing how it has outlived its niche thanks to cultural brokers that appropriate the work across generational, linguistic, national, and cultural boundaries.

INDEXICALS

This book explains this appropriation by studying the smalls units of significance that I call indexicals.[35] "This," "you," "here," "now," and "the people" are examples of indexicals. "This," for instance, indexes something the speaker points to, the expression "you" indexes a person in front of the speaker, and so on. They are everyday expressions that depend on the situation in which people use them for other participants to understand what the expression is indexing but not necessarily what it means.[36] These expressions are pervasive in human communication because "human cognitive capacity is limited" and because social reality is full of information. The solution to these cognitive and social barriers is "routine" (repetitive behavior) because, again, "the world is too complex for [individuals] to have to renegotiate all of it (or even very much of it) all the time. Most of the time it is easier to stay where one is familiar."[37] Repeating these everyday expressions allows individuals to cut, negotiate, and internalize a large amount of information into more manageable and familiar pieces that help them create routine; that is, people can use these units to communicate with other people in customary ways or to make sense of ordinary social situations.

In literature, indexicals from classics are present in everyday life situations, too. Even people who have not read (and never will) the classic often use these indexicals because they have become traditional ways of making sense of social situations. For example, references to "To be, or not to be," down the rabbit hole, or Big Brother occur daily in face-to-face and online interactions as well as in popular and mass media communication. Moreover, these situations are foreign to the niche where the cultural object was made. For example, a 2018 article in the *New York Times* used the expression Quixotic (from a seventeenth-century Spanish book) to help readers better understand a modern-day hitchhiker's adventures in Africa. Repeated use of these familiar expressions over generations and across national, linguistic, and cultural boundaries creates patterns of meaningfulness that transcend the niche in which the object was created. Use of these indexicals makes it possible to recognize certain literary works as meaningful decades or centuries later in other countries, languages, and cultures. In the case of a classic, there are at least four such patterns: lived experience, universalization, artistic commensuration, and entrenched criticism.[38] Macondo, the ascent of Remedios the Beauty to heaven, and the novel's opening sentence, among others, have become indexical expressions that people in over ninety countries have used for decades, sometimes unaware they come from a 1967 Caribbean novel.

COUNTERFACTUALS

Is the classic born to be one? The study of counterfactuals helps to answer this question. Counterfactual analysis is common in the social, human, and natural sciences.[39] But it is rare for cultural objects. Studies dealing with the consecration of a literary work as a classic rarely compare it to cases that have key similarities, such as the same style, literary agent, or critical reception. Shakespeare studies have led the way in the field of literature. Some scholars claim that Thomas Middleton's plays are as good as Shakespeare's. But old and new audiences have difficulties appreciating the higher or equal value of other plays from that era due to more than four hundred years of history and the social process that has shaped readers' taste to prefer Shakespeare's plays.[40] I call cases such as Middleton's plays literary counterfactuals: works that had conditions to become a classic but did not. Their study is valuable for three reasons. First, it provides extra arguments to deny the claim that a work of art becomes a classic because its author was a genius or because its contents were more "universal" than those of similar literary works.[41] Second, it reaffirms the point that the transformation of a cultural object into a classic is not inevitable.[42] And third, comparing literary counterfactuals offers a more exhaustive inventory than prior research of the factors involved in the consecration of a classic.

You, the reader, may have noticed that throughout this book I referred to counterfactual situations for *One Hundred Years of Solitude*. For example, what would have happened if García Márquez had finished the first manuscript of this novel, then entitled "The House," and published it in 1955, more than a decade before he ever heard about the New Latin American Novel or received the support of his Mafia Group friends? My intention with these counterfactual situations was to show the obstacles that the novel had to overcome to be imagined, produced, and circulated in the long term. Clearly, if this novel had been published in Colombia and before 1967, it would have fallen into the same global obscurity as the works of Héctor Rojas Herazo and Eduardo Caballero Calderón. Both were García Márquez's talented contemporaries (Rojas Herazo was also his close friend). And like him, they wrote touching rural stories using a realist style. But unlike him, their works of art and many others now, to paraphrase poet Thomas Gray, waste their sweetness on the desert of oblivion. Only classics ascend to glory.

ACKNOWLEDGMENTS

My Newtonian moment, if I may call it that, happened in the fall of 2007. I had just started my doctorate at Harvard University in Cambridge. What impressed me most was not the university but the rain. That fall it rained day after day. And on one of those long rainy days I was walking to Widener Library under my umbrella when all of a sudden I said to myself out loud, "It rains like in Macondo." Little did I suspect that my reaction was the idea for this book. Back then, I simply wondered why I said that. I was neither in Latin America nor had I ever been there. And more than ten years had passed since I read *One Hundred Years of Solitude*. Yet the memory of Macondo's never-ending rain hit me, randomly, right there, watching it rain in Cambridge. And this new memory, a mixture of fiction and real life, chased me for a year until I met with my advisor, Michèle Lamont, to discuss ideas for my doctoral project, and she suggested that I work on *One Hundred Years of Solitude*. What I never told her, and she will find out by reading these lines, is that I had a project about this novel among my list of ideas.

This book is, as it could not be otherwise, a work of imagination, too. As I wrote it, other memories came to me. I recalled Miguel Ángel Cabrera's teaching on the presence of social theory in literature, Keith Baker explaining to me how intellectual conditions make events imaginable (or thinkable), Roger Chartier expanding my view of reading practices and the agents involved in the making of texts, Saskia Sassen compelling me to rethink the global, and William Sewell's suggestions on how to connect semiotics to tangible, social practices. Michèle Lamont, who had the hardest of tasks, helped me achieve cohesion in this array of ideas and also to develop a framework firmly grounded in cultural sociology.

Filiz Garip was present at this project's birth and, despite the enormity of the task ahead, she has guided me through it until the end. I want to thank Mario Santana and Gerald Martin, whose books helped me to write mine. Mario wrote an outstanding study on the reception of the Latin American Boom in Spain and for years has supported me in countless ways. Gerald wrote an extraordinary biography of García Márquez from which I have learned immensely, as he has understood the writer's imagination in ways that no one ever has.

I conducted research for this book in Colombia, Mexico, Spain, France, Scotland, Venezuela, and the United States. In Colombia in particular, I thank Jaime Abello and his amazing team at the Gabo Foundation, Guillermo Angulo, Ariel Castillo, Tita Cepeda, Jorge Orlando Melo, Nicolás Pernett (who commented on the full manuscript), Sergio Sarmiento at Biblioteca Luis Ángel Arango, Julio Oñate, and Kike Mojica, my guide in García Márquez's hometown of Aracataca. In the United States, I thank Stephen Enniss and his exceptional team at the Harry Ransom Center, which gave me the opportunity to be among the first researchers to work with the Gabriel García Márquez Papers. In Mexico, I thank Diego García Elío and Gonzalo García Barcha for their generosity and support as this book entered its final stages.

This book is also a work of collaboration. I was lucky to share my research in progress with colleagues in eight countries. I wish I could name them all. Their generosity proves how much transnational collaborators can improve researchers' ideas. My thanks to Ignace Adant, Jullianne Ballou, Bart Bonikowski, Anna Casas, Paola Castaño, Clayton Childress, Bruno Cousin, Juan Díez Medrano, Juan Manuel García Ramos, Dunia Gras Miravet, Rosario Hubert, Ian MacMillen, Peter Marsden, Stiliana Milkova, Harry Morales, Christopher Muller, Reynaldo Riva, Bécquer Seguin, Mariano Siskind, Diana Sorensen, Ilan Stavans, Eugenio Suárez-Galbán Guerra, Lyubomir Uzunov, and Christopher Winship. My gratitude to my wonderful and supportive colleagues in Sociology at Whitman College, Alissa Cordner, Keith Farrington, Michelle Janning, Helen Kim, and Gilbert Mireles. At Whitman, I also thank Sharon Alker, Carlos Vargas, and several students who shared their excitement as the newest generation of readers of *One Hundred Years of Solitude*, especially to Zidane Galant-LaPorte who read and commented on the full manuscript. My thanks to Hsin-Chao Wu, Huan Jin, and Wenping Xue who helped with Chinese data, Dong-Kyun Im with Korean, and Shiori Yamada with Japanese.

My editor Eric Schwartz, associate editor Lowell Frye, and the incredible team at Columbia University Press guided this book through the stage of production and also celebrated its completion by having a book club on *One Hundred Years of Solitude*. My thanks to the anonymous manuscript reviewers, whose role as invisible collaborators improved the final text. During these final revisions, Stefan Beljean, Erin Goodman, Gustavo Guerrero, Peggy Levitt, Benjamin Loy, Ricardo Maldonado, Thomas Medvetz, Oleski Miranda (who also did invaluable research for me in Venezuela), Gesine Müller, Arturo Rodríguez Morató, Natalia Ruiz Junco, Ignacio Sánchez Prado, and Mario Santana read different parts of the manuscript.

My special thanks to Carmen Balcells, who kindly answered questions about the origins of her agency, to Luis Harss, who helped me better understand the history of the Latin American Boom, to Don Klein for giving me full access to his unequaled database of editions of García Márquez's works worldwide, and to Héctor J. Delgado for showing me the precious galley proofs of *One Hundred Years of Solitude*. Jeffrey Alexander, Philip Smith, Ronald Jacobs, and Shai Dromi enthusiastically supported the publication of the article at the center of this book in the newly born *American Journal of Cultural Sociology*. At the onset of this research, I spent months asking writers the same question again and again: How does a literary work become a classic? I thank Bernado Atxaga, Jean-Marie Le Clézio, Orhan Pamuk, José Luís Peixoto, Carlos Ruiz Zafón, and the irreplaceable Carlos Fuentes for kindly sharing with me their views on this question. For research funding, I thank the Graduate School of Arts and Sciences, Sociology Department, David Rockefeller Center for Latin American Studies at Harvard University, Andrew W. Mellon Foundation, and Harry Ransom Center at the University of Texas at Austin.

For more than a decade, I have talked to people from all walks of life about my research in the most unexpected occasions. This novel entered a conversation, for example, during dinner on the terrace of a Hoboken apartment facing Manhattan and a conversation at a farm in Walla Walla when we were talking about what kinds of apples Ancient Romans ate. An anonymous commuter talked to me about the novel on a bus in Edinburgh, an excited Harvard University undergraduate told me that he had three copies of it in his dorm room, two colleagues eagerly questioned me about it at a job interview in Abu Dhabi, a relative pointed at a banner of García Márquez (promoted as the author of that novel) at the annual book fair in my hometown of La Laguna, and, after revising the manuscript of *Ascent to Glory*, the editorial services manager shared with me his fond memories reading the novel for the first time. The reactions of these and other people when they found out I was working on *One Hundred Years of Solitude* enlightened me about the ways in which this novel has become a global classic. And seeing these ways and learning about others convinced me about classics' power to be a part of people's lives like very few objects of human culture.

This book brought me the friendship of José Montelongo, whose ideas, support, and feedback resonate throughout these pages. My thanks to María Candelaria Acuña Bennasar, Joan Bocanegra, Balraj Gill, Aníbal Martel, Patricia Martín, Thenesoya Martín, Carlos Rodríguez Morales, Ángel Ruiz, and other relatives and friends for their support and love over the years. And my gratitude and love to my wife Jenny Rodríguez-Peña, whose magical smile showed me in Callao that many things can have a second opportunity on earth.

NOTES

INTRODUCTION

1. García Márquez and Mendoza 1982; Martin 2009; Saldívar 2005; Vargas Llosa 1971. On myth and art, see Eyerman and McCormick 2006.
2. Knopf cited in Hirsch 1972: 648.

1. IMAGINING A WORK OF ART

1. *Primera Plana* 234 (June 20, 1967).
2. Roh 1927: 301.
3. Carpentier cited in Siskind 2014: 74, see also 63–72.
4. Letter of García Márquez to Plinio Apuleyo Mendoza. July 1, [1964], 1, Harry Ransom Center (hereafter, HRC). García Márquez cited in Carballo 1963: xx. Nobel award statements for 1967 and 1982 in https://www.nobelprize.org/prizes/literature (accessed on September 10, 2019).
5. Mamani Macedo 2017; Santana-Acuña, "Aesthetic Labeling," forthcoming. The invention of Latin American literature is an important case of study because, unlike literary traditions whose boundaries coincide with those of their corresponding nation-states (for example, French, Italian, or German literature), the boundaries of *literatura latinoamericana* do not match national boundaries. Latin American literature is arguably the most successful supranational literary tradition created in the twentieth century. The success of *One Hundred Years of Solitude* played a central role in the consolidation of this tradition. Research on the making of these supranational traditions is scarce (see Díez Medrano 2003). This chapter shows that Latin American literature could only emerge as a supranational tradition thanks to transnational collaboration across national spaces of cultural production.
6. *Primera Plana* 189 (August 9, 1966): 66.
7. Quote in Spender and Lasky 1965: 4; Casanova 1999: 253; Siskind 2014.
8. De Torre and Carpentier cited in Alemany Bay 1998: 71, 95; Torres Caicedo (1879) cited in Ardao 1980: 149, 232.
9. Quote in Ardao 1980: 135; González Echevarría 2012: 19; Rama 1982. Torres Caicedo's *Ensayos biográficos y de crítica literaria* (1868) referred mainly to "American literature." So did Antonio

Batres Jáuregui in *Literatura americana* (1879) and contributors to Ernesto Nelson's *The Spanish American Reader* (1916). The label *literatura hispanoamericana* appeared more frequently in books published in Spain but not in Latin America, where *literatura latinoamericana* became the dominant label. Ngram Viewer searches do not distinguish by country of publication. If searches included only books published in Latin America (not in Spain), the results for this label, shown in figure 1.1, will be more similar to those in figure 1.2. For results for this label in French, German, and Italian, see Santana-Acuña, "Aesthetic Labeling," forthcoming.

10.　Quotes in Rama 1982: 206.

11.　On cosmopolitanism, Cheah 2016; Fojas 2005; Rama 1982; Siskind 2014. Reference to critics of Borges in Fuentes 1976: 26. Borges's lecture cited in Siskind 2014: 5. Borges cited in Harss 1966: 38.

12.　The clash of local traditions and outside influences (especially those from Western culture) is a pervasive problem in the region's literature. This clash is understood as a conflict between civilization/barbarism and Europe/America. Fuentes 1976; González Echevarría 2012: 7; Harss 1966: 35, 37; Martin 1989; Siskind 2014. Vargas Llosa cited in *Primera Plana* 189 (August 9, 1966): 68.

13.　Fuentes 1976: 37, see also 9–10; Rodríguez Monegal 1965d: 54. Cf. González Echevarría 2012: 16.

14.　Fuentes 1976: 81; Rama 1982: 68 (quote), see also 44–45, 77–78, 131–32.

15.　Fuentes cited in García Márquez 2001a: 447; censor cited in Herrero-Olaizola 2007: xiv; Harss cited in Martínez 2008.

16.　Martin 2008: 482. See also Martin 1989.

17.　As Becker (2008 [1982]) argued, aesthetics is more an activity than a body of doctrine. The case of Latin American literature is important because it shows how collaboration in art happens across generations, rather than the customary focus on collaboration in a group or generation (cf. Becker 2008 [1982]; Farrell 2001). Findings in this section do not align with field theory's approach to cultural production (Bourdieu 1992; Casanova 1999; Sapiro 1999). This approach claims that the shape of any given field of cultural production is ultimately the product of struggle and conflict. In the literary field, competition between writers, critics, and generations explains what and who gets published and ultimately consecrated. The consolidation and international success of a Latin American literary tradition suggests otherwise. Collaboration, not conflict, drove the actions of leading cultural producers in 1960s; then, struggles were more allegoric than structural. Struggles from the 1970s onward ruined the homogeneity that had catapulted Latin American literature into the global scene. See also chapter 5.

18.　Rama 1982: 260, 285 (Carpentier quote).

19.　I offer a different chronology for each generation and emphasize the importance of literary format as a defining feature of each generation (cf. Rama 1982). I built on Karl Manheim (2000: 279), who argued that generations, more than by chronological boundaries, are unified by a "style," which depends on "the trigger action of the social and cultural process."

20.　For an exception, see Gras Miravet 2015. Each generation had its antagonists, too: Ciro Alegría (Short Form Generation), José María Arguedas (Hybrid Generation), and Manuel Scorza (Novel Generation). Yet their opposition to Latin American cosmopolitanism helped to sharpen the boundaries of Latin American literature. See also chapter 5.

21.　Harss cited in Martínez 2008; Altamirano 2010; Rama 1982; Lamont 2009.

22.　Rojas cited in Alburquerque Fuschini 2000: 345; Gras Miravet 2015; Kerr 2007: 76.

23.　Rama 1982: 44–45; Bocaz Leiva 2013: 1060; Donoso 1972; Fuentes 2017; Herrero-Olaizola 2007: 97, 147, 194–95; Piazza 1968. See also chapter 8.

24.　Quote in Rama 1982: 124; Rodríguez Monegal 1967a. See also Huerta 2013.

25.　Weiss 2014. Paris was a cultural meeting point for Spanish, Irish, Russian, and U.S. artists, too (Casanova 1999). Living in Paris was also a rite of passage for the region's literary critics such as Rodríguez Monegal and Rama.

26.　Vargas Llosa cited in *Primera Plana* 189 (August 9, 1966): 66. Porrúa 2014.

27. Reyes 1997: 82, 90.

28. Asturias cited in Huerta 2013: §21, n. 17; Rama 1982: 38; Santana 2000.

29. Quote in Fuentes 1976: 32. Anderson 1996: 7; Martínez 1999; Rama 1982: 162; González Echevarría 1996. Regarding the concept of aesthetic liberation, I built on McAdam's (1982) cognitive liberation to refer to the period when a collective becomes aware of its agency to intervene in a large-scale cultural process such as the rise of the New Latin American Novel.

30. Rodríguez Monegal 1984: 30 (quote), 34. See also Rama 1982: 159, 220.

31. Costa Picazo 2001: 20, 28; Hallewell 1987: 142; Harss 1966: 36. Tate's critique in Fuentes 1976. Fuentes cited in García Márquez 2001a: 445. Faulkner's deep influence in the region's literary imaginary was the subject of academic research as early as 1956 (Frisch 1993). Latin American translations in *Sur* magazine and by publishers Sudamericana, Futuro, and Rueda included *Sanctuary*, *The Wild Palms*, *The Unvanquished*, *The Sound and the Fury*, *Pylon*, *Knight's Gambit*, *Intruder in the Dust*, *Absalom, Absalom!*, *These 13*, and *Victory and other stories*.

32. Bethell 1998; Martin 2008: 480; Rama 1982: 243-44; Sorensen 2007. Other Latin American cultural poles were outside the region: Madrid, Barcelona, Paris, and New York. This transnational development departs from field theory's emphasis on the consolidation of an art field as a national development (Bourdieu 1992; cf. Buchholz 2016). Latin American literature emerged in a decentralized environment that was multilingual, multiethnic, and multinational.

33. Harss 1967: 28-29; Alburquerque Fuschini 2000: 338-339, 343 (open letter); Donoso 1972: 42, 35 (general complaint).

34. Harss 1966: 41 (quote); Castellet cited in Santana 2009: 295; Alburquerque Fuschini 2000: 348; Campuzano 1996: 216-19; Cohn 2012: 73; Iber 2015; Martin 2008: 481; Mignolo 2005: 91; Mudrovcic 1997: 134; Sorensen 2007.

35. Cobb 2008; Cohn 2004; Cohn 2006; Franco 2002; Huerta 2013: §50; Iber 2015; Mignolo 2005; Saunders 2000. The rise of the lettered region also challenges the claim that the literary field of Latin America achieved its autonomy from economic and political forces, while in fact it was under the constraint of contemporary politics, especially the Cuban Revolution and Cold War, and economics, especially the rise of the region's middle classes (cf. Sánchez Prado 2018).

36. González Echevarría 1996. Reid cited in Donoso 1972: 80.

37. Herrero-Olaizola 2007: 7-8; Iber 2015; Martin 2009.

38. Arenal 2011: 43; Aznar Soler 2010; Aznar Soler and López García 2016; González Calleja and Pardo Sanz 1993; Hallewell 1987: 146; Herrero-Olaizola 2007; Morcillo 2016.

39. Bocaz Leiva 2013: 1062; Huerta 2013; Louis 2013: 79; Paternostro 2014: 162; Piatier 1965; Rama 1982: 260-261. In 1962, Gallimard moved Latin American authors from the more regional collection *La Croix du Sud* to the cosmopolitan *Du monde entier*.

40. U.S. professor cited in Faber 2008: 19; Henríquez Ureña cited in Gabilondo 2009: 805. "One should only speak of *Latin culture* or, strictly speaking, *neo-Latin* (*novolatina*)." Emphasis in original.

41. Childress, Rawlings, and Moeran 2017; Sapiro 2016a.

42. Aznar Soler and López García 2016. Nobel award statements for 1945, 1956, 1960, 1967, and 1971 at https://www.nobelprize.org/prizes/literature (accessed on September 10, 2019). García Márquez 2015b.

43. Cobb 2008; Cohn 2004.

44. Alburquerque Fuschini 2000: 349; Piazza 1968: 122; Rama 1982: 156, 264-65; Rodríguez Carranza 2004; Sosnowski 1999. The editorial boards of these periodicals became another place for the reunion of writers, critics, and scholars from different countries and generations.

45. The following periodicals published or reviewed work by García Márquez before *One Hundred Years of Solitude*: *Primera Plana* (Argentina), *México en la Cultura*, *Revista Mexicana de literatura*, *La Cultura en México*, *Diálogos* (Mexico), *Marcha* (Uruguay), *Mito*, *Crónica*, *Eco* (Colombia), *Papel Literario* (Venezuela), *Amaru* (Peru), *Mundo Nuevo* (France), and *Life en Español* (United States).

46. Rama 1982: 265; López Llovet de Rodrigué 2004: 43.

47. Benedetti 1970: 21.

48. *Primera Plana:* October 26, 1965: 37, August 2, 1966: 13, and August 9, 1966: 66. Reference to *One Hundred Years of Solitude* (November 30, 1965): 55. See also King 2012: 429, 431, 436–37.

49. Donoso 1972: 121-22 (appearance); Rodríguez Monegal 1984: 31 (intention). See also Mudrovcic 1997.

50. "Latin American reality" cited by Rodríguez Monegal 1967b: 4. Indigenist and *costumbrista* writers were not prevalent in *Mundo Nuevo.* See, for example, issue number 11 (May 1967).

51. Sommer 1991: 1; Rama 1982: 32; Fuentes 1976: 32.

52. Rama 1982.

53. Rodríguez Monegal 1965a; Rodríguez Monegal 1965b; Rodríguez Monegal 1965c: 109; Rodríguez Monegal 1965d: 22.

54. Caillois cited in Piatier 1965: 12; Cohen 1965: 867.

55. J. E. Rivera regarded *The Vortex* as a major literary achievement, and he was long frustrated by its poor reception (González Echevarría 2012: 87). For *Los Sangurimas,* see chapter 8. Susan Sontag, among other influential gatekeepers, have praised *Pedro Páramo*, which nevertheless did not come close to the success of most New Latin American Novels, let alone *One Hundred Years of Solitude.*

56. Rodríguez Monegal 1967b: 4. *Primera Plana* 234 (June 20, 1967).

2. THE PUBLISHING INDUSTRY MODERNIZES

1. Letter of García Márquez to Lastra, March 14, 1967, 1, Pedro Lastra Collection (hereafter, PLC).

2. Vargas Llosa cited in Herrero-Olaizola 2007: 40. Fernando Alegría in Anonymous 1967/1968: 81–82; Benedetti 1970: 14; Herrero-Olaizola 2007: 18; Orthofer 2016: 404-407, 416–18; Rama 1982: 57–58. Cf. Griswold 1981 on piracy.

3. Fuentes 1977: 44:50. Lettered minority in Rama 1982: 56–57, 142–43. Benedetti 1970: 14–15. Favorable terms of trade in Martin 2008: 493. Between the 1940s and 1960s, the number of illiterate people decreased in almost all countries of Latin America, including Brazil, while the number of college students grew. On illiteracy, see Padua 1979.

4. The production of culture approach (Peterson and Anand 2004) in particular has overlooked how the production of works of art transforms the aesthetic imagination and practices of gatekeepers. Cf. Hamann and Beljean 2019; Marling 2016; Rama 1982: 30–31.

5. The case of Latin American literature offers new insights into the study of cultural production, because the book industry that internationalized New Latin American Novels was not present in a single country in the region and it also included Spain. Thus, the production of these novels was beyond the control of a single art world, cultural industry, or field. The making of these novels cannot be reduced to the dynamics of national and monolingual art worlds, cultural industries, or fields as approaches to cultural production suggest. This case also contributes to research on global cultural production (Buchholz 2016; Karush 2016; Phillips 2013).

6. The case of Latin American literature offers insights to explain the connection between transnational print culture and supranationalism. It helps to understand how the circulation of region-spanning publications can create among readers the perception of a supranational entity: Latin America. The success of Latin American literature in connection to the modernization of the Spanish publishing industry reaffirms that print capitalism (the spread of printed means of communication such as newspapers) is also a key component of supranational awareness.

7. Donoso 1972; García San Martín 2013; González Echevarría 2012: 19; Rama 1982: 47–52. On the role of non-professionals in literature, see Lahire 2006. García Márquez statement in letter to

Lastra, March 14, 1967, 1. On early circulation of *One Hundred Years of Solitude*, see García Márquez Papers (hereafter, GGMP), HRC, cont. 53.2.

8. The novels of foundational fiction were the exception in a literary scene dominated by poetry during the nineteenth century. Rama 1982: 30–31; Sommer 1991; Borges cited in Rama 1982: 288; Marco and Gracia García 2004: 836; Rulfo 1977: 30:35-30:55; López Llovet de Rodrigué 2004: 41.

9. For instance, Jaime García Terrés (1924–1996) had a privileged position in Mexico's cultural industry. He was director of the regional publishing company Fondo de Cultura Económica. He helped peers to find jobs. He did so for García Márquez upon his arrival to Mexico City. Yet his work—he wrote poetry and essays—had no circulation outside Mexico.

10. Rama 1982: 169, 297.

11. As this case suggests, transnational print capitalism is an under-examined factor in the development of national communities, fields, and cultural industries (cf. Anderson 2006; Bourdieu 1992; Corse 1997).

12. Report cited in Herrero-Olaizola 2007: 8, capitals in original.

13. Hallewell 1987: 141–42; Ana María Cabanellas in Lago Carballo and Gómez-Villegas 2006: 92, 108.

14. Gil-Mugarza: 156, 173, 184; Hallewell 1987: 145.

15. Research on cultural production often departs from situations in which raw materials used to produce cultural goods are plentiful and their supply undisturbed (for instance, paper, steel, chemicals, etc.). However, it is important to address how limited availability of raw materials obliges producers to make changes in the supply of these materials and how these changes can have a long-lasting impact on the evolution of a given creative industry (Chartier 2005; Griswold 1986; Kafka 2012; Sapiro 1999).

16. In most of Latin America, the solution to paper scarcity was to use low-quality paper. In Mexico, it "never had a good quality," according to Joaquín Díaz Canedo, founder of Joaquín Mortiz Press. The November 24, 1965, issue of *La Cultura en México* alerted that poor-quality and expensive paper was an obstacle to the national publishing industry. *El Tiempo* of Colombia reported similar problems of paper supply in its supplement *El Colombiano Literario* (June 12, 1955), 4. Xavier Moret in Carreira 1994; Herrero-Olaizola 2007: 9, 179, 201 n. 5; Lago Carballo and Gómez-Villegas 2006: 39.

17. Herrero-Olaizola 2007: 18, 38, 179. Aguirre 2015.

18. Herrero-Olaizola 2007: 178, 180, 185 n. 3.

19. Gil-Mugarza 2014.

20. Aguirre 2015; Herrero-Olaizola 2007: 6, 39.

21. Santana 2000: 43.

22. Gil-Mugarza 2014: 177.

23. Unlike the Spanish government, the Argentine government did not help its publishing industry to be competitive abroad (Hallewell 1987: 145).

24. Editor Pedro Altares cited in Moret 2002: 290. Censorship practices are an important challenge to the view of fields as sites of cultural production driven by competition and conflict. Under censorship, artists, gatekeepers, and consumers have no other option but to adapt to the political climate if they want to create, publish, and consume cultural goods. More importantly, in Spain, they ended up internalizing the logic of censors (Herrero-Olaizola 2007; Larraz Elorriaga 2014).

25. Percentage of rejections according to publisher Carlos Barral in Herrero-Olaizola 2007: 40. Abellán 1980; Larraz Elorriaga 2014; report cited in Herrero-Olaizola 2007: 46; Latin American critic José Miguel Oviedo cited in Santana 2009: 287.

26. Santana 2000.

27. Herrero-Olaizola 2007: xiv, xxv, 185; Larraz Elorriaga 2014.

28. For exceptions, see Griswold 1981; Herrero-Olaizola 2007; Larraz Elorriaga 2014; Radway 1997; Schiffrin 2000. Different levels of censorship existed in most democratic countries at this time. In the United Kingdom, obscenity laws were controversially reformed as late as 1959.

29. Censors cited in Herrero-Olaizola 2007: xiv, xxi, 41.

30. Censors cited in Herrero-Olaizola 2007: xiv, 162; letters of García Márquez to Vargas, June 21, 1963, and to Mendoza, [late 1962] and June 14, [1963], HRC. García Márquez publicly protested the changes in the text of *In Evil Hour*, and the controversy helped to sell the 5,000 copies. On the controversy, see Santana-Acuña, "Spain," forthcoming. Linotypists and Vargas Llosa in Ayén 2014. In Latin America, the reader for Joaquín Mortiz Press "enthusiastically" recommended Puig's novel "for [its] original and effective structure" (Anderson 1996: 24).

31. Cabrera Infante even referred to censors' role as co-authorship. Censors cited in Herrero-Olaizola 2007: 91, 97. On rejection and originality, see Lamont 2009; Sapiro 2016a; Santana-Acuña, "Spain," forthcoming.

32. Key authors included Cela, Delibes, Luis Romero, José Suárez Carreño, Ignacio Aldecoa, Ana María Matute, Sánchez Ferlosio, and the early Juan Goytisolo (later associated with the New Latin American Novel). In the mid-1950s, French publisher Gallimard released a collection of social-realist literature from Franco's Spain (Pavlovic 2011: 25; Santana 2000: 40, 50).

33. Goytisolo cited in Pavlovic 2011: 25, 31.

34. Castellet cited in Pavlovic 2011: 79, 67.

35. Santana 2000: 64.

36. Pavlovic (2011) uses field theory to explain the success of Seix Barral. But she overlooks that its success was transnational and beyond any existing national fields.

37. Furthermore, Seix Barral promoted its Latin American writers as Spaniards and, decisively, as modernizers of Spanish literature (Santana 2000).

38. Barral cited in Pavlovic 2011: 66.

39. Catalogue cited in Herrero-Olaizola 2007: xxiii, 19.

40. Soon publishers from Sweden, Norway, Denmark, Holland, Japan, and Portugal joined. At first, however, the Formentor Group promoted social realist literature from Spain (Santana 2000).

41. Herrero-Olaizola 2007: 18.

42. Borges 1970: 94; Pavlovic 2011: 48, 62; Santana 2000: 50–52, 59–62.

43. Scholarship on cultural production can benefit from further analysis of the Seix Barral case. The publisher, which entered the Latin American publishing market, helped to create conditions in Spain that permitted a foreign, Latin American book publisher such as Sudamericana (with its branch EDHASA) to succeed. According to field theory, only the winner inside a field is the one that reaps the benefits. But in the case of *One Hundred Years of Solitude*, to follow the language of field theory, an outsider and competitor reaped the benefits by succeeding in Spain as well as Latin America. Vargas Llosa cited in Herrero-Olaizola 2007: 180.

44. Onetti 1976: 9:50–10:30.

45. For a review of scholarship on migrations and cultural industries, see Aznar Soler and López García 2016: xxxi-liv.

46. Arenal 2011: 43; Aznar Soler and López García 2016; Férriz Roure 1998; González Calleja and Pardo Sanz 1993; González Echevarría 1996; Hallewell 1987; Lago Carballo and Gómez-Villegas 2006; López Llovet de Rodrigué 2004.

47. Paternostro 2014: 62; Anderson 1996. These transnational publishing ventures question the classic view of fields as self-contained national units. Cf. Buchholz 2016.

48. For a detailed list of these periodicals, see Aznar Soler and López García 2016.

49. Fiorillo 2002: 219.

50. González Echevarría 1996; Rodríguez Monegal 1972; Rodríguez-Carranza 2004. Ana María Cabanellas in Anderson 1996: 7; Lago Carballo and Gómez-Villegas 2006: 92; Rama 1982: 274; King 2012: 436; Monsiváis cited in Lago Carballo and Gómez-Villegas 2006: 211.

51.   Cabrera Infante cited in Herrero-Olaizola 2007: 78, 94. Letter of García Márquez to Lastra, March 14, 1967, 1, PLC.

52.   López Llausàs cited in López Llovet de Rodrigué 2004: 27. Letter of García Márquez to Lastra, March 14, 1967, 1, PLC.

53.   López Llovet de Rodrigué 2004: 41; Martínez 1999; Rama 1982: 294-95.

54.   Mexican Fondo de Cultura Económica opened in Spain in 1962. It soon faced a censorship ban on two of its best-selling titles, *Pedro Páramo* and *The Death of Artemio Cruz* (Lago Carballo and Gómez-Villegas 2006: 126, 130).

55.   Balcells cited in Paternostro 2014: 137 and in Herrero-Olaizola 2007: 177. Boundary-spanning agent in Hirsch 1972: 650. Donoso 1972; Paternostro 2014: 74; Santana 2000. On dealers' role, see Santana-Acuña 2016a; Santana-Acuña 2016b; Velthuis 2005; White and White 1993. On literary agents, see Thompson 2010.

56.   Anderson 1996: 13; López Llausàs cited in López Llovet de Rodrigué 2004: 34.

57.   Letter of Fuentes to Donoso, November 12, 1962, cited in Bocaz Leiva 2013: 1062.

58.   For my analysis, I used the contracts in GGMP, HRC, especially cont. 66.9, 66.11. The Carmen Balcells Archives were unavailable to researchers at the time I wrote this book.

59.   GGMP, HRC, cont. 54.1. The agency did not start to deal with another important source of revenue, the film rights of its clients' works, until the 1970s.

60.   Donoso 1972: 116.

61.   Martínez 1999; Martínez 1967: 54; Vargas Llosa cited in Herrero-Olaizola 2007: 40; Cortázar cited in Rama 1982: 269; García Márquez cited in interview with Monsalve 1968: 4; Bourdieu 2012; González Echevarría 2012: 47; Jimeno Revilla 2015; Rama 1982: 56-57, 142-43, 259-320.

62.   Cartas a la redacción, *Life en Español* (June 21, 1965): 3.

63.   Benedetti 1970: 14-15.

64.   Rodríguez Monegal cited in *Primera Plana* 189 (August 9, 1966): 66. King 2012: 436. *Primera Plana* 155 (October 26, 1965): 1. Herrero-Olaizola 2007; Lago Carballo and Gómez-Villegas 2006: 187; Santana 2000.

65.   Citations of Biblioteca Básica de Cultura Latinoamericana taken from its edition of *Leaf Storm*.

66.   Herrero-Olaizola 2007: 38; Jimeno Revilla 2015: I-2, gráfico 18; Radway 1997; Santana 2000: 35; Ayén 2014: Loc. 1071; Santana-Acuña, "Spain," forthcoming.

67.   Contract with Veracruzana, July 19, 1961. GGMP, HRC, cont. 66.9. He received an advance of 1,000 pesos and royalties for 10 percent of the price of the cover. Letters from García Márquez to Mendoza, August 9, [1961], [late 1962], and September 1, 1963; to Francisco Porrúa, October 30, 1965, 1, HRC.

68.   Sales of his early works soared after the publication of *One Hundred Years of Solitude*. Yet numerous writers and scholars consider his novella *No One Writes to the Colonel*, which sold few copies upon its release, to be aesthetically superior to *One Hundred Years of Solitude* (Martin 2009; Swanson 2010).

69.   On the Balcells visit, see *La Cultura en México* 179 (July 21, 1965: xx). The contract with García Márquez is dated August 6, not in July (Ayén 2014). García Márquez's contracts, GGMP, HRC, cont. 66.9, 66.11.

70.   Porrúa cited in García Márquez 2001a: 59 and Herrero-Olaizola 2007: 124; ERA publisher cited in Paternostro 2014: 144. Eloy Martínez cited in García Márquez 2001a: 64-65.

71.   When Porrúa and García Márquez met in 1967, after the publication of *One Hundred Years of Solitude*, they discovered they shared similar taste in literature and music (Porrúa 2014).

72.   Letter of Fuentes to García Márquez, November 19, 1965, 1, Carlos Fuentes correspondence (hereafter, CFC); Barral cited in Herrero-Olaizola 2007: 120.

73.   Letter of Fuentes to García Márquez, April 15, 1966, 1, CFC; Schavelzon 2002.

74.   Censorship file for *One Hundred Years of Solitude*, AGA 66/02529, exp. 1184.

75.   This finding suggests that the interpretation of meaning and aesthetics are not exclusive to the text. Rather they are socially constructed during the interaction between the text and the aesthetic-moral frameworks readers use to make sense of the text.

76.   Censorship file for *One Hundred Years of Solitude*, AGA 73/2026, exp. 6990.

3. A NOVEL IN SEARCH OF AN AUTHOR

1.   Poniatowska 1973: 203.

2.   This chapter seeks to fill a gap in the art world's approach in particular: how do conventions travel? Part of García Márquez's appeal to new art groups was that he imported conventions that he shared with these groups. He also recombined previous conventions with new ones. This *bricolage* of conventions or *convention-work* is not addressed in the art world's scholarship, which looks at small worlds. Bourdieu (1992) explained how conventions travel by looking at the circulation of ideas but he did not clarify how individuals and objects become carriers of ideas.

3.   Becker 2008 [1982]: 229.

4.   Collaboration has a measurable impact on how artists imagine the work of art. Contrary to the emphasis on competition and adaptation (Bourdieu 1992; Peterson 1997), new scholarship shows the impact of collaboration on the production of cultural goods (Halley and Sonolet 2017; Rodríguez Morató and Santana-Acuña 2017).

5.   García Márquez 2002; Martin 2009; Mejía Vélez 1972; Saldívar 2005.

6.   García Márquez 2002; Martin 2009; Sims 1992: 39 (quote).

7.   He hang out with journalists Guillermo Cano and José Salgar (from *El Espectador* newspaper), Enrique Santos Calderón (*El Tiempo* newspaper and founder of *Alternativa* magazine), radio broadcaster Álvaro Castaño Castillo, and writers Gonzalo Mallarino and Plinio Apuleyo Mendoza (Paternostro 2014: 99, 270).

8.   García Márquez 2002; Martin 2009.

9.   Columns in García Márquez 2015b: 240, 528; García Márquez cited in Restrepo 1955b: 1.

10. García Márquez 2001a: 167; García Márquez 2002: 386–89 (quote); Sims 1992.

11. García Márquez 2002: 389 (challenge); Paternostro 2014: 104, 112; García Márquez cited in Restrepo 1955b: 1.

12. Letter of García Márquez to Félix Restrepo, May 22, 1962, 1–2, and letter of García Márquez to Apuleyo Mendoza, May 1962, HRC; Censorship file, *One Hundred Years of Solitude*, AGA 66/02529, exp. 1184.

13. In 1948, Rojas Herazo published a literary column on a solitary general and hero of the civil war; a character similar to Colonel Buendía in *One Hundred Years of Solitude*. García Usta 2015: 39–40, 85, 317–18; García Márquez 2015b: 686–88.

14. García Márquez 2001a: 537.

15. Although not a group member, another formative influence on García Márquez and other members was writer Félix Fuenmayor (Fiorillo 2002: 21; García Márquez 2001a: 514, 544).

16. Fiorillo 2002: 96–97, 100; García Márquez 2001a: 553; Illán Bacca 2012; Martin 2009: 127; Paternostro 2014: 69.

17. Restrepo 1955b.

18. Fradinger forthcoming.

19. Other techniques imported from Faulkner include soliloquies, usage of indirect style, chronological distortion, and personal punctuation of the text. García Márquez also understood the aesthetic importance of word and sentence repetition, use of negative ultimates, intertextuality, long sentences and abundant subordinate clauses, and reliance on abstract nouns as subject of sentences, for instance, solitude, nostalgia, silence (Costa Picazo 2001: 24–27, 30–31, 34).

20. Restrepo 1955b: 1.

21. García Márquez 2001a: 449–50; Miliani 1965: 4 (certain sense); Restrepo 1955b: 1 (my novel). The group's strong support of Faulkner partly explains why García Márquez did not develop a taste for French intellectuals à la Sartre, expressing in his columns a dislike for contemporary French literature of this time, with the exception of Camus. On his initial criticism of Sartre, see García Usta 2015: 115.

22. García Márquez 2001a: 346. On May 15, 1949, his friend Rojas Herazo reported in his note in *El Universal* to be finishing up *Ya cortamos el heno* and García Márquez received input from him on the title and the manuscript (García Márquez 2001a: 110, 142). For *In Evil Hour*, see García Márquez correspondence, HRC.

23. García Márquez 2001a: 466. As he explained in an interview, "originality is not the important thing, but the way of telling the story. Antigone and Prometheus. The great myths of Greek antiquity are rewritten every century because they are immortal stories" (Muñoz 2012).

24. García Márquez 1952: 16.

25. García Márquez 2001a: 151, 309, 137; García Usta 2015.

26. García Márquez 2001a: 274; García Usta 2015: 76; Martin 2009: 441; Paternostro 2014: 61.

27. I used one surviving copy of *Comprimido* at the Biblioteca Luis Ángel Arango and the facsimile of *Crónica* in Bayona, Gilard, and de Cepeda 2010. García Usta 2015: 61–62; Paternostro 2014: 58.

28. According to Enrique Scopell, they recommended him to send the manuscript of *Leaf Storm* to publishers in Mexico and Spain but not Colombia (Paternostro 2014: 96). Cepeda Samudio cited in Martin 2009: 151. By mail, members continued to give each other feedback. In 1962 García Márquez said he had read the original of Cepeda Samudio's *La casa grande* and called it "an excellent novel" (Angulo 1962: 1).

29. García Márquez 2015b; Martin 2009: 169; Salgar cited in Paternostro 2014: 103, see also 107.

30. Film reviews in García Márquez 2015a: 160, 412–13; García Márquez 2015b: 423. For García Márquez and cinema, see Fiddian 2010; Rocco 2014.

31. García Márquez, Ruiz Rivas, and Truque 1954: 9.

32. Reviews in Ariete 1955: 4; Restrepo 1955a: 4. For history of its editions, Don Klein database. Contract of *Leaf Storm*, Guillermo Cano Collection, HRC.

33. Martin 2009: 200–207; Saldívar 2005.

34. Fiorillo 2002: 173; García Márquez 2001a: 533.

35. Fiorillo 2002: 107; Martin 2009: 186–88; Paternostro 2014: 114, 118–19; Vargas Llosa 1971: 399.

36. Martin 2009: 180, see also 199.

37. Guillermo Cano correspondence, 1955–1957, HRC. Fiorillo 2002: 107; Paternostro 2014: 119.

38. Chacón 1970: 26; Garmendia 1989: 252–53; Martin 2009: 225–41; Zapata 2007: 19, 34.

39. Latcham 1958: 29; Vargas Llosa 1971.

40. Chacón 1970: 24–25; Garmendia 1989: 252–53; Paternostro 2014: 122; Vargas Llosa 1971: 42–48.

41. Chacón 1970: 26, 30, 266. During the time García Márquez lived in Caracas, along with the novel fragment by Carpentier and work by Venezuelan authors, the Sardio Group published work by minor French authors, Asturias, Beckett, Paz, and Juan Goytisolo.

42. Martin 2009: 222, 231–35; Vargas Llosa 1971: 42–48; Zapata 2007: 55–56, 75, 83.

43. "Anteproyecto para la creación del Instituto de Cine de Barranquilla," Patricia Cepeda Samudio Archive, Barranquilla. Letters of García Márquez to Germán Vargas, April 26, [1961] and to Álvaro Cepeda Samudio, April 26, [1961], HRC.

44. García Márquez 2001a: 435; Poniatowska 1973: 193. Luis Harss, personal communication, 2017.

45. Letters of García Márquez to Mendoza, May 29, [1961], 1 (prospects) and to Masetti, May 2, 1961, HRC. He made very clear to his friends he did not want to do daily journalism again. Letters to Álvaro Cepeda Samudio, May 23 and July 21, [1961], HRC.

46.   García Márquez's piece appeared in *México en la Cultura* 643 (July 9, 1961): 10. Regular contributors to this magazine included Fernando Benítez, José Emilio Pacheco, Juan Vicente Melo, Carlos Fuentes, Emmanuel Carballo, Emilio García Riera, Carlos Monsiváis, and Rosario Castellanos, among others. It also included Spanish exiles as staff and contributors: Rojo, Aub, and García Ascot (Camposeco 2015: 105-6).

47.   Letters of García Márquez to Mendoza, August 13, August 5, and August 9 (cream) and July 10, [1961]; to Cepeda Samudio, July 21, [1961], HRC.

48.   Piazza 1968: 122, 156.

49.   Martin 2008: 484, see also 480.

50.   Fuentes 1962; Fuentes 1964.

51.   Other members included Estela Matute, Rocío Sanz, Huberto Batis, Luis Guillermo Piazza, Vicente Rojo, José Luis Cuevas, Juan Ibáñez, Bertha (Chaneca) Maldonado, Arnold Belkin, Sergio Pitol, Yuriria Iturriaga, Juan Bañuelos, Vicente Leñero, Montes de Oca, Sergio Fernández, Salvador Ortega, Joaquín Rodríguez, Héctor García, Ricardo Vinós, José Estrada, and Manuel Barbachano (Fuentes 2017; Piazza 1968; Vargas Llosa 1971).

52.   Mendoza in García Márquez 2001a: 580; Mauleón and Aguilar 2002: 176; Paternostro 2014: 64 (mesmerized).

53.   Donoso 1972: 102, 104-5; Martin 2009: 282; Piazza 1968.

54.   Díaz Ruíz 2014: 26-27; Martin 2009.

55.   Letters of García Márquez to Mendoza, June 30, August 9, and December 4, [1961], and [May 1962]; to Cepeda Samudio, July 21 and December 4, [1961], HRC. Alatriste cited in Martin 2009: 270.

56.   Letters of García Márquez to Apuleyo Mendoza, August 9, [1961], September 26, [1961], [May 1962], [September 1962], April 17, [1963], June 14, [1963], and September 1, [1963]; to Cepeda Samudio, December 4, [1961] and March 20, 1962; and to Germán Arciniegas, June 21, 1963, HRC. Fuentes 2017; Martin 2009: 167, 187, 270-75; Rocco 2014; Vargas Llosa 1971: 66-71.

57.   He received 180,000 pesos for *The Golden Cockerel*. He sent the script on the *charro* to his friends asking for feedback, because it reminded him of Macondo and he saw this as a problem. Letters of García Márquez to Mendoza, June 14 and September 1, [1963], [December 1964], and May 22, [1965], HRC.

58.   Letters of García Márquez to Mendoza, May 1962, June 14, [1963], September 1, [1963], and December 8, [1963], HRC.

59.   Benedetti 1966: 88.

60.   Martin 2009: 463 (García Marketing); Pachón Castro 1966: 15 (newspaper). Letter of García Márquez to Mendoza, May 1966.

61.   Letters of García Márquez to Mendoza, September 26, [1961], [May 1962], April 17, [1963], June 14, [1963], and October [1964]; to Cepeda Samudio, December 4, [1961] and March 20, 1962; and to Arciniegas, June 21, 1963, HRC; Carballo 1963: xx (biography).

62.   His friends in Barranquilla called his voluminous work in progress "the huge thing" (*mamotreto*) (García Márquez 2001a: 74; Martin 2009; Vargas 1967: 22; Vargas Llosa 1971). García Márquez in letter to Mendoza, August 13, [1961], 3, 4, HRC; García Márquez in Poniatowska 1973: 202 (wanted).

63.   The trip to Aracataca in 1950 opens the writer's autobiography (García Márquez 2002). His biographers Martin and Saldívar are divided about the date of this transformative trip. Most likely, there was more than one of these transformative trips (Martin 2009: 132, 136; Saldívar 2005). García Márquez cited in Fiorillo 2002: 216. Text of "The Buendía House" in Bayona, Gilard, and de Cepeda 2010: 241.

64.   Fiorillo 2002: 221; García Márquez 2015b (e.g. "La hija del coronel," "El hijo del coronel," "El regreso de Meme"). García Márquez 2001a: 241-75; Martin 2009: 119; Sims 1992: 35.

65.   Texts in García Márquez 2015b and manuscripts in Biblioteca Luis Ángel Arango.

66.   García Márquez 1952: 16.

67.   García Márquez 2001a: 142, see also 74, 156, 235, 274; Martin 2009: 158; Mejía Vélez 1972; Pater-
      nostro 2014: 82, 96–97, 150 (tenacious); Poniatowska 1973: 203 (dificulty). It is unclear whether
      he simply set the manuscript aside or destroyed this and other versions. But later evidence from
      his personal archives suggests that García Márquez's writing method involved keeping materials
      until the work was finished. He brought manuscripts with him everywhere he went.

68.   García Márquez 2001a: 409–11; Martin 2009: 200.

69.   García Márquez 1958: 31; García Márquez 1982: 39.

70.   Letter of García Márquez to Mendoza, August 13 [1961], 3, HRC.

71.   In the 2000s, García Márquez said that in *Pedro Páramo* (influenced by Faulkner's *Wild Palms*) he
      found key elements to write *One Hundred Years of Solitude* (Billon 2005: 64; Martin 2009: 265). Let-
      ters of García Márquez to Mendoza, August 13, [1961], 3–4 (incredible and angels) and December 4,
      [1961]; to Cepeda Samudio, December 4, [1961]; and to Germán Vargas, June 21, 1963, HRC.

4. NETWORKED CREATIVITY AND THE MAKING OF A WORK OF ART

1.   Poniatowska 1973: 201.

2.   García Márquez cited in Fiorillo 2002: 218; Rodríguez Monegal cited in Zapata 2007: 146; García
      Márquez correspondence with Mendoza, 1963–1965, HRC; Carballo cited in Paternostro 2014:
      137; García Márquez cited in Font Castro 1971: 36.

3.   Cf. Accominotti 2009; Christakis and Fowler 2009; Padgett and Powell 2012.

4.   Martin 2008: 484 (mesmerized); Poniatowska 1965: i.

5.   Second edition of *Leaf Storm* (c. 1959): back cover; Angulo 1962; Latcham 1961; Latcham 1958: 38;
      Volkening 1963.

6.   Carballo 1963: xx.

7.   Benedetti 1965: 11; Rama 1964a: 28; Rama 1964b.

8.   Benedetti 1966: 88.

9.   Harss 1967: 311–12. Personal communication with Harss, 2017.

10.   Miliani 1965: 4; Piatier 1965: 12.

11.   Scrapbooks, GGMP, HRC; Volkening 1963: 280–81, 288, 300–301. García Márquez recom-
      mended Volkening's essay to other critics, such as Pedro Lastra, interested in writing about him.

12.   Rama cited in García Márquez 2001a: 453. García Márquez's strategy was not unique. Chilean
      writer Donoso recruited Uruguayan critic Rodríguez Monegal, who gave him feedback on his
      work in progress (see chapter 8).

13.   Contracts: René Julliard (November 27, 1962), Feltrinelli (February 8, 1965) but released it four
      years later, and Meulenhoff (February 22, 1966); letters of García Márquez to Mendoza, [late
      1962], April 17, [1963], December 8, [1963], July 1, [1964], and March 17, [1967], HRC. The contract
      with Balcells is dated August 6, 1965. Ayén 2014: Loc. 498; Martin 2009: 284.

14.   He said to Vargas Llosa the epiphany happened in January 1965. Elsewhere, he said it was in
      October (García Márquez 2015c; Vargas Llosa 1971).

15.   Porrúa 2014. Letter of García Márquez to Porrúa, October 30, 1965; *One Hundred Years of Solitude*
      contract, HRC.

16.   Martin 2009: 284 (shit). Contract with Harper & Row, GGMP, HRC, cont. 66.9, p. 2. Letter of
      García Márquez to Fuentes, May 8, [1967], CFC.

17.   Letter of García Márquez to Mendoza, November 13, [1965], HRC.

18.   Letter of Fuentes to García Márquez, April 15, 1966, 1, CFC. Letters of García Márquez to Men-
      doza, July 1, [1964] and [December 1964], HRC.

19.   Miliani 1965: 4.

20. The art worlds approach presents artists and their success as the result of their belonging to a single art world (Becker 2008 [1982]). This does not apply to the making of *One Hundred Years of Solitude* and other best-selling New Latin American Novels.

21. Donoso 1972: 107; Poniatowska 1973: 220.

22. Fuentes 1965: vii. *La Cultura en México* featured his talk in a twelve-page article that included six pages of photographs.

23. Elío cited in Gordon 2002: 13:40–13:50; Elío cited in Mauleón and Aguilar 2002: 178.

24. Miliani 1965: 4; Pachón Castro 1966: 15.

25. García Márquez and Mendoza 1982: 111 (first sentence). During the writing of *One Hundred Years of Solitude*, García Márquez did not cut himself off from income, especially from filmmaking. At some point in 1966, he worked on the adaptation of one segment in the movie *Juego peligroso*, released on July 20, 1967. He also participated in *4 contra el crimen*, released on April 25, 1968; Pachón Castro 1966: 15; Poniatowska 1973: 196; Paternostro 2014: 140. Letter of García Márquez to Fuentes, December 25, [1965], HRC. In 2019, I interviewed a neighbor of García Márquez who recalled helping the writer's wife with food supplies.

26. Letters to Mendoza, [December 1964] and May 22, 1965, HRC.

27. Letter of García Márquez to Vargas Llosa, October 1, [1966], Mario Vargas Llosa correspondence (hereafter, MVLC). Elie 2015; García Márquez 2001b: 20–21; Martin 2009: 293; Schoo 1967: 53; Carballo cited in Paternostro 2014: 140, see also 141.

28. Poniatowska 1973: 213.

29. Letter of García Márquez to Vargas Llosa, October 1, [1966], MVLC. Poniatowska 1973: 198.

30. Harss 1967: 339; Elío cited in Paternostro 2014: 141. Letters of García Márquez to Fuentes, October 30, [1965], CFC and to Mendoza, November 13, [1965], HRC.

31. Letters of García Márquez to Fuentes, December 25, [1965], February 17 and May 21, [1966], CFC; to Mendoza, June 27, [1966], HRC; to Vargas Llosa, October 1, [1966], MVLC; Blanco Castilla 1966.

32. Letters of García Márquez to Fuentes, February 17, [1966], CFC.

33. Letters of García Márquez to Cano, April [1967] and to Angulo, June 20, [1966], HRC. *El Nacional*, Mexico City, June 15, 1965, 6.

34. Letters of García Márquez to Fuentes, July 30 and September 30 [1966], CFC and to Mendoza, July 22, [1966] and August 24, [1966], HRC. "5000 años de Celanese Mexicana," HRC; I thank Gonzalo García for bringing this document to my attention. See also below, note 57.

35. García Márquez 1976: 20:00–20:15 (great time). Letters of García Márquez to Fuentes, December 7, [1966], CFC; to Mendoza, March 17, [1967], HRC; and to Vargas Llosa, May 12, [1967] MVLC; Elío cited in Mauleón and Aguilar 2002: 180 (bad). Neighbor in Cerrada de La Loma, Mexico City, personal communication, February 23, 2019.

36. Carballo cited in García Márquez 2001b: 28 (very soon); García Márquez and Mendoza 1982: 104 (friends); Martin 2009: 296; Paternostro 2014: 22 (everyone); Poniatowska 1973: 196; Vargas Llosa 1971: 78ss.

37. Poniatowska 1973: 208; letter of García Márquez to Mendoza, [December 1964], HRC.

38. Font Castro 1971: 36.

39. Miliani 1965: 4; letter to Mendoza, July 22, [1966], HRC.

40. Excerpts of *Explosion in a Cathedral* reproduced in Fuentes 1964: xvi. English translation by John Sturrock, passages XX and XLVII.

41. Letters of García Márquez to Mendoza, July 1, [1964] and July 22, [1966], HRC. García Márquez 2001a: 590–91 (flavor). He did not fully acknowledge the big influence of Carpentier's novel on his. The influence is clear even in the title. Literally translated, the title of Carpentier's novel should be *The Century of Lights* in English. The title of García Márquez's novel about "the century of solitude" is *One Hundred Years of Solitude*.

42. Miliani 1965: 4.

43. Poniatowska 1973: 201 (my emphasis). See also Paternostro 2014: 143.

44. The García Rieras occasionally took García Marquez's family to their home Sunday evenings. They also received invitations from the Alcorizas. Betancur 1989: 44 (version); Elío cited in García Márquez 2001a: 73-74; García Márquez 2001b: 20-21, 26, 30; Martin 2009: 149; Paternostro 2014: 141, see also 136, 139; Poniatowska 1973: 196; Vargas Llosa 1971: 79ss.

45. Barcha's feedback in Font Castro 1971: 35; Elío cited in Paternostro 2014: 141-42. See also Mauleón and Aguilar 2002: 180 and Gordon 2002: 10:50-15:15.

46. Letter of García Márquez to Mendoza, July 22, [1966], HRC; Díaz Sosa 1967: 4.

47. Carballo directed *Revista de la Universidad de México*, was member of the editorial board of *Casa de las Américas* magazine. With Fuentes, he created *Revista Mexicana de Literatura*, which published short stories by García Márquez. He contributed literary criticism on national and international titles as well as interviews with writers to supplements *México en la cultura* and *La Cultura en México* (Alburquerque Fuschini 2000: 349; Camposeco 2015: 112, 114).

48. Carballo cited in Ferreyra 2014 and in Paternostro 2014: 22, 142-44 (my emphasis).

49. Araiza invited some friends over to read chapters as she was typing them. Most probably, her comments to García Márquez were also informed by what her friends said. García Márquez 2001b: 32; Martin 2009: 294; Poniatowska 1973: 200.

50. Elío in Mauleón and Aguilar 2002: 180; Mutis cited in Muñoz 2012; Balcells cited in Paternostro 2014: 175. He told his stories when they were fairly clear in his mind, as he was superstitious. "Interviewer: Could you tell me something else? García Márquez: I can't because it brings bad luck to the story" (Muñoz 2012).

51. Poniatowska 1973: 196-97.

52. Font Castro 1971: 36; letters of Fuentes to García Márquez, April 15 and August 26, 1966, CFC.

53. Letter to Mendoza, July 22, 1966, HRC; Harss cited in Fontana 2012. See also Paternostro 2014: 162.

54. Letter of García Márquez to Fuentes, March 4, [1967], CFC.

55. Vargas cited in Fiorillo 2002: 111; see also 273. Letters of García Márquez to Angulo, December 16, [1966] and to Mendoza, March 17, [1967], HRC, my emphasis.

56. *Critique génétique* is mostly a descriptive analysis of the text and implies that creativity is an individual effort. My analysis, on the contrary, shows how the writer's social network informs his creativity during the genesis of the manuscript. Cf. de Biasi 2011.

57. In late August or September 1966, García Márquez gave the final typescript to Sudamericana, a total of 490 sheets. It is unclear whether he actually mailed it, his friend Mutis took it with him to Buenos Aires, or he did both. Back then, photocopying was still a new and expensive technology. To make multiple copies, the standard procedure was to use carbon copy paper. García Márquez's typist typed the text on regular paper and made of at least three carbon copies of each sheet. The original on regular paper was sent to the publisher and it is lost. One carbon copy is what I call the Ransom typescript (previously owned by García Márquez). The second carbon copy is the Cepeda typescript, kept by the Cepeda Samudio family, which is the copy that García Márquez sent in December 1966 to his friends in Colombia to receive their feedback. There is a photocopy of this typescript at the Harry Ransom Center. The third carbon copy is the Carballo typescript, which García Márquez gave as a gift to Carballo and is now at the Museo Soumaya in Mexico City.

58. Letter of García Márquez to Vargas Llosa, March 20, 1967, MVLC.

59. Fragments of "The House" in García Márquez 2015b. Harss 1967: 319; Miliani 1965: 4. On tropical gothic, see Suárez 2015.

60. Rama 1964b: 22; Volkening 1963: 290.

61. Fuentes 1965: v; Rulfo (1977: 39:53) said *Pedro Páramo* "in reality is a novel of ghosts." The gothic appears also in Buñuel's 1961 film *Viridiana*.

62. García Márquez 1967a: 26 (my emphasis). Likely, his gothic has some of its roots in rural and traditional forms of Catholicism (and indigenous culture) in Latin America, where some communities customarily refer to miracles as an everyday thing, have countless superstitions, and treat saints like real human beings. Cf. González Echevarría 2014: 343.

63. Letter of García Márquez to Fuentes, October 30, [1965], CFC.

64. Miliani 1965: 4.

65. Harss 1967: 339.

66. In the Miliani interview, García Márquez stated that the third generation promoted thirty-two civil wars and lost them all. In the Harss letter, the Colonel alone, now a member of the second generation, promoted these wars (Harss 1967: 340).

67. Letters of García Márquez to Fuentes, October 30, [1965], CFC, and to Porrúa, October 30, 1965, HRC.

68. Harss 1967: 340; Pachón Castro 1966: 15. In 1955, in the last pages of *Leaf Storm*, García Márquez wrote that a "final wind will sweep Macondo." I thank Nicolás Pernett for pointing this out.

69. González Bermejo 1970; Pachón Castro 1966: 15; Elío cited in Paternostro 2014: 145.

70. García Olaya 1967; González Bermejo 1970; Osorio Tejeda 1968; Vargas 1967.

71. He selected words that sounded better in a specific sentence: "ulcerados" (novel, p. 74) instead of "llagados" (typescript, p. 95), "orgullo" (novel, p. 180) instead of "idealismo" (typescript, p. 245), "hígado colonial" (novel, p. 322) instead of "organismo colonial" (typescript, p. 448).

72. Changes in syntax applied mostly to pronouns and verbs. For instance, "Este" (typescript, p. 126) was replaced with "Esto" (novel, p. 95); "lo" (typescript, p. 133) was replaced with "le" (novel, p. 100); "nunca llevara" (typescript, p. 321) was replaced with "nunca llevaría" (novel, p. 233); and "escandalizó" (typescript, p. 325) was replaced with "escandalizaba" (novel, p. 236).

73. Ayén and Ayala-Dip 2014: 8:15–8:58.

74. Fuentes 1966: vii.

75. Letter of Fuentes to García Márquez, January 24, 1967, CFC. Rodríguez Monegal 1967a: 621.

76. Scholarship on cultural production studies artists as if they have little or no impact on how critics are going to interpret their works (Casanova 1999; Childress 2017; Chong 2020). The case of *One Hundred Years of Solitude* reveals the strong influence that artists exerted on critics' assessment of the novel prior to its publication.

77. García Márquez 1966: 5-D; Vargas 1967: 21–22.

78. Letter of García Márquez to Vargas [1967], HRC. In return, García Márquez did the same for his peers. For example, he promoted Cepeda Samudio's *La casa grande* as a New Latin American Novel (see chapter 8).

79. Letters of García Márquez to Lastra, May 30, 1967, PLC, and to Vargas, May 30, [1967], HRC.

80. Letters of Rodríguez Monegal to Porrúa, October 14, 1966, and to García Márquez, December 12, 1966, Emir Rodríguez Monegal correspondence (hereafter, ERMC).

81. *Primera Plana*: May 23, 1967: 64 and June 20, 1967: 1, 52. Most likely, coverage of the novel in this magazine helped to finish off the first edition.

82. Rodríguez Monegal 1984: 34. *Primera Plana* 83 (June 9, 1964): 3 and 233 (June 13, 1967): 1.

83. Donoso 1972: 77; Buzzi cited in García Márquez 1997: 42.

84. Elío in Paternostro 2014: 22; Porrúa 2014; see also Santana-Acuña 2020.

85. Letters of García Márquez to Mendoza, July 22, [1966] and March 17, 1967, HRC, and to Lastra, March 14, 1967, PLC.

86. Letter of García Márquez to Mendoza, July 22, [1966], HRC. See also Angulo in Paternostro 2014: 22.

87. Letters of García Márquez to Angulo, June 20, [1966], to Mendoza, July 22, [1966] and March 17, [1967], HRC; to Lastra, March 14, [1967], PLC; and to Vargas Llosa, March 20, 1967, MVLC.

88. López Llovet de Rodrigué 2004: 52. On initial sales of novel, see letter of García Márquez to Fuentes, July 12, [1967]; Zapata 2007: 17; scrapbook, GGMP, HRC, oversize box (osb) 7; Fiorillo 2002: 273 (quotas).

89. This suggests a different path to success than field theory's emphasis on competition among cultural producers (Bourdieu 1992). Some cultural goods can more easily reach a top position in their field when market competition is lacking and cooperation prevails.

90. Santana-Acuña 2020. Sudamericana ad, *Primera Plana* (June 13, 1967): 67. As important as they were, sales of *One Hundred Years of Solitude* did not come close to those of the Beatles' *Sgt. Pepper's Lonely Hearts Club Band*. Released in Argentina in August, 40,000 copies sold out in Buenos Aires in just fifteen days. See *Primera Plana* (September 12, 1967): 60.

91. García Márquez 1967b; García Márquez in Ortega 1967: 10–11. But a year earlier, before *One Hundred Years of Solitude* was published, he said "Jorge Luis Borges is fabulous" (Pachón Castro 1966: 15). Díaz Sosa 1967: 4.

92. Copies per printing: 1st 7,940; 2nd 10,053; 3rd 11,880; 4th 12,420; 5th 16,110; 6th 15,220; 7th 5,924; Cuban edition 15,000 (see Santana-Acuña 2020). Coverage of release in Peru and elsewhere, scrapbook, GGMP, HRC, osb 7.

93. Herrero-Olaizola 2007: 131–34; Santana-Acuña 2020; Santana-Acuña, "Spain," forthcoming.

94. Research in sociology of art and sociology of literature has not fully addressed the question of how pre-existing meanings can shape the reception of a work of art (Griswold 1987; Santana-Acuña, "Aesthetic Labeling," forthcoming). Cf. Casanova 1999; Chong 2013; Chong 2020.

95. Reception among the first generation of U.S. reviewers shows similarities. See Marling 2016: 38–41.

96. Alat 1967: 11; *Análisis* 1967: 51; *Primera Plana* 1967: 59; Pinto 1967a: 15.

97. Miguel Otero Silva in Anonymous 1967/1968: 77; García Olaya 1967: 17; Rama 1967: 31; Rodríguez Monegal 1967a: 11.

98. *Atlas* 1967: 59; Franco 1967: 1054; Olivari 1967: s.d.; Orbegozo 1967: 10–11.

99. Ayax [1968]; Oviedo 1967: 3.

100. García Ascot 1967: vi; Carballo in García Márquez 1998: 14–15; Porrúa 2014; Rodríguez Monegal 1967a: 12; Vargas 1967: 21–22.

101. That label was not applied to García Márquez's early work either. In two essays published in 1964, Rama referred to his works as "hallucinated realism," "realist and fantastic," and "the grotesque" (Rama 1964b: 22; Rama 1982: 92). When dealing with *One Hundred Years of Solitude*, his older works were labeled as "the supernatural" (*Primera Plana* 1967: 59).

102. For instance, "the true 'chronicle of the marvelous real'" (Valente 1969: 7), "marvelous real" (*Primera Plana* 1967:59; Oviedo 1967: 3), and "samples of the marvelous-real" (Arenas 1969: 37).

103. Alone 1969: 33; *Análisis* 1967: 51.

104. Castro Arenas 1967: 14; Domínguez in Simón Martínez 1969: 146. Before the release of *One Hundred Years of Solitude*, only Venezuelan critic Miliani 1965: 4 referred to García Márquez (but not to any of his works) as "restrained and sober craftsman of magical realism."

105. *Atlas* 1967: 59; Arciniega 1968: 7; Campos 1968: 12; Fell 1968: vii; Franco 1967: 1054; García-Peña 1969: 29; Gómez 1968: 38; González 1968: 3; Lleras 1969: 8; Oviedo 1967: 3; Pinto 1967b: 15; Rodríguez Martínez 1969: 17; Toro Martínez 1968: C-1; Vargas Llosa 1969: 20.

106. Holgín 1967: 137; Carballo in García Márquez 1998: 23; Gimferrer 2004: 125; Llorca 1968: 14; Oviedo 1967: 3; Rodríguez Monegal 1968: 3.

107. García Márquez stated his novel "completely lacks seriousness" (García Márquez and Mendoza 1982: 104).

108. Burgos Cantor 1967: 17; Franco 1967: 1054; Fuentes 1966: 7; Fuentes 1976: 59; Montero Castro 1967/1968: 135; Toro Martínez 1968: C-1.

109. *El Espectador* 1967: s.d.; Gómez 1968: 38; Coneo 1967: s.d.; Zalamea 1967.

110. Porrúa cited in Jarque 1997; Martin 2009. For Matthew Effect, see Merton 1968.

111. On effects of structural dislocation, see Sewell 2005.

112. On semantic structure, see Hoffman et al. 2018.

113. Anderson 1996: 36.
114. Restrepo 1955b: 1.

PART II: BECOMING A GLOBAL CLASSIC

1. Sales numbers for *One Hundred Years of Solitude* can be found in the Gabriel García Márquez Papers (GGMP), Harry Ransom Center (HRC), MS-5353, cont. 66.9. Beyond that, there is no reliable way of measuring book sales in most countries before the creation of Nielsen's BookScan in 2001.
2. Corse and Griffin 1997: 174; Kapsis 1992; Peterson 2003; Santoro 2002; Sassoon 2001.
3. Apter 2013; Lizé 2016; Rossman 2012; Sgourev and Althuizen 2017; Verboord 2009; Verboord 2011; Verboord and van Rees 2009.
4. Cf. Childress 2017; Chong 2020; DiMaggio 1982; Griswold 1986; Griswold 2000; Griswold 2008; Lena and Pachucki 2013; Sapiro 1999.

5. CONTROVERSY, CONFLICT, COLLAPSE

1. Benedetti 1970: 49.
2. Ayén 2014; Cohen 2007; Marco and Gracia García 2004: 1003.
3. Benedetti 1970: 44-48.
4. Borges cited in Marco and Gracia García 2004: 835-36.
5. Martínez 2008.
6. Franco 2002; González Echevarría 2012: 101; Martin 1989; Martin 2008: 485; Vargas Llosa 1971. See also Müller and Gras Miravet 2015a: 10.
7. Casal 1971; Martin 2008: 491 (crisis).
8. Fuentes cited in Sheridan 2018: 33.
9. Martin 2008: 493; Siskind 2014; Sorensen 2007.
10. Arguedas 1969: 34; González cited in Blanco Amor 1976: 16; Cortázar 1969; Franco 2006; Moraña 2006; Rama 1982: 235.
11. Cabrera Infante 1980: 10-12; Cornejo Polar and Moraña 1998; D'Allemand 2001; Mignolo 2005: 59 (elites); Verdesio 2003. To García Márquez's credit, he also stated "Latin American literature is a reflection of different realities, and what it is reflecting, as a whole, is the immense variety of Latin American countries" (Marco and Gracia García 2004: 1110).
12. Cornejo Polar and Moraña 1998; Lienhard 1986; Mignolo 2005; Moraña 2005. Released in 1971, Eduardo Galeano's *Open Veins of Latin America* became a key text in postcolonial studies as the Latin American equivalent to Fanon's *Wretched of the Earth* (1961).
13. Ardao 1980: 134; Gallo 2014; Hoyos 2015; Jorge 2004; Segala 1999.
14. Allemany Bay 2013; D'Allemand 2001; Mignolo 2005; Rama 1982: 216.
15. I am using Thomas Kuhn's terminology in *The Structure of Scientific Revolutions* (1962). Literary criticism also started to become canonical with the publication of books such as *La crítica de la novela iberoamericana contemporánea* (1973).
16. Cabrera Infante 1980: 13-17; Collazos 1970; Donoso 1972; Borges cited in Marco and Gracia García 2004: 837; Carpentier and Vargas Llosa cited in Rama 1982: 267, 285.
17. Sollers cited in *Mundo Nuevo* 6 (December 1966): 93; Cocciolo cited in Blanco Amor 1976: 14-15.
18. Gironella, Zaldibea, and Grosso cited in Marco and Gracia García 2004: 59, nn. 17, 144, 136-40; Tola de Habich and Grieve 1971: 158. See also Fuentes 1976: 67.
19. Blanco Amor 1976: 20 (González cited), 24; Rama 1982: 281-82.

20. Donoso 1981: 13; Rama 1982; Rodríguez Monegal 1972. A decade later, Rodríguez Monegal 1984: 35 said that this book's goal was to "bury" the Boom.
21. Porrúa cited in Ayala-Dip 2014; Martin 2008; Rama 1982.
22. Fuguet and Gómez 1996; see also Santana-Acuña 2014.
23. Hoyos 2015; Martin 2009; Rama 1982.
24. A clear example is Piazza's *La mafia* (1967). Released two months after *One Hundred Years of Solitude*, this Mexican *nouveau roman* is an insider's friendly satire of Mafia writers and their cultural milieu.
25. Letter of Gullón to Rodríguez Monegal, September 13, 1966, ERMC.
26. Bocaz Leiva 2013: 1050, n. 2; Donoso 1972; Rama 1975; Rama 1982: 284–90; Siebenmann 1979: 17.
27. Ayén 2014; Cabrera Infante 1980; Donoso 1972; Herrero-Olaizola 2007; Martin 2009; Rama 1982.
28. Jimeno Revilla 2015; Santana 2000.
29. Martin 2009: 341 (bullshit). For the Balzac controversy, see newspaper clippings in GGMP, HRC, osb 7.
30. Puig cited in Herrero-Olaizola 2007: 166.
31. Kerr 2007: 78; Müller and Gras Miravet 2015b: 10; Sheridan 2018: 45; Vilas 2015: 12.
32. Aguilar 2017; Henseler 2003; Martin 2008: 493; Rama 1982: 169. Initially, influential female critics Sylvia Molloy, Josefina Ludmer, and Sara Castro-Klarén wrote criticism of male Boom writers but not female writers.
33. Ferré 1994: 897.
34. Anderson 1996: 36; Herrero-Olaizola 2007: 32–33.
35. García Márquez cited in Marco and Gracia García 2004: 1028.
36. Donoso 1972: 200–201, 208; Fuentes 1977: 47:50–47:53; Martin 2008: 486; Orthofer 2016: 388.
37. Donoso 1972: 121–22; Martin 2008: 486; Mudrovcic 1997.
38. Arguedas 1969; Collazos 1970; Cortázar 1969; Franco 2006; Moraña 2006; Rama 1982: 235.
39. Martínez cited in Blanco Amor 1976: 22; Harss cited in Rama 1982: 283.
40. Cobb 2008; Cohn 2006; Cohn 2012; Iber 2015; Mudrovcic 1997.
41. Letter of García Márquez to Donoso about Era [1968], HRC. Donoso 1972: 118. The transformation of the publishing industry in the 1970s was certainly connected to the slowdown of the world economy and publishing industries after the oil crisis of 1973 as well as to censorship by dictatorships in Latin American literature and universities (Rodríguez Monegal 1984: 30, 35–36).
42. Donoso 1972: 200; Gil-Mugarza 2014: 178, 185; Landeros 1965.
43. Paradoxically, this organizational change happened hand in hand with the establishment of large corporate publishing conglomerates, including literary agents, publishers, and distributors (Sapiro 2016a; Thompson 2010; Verboord 2011). Latin American literature might have been a forerunner of what became a global pattern in the organization of the publishing industry since the 1970s.
44. Rama 1982: 304; Santana 2000.
45. Donoso cited in Anderson 1996: 23, n. 16.
46. Herrero-Olaizola 2007: 14, 22; Santana 2000: 61. Seix Barral's competitor in the 1960s, Destino Press was also absorbed by Planeta Press.
47. Ayén 2014: Locs. 1005-91; Ayén and Ayala-Dip 2014: 25–35; Herrero-Olaizola 2007: 131 (household item); Porrúa cited in Lennard 2009.
48. On sales, Santana-Acuña 2020. On Rabassa, Fox 2016. On faulty translations, Díaz Martínez 2020. More data on translations in Santana-Acuña 2014.
49. Fau 1980; Fau and González 1986; González 1994; González 2003; González [s.d.]; Klein 2003.
50. Balcells cited in Elie 2015; Martin 2009: 329.

6. A NOVEL WITHOUT BORDERS

1. Rushdie cited in Elie 2015.
2. Anonymous 2017: 13; Toly 2019: 72. Profile of Smith, https://vu.linkedin.com/in/natalie-smith -27918857/de and *Oyla* 2018 article, https://oyla.xyz/article/blagodatnoe-more-nescastij [Accessed September 10, 2019].
3. Gerald Martin (2009: xix) calls *One Hundred Years of Solitude* the "world's first truly 'global' novel."
4. García Márquez and Mendoza 1982; Martin 2009: 285–86; Poniatowska 1973: 208; Vargas 1967: 22.
5. García Márquez 2001a; Martin 2009: 587, nn. 56, 57; Vargas 1967; Vargas Llosa 1971.
6. "Why Should You Read *One Hundred Years of Solitude?*" https://www.ted.com/talks/francisco_diez _buzo_one_hundred_years_of_solitude?language=en [Accessed September 10, 2019].
7. García Márquez cited in Poniatowska 1973: 196.
8. García Márquez 1976: 20:00–20:10; Marco and Gracia García 2004: 1029.
9. Elie 2015.
10. Pernett 2014; García Márquez cited in Poniatowska 1973: 218; Rama 1982: 215-17.
11. Fuentes 1976: 59, 61, 64; González Echevarría 2012: 106; Jameson 2017; Stavans cited in Martin 2009: 539, n. 4; Vargas Llosa 1971.
12. Benedetti 1970; Parkes cited in Esposito 2017; Hart and Ouyang 2005a; Johnson 1996; Marco and Gracia García 2004; Martin 2009; Santana 2000; Shaw 2010; Speer 2018; Vargas Llosa 1971; Zeng 2009. Porrúa cited in Lennard 2009.
13. Orthofer 2016: 420; Siskind 2014.
14. Siskind 2014: 61-71.
15. Cf. Peterson 2003; Santoro 2002.
16. Porrúa 2014.
17. Siskind 2014: 95.
18. Camayd-Freixas 1998; Duncan 2007: 194-207; Martin 1989: 141 (dangerous); Menton 1998; "Universal tendency" cited in Siskind 2014: 91. Cooper 1998; Haber 2003; Hart and Ouyang 2005a; Vargas Llosa 1971; Young and Hollaman 1984; Zamora and Faris 1995. Mo Yan Nobel in https:// www.nobelprize.org/prizes/literature/2012/yan/facts/ [Accessed September 10, 2019].
19. *El País* 2014; Jameson 2017; Orthofer 2016: 399, 388; Siebenmann 1979: 19. See also Zamora and Faris 1995; Teodosio Fernández (1992) in Alemany Bay 1998: 93-94; Bloom 2003; Bloom 2009; Hart and Ouyang 2005b; Valdés and Valdés 1990.
20. Arreola was well known and respected in Mexico (despite not being a member of Fuentes's Mafia) but not well positioned internationally. It did not help him that he did not publish actively during the 1960s. Carpentier, on the contrary, was well positioned internationally and was quite prolific in the 1960s. On Garro, see Rosas Lopátegui 2002.
21. Orthofer 2016: 406–7 (Aguilera-Malta), 411 (Rulfo).
22. Morrison and Rushdie cited in Elie 2015. Toni Morrison teaching files, Princeton University Special Collections.
23. Díaz cited in Elie 2015; Ghosh and Aldama 2002; Mailer 2004: 50. See also Hoyos 2015; Müller and Gras Miravet 2015a.
24. Jordison 2017; Toly 2019.
25. Siskind 2014: 61.
26. On commensuration, see Espeland and Stevens 2003.
27. In Latin America, borrowings and imitations of *One Hundred Years of Solitude* include, among others, *Los viernes de la eternidad* (1971) and *Los tumultos* (1974) by Granata, *El bazar de los idiotas* by Gardeazábal (1974), *Yo, el Supremo* by Roa Bastos (1974), *Redoble muy largo* by Echeverría (1974), "Luna caliente" (1983) by Giardinelli, and *Daimón* (1978), *Los perros del paraíso* (1983), and *El largo atardecer del caminante* (1992) by Posse.

28.   Arturo Uslar Pietri in Anonymous 1967/1968: 92.

29.   Farr and Harker 2008.

30.   Kakutani 2017 (Malia); Martin 2009: 426, 528; Moreno Blanco 2017. On book clubs, Childress 2017; Radway 1997.

31.   Müller 2018; Santana 2000; Valdés and Valdés 1990.

32.   Fau 1980; Müller 2018; Perés 1969: 416; Santana 2000.

33.   Donoso 1972: 153, 192 (classic); Fau 1980; Fau and González 1986; González 1994; González 2003; González [s.d.]; Martin 2008: 480 (par excellence); Martin 2009; Valdés and Valdés 1990. On area studies and journals, see Faber 2008; Huerta 2013; Santana 2000. On academic careers, see Lamont 2009. Tangential use, see Moretti 1996.

34.   Verboord 2009; Verboord and van Rees 2009.

35.   After the Ransom Center acquisition, two Colombian organizations made major purchases of García Márquez materials. The Biblioteca Luis Ángel Arango bought manuscripts dating from the early 1950s and papers from his friend Cepeda Samudio. The National Library acquired the complete collection of García Márquez's works in different international editions, about three thousand volumes.

36.   For examples across decades, see scrapbooks, GGMP, HRC, osb 6, 7, 12, and 13. See also chapter 7.

37.   Poniatowska 1973: 226; Santana Acuña 2017. Scrapbooks, GGMP, HRC, osb 12.

38.   Casanova 1999; Heilbron 1999; Sapiro 2016a.

39.   1969: Chianciano Prize (Italy) and Best Foreign Novel (France). 1970: Best book of the year, *New York Times* (United States). 1971: Honorary PhD, Columbia University (United States). 1972. Rómulo Gallegos Prize (Venezuela). 1973: Neudstadt International Prize (United States).

40.   Nobel Award Statement. 1982. https://www.nobelprize.org/prizes/literature/1982/summary/ [Accessed September 10, 2019].

41.   Picasso cited in Wikipedia entry, "Cien años de soledad." https://es.wikipedia.org/w/index .php?title=Cien_a%C3%B1os_de_soledad&oldid=112102790 [Accessed September 10, 2019].

42.   *New York Times* (March 9, 2010). The selected German text was the opening of Kafka's *The Metamorphosis* and the French text was a fragment from *The Little Prince*.

43.   Klein 2003; Klein online database; Siskind 2014: 94–5.

44.   For editions, Fau 1980; Fau and González 1986; González 1994; González 2003; González [s.d.]; Klein 2003. See also catalogue of the Biblioteca Nacional de Colombia and Klein online database.

45.   Herrero-Olaizola 2007: 194, 203; Martin 2009.

46.   *One Hundred Years of Solitude* as an audiobook: https://www.newkerala.com/news/read/1965 /intercontinental-hotels-amp-resorts-launches-a-curated-audible-book-collection-inspired -by-the-intercontinental-life.html; drink: https://www.caskers.com/hyakunen-no-kodoku-barrel -aged-barley-shochu-100-years-of-solitude-kuroki-honten; and dish: https://www.youtube.com /watch?v=IaoPIw-vsZA [Accessed September 10, 2019].

47.   Sparky Sweets, Thug Notes: https://www.youtube.com/watch?v=H6I4vlLOIyM; Green Brothers, Crash Course, Crash Course: https://www.youtube.com/watch?time_continue=13&v=YWNcCs__vQg [Accessed September 10, 2019].

48.   Forbes et al. 2015: 13.

49.   Index Translationum: http://www.unesco.org/xtrans/bsstatexp.aspx?crit1L=5&nTyp=min&topN =50&lg=0 [Accessed September 10, 2019]. Scrapbooks, GGMP, HRC, osb 6, 7, 12, and 13. Marco and Gracia García 2004: 663, 688, 976–78, 982, 999; Martin 2009: 401, 529, 535.

50.   García Márquez cited in Poniatowska 1973: 215. Marco and Gracia García 2004: 1033, 1112; Martin 2009: 364–68, 563, n. 37. Scrapbooks, GGMP, HRC, osb 6, 7, 12, and 13.

51.   Donoso 1972: 188, 195; Martin 2009: 371, 377, 410, 492. See also Espmark 1991.

52.   Bell-Villada 2006; Greenberg 2009 (theme park); Herrero-Olaizola 2007: 176–77; Martin 2009: 425 (spectacle), 463, 494, 528; Stone 1981. *Vanity Fair* published *Chronicle of a Death Foretold* in full as

a premiere, repeating what Hemingway did in *Life* magazine with *The Old Man and the Sea*. On US$50,000 charge see GGMP, HRC, cont. 53.4.

53. GGMP, cont. 62, and Photograph Albums, Subseries A, HRC. Arenas 1981; Castro 2002; Martin 2009: 391-431; Carballo cited in Mauleón and Aguilar 2002: 180; Valdéz 2010.

54. Anonymous 2018; Martin 2009: 446-52, 519.

55. Similar branding has been found for van Gogh and Beethoven (DeNora 1995; Heinich 1991). Cf. Bartmanski 2012; Lamont 1987.

56. Martin 2009: 414, 421, 540; Müller 2018: 169; Paternostro 2014: 92.

57. Müller 2018: 162-63.

58. Gates 2019; NPR 2018: 0:28-0:30; Paternostro 2014: 14 (beloved); Varela 2014.

7. INDEXING A CLASSIC

1. In this chapter, citations and years in brackets refer to data from the online dataset that I collected for the six elements under analysis between 1967 and 2020. For dataset, go to: https://drive .google.com/open?id=1dmmKquw3ZJPG1eEVKosbpulZysZ4FQjU.

2. Santana-Acuña 2014. See also Bar-Hillel 1954; Fontdevila 2010; Garfinkel 1967; Silverstein 1976.

3. Collins and Guillén 2012: 539. Regarding negative reputation for writers such as Faulkner and Orwell, see Rodden 2002 and Schwartz 1988.

4. Others examples are the galleon abandoned in the jungle, José Arcadio's long penis, the four-year-long rain, the insomnia plague, the banana strike and massacre, and the novel's ending.

5. Fox 2016.

6. Leonard 1982: C-31.

7. Vineberg 1982: 10.

8. Fuentes 1976: 58.

9. Zapata 2007: 87; see also image of bottle.

10. Zapata 2007: 77; see also image of album cover.

11. Similar evidence about the universalization of Macondo was found for years 1971, 1978, 2006, 2007, and 2012.

12. Barcia 2007.

13. Other supernatural events indexed by transnational audiences are the priest's levitations in chapter 5, the death of José Arcadio, patriarch of the Buendía family, in chapter 7, and the four-year, non-stop rainfall on Macondo in chapter 16.

14. García Márquez 2001b; García Márquez and Vargas Llosa 1968.

15. Unlike this neighbor, U.S. critic John Leonard wrote, "I believe [in] Remedios the Beauty, plucked up by the wind and flown to God" [1970].

16. Zeng 2009.

17. Martínez cited in Martin 2009: 309.

18. Zapata 2007: 132.

19. Zapata 2007: 133.

20. Cf. Heinich 1991.

21. Another pattern is the adscription of García Márquez to different schools of thought. For Argentine writer Graciela Maturo, García Márquez is a Neo-Platonist [1977]. For Cuban writer A. Benítez Rojo (hinting at Postmodernism), he "manipulates the Western literary discourse" [1987]. And for South African writer and Nobel laureate J. M. Coetzee, he is a psychological realist [2006].

22. Like "Macondian," the adjective "Marquezian" has entered into language [1999] and is spreading (Elie 2015; Martin 2009).

8. ASCENT TO GLORY FOR FEW, DESCENT TO OBLIVION FOR MOST

1. Trollope 1950 [1883]: 70.

2. Counterfactual thought about literature is rare (Cohen 1999; Jauss 1982). Studies of counterfactual history in literary works are more common (Widmann 2009).

3. This chapter mentions in endnotes another twenty-five counterfactuals in literature.

4. *Los Sangurimas* is not an isolated case. Comparable cases include *Cuatro años a bordo de mí mismo* (1934) by Colombian Eduardo Zalamea Borda (1907-1963), one of García Márquez's mentors; *Broad and Alien Is the World* (1941) by Ciro Alegría (1909-1967), which Spanish writer Jesús Fernández Santos considered to be superior to *One Hundred Years of Solitude* (Tola de Habich and Grieve 1971: 146); and *El girasol* (1956) by Colombian Eduardo Santa (b. 1927).

5. Gilard 1976; González 1988; Levine 1975; Wishnia 1999: 38, 32 (quotes).

6. Gilard 1976: 183; González 1988: 740.

7. This was also the case of Colombian writer Carlos Arturo Truque. Born in 1927, like García Márquez, he passed away at forty-three. He was one of the three young and promising authors, along with García Márquez and Guillermo Ruíz Rivas, selected for *Tres cuentos colombianos* in 1954. Like Cepeda Samudio and García Márquez, Faulkner influenced Truque's rural realist short stories. See, for example, *El día que terminó el verano y otros cuentos* (1973).

8. Latcham 1958: 38; Rama 1982: 203.

9. Carrión de Fierro 1993; Gilard 1976: 183 (quote); Joset 1990; Robles 1976; Robles cited in González 1988: 742. Efforts to consecrate in retrospect other literary works were more successful during the peak of the New Latin American Novel. See, for example, *Adam Buenosayres* (1948) by Leopoldo Marechal (Rama 1982: 169, 297). On retrospective consecration, see Haskell 1980 and Schmutz 2005.

10. Vargas cited in Fiorillo 2002: 163; García Márquez 2015b: 325.

11. Letter of García Márquez to Cepeda Samudio, May 30, [1962], HRC. In terms of literary imagination, García Márquez shared similarities with Héctor Rojas Herazo, his close friend in Cartagena. Both from a small town, they worked at the same newspaper, *El Universal*, and wrote about rural themes. Rojas Herazo helped García Márquez with the drafts of two early novels, "La casa" and "Ya cortamos el heno." See, for example, Rojas Herazo's *Respirando el verano* (1962) and *En noviembre llega el obispo* (1967). Similarities in terms of literary imagination are also present in the contemporary works *El camino en la sombra* (1965) by José Antonio Osorio Lizarazo and *Neblina azul* (1949) by Jorge Lee Biswell Cotes.

12. Bancelin 2012; Cepeda Samudio 1991; Fiorillo 2002.

13. García Márquez 2015a: 237.

14. García Márquez correspondence with Cepeda Samudio, 1961, HRC; Olaciregui 2018; Rama 1964b: 22.

15. Letter of García Márquez to Cepeda Samudio, December 4, [1961], HRC. Cepeda Samudio's accusation in Fiorillo 2002: 197. In a column published on August 26, 1981, "El cuento del cuento," García Márquez gave credit to Cepeda Samudio for giving him "the final solution" to *Chronicle of a Death Foretold*. The evidence suggests that Álvaro Mutis and García Márquez engaged in similar exchanges about ideas for their work in person (Betancur 1989).

16. Letter of García Márquez to Cepeda Samudio about manuscript of *One Hundred Years of Solitude*, December 16, [1966], HRC. The Ransom Center has a photocopy of this manuscript.

17. Cepeda Samudio 1991: x-xii; Gilard 1976; Vargas Llosa 1971: 10-13.

18. Vargas and Scopell cited in Fiorillo 2002: 112, 130, 163-64.

19. Rama and Cepeda Samudio cited in Olaciregui 2018.

20. Letter of García Márquez to Cepeda Samudio, May 23, [1961], HRC. Bancelin 2012.

21. García Márquez in Cepeda Samudio 1967; Herrera 2012.

22. Gilard in Cepeda Samudio 1984: 11; Cepeda Samudio 2015: back cover.

23. Lezama Lima cited in *Primera Plana* 250 (May 7–13, 1968): 59; Guerrero 2020.

24. Coverage of *Paradiso* in *Primera Plana* 250 (May 7–13, 1968): cover, 1, 61 (maestro). Vargas Llosa in *La Cultura en México* 270 (April 19, 1967): i–vii). Not everything, of course, was praise. Luis Harss was among the critics, and he called out Lezama Lima for "bookish and cumbersome prose" and said his language was "onanist" (cited in Martínez 2008).

25. Blanco Amor 1976: 14; Gimferrer and Conte in Marco and Gracia García 2004: 473, 597; Cela, Caballero Bonald, and García Hortelano in Tola de Habich and Grieve 1971; Vargas Llosa in *Mundo Nuevo* 16 (October 1967): 89.

26. Cf. Bloom 1994; Corse and Griffin 1997; Corse and Westervelt 2002.

27. Lezama Lima admired baroque writer Luis de Góngora, the seventeenth-century poet of the Spanish Gold Age, also praised by Fuentes and other members of the New Latin American Novel.

28. Lezama Lima 1973: 9. Translation by Gregory Rabassa, chapter 1.

29. Donoso 1972: 66; González Echevarría 2012: 112; Guerrero 2020 (Proust); Orthofer 2016: 421 (great).

30. Cecilia García Huidobro cited in *Clarín* 2012; Kerr 2007. A similar case is that of Peruvian Julio Ramón Ribeyro. In letters to Chilean critic Pedro Lastra, he complained about the same thing García Márquez did to Lastra before the success of *One Hundred Years of Solitude*: invisibility.

31. Kerr 2007; Latcham 1958: 50; Piazza 1968; Rama 1982: 191. Correspondence between Rodríguez Monegal and Donoso analyzed in Bocaz Leiva 2013. *Guardian* cited in September issue of *Encounter* (1965): 103.

32. Bocaz Leiva 2013; Kerr 2007. Attendance at the book party is taken from names in a signed copy of *Coronation* at the Harry Ransom Center. *Daily Telegraph* cited in September issue of *Encounter* (1965): 103.

33. Bocaz Leiva 2013: 1054.

34. Donoso 1976: 4:30–4:35. According to Donoso's wife, they had twenty-one homes in twenty years of marriage (Donoso 1972: 148).

35. Bocaz Leiva 2013: 1056; Rama 1982: 191, 194.

36. Bloom 1994; González Echevarría 2012: 111.

37. Donoso 1965: xiii–xiv; Piazza 1968: 22.

38. Donoso 1972: 159; Harss cited in Martínez 2008; Herrero-Olaizola 2007: 23.

39. Baroja in Donoso 2016. Censors on Donoso in Herrero-Olaizola 2007: 23–24. Censors on *One Hundred Years of Solitude*, see chapter 2.

40. Barral 1983: 198; Donoso 2011.

41. Latcham 1958: 42; Rama 1982: 37, 208; Vilas 2015: 13.

42. Vargas Llosa 1996: 16.

43. Vargas Llosa 1996.

44. Arguedas 1974: 165; Harss cited in Martínez 2008. Arguedas against professionalism in Rama 1982: 251.

45. A writer needs to be alive to promote her work. A similar case is Macedonio Fernández's *The Museum of Eterna's Novel* (1967). He passed away in 1964, before Harss started to work on *Into the Mainstream* and when regional and international interest in the New Latin American Novel was growing. The novel's posthumous release had coverage comparable to *One Hundred Years of Solitude* in mainstream media such as *Primera Plana* (see also Rodríguez Monegal 1972: 80). Had Fernández been alive in 1967, he would have been added to the canon of the New Latin American Novel, and his novel, which has influenced successful writers such as Roberto Bolaño, would have a higher literary value.

46. Rama 1982: 252.

47. Arguedas (1992: 93) did not accept that social change could be positive for indigenous people.

48.   Rama 1982: 251.

49.   Castro-Klarén 2017; Cornejo Polar and Moraña 1998; Moraña 2006.

CONCLUSION

1.   Herrero-Olaizola 2007: 203.

APPENDIX: WHY AND HOW TO STUDY CLASSICS?

1.   Bayard 2007; Bourdieu 1992; Chartier 2005; Coser 1963; Edling and Rydgren 2011; Elster 2007; Greenblatt 2004; Kuzmics and Mozetic 2003; Lepenies 1988; Longo 2015; Runciman 1989; Tompkins 1985.

2.   For exceptions in sociology, see especially Childress 2017; DeNora 1995; Griswold 1986.

3.   Bourdieu 1992; Bourdieu 2012; Bourdieu 2013; Chartier 1996; Coser 1963; Durkheim 1968 [1912]; Edling and Rydgren 2011; Elias 1993; Elster 2007; Escarpit 1986; Griswold 1986; Kuzmics and Mozetic 2003; Lepenies 1988; Longo 2015; Radway 1997; Runciman 1989; Simmel 2005; Tompkins 1985; Weber 2015.

4.   For approaches to the novel form, reading practices, and classic texts and authors, see Chartier 1992; Chartier 2011; Greenblatt 2004; Greenblatt 2011; Greenblatt 2017; Moretti 1996; Moretti 2006; Thumala Olave 2018. On the role of gatekeepers, entrepreneurs, and organizations in art production, see Chong 2020; DiMaggio 1982; Griswold 2016; Marling 2016; Peterson 1997; Thompson 2010. On conventions, scripts, and collaboratives circles in art making and reception, see Becker 2008 [1982]; Benzecry 2011; Farrell 2001; Fine 2001; Menger 2009. On materiality and agency of works of art, see DeNora 2006; Domínguez Rubio 2012; Griswold, Mangione, and McDonnell 2013; Latour 2005; Levitt 2015. On fields of cultural production, see Buchholz 2016; Childress 2017; Leschziner 2015; Prior 2013; Sapiro 1999. On art circulation as a form of consecration, see Heinich 1991; Karush 2016; Phillips 2013. And on culture and social blueprint, see Christakis 2019. For an overview of recent approaches to the sociological study of art, see Rodríguez Morató and Santana-Acuña forthcoming.

5.   Goffman 1990: 9.

6.   Bouchard 2017; Durkheim 1968 [1912]; Taylor 2004.

7.   Elsewhere, I made the distinction between meaning and meaningfulness to show that people can agree that something is meaningful but not about its meaning (Santana-Acuña 2014).

8.   Chong 2020; Damrosch 2003; Darnton 1982; Sapiro 2016b.

9.   Cultural brokers are key to bridging ties over cultural or structural holes. Cf. Burt 1995; Pachucki and Breiger 2010.

10.   The influence of secondary school institutions and textbooks is shrinking. Influence is growing in popular entertainment and the digital sphere (Allen and Lincoln 2004; Baumann 2001; Bennett et al. 2009; Bromberg and Fine 2002; Thompson 2010; Verboord and van Rees 2009).

11.   To advance in this direction, I analyzed expert criticism alongside lay criticism to show a more horizontal, interdependent relationship between the two (Cheah 2016: 29–30; Kiely 1970 Corse and Griffin 1997; Corse and Westervelt 2002; Levitt forthcoming).

12.   On genius, see Sassoon 2001. On social conditions of art making, see DeNora (1995) on Beethoven and Heinich (1991) on Van Gogh. Integrated professional in Becker 2008 [1982]: 229. On networks and innovation, see Accominotti 2009; Christakis and Fowler 2009; Padgett and Powell 2012.

13.   Cf. Casanova 1999; Santana-Acuña 2014; Sassoon 2001.

14.   Müller 2018; Siskind 2014.

15. Casanova 1999; Cheah 2016; Damrosch 2003; Moretti 1996; Palumbo-Liu, Robbins, and Tanoukhi 2011.

16. Apter 2013; Cheah 2016.

17. Bloom 1994; Moretti 1996; Siskind 2014.

18. Santana-Acuña, "Aesthetic Labeling," forthcoming. On the move from the national to the global, see Sassen 2006.

19. Archer and Jockers 2016; Blatt 2017.

20. Alexander 2010; Alexander, Jacobs, and Smith 2012; Biernacki 2012; Chartier 2005; Griswold 1987; Lamont 1992: 178; Reed 2011; Santoro 2002.

21. Buchholz 2016; Greenblatt and Gallagher 2000; Sapiro 1999; Sapiro 2003.

22. Becker, Faulkner, and Kirshenblatt-Gimblett 2006: 3.

23. Acord and Denora 2008; Bennett and Joyce 2010; Born 2010; Cheah 2016; de la Fuente 2007; DeNora 2000; DeNora 2006; Domínguez Rubio 2012; Gell 1998; Greenblatt 2004; Griswold, Mangione, and McDonnell 2013; Hennion 1993; Latour 2005; Mukerji 2009; Strandvad 2012; Wagner-Pacifici 2010; Witkin 1997.

24. Bourdieu and Chartier 2010; Chartier and Bourdieu 1985.

25. Bevers 2005; Bloom 1994; Guillory 1993; Lauter 1991.

26. Researchers in literary studies acknowledge that the classic is related to canonization but "is not entirely reducible to it" (Mukherjee 2010: 1028). In sociology, sacralization (DiMaggio 1992) seeks to free cultural objects from the rigidity of canonical analysis. Unlike the approach in this book, sacralization emphasizes the object's dependence on its cultural niche for later success.

27. Cf. Bloom 1994: 15; Guillory 1993: 6.

28. Bourdieu 2016: 207.

29. Becker 2008 [1982]; Farrell 2001; Lahire 2006.

30. Recent studies also suggest that effective cultural production may require a combination of the three (Childress 2017; Lena and Pachucki 2013), contrary to the emphasis on either competition (Bourdieu 1992), collaboration (Becker 2008 [1982]), or adaptation (Peterson 1997).

31. Marling 2016; Menger 2009; Sapiro 2003.

32. See Haskell 1980; Lamont 2012; Weber 1986.

33. Evans 1995; Granovetter 1985; Patterson 2010. Yet contributions have not studied the embeddedness of cultural objects (Mica and Wisniewski 2012) and even less their disembeddedness (Polanyi 2001). The exception is studies of the cultural dimensions of embeddedness in markets (Dequech 2003; Krippner 2002; Krippner and Alvarez 2007; Spillman 1999).

34. Cf. Glaeser 2011; Greenblatt 1990; McDonnell, Bail, and Tavory 2017.

35. Bar-Hillel 1954; Fontdevila 2010; Silverstein 1976. Indexical expressions are similar to deictic expressions—words that require additional information to be understood. The main difference is that deictic expressions are associated with spatiotemporal references, while indexical expressions include a wider range of references (e.g., the arts). In short, I consider deictic expressions a subcategory of indexical expressions. The link between indexicals and meaning remains under debate in linguistics (Giorgi 2010).

36. The indexical analysis presented in this section is primarily concerned with identifying agreement about meaningfulness (which reveals the existence of an underlying indexical order), despite the existence of disagreements about the meanings of the book elements under analysis.

37. Collins 1981: 996, 1012.

38. These patterns confirm that indexical usage contributes to the making of macro-sociological orders (Silverstein 2003).

39. Ferguson 1997; Morgan and Winship 2007; Ragin 2008.

40. Greenblatt 2004; Griswold 1986; Shakespeare 2016; Taylor 1989; Taylor and Henley 2012.

41. Davis 2007.

42. Cf. Archer and Jockers 2016; Blatt 2017.

REFERENCES

PRIMARY SOURCES

Gabriel García Márquez Papers (GGMP), Guillermo Cano Collection, Plinio Apuleyo Mendoza Collection, Harry Ransom Center (HRC), University of Texas at Austin.

Patricia Cepeda Samudio Archive, Barranquilla, Colombia.

Pedro Lastra Collection (PLC), Special Collections, University of Iowa.

Censorship files for *One Hundred Years of Solitude*, Archivo General de la Administración (AGA).

Correspondence of Carlos Fuentes (CFC), José Donoso (JDC), Emir Rodríguez Monegal (ERMC), and Mario Vargas Llosa (MVLC), Special Collections, Princeton University.

Galley Proofs of *One Hundred Years of Solitude*, Héctor Joaquín Delgado Collection, Mexico City.

First editions of García Márquez's works, Dr. Don Klein Bibliographical database.

García Márquez, Gabriel. *Cien años de soledad* (editions: 1967 and 1971. Buenos Aires: Sudamericana; 1991. Madrid: Cátedra; and 2007, Madrid and Mexico City: Real Academia Española y Asociación de Academias de la Lengua Española).

UNESCO Basic Facts and Figures (1952–1962).

UNESCO Statistical Yearbook (1963–1973).

For online database with sources in chapter 7, go to: https://drive.google.com/open?id=1dmmKquw3 ZJPG1eEVKosbpulZysZ4FQjU

PERIODICALS (SELECTION)

Amaru, Peru (1967); *Casa de las Américas*, Cuba (1960–1965); *Diálogos*, Mexico (1967); *Eco*, Colombia (1967); *Encuentro Liberal*, Colombia (1967); *El Espectador*, Colombia (1952–1955, 1966–1970); *El Tiempo*, Colombia (1944, 1955, 1962); Ercilla, Chile (1963–1965); *La Cultura en México, Siempre!*, Mexico (1961–1967); *La Familia*, Mexico (1961–1964); *La Quinzaine Littéraire*, France (1968); *Le Monde*, France (1965–1968); *Libre*, France (1971–1972); *Life en Español*, United States (1965); *Marcha*, Uruguay (1960–1970); *México en la Cultura, Novedades*, Mexico (1961); *Mundial. Revista Gráfica*, Spain (1922); *Mundo Nuevo*, France (1966–1971); *Papel Literario, El Nacional*, Venezuela (1966–1971); *Papeles. Revista del Ateneo de Caracas*, Venezuela (1967–1968); *Primera Plana*, Argentina (1965–1969); *Repertorio Americano*, Costa Rica (1926); *Revista Mexicana de literatura*, Mexico (1962–1965); *Sucesos para Todos*, Mexico (1961–1964); *National Observer*, United States (1970); *New York Times*, United States (1970–2018); *Times Literary Supplement*, United Kingdom (1965, 1967).

BIBLIOGRAPHY

Abellán, Manuel Luis. 1980. *Censura y creación literaria en España: 1939–1976*. Barcelona: Edicions Península 62.

Accominotti, Fabien. 2009. "Creativity from Interaction: Artistic Movements and the Creativity Careers of Modern Painters." *Poetics* 37(3): 267–94.

Acord, Sophia K., and Tia Denora. 2008. "Culture and the Arts: From Art Worlds to Arts-in-Action." *Annals of the American Academy of Political and Social Science* 619: 223–37.

Aguilar, Gonzalo. 2017. "Clarice Lispector in the Foreign Legion." *Journal of World Literature* 2(1): 80–91.

Aguirre, Carlos. 2015. *La ciudad y los perros: biografía de una novela*. Lima: Fondo Editorial PUCP.

Alat (Alfonso La Torre). 1967. "García Márquez: 'Forjamos la gran novela de América'." *Expreso* (Lima), September 8, 11.

Alburquerque Fuschini, Germán. 2000. "La red de los escritores latinoamericanos en los años sesenta." *Universum* 15: 337–50.

Alemany Bay, Carmen. 1998. *La polémica del meridiano intelectual de Hispanoamérica (1927): estudios y textos*. Alicante: Universidad de Alicante.

Alexander, Jeffrey. 2010. "Iconic Consciousness: The Material Feeling of Meaning." *Thesis Eleven* 103(1): 10–25.

Alexander, Jeffrey, Ronald N. Jacobs, and Philip Smith (Eds.). 2012. *The Oxford Handbook of Cultural Sociology*. New York, NY: Oxford University Press.

Allemany Bay, Carmen. 2013. "La narrativa sobre el indígena en América Latina. Fases, entrecruzamientos, derivaciones." *Acta Literaria* 47: 85–99.

Allen, Michael Patrick, and Anne E. Lincoln. 2004. "Critical Discourse and the Cultural Consecration of American Films." *Social Forces* 82(3): 871–94.

Alone. 1969. "Cien años de soledad." *Coral* 9: 33–34.

Altamirano, Carlos. 2010. "Élites culturales en el siglo XX latinoamericano." In *Historia de los intelectuales en América Latina*, ed. Carlos Altamirano, 9–28. Buenos Aires: Katz.

Análisis (Buenos Aires). 1967. "Historia mágica del continente." 340 (September 18): 50–52.

Anderson, Benedict. 2006. *Imagined Communities: Reflections on the Origin and Spread of Nationalism*. London: Verso.

Anderson, Danny. 1996. "Creating Cultural Prestige: Editorial Joaquín Mortiz." *Latin American Research Review* 31(2): 3–41.

Angulo, Guillermo. 1962. "Habla el ganador del concurso literario." *Lecturas Dominicales, El Tiempo*, April 29, 1, 3.

Anonymous. 1967/1968. "Los novelistas y sus críticos (en el XIII Congreso Interamericano de Literatura)." *Papeles. Revista del Ateneo de Caracas* 5: 70–103.

——. 2014. "¿Cómo se dio a conocer la mágica 'Cien años de soledad'?" *El País* (Cali), April 17.

——. 2017. "Ticker." *Time*, October 30.

——. 2018. "6 razones para postular al Premio Gabo 2018." March 15.

Apter, Emily. 2013. *Against World Literature: On the Politics of Untranslatability*. London: Verso.

Archer, Jodie, and Matthew L. Jockers. 2016. *The Bestseller Code: Anatomy of the Blockbuster Novel*. New York, NY: St. Martin's.

Arciniega, Rosa. 1968. "Novela al tope del mástil." *El Sol* (León de los Aldama), May 27, 7.

Ardao, Arturo. 1980. *Génesis de la idea y el nombre de América Latina*. Caracas: Centro de Estudios Latinoamericanos Rómulo Gallegos.

Arenal, Celestino del. 2011. *Política exterior de España y relaciones con América Latina: iberoamericanidad, europeización y atlantismo en la política exterior española*. Madrid: Fundación Carolina.

Arenas, Reinaldo. 1969. "*Cien años de soledad* en la ciudad de los espejismos." *Coral* 9: 35-39.

——. 2001 [1981]. "García Márquez ¿esbirro o es burro?" In *Necesidad de libertad–Grito luego existo*, 73-76. Miami: Ediciones Universal.

Arguedas, José María. 1969. "Inevitable comentario a unas ideas de Julio Cortázar." *El Comercio* (Lima), June 1, 34.

——. 1974. *Yawar fiesta*. Buenos Aires: Losada.

——. 1992. *Una recuperación indigenista del mundo peruano: una perspectiva de la creación latinoamericana*. Barcelona: Anthropos.

Ariete. 1955. "La horajasca" (Tertulia). *El Colombiano Literario, El Colombiano* (Medellín), September 25, 4.

Atlas: A Window on the World. 1967. "The Total Novel." November: 59-62.

Ayala-Dip, Ernesto. 2014. "Fallece Paco Porrúa, el editor de 'Cien años de soledad' y 'Rayuela'." *El País* (Madrid). December 20, 2014.

Ayax (García-Peña, Roberto). [1968]. "Rastro de los hechos." *El Tiempo* (Bogotá). Location: GGMP, HRC, osb 7.

Ayén, Xavi. 2014. *Aquellos años del boom. García Márquez, Vargas Llosa y el grupo de amigos que lo cambiaron todo*. Barcelona: RBA.

Ayén, Xavi, and Ernesto Ayala-Dip. 2014. "Presentación de *Aquellos años del Boom*." Barcelona: Librería La Central.

Aznar Soler, Manuel. 2010. *República literaria y revolución: 1920–1939*. Sevilla: Renacimiento.

Aznar Soler, Manuel, and J. Ramón López García (Eds.). 2016. *Diccionario biobibliográfico de los escritores, editoriales y revistas del exilio republicano de 1939*. Sevilla: Renacimiento.

Bancelin, Claudine. 2012. *Vivir sin fórmulas: la vida intensa de Álvaro Cepeda Samudio*. Madrid: Planeta.

Bar-Hillel, Yehoshua. 1954. "Indexical Expressions." *Mind* 63(251): 359-79.

Barcia, Pedro. 2007. "*Cien años de soledad* en la novela hispanoamericana." In *Cien años de soledad*, ed. Real Academia Española, 477-94. Madrid and Mexico City: Real Academia Española y Asociación de Academias de la Lengua Española.

Barral, Carlos. 1983. *Penúltimos castigos*. Barcelona: Seix Barral.

Bartmanski, Dominik. 2012. "How to Become an Iconic Social Thinker: The Intellectual Pursuits of Malinowski and Foucault." *European Journal of Social Theory* 15(4): 427-53.

Baumann, Shyon. 2001. "Intellectualization and Art World Development: Film in the United States." *American Sociological Review* 66(3): 404-26.

Bayard, Pierre. 2007. *Comment parler des livres que l'on n'a pas lus?* Paris: Minuit.

Bayona, J.F., J. Gilard, and T. de Cepeda (Eds.). 2010. *Crónica: su mejor "week-end": semanario literario-deportivo de Barranquilla (1950–1951): textos rescatados*. Barranquilla: Ediciones Uninorte.

Becker, Howard. 2008 [1982]. *Art Worlds*. Berkeley, CA: University of California Press.

Becker, Howard, Robert Faulkner, and Barbara Kirshenblatt-Gimblett (Eds.). 2006. *Art from Start to Finish: Jazz, Painting, Writing, and Other Improvisations*. Chicago, IL: University of Chicago Press.

Bell-Villada, Gene H. (Ed.). 2006. *Conversations with Gabriel García Márquez*. Jackson: University Press of Mississippi.

Benedetti, Mario. 1965. "Dinamismo interior de una tormenta." *La Mañana* (Montevideo), November 5, 11.

——. 1970. *Letras del continente mestizo*. Montevideo: Arca.

Benedetti, Mario, et al. 1966. *Los diez mandamientos*. Buenos Aires: Editorial Jorge Álvarez.

Bennett, Tony, and Patrick Joyce (Eds.). 2010. *Material Powers: Cultural Studies, History and the Material Turn*. New York, NY: Routledge.

Bennett, Tony, Mike Savage, Elizabeth Bortolaia Silva, Alan Warde, Modesto Gayo-Cal, and David Wright (Eds.). 2009. *Culture, Class, Distinction*. New York, NY: Routledge.

Benzecry, Claudio. 2011. *The Opera Fanatic: Ethnography of an Obsession*. Chicago, IL: University of Chicago Press.

Betancur, Belisario. 1989. "García Márquez en el laberinto del general." *El País* (Madrid), March 10, 44-45.

Bethell, Leslie. 1998. *A Cultural History of Latin America: Literature, Music, and the Visual Arts in the 19th and 20th Centuries*. Cambridge: Cambridge University Press.

Bevers, Ton. 2005. "Cultural Education and the Canon: A Comparative Analysis of the Content of Secondary School Exams for Music and Art in England, France, Germany, and the Netherlands, 1990-2004." *Poetics* 33(5-6): 388-416.

Biernacki, Richard. 2012. *Reinventing Evidence in Social Inquiry: Decoding Facts and Variables*. New York, NY: Palgrave Macmillan.

Billon, Yves. 2005. *Gabriel García Márquez: la escritura embrujada*. Madrid: Fuentetaja.

Blanco Amor, José. 1976. *El final del 'boom' literario y otros temas*. Buenos Aires: Ediciones Cervantes.

Blanco Castilla, Amado. 1966. "Diez horas cantando vallenatos." *El Tiempo* (Bogotá), March 19, 14.

Blatt, Ben. 2017. *Nabokov's Favorite Word Is Mauve: What the Numbers Reveal about the Classics, Bestsellers, and Our Own Writing*. New York, NY: Simon & Schuster.

Bloom, Harold. 1994. *The Western Canon: The Books and School of the Ages*. New York, NY: Harcourt Brace.

——(Ed.). 2003. *Gabriel García Márquez's* One Hundred Years of Solitude. New York, NY: Bloom's Literary Criticism.

——(Ed.). 2009. *Gabriel García Márquez's* One Hundred Years of Solitude. New York, NY: Bloom's Literary Criticism.

Bocaz Leiva, María Laura. 2013. "La integración de José Donoso a la plataforma del Boom: intercambio epistolar inédito de José Donoso con Emir Rodríguez Monegal y Carlos Fuentes en la década del 60." *Revista Iberoamericana* 79(244-245): 1049-68.

Borges, Jorge Luis. 1970. "Autobiographical Notes." *New Yorker*, September 11, 40-94.

Born, Georgina. 2010. "The Social and the Aesthetic: For a Post-Bourdieuian Theory of Cultural Production." *Cultural Sociology* 4(2): 171-208.

Bouchard, Gérard. 2017. *Social Myths and Collective Imaginaries*. Toronto: University of Toronto Press.

Bourdieu, Pierre. 1992. *Les Règles de l'art : genèse et structure du champ littéraire*. Paris: Seuil.

——. 2012. *La Distinction : critique sociale du jugement*. Paris: Minuit.

——. 2013. *Manet : une révolution symbolique*. Paris: Seuil.

——. 2016. *Questions de sociologie*. Paris: Minuit.

Bourdieu, Pierre, and Roger Chartier. 2010. *Le Sociologue et l'historien*. Paris: Agone.

Bromberg, Minna, and Gary A. Fine. 2002. "Resurrecting the Red: Pete Seeger and the Purification of Difficult Reputations." *Social Forces* 80(4): 1135-55.

Buchholz, Larissa. 2016. "What Is a Global Field? Theorizing Fields Beyond the Nation-State." *The Sociological Review Monographs* 64(2): 31-60.

Burgos Cantor, Roberto E. 1967. "Cien años de soledad." *El Espectador* (Bogotá), September 24, 17.

Burt, Ronald. 1995. *Structural Holes: The Social Structure of Competition*. Cambridge, MA: Harvard University Press.

Cabrera Infante, Guillermo. 1980. "Include Me Out." In *Requiem for the 'Boom'—Premature?: A Symposium*, ed. Rose S. Minc and Marilyn R. Frankenthaler, 9-20. Montclair, NJ: Montclair State University.

Camayd-Freixas, Erik. 1998. *Realismo mágico y primitivismo: relecturas de Carpentier, Asturias, Rulfo y García Márquez*. Lanham, MD: University Press of America.

Campos, Jorge. 1968. "García Márquez: fábula y realidad." *Ínsula* 258: 11-12.

Camposeco, Víctor Manuel. 2015. *México en la Cultura, 1949-1961: renovación literaria y testimonio crítico*. Mexico City: Consejo Nacional para la Cultura y las Artes.

Campuzano, Luisa. 1996. "La revista *Casa de las Américas*, 1960-1995." *Nuevo Texto Crítico* 16/17(July 1995-June 1996): 215-37.

Carballo, Emmanuel. 1963. "Gabriel García Márquez: entre la esperanza y el desconsuelo." *La Cultura en México* 87: xx.

Carreira, G. G. 1994. *Historia del papel en España*. Lugo: Servicio de Publicaciones, Diputación Provincial de Lugo.

Carrión de Fierro, Fanny. 1993. *José de la Cuadra, precursor del realismo mágico hispanoamericano*. Quito: Ediciones de la Pontificia Universidad Católica del Ecuador.

Casal, Lourdes. 1971. *El caso Padilla; literatura y revolución en Cuba*. Miami: Ediciones Universal.

Casanova, Pascale. 1999. *La République mondiale des lettres*. Paris: Seuil.

Castro Arenas, Mario. 1967. "García Márquez de paso en Lima." *Siete Días* suplemento, *La Prensa* (Lima), September 10, 14.

Castro, Fidel. 2002. "La novela de sus recuerdos." *Granma Internacional*, December 8: 8.

Castro-Klarén, Sara. 2017. "Desenredando los nudos: Vargas Llosa y Arguedas en *La utopía arcaica*." In *Migración y frontera: experiencias culturales en la literatura peruana del siglo XX*, ed. Javier García Liendo, 117-47. Madrid: Iberoamericana Vervuert.

Cepeda Samudio, Álvaro. 1967. *La casa grande*. Buenos Aires: Editorial Jorge Álvarez.

—. 1984. *Le maître de la Gabriela*. Paris: P. Belfond.

—. 1991. *La casa grande*. Austin: University of Texas Press.

—. 2015. *Obra literaria*. Córdoba and Poitiers: Alción Editora and CRLA-Archivos.

Chacón, Alfredo (Ed.). 1970. *La izquierda cultural venezolana, 1958–1968: ensayo y antología*. Caracas: Editorial D. Fuentas.

Chartier, Roger. 1992. *L'Ordre des livres : lecteurs, auteurs, bibliothèques en Europe entre XIVe et XVIIIe siècle*. Aix-en-Provence: Alinea.

—. 1996. *Culture écrite et société : l'ordre des livres, XIVe-XVIIIe siècle*. Paris: Albin Michel.

—. 2005. *Inscrire et effacer : culture écrite et littérature (XIe-XVIIIe siècle)*. Paris: Gallimard and Seuil.

—. 2011. *Cardenio entre Cervantès et Shakespeare : histoire d'une pièce perdue*. Paris: Gallimard.

Chartier, Roger, and Pierre Bourdieu. 1985. "Comprendre les pratiques culturelles." In *Pratiques de la lecture*, ed. Roger Chartier and Alain Paire, 217-39. Marseille: Rivages.

Cheah, Pheng. 2016. *What Is a World? On Postcolonial Literature as World Literature*. Durham, NC: Duke University Press.

Childress, Clayton. 2017. *Under the Cover: The Creation, Production, and Reception of a Novel*. Princeton, NJ: Princeton University Press.

Childress, Clayton, Craig Rawlings, and Brian Moeran. 2017. "Publishers, Authors, and Texts: The Process of Cultural Consecration in Prize Evaluation." *Poetics* 60: 48-61.

Chong, Phillipa. 2013. "Legitimate Judgment in Art, the Scientific World Reversed? Maintaining Critical Distance in Evaluation." *Social Studies of Science* 43(2): 265-81.

—. 2020. *Inside the Critics' Circle: Book Reviewing in Uncertain Times*. Princeton, NJ: Princeton University Press.

Christakis, Nicholas. 2019. *Blueprint: The Evolutionary Origins of a Good Society*. New York, NY: Little, Brown Spark.

Christakis, Nicholas, and James Fowler. 2009. *Connected: The Surprising Power of Our Social Networks and How They Shape Our Lives*. New York, NY: Little, Brown and Co./Hachette Book Group.

Clarín (Buenos Aires). 2012. "Los Donoso, el novelesco y trágico desenlace de una familia." March 11.

Cobb, Russell. 2008. "The Politics of Literary Prestige: Promoting the Latin American 'Boom' in the Pages of *Mundo Nuevo*." *A Contracorriente* 5(3): 75-94.

Cohen, John Michael. 1965. "Southern Crosses." *Times Literary Supplement* (London), September 30, 867-68.

Cohen, Margaret. 1999. *The Sentimental Education of the Novel*. Princeton, NJ: Princeton University Press.

Cohen, Noam. 2007. "García Márquez's Shiner Ends Its 31 Years of Quietude." *New York Times*, March 29.

Cohn, Deborah. 2004. "William Faulkner's Ibero-American Novel Project: The Politics of Translation and the Cold War." *The Southern Quarterly* 42(2): 5–18.

——. 2006. "A Tale of Two Translation Programs: Politics, the Market, and Rockefeller Funding for Latin American Literature in the United States during the 1960s and 1970s." *Latin American Research Review* 41(2): 139–64.

——. 2012. *The Latin American Literary Boom and U.S. Nationalism during the Cold War*. Nashville, TN: Vanderbilt University Press.

Collazos, Oscar. 1970. *Literatura en la revolución y revolución en la literatura*. Mexico City: Siglo Veintiuno Editores.

Collins, Randall. 1981. "On the Microfoundations of Macrosociology." *American Journal of Sociology* 86(5): 984–1014.

Collins, Randall, and Mauro Guillén. 2012. "Mutual Halo Effects in Cultural Production: The Case of Modernist Architecture." *Theory and Society* 41(6): 527–56.

Coneo, José María. 1967. "Cartas al director: inventario de muertos." *Magazine Dominical, El Espectador* (Colombia), September 3.

Cooper, Brenda. 1998. *Magical Realism in West African Fiction: Seeing with a Third Eye*. London: Routledge.

Cornejo Polar, Antonio, and Mabel Moraña. 1998. *Indigenismo hacia el fin del milenio: homenaje a Antonio Cornejo-Polar*. Pittsburgh, PA: Instituto Internacional de Literatura Iberoamericana, University of Pittsburgh.

Corse, Sarah. 1997. *Nationalism and Literature: The Politics of Culture in Canada and the United States*. Cambridge: Cambridge University Press.

Corse, Sarah, and Monica Griffin. 1997. "Cultural Valorization and African American Literary History: Reconstructing the Canon." *Sociological Forum* 12(2): 173–203.

Corse, Sarah, and Saundra Westervelt. 2002. "Gender and Literary Valorization: The Awakening of a Canonical Novel." *Sociological Perspectives* 45: 139–61.

Cortázar, Julio. 1969. "Un gran escritor y su soledad: Julio Cortázar." *Life en Español* 33(7): 43–55.

Coser, Lewis. 1963. *Sociology Through Literature: An Introductory Reader*. Englewood Cliffs, NJ: Prentice-Hall.

Costa Picazo, Roberto. 2001. "La traducción de Faulkner al castellano." *Anclajes* 5 (December): 19–39.

D'Allemand, Patricia. 2001. *Hacia una crítica cutural Latinoamericana*. Lima: CELACP and Latinoamericana Editores.

Damrosch, David. 2003. *What Is World Literature?* Princeton, NJ: Princeton University Press.

Darnton, Robert. 1982. *The Literary Underground of the Old Regime*. Cambridge, MA: Harvard University Press.

Davis, Theo. 2007. *Formalism, Experience, and the Making of American Literature in the Nineteenth Century*. Cambridge: Cambridge University Press.

de Biasi, Pierre-Marc. 2011. *Génétique des textes*. Paris: CNRS.

de la Fuente, Eduardo. 2007. "The 'New Sociology of Art': Putting Art Back into Social Science Approaches to the Arts." *Cultural Sociology* 1(3): 409–25.

DeNora, Tia. 1995. *Beethoven and the Construction of Genius: Musical Politics in Vienna, 1792–1803*. Berkeley, CA: University of California Press.

——. 2000. *Music in Everyday Life*. Cambridge: Cambridge University Press.

——. 2006. "Music as Agency in Beethoven's Vienna." In *Myth, Meaning, and Performance: Toward a New Cultural Sociology of the Arts*, ed. Ron Eyerman and Lisa McCormick, 103–19. Boulder, CO: Paradigm.

Dequech, David. 2003. "Cognitive and Cultural Embeddedness: Combining Institutional Economics and Economic Sociology." *Journal of Economic Issues* 37(2): 461–70.

Díaz Martínez, Liset. 2020. "Gabriel García Márquez traducido: observaciones sobre la variación." In *Literatura latinoamericana mundial: dispositivos y disidencias*, ed. Gesine Müller, Gustavo Guerrero, Benjamin Loy, and Jorge Locane, 147–72. Berlin: De Gruyter.

Díaz Ruiz, Ignacio. 2014. "García Márquez en México: 1961–1967. Cornucopia y encrucijada." *Revista de la Universidad de México* 123: 24–32.

Díaz Sosa, Carlos. 1967. "Gabriel García Márquez: al trabajar en la escritura misma surgió la narrativa latinoamericana." *Papel Literario de El Nacional* (Caracas), September 3, 4.

Díez Medrano, Juan. 2003. *Framing Europe: Attitudes to European Integration in Germany, Spain, and the United Kingdom*. Princeton, NJ: Princeton University Press.

DiMaggio, Paul. 1982. "Cultural Entrepreneurship in Nineteenth-Century Boston." *Media, Culture and Society* 4(1): 33–50.

—. 1992. "Cultural Boundaries and Structural Change: The Extension of the High Culture Model to Theater, Opera, and Dance, 1900–1940." In *Cultivating Differences*, ed. Michèle Lamont and Marcel Fournier, 21–57. Chicago, IL: University of Chicago Press.

Domínguez Rubio, Fernando. 2012. "The Material Production of the Spiral Jetty: A Study of Culture in the Making." *Cultural Sociology* 6(2): 143–61.

Donoso, José. 1965. " 'Beber un caliz' de Ricardo Garibay." *La Cultura en México* 629: xiii–xiv.

—. 1972. *Historia personal del 'Boom'*. Barcelona: Anagrama.

—. 1976. "A fondo: José Donoso." *A fondo*, interview with Joaquín Soler Serrano. Madrid: Radio Televisión Española.

—. 1981. *El jardín de al lado*. Barcelona: Seix Barral.

—. 2016. *Diarios tempranos: Donoso in progress, 1950–1965*. Santiago: Universidad Diego Portales.

Donoso, Pilar. 2011. *Correr el tupido velo*. Providencia, Chile: Alfaguara.

Duncan, Ian. 2007. *Scott's Shadow: The Novel in Romantic Edinburgh*. Princeton, NJ: Princeton University Press.

Durkheim, Émile. 1968 [1912]. *Les Formes élémentaires de la vie religieuse: le système totémique en Australie*. Paris: Presses Universitaires de France.

Edling, Christofer, and Jens Rydgren (Eds.). 2011. *Sociological Insights of Great Thinkers: Sociology Through Literature, Philosophy, and Science*. Santa Barbara, CA: Praeger.

Elias, Norbert. 1993. *Mozart: Portrait of a Genius*. Berkeley, CA: University of California Press.

Elie, Paul. 2015. "The Secret History of *One Hundred Years of Solitude*." *Vanity Fair*, December 9.

Elster, Jon. 2007. *Explaining Social Behavior: More Nuts and Bolts for the Social Sciences*. Cambridge: Cambridge University Press.

Escarpit, Robert. 1986. *Sociologie de la littérature*. Paris: Presses Universitaires de France.

El Espectador (Bogotá). 1967. "Esa novela no la leo." September 21.

Espeland, Wendy, and Mitchell Stevens. 2003. "Commensuration as a Social Process." *Annual Review of Sociology* 24: 313–43.

Espmark, Kjell. 1991. *The Nobel Prize in Literature: A Study of the Criteria Behind the Choices*. Boston, MA: G. K. Hall.

Esposito, Scott. 2017. "Why Is *One Hundred Years of Solitude* Eternally Beloved?" *Literary Hub*, June 6.

Evans, Peter. 1995. *Embedded Autonomy: States and Industrial Transformation*. Princeton, NJ: Princeton University Press.

Eyerman, Ron, and Lisa McCormick. 2006. "Introduction." In *Myth, Meaning, and Performance: Toward a New Cultural Sociology of the Arts*, ed. Ron Eyerman and Lisa McCormick, 1–12. Boulder, CO: Paradigm.

Faber, Sebastiaan. 2008. "Economies of Prestige: The Place of Iberian Studies in the American University." *Hispanic Research Journal* 9(1): 7–32.

Farr, C. K., and J. Harker. 2008. *The Oprah Affect: Critical Essays on Oprah's Book Club*. Albany, NY: State University of New York Press.

Farrell, Michael P. 2001. *Collaborative Circles: Friendship Dynamics and Creative Work*. Chicago, IL: University of Chicago Press.

Fau, Margaret. 1980. *Gabriel García Márquez: An Annotated Bibliography, 1947–1979*. Westport, CT: Greenwood Press.

Fau, Margaret, and Nelly de González. 1986. *Bibliographic Guide to Gabriel García Márquez, 1979–1985.* New York, NY: Greenwood Press.

Fell, Claude. 1968. "Cent années de solitude." *Le Monde,* Mars 23, vii.

Ferguson, Niall (Ed.). 1997. *Virtual History: Alternatives and Counterfactuals.* London: Picador.

Ferré, Rosario. 1994. "The Bitches' Colloquy." *Callaloo* 17(3): 889–99.

Ferreyra, Carlos. 2014. "Emmanuel en la memoria." *Crónica* (Mexico City), April 24.

Férriz Roure, Teresa. 1998. *La edición catalana en México.* Zapopan: Colegio de Jalisco.

Fiddian, Robin. 2010. "Entre la pantalla y el libro: Gabriel García Márquez y el cine." *Arbor* 186(741): 69–77.

Fine, Gary Alan. 2001. *Difficult Reputations: Collective Memories of the Evil, Inept, and Controversial.* Chicago, IL: University of Chicago Press.

Fiorillo, Heriberto. 2002. *La Cueva: crónica del Grupo de Barranquilla.* Barranquilla: Editorial Heriberto Fiorillo.

Fojas, Camilla. 2005. *Cosmopolitanism in the Americas.* West Lafayette, IN: Purdue University Press.

Font Castro, José. 1971. "Anecdotario de una Semana Santa con Gabriel García Márquez en Caracas." *Momento* (Caracas). 771(April): 34–37.

Fontana, Antonio. 2012. "'Cien años de soledad' me pareció una larga anécdota." *ABC Cultural, ABC* (Madrid), October 27, 4–7.

Fontdevila, Jorge. 2010. "Indexes, Power, and Netdoms: A Multidimensional Model of Language in Social Action." *Poetics* 38(6): 587–609.

Forbes, A. G., A. Burbano, P. Murray, and G. Legrady. 2015. "Imagining Macondo: Interacting with García Márquez's Literary Landscape." *IEEE Computer Graphics and Applications* 35(5): 12–19.

Fox, Margalit. 2016. "Gregory Rabassa, a Premier Translator of Spanish and Portuguese Fiction, Dies at 94." *New York Times,* June 15.

Fradinger, Moira. Forthcoming. *Antígonas: A Latin American Itinerary.* Oxford: Oxford University Press.

Franco, Jean. 1967. "Stranger in Paradise." *Times Literary Supplement* (London), November 9, 1054.

—. 2002. *The Decline and Fall of the Lettered City: Latin America in the Cold War.* Cambridge, MA: Harvard University Press.

Franco, Sergio R. 2006. *José María Arguedas: hacia una poética migrante.* Pittsburgh, P.A.: Instituto Internacional de Literatura Iberoamericana.

Frisch, Mark. 1993. *William Faulkner: su influencia en la literatura hispanoamericana: Mallea, Rojas, Yáñez y García Márquez.* Buenos Aires: Corregidor.

Fuentes, Carlos. 1962. "Faulkner: entre el dolor y la nada." *La Cultura en México* 24: i–v.

—. 1964. "La nueva novela latinoamericana." *La Cultura en México* 128: i–xvi.

—. 1965. "No creo que sea obligación del escritor engrosar las filas de los menesterosos." *La Cultura en México* 189: i–xii.

—. 1966. "Gabriel García Márquez: *Cien años de soledad.*" *La Cultura en México* 228: vii.

—. 1976. *La nueva novela hispanoamericana.* Mexico City: Joaquín Mortiz.

—. 1977. "A fondo: Carlos Fuentes." *A fondo,* interview with Joaquín Soler Serrano. Madrid: Radio Televisión Española.

—. 2017. *Luis Buñuel o La mirada de la medusa.* Madrid: Fundación Banco Santander.

Fuguet, Alberto, and Sergio Gómez. 1996. *McOndo.* Barcelona: Grijalbo Mondadori.

Gabilondo, Joseba. 2009. "Genealogía de la 'raza latina': para una teoría atlántica de las estructuras raciales hispanas." *Revista iberoamericana* 75(228): 795–818.

Gallo, Rubén. 2014. *Proust's Latin Americans.* Baltimore, MD: Johns Hopkins University Press.

García Ascot, Jomí. 1967. "'Cien años de soledad' una novela de Gabriel García Márquez solo comparable a 'Moby Dick'." *La Cultura en México* 281: vi–vii.

García Márquez, Eligio. 1997. "El enigma de Buenos Aires." *Cambio 16* 207: 42–43.

—. 2001a. *Tras las claves de Melquíades: historia de Cien años de soledad.* Bogotá: Norma.

García Márquez, Gabriel. 1952. "La mujer que llegaba a las seis" and "Auto-Crítica." *Dominical, El Espectador* (Bogotá), March 30, 16, 23, 25.

—. 1958. "Nagy: ¿héroe o traidor?" *Élite* (Caracas), June 28: 28–31.

—. 1966. "Desventuras de un escritor de libros." *El Espectador* (Bogotá), July 1966, 5-D.

—. 1967a. *Cien años de soledad*. Buenos Aires: Editorial Sudamericana.

—. 1967b. "Quiero comprometer a mis lectores en vez de ser un escritor comprometido." *Últimas Noticias* (Caracas), August 4, 20.

—. 1976. "Entrevista con Germán Castro Caycedo." Colombia: RTI.

—. 1982. *El coronel no tiene quien le escriba*. Bogotá: La Oveja Negra.

—. 1998. *Voz de autor. Cien años de Soledad*. Mexico City: Universidad Nacional Autónoma de México.

—. 2001b. "La novela detrás de la novela." *Cambio* (Bogotá), July 19: 18–38.

—. 2002. *Vivir para contarla*. Barcelona: Mondadori.

—. 2015a. *Entre cachacos*. Bogotá: Penguin Random House.

—. 2015b. *Textos costeños*. Bogotá: Penguin Random House.

—. 2015c. *Notas de prensa, 1980–1984*. Bogotá: Penguin Random House.

García Márquez, Gabriel, and Plinio Apuleyo Mendoza. 1982. *El olor de la guayaba: conversaciones con Plinio Apuleyo Mendoza*. Barcelona: Bruguera.

García Márquez, Gabriel, Guillermo Ruiz Rivas, and Carlos Arturo Truque. 1954. *Tres cuentos colombianos*. Bogotá: Minerva.

García Márquez, Gabriel, and Mario Vargas Llosa. 1968. *La novela en América latina: diálogo*. Lima: Universidad Nacional de Ingeniería.

García Olaya, F. 1967. "Gabriel García Márquez o Todos los caminos conducen a Macondo." *El Catolicismo* (Bogotá), August 27, 17.

García San Martín, Álvaro. 2013. "Francisco Bilbao, entre el proyecto latinoamericano y el gran molusco." *Latinoamérica. Revista de Estudios Latinoamericanos* 56: 141–62.

García Usta, Jorge. 2015. *Cómo aprendió a escribir García Márquez*. Bogotá: Collage Editores.

García-Peña, Roberto. 1969. "*Cien años de soledad*: gran novela de América." *Coral* 9: 29–30.

Garfinkel, Harold. 1967. *Studies in Ethnomethodology*. Englewood Cliffs, NJ: Prentice-Hall.

Garmendia, Salvador. 1989. *Los pequeños seres, Memorias de Altagracia y otros relatos*. Caracas: Biblioteca Ayachuco.

Gates, Henry Louis. 2019. "By the Book: Henry Louis Gates Jr. (Sunday Book Review)." *New York Times*. March 28, 7.

Gell, Alfred. 1998. *Art and Agency: An Anthropological Theory*. Oxford: Clarendon Press.

Ghosh, Amitav, and Frederick Aldama. 2002. "An Interview with Amitav Ghosh." *World Literature Today* 76: 84.

Gil-Mugarza, Guillermo. 2014. "Las letras y los números. La producción española de libros en el siglo XX a través de las fuentes estadísticas." *Revista de Historia Industrial* 56: 151–86.

Gilard, Jacques. 1976. "De *Los Sangurimas* a *Cien años de soledad*." *Universidad de Medellín* 21: 183–96.

Gimferrer, Pere. 2004. "Sobre *Cien años de soledad*." In *La llegada de los bárbaros: la recepción de la narrativa hispanoamericana en España, 1960–1981*, ed. Joaquín Marco and Jordi Gracia García, 473–75. Barcelona: EDHASA.

Giorgi, Alessandra. 2010. *About the Speaker: Towards a Syntax of Indexicality*. Oxford: Oxford University Press.

Glaeser, Andreas. 2011. *Political Epistemics: The Secret Police, the Opposition, and the End of East German Socialism*. Chicago, IL: University of Chicago Press.

Goffman, Erving. 1990. *The Presentation of Self in Everyday Life*. New York, NY: Doubleday.

Gómez, Eduardo. 1968. "*Cien años de soledad*. Novela de García Márquez." *Enfoque Internacional* II:1 (January): 38.

González, Galo F. 1988. "José de la Cuadra: Nicasio Sangurima, un patriarca olvidado." *Revista iberoamericana* 54(144-45): 739-51.

González, Manuel Pedro. 1968. "Apostillas a una novela insólita." *Papel Literario de El Nacional* (Caracas), January 2, 3.

González, Nelly de. 1994. *Bibliographic Guide to Gabriel Garcia Márquez, 1986–1992*. Westport, CT: Greenwood Press.

—. 2003. *Bibliographic Guide to Gabriel Garcia Márquez, 1992–2002*. Westport, CT: Praeger.

—. [s.d.]. "Bibliographic Guide to Gabriel García Márquez, 2002-on."

González Bermejo, Ernesto. 1970. "García Márquez." *Magazín Dominical, El Espectador* (Bogotá), November 29, 1, 3-7.

González Calleja, Eduardo, and Rosa María Pardo Sanz. 1993. "De la solidaridad ideológica a la cooperación interesada (1953-1975)." In *España/América Latina: un siglo de políticas culturales*, ed. Pedro Pérez-Herrero and Nuria Tabanera, 120-60. Madrid: AIETI-OEI.

González Echevarría, Roberto. 1996. "A Brief History of the History of Spanish American Literature." In *The Cambridge History of Latin American Literature*, ed. Enrique Pupo-Walker and Roberto González Echevarría, 7-32. Cambridge: Cambridge University Press.

—. 2012. *Modern Latin American Literature: A Very Short Introduction*. Oxford: Oxford University Press.

—. 2014. *Oye mi son: Ensayos y testimonios sobre literatura hispanoamericana*. Sevilla: Renacimiento.

Gordon, José. 2002. "La increíble historia del Gabo y sus amigos desalmados." *Luz Verde, Canal 22* (Mexico City).

Granovetter, Mark. 1985. "Economic Action and Social Structure: The Problem of Embeddedness." *American Journal of Sociology* 91(3): 481-510.

Gras Miravet, Dunia. 2015. "El boom desde dentro: Carlos Fuentes y las redes informales de promoción cultural." In *América Latina y la literatura mundial: mercado editorial, redes globales y la invención de un continente*, ed. Gesine Müller and Dunia Gras Miravet, 197-221. Madrid and Frankfurt am Main: Iberoamericana.

Greenberg, Michael. 2009. "Looking for the Patriarch." *The New York Review of Books*, July 16.

Greenblatt, Stephen. 1990. "Resonance and Wonder." *Bulletin of the American Academy of Arts and Sciences* 43(4): 11-34.

—. 2004. *Will in the World: How Shakespeare Became Shakespeare*. New York, NY: Norton.

—. 2011. *The Swerve: How the World Became Modern*. New York, NY: Norton.

—. 2017. *The Rise and Fall of Adam and Eve*. New York, NY: Norton.

Greenblatt, Stephen, and Catherine Gallagher. 2000. *Practicing New Historicism*. Chicago, IL: University of Chicago Press.

Griswold, Wendy. 1981. "American Character and the American Novel: An Expansion of Reflection Theory in the Sociology of Literature." *American Journal of Sociology* 86(4): 740-65.

—. 1986. *Renaissance Revivals: City Comedy and Revenge Tragedy in the London Theatre, 1576–1980*. Chicago, IL: University of Chicago Press.

—. 1987. "The Fabrication of Meaning: Literary Interpretation in the United States, Great Britain, and the West Indies." *American Journal of Sociology* 92(5): 1077-117.

—. 2000. *Bearing Witness: Readers, Writers, and the Novel in Nigeria*. Princeton, NJ: Princeton University Press.

—. 2008. *Regionalism and the Reading Class*. Chicago, IL: University of Chicago Press.

—. 2016. *American Guides: The Federal Writers' Project and the Casting of American Culture*. Chicago, IL: Chicago University Press.

Griswold, Wendy, Gemma Mangione, and Terence McDonnell. 2013. "Objects, Words, and Bodies in Space: Bringing Materiality into Cultural Analysis." *Qualitative Sociology* 36(4): 343-64.

Guerrero, Gustavo. 2020. "José Lezama Lima en Francia: apuntes sobre la mediación editorial, la traducción y la recepción de *Paradiso*." In *Literatura latinoamericana mundial: dispositivos y disidencias*, ed. Gustavo Guerrero, Gesine Müller, Benjamin Loy, and Jorge Locane, 46-53. Berlin: De Gruyter.

Guillory, John. 1993. *Cultural Capital: The Problem of Literary Canon Formation*. Chicago, IL: University of Chicago Press.

Haber, Erika. 2003. *The Myth of the Non-Russian: Iskander and Aitmatov's Magical Universe*. Lanham, MD: Lexington Books.

Hallewell, Laurence. 1987. "The Impact of the Spanish Civil War on Latin American Publishing." In *Intellectuals Migrations: Transcultural Contributions of European and Latin American Emigrés*, ed. Anonymous, 139–50. Madison: SALALM Secretariat and University of Wisconsin-Madison.

Halley, Jeffrey A., and Daglind E. Sonolet (Eds.). 2017. *Bourdieu in Question: New Directions in French Sociology of Art*. Leiden, Netherlands: Brill.

Hamann, Julian, and Stefan Beljean. 2019. "Career Gatekeeping in Cultural Fields." *American Journal of Cultural Sociology*. https://doi.org/10.1057/s41290-019-00078-7

Harss, Luis. 1966. *Los nuestros*. Buenos Aires: Editorial Sudamericana.

—. 1967. *Into the Mainstream: Conversations with Latin-American Writers*. New York, NY: Harper & Row.

Hart, Stephen, and Wen-chin Ouyang (Eds.). 2005a. *A Companion to Magical Realism*. Woodbridge, UK: Tamesis.

—. 2005b. "Introduction: Globalization of Magical Realism: New Politics of Aesthetics." In *A Companion to Magical Realism*, ed. Stephen Hart and Wen-Chin Ouyang, 1–22. Woodbridge, UK: Tamesis.

Haskell, Francis. 1980. *Rediscoveries in Art: Some Aspects of Taste, Fashion, and Collecting in England and France*. Ithaca, NY: Cornell University Press.

Heilbron, Johan. 1999. "Towards a Sociology of Translation." *European Journal of Social Theory* 2(4): 429–44.

Heinich, Nathalie. 1991. *La Gloire de Van Gogh : essai d'anthropologie de l'admiration*. Paris: Minuit.

Hennion, Antoine. 1993. *La Passion musicale : une sociologie de la médiation*. Paris: Métailié.

Henseler, Christine (Ed.). 2003. *Contemporary Spanish Women's Narrative and the Publishing Industry*. Urbana, IL: University of Illinois Press.

Herrera, Javier. 2012. "Una incursión en la Ciénaga de García Márquez: el proyecto de adaptación de *La casa grande* de Álvaro Cépeda por Luis Alcoriza." *Revista Brasileira do Caribe* 12(24): 531–47.

Herrero-Olaizola, Alejandro. 2007. *The Censorship Files: Latin American Writers and Franco's Spain*. Albany, NY: State University of New York Press.

Hirsch, Paul. 1972. "Processing Fads and Fashions: An Organization-Set Analysis of Cultural Industry Systems." *American Journal of Sociology* 77(4): 639–59.

Hoffman, Mark Anthony, Jean-Philippe Cointet, Philipp Brandt, Newton Key, and Peter Bearman. 2018. "The (Protestant) Bible, the (Printed) Sermon, and the Word(s): The Semantic Structure of the Conformist and Dissenting Bible, 1660–1780." *Poetics* 68: 89–103.

Holgín, Andrés. 1967. "Cien años de soledad." *Razón y fábula* (September-October): 137–138.

Hoyos, Héctor. 2015. *Beyond Bolaño: The Global Latin American Novel*. New York, NY: Columbia University Press.

Huerta, Mona. 2013. "Le Latino-américanisme français en perspective." *Caravelle* (December): 39–62.

Iber, Patrick. 2015. *Neither Peace nor Freedom: The Cultural Cold War in Latin America*. Cambridge, MA: Harvard University Press.

Illán Bacca, Ramón. 2012. *Escribir en Barranquilla*. Barranquilla: Editorial Universidad del Norte.

Jameson, Fredric. 2017. "No Magic, No Metaphor." *London Review of Books*, June 7, 21–32

Jarque, Fietta. 1997. " 'Cien años de soledad,' treinta años de leyenda." *El País* (Spain), June 6, 1997.

Jauss, Hans Robert. 1982. *Toward an Aesthetic of Reception*. Minneapolis, MN: University of Minnesota Press.

Jimeno Revilla, Raquel. 2015. "El proyecto artístico-cultural de Círculo de Lectores: la creación de un nuevo público lector (1962–1992)." Madrid: Universidad Autónoma de Madrid.

Johnson, Dane. 1996. "The Rise of Gabriel Garcia Marquez and Toni Morrison." In *Cultural Institutions of the Novel*, ed. Deidre Lynch and William Beatty Warner, 129–56. Durham, NC: Duke University Press.

Jordison, Sam. 2017. "Can *One Hundred Years of Solitude* Be Read as More than Just Fantasy?" *Guardian*, May 16.

Jorge, Volpi. 2004. "El fin de la narrativa latinoamericana." *Revista de Crítica Literaria Latinoamericana* 30(59): 33–42.

Joset, Jacques. 1990. "Oralidad y textualidad en *Los Sangurimas* de José de la Cuadra." *La Torre* 13: 71–78.

Kafka, Ben. 2012. *The Demon of Writing: Powers and Failures of Paperwork*. New York, NY: Zone Books.

Kakutani, Michiko. 2017. "Obama's Secret to Surviving the White House Years: Books." *New York Times*, January 16.

Kapsis, Robert. 1992. *Hitchcock: The Making of a Reputation*. Chicago, IL: University of Chicago Press.

Karush, Matthew B. 2016. *Musicians in Transit: Argentina and the Globalization of Popular Music*. Durham, NC: Duke University Press.

Kerr, Lucille. 2007. "Corresponding Archives: Letters from the Latin American Literary Front." *Symposium: A Quarterly Journal in Modern Literatures* 61(1): 75–96.

Kiely, Robert. 1970. "Memory and Prophecy, Illusion and Reality Are Mixed and Made to Look the Same." *New York Times Book Review*, March 8, 5, 24.

King, John. 2012. " 'Ya nunca más seríamos lo que éramos': Tomás Eloy Martínez and *Primera Plana* in the 1960s." *Bulletin of Latin American Research* 31(4): 426–44.

Klein, Don. 2003. *Gabriel García Márquez: una bibliografía descriptiva en conmemoración de los cincuenta años de la publicación de sus escritos, 1947–1997*. Bogotá: Editorial Norma.

Krippner, Greta R. 2002. "The Elusive Market: Embeddedness and the Paradigm of Economic Sociology." *Theory and Society* 30(6): 775–810.

Krippner, Greta R., and Anthony S. Alvarez. 2007. "Embeddedness and the Intellectual Projects of Economic Sociology." *Annual Review of Sociology* 33(1): 219–40.

Kuzmics, Helmut, and Gerald Mozetic. 2003. *Literatur als Soziologie: zum Verhältnis von literarischer und gesellschaftlicher Wirklichkeit*. Konstanz: UVK.

Lago Carballo, Antonio, and Nicanor Gómez-Villegas (Eds.). 2006. *Un viaje de ida y vuelta: la edición española e iberoamericano (1936–1975)*. Madrid: Siruela.

Lahire, Bernard. 2006. *La Condition littéraire : la double vie des écrivains*. Paris: Découverte.

Lamont, Michèle. 1987. "How to Become a Dominant French Philosopher: The Case of Jacques Derrida." *American Journal of Sociology* 93(3): 584–622.

—. 1992. *Money, Morals, and Manners: The Culture of the French and American Upper-Middle Class*. Chicago, IL: University of Chicago Press.

—. 2009. *How Professors Think: Inside the Curious World of Academic Judgment*. Cambridge, MA: Harvard University Press.

—. 2012. "Toward a Comparative Sociology of Evaluative and Valuation Practices." *Annual Review of Sociology* 38: 201–21.

Landeros, Carlos. 1965. "Una encuesta sobre la industria editorial." *La Cultura en México* 197: iii–xii

Larraz Elorriaga, Fernando. 2014. *Letricidio español. Censura y novela durante el franquismo*. Gijón, Spain: Trea.

Latcham, Ricardo A. (Ed.). 1958. *Antología del cuento hispanoamericano contemporáneo*. Santiago de Chile: Zig-Zag.

—. 1961. "Denuncia y violencia en la novela." *Marcha* (suplemento), December 29: 2, 4.

Latour, Bruno. 2005. *Reassembling the Social: An Introduction to Actor-Network-Theory*. New York, NY: Oxford University Press.

Lauter, Paul. 1991. *Canons and Contexts*. New York, NY: Oxford University Press.

Lena, Jennifer C., and Mark A. Pachucki. 2013. "The Sincerest Form of Flattery: Innovation, Repetition, and Status in an Art Movement." *Poetics* 41(3): 236–64.

Lennard, Patricio. 2009. "Confieso que he leído." *Pagina 12*, June 7.

Leonard, John. 1982. "The Mosquito Coast." *New York Times*, February 11, Section C, 31.

Lepenies, Wolf. 1988. *Between Literature and Science: The Rise of Sociology*. Cambridge and Paris: Cambridge University Press and Éditions de la Maison des sciences de l'homme.

Leschziner, Vanina. 2015. *At the Chef's Table: Culinary Creativity in Elite Restaurants*. Palo Alto, CA: Stanford University Press.

Levine, Suzanne Jill. 1975. *El espejo hablado: un estudio de* Cien años de soledad. Caracas: Monte Ávila Editores.

Levitt, Peggy. 2015. *Artifacts and Allegiances: How Museums Put the Nation and the World on Display*. Oakland, CA: University of California Press.

—. Forthcoming. "Scale-Shifting: Explaining Migration between National, Regional, and Global Literary Fields." *Journal of World Literature*.

Lezama Lima, José. 1973. *Paradiso*. Mexico City: Ediciones Era.

Lienhard, Martín. 1986. "La legitimación indígena en dos novelas centroamericanas: 'Balún Canán' (R. Castellanos) y 'Hombres de maíz' (M.A. Asturias)." In *Identidad cultural de Iberoamérica en su literatura*, ed. Saúl Yurkievich, 265-77. Madrid: Editorial Alhambra.

Lizé, Wenceslas. 2016. "Cultural Consecration and Legitimation–Modes, Agents and Processes." *Poetics* 59(December): 1-4.

Lleras, Antonio. 1969. "Cien años de soledad." *Coral* 9: 8-9.

Llorca, Carmen. 1968. "Las novelas de García Márquez." *Diario SP* 165 (March 20): 14.

Longo, Mariano. 2015. *Fiction and Social Reality: Literature and Narrative as Sociological Resources*. Farnham, UK: Ashgate Publishing Limited.

López Llovet de Rodrigué, Gloria. 2004. *Sudamericana: Antonio López Llausás, un editor con los pies en la tierra*. Buenos Aires: Dunken.

Louis, Annick. 2013. "Étoiles d'un ciel étranger : Roger Caillois et l'Amérique Latine." *Littérature* 170(June): 71-81.

Mailer, Norman. 2004. *The Spooky Art: Some Thoughts on Writing*. New York, NY: Random House.

Mamani Macedo, Mauro (Ed.). 2017. *Sitio de la Tierra: Antología del vanguardismo literario andino*. Lima: FCE.

Mannheim, Karl. 2000. *Essays on the Sociology of Knowledge*. London: Routledge.

Marco, Joaquín, and Jordi Gracia García (Eds.). 2004. *La llegada de los bárbaros: la recepción de la narrativa hispanoamericana en España, 1960–1981*. Barcelona: EDHASA.

Marling, William. 2016. *Gatekeepers: The Emergence of World Literature and the 1960s*. New York, NY: Oxford University Press.

Martin, Gerald. 1989. *Journeys Through the Labyrinth: Latin American Fiction in the Twentieth Century*. London: Verso.

—. 2008. "The 'Boom' of Spanish-American Fiction and the 1960s Revolutions (1958-75)." In *A Companion to Latin American Literature and Culture*, ed. Sara Castro-Klarén, 478-94. Malden, MA: Wiley-Blackwell.

—. 2009. *Gabriel García Márquez: A Life*. New York, NY: Alfred A. Knopf.

Martínez, Tomás Eloy. 1967. "La gran novela." *Primera Plana* (Buenos Aires), April 18: 54-55.

—. 1999. "Los sueños de un profeta." *La Nación* (Buenos Aires), September 4.

—. 2008. "¿Qué se hizo de Luis Harss?" *La Nación* (Buenos Aires), January 26.

Mauleón, Héctor de, and Julio Aguilar. 2002. "Memoria de orquídea tropical." *Cambio* (Bogotá), October 7: 176-80.

McAdam, Doug. 1982. *Political Process and the Development of Black Insurgency, 1930–1970*. Chicago, IL: University of Chicago Press.

McDonnell, Terence E., Christopher A. Bail, and Iddo Tavory. 2017. "A Theory of Resonance." *Sociological Theory* 35(1): 1-14.

Medina Portillo, David (Ed.). 2017. *A cincuenta años de* Cien años de soledad. *Contexto, correspondencia y recepción*. Mexico City and Bogotá: El Equilibrista, Universidad de Guadalajara and Ministerio de Cultura de Colombia

Mejía Vélez, Álvaro. 1972. "Gabriel García Márquez visto por su hermana monja, sor Aida, o Remedios la Bella." *El Correo* (Medellín), July 11, 4–5.

Menger, Pierre-Michel. 2009. *Le Travail créateur : s'accomplir dans l'incertain*. Paris: Seuil-Gallimard.

Menton, Seymour. 1998. *Historia verdadera del realismo mágico*. Mexico City: Fondo de Cultura Económica.

Merton, Robert. 1968. "The Matthew Effect in Science." *Science* 159(3810): 56–63.

Mica, Adriana, and Rafal Wisniewski. 2012. "Workshop on Embeddedness and Embedding." *Polish Sociological Review* 179: 443–46.

Mignolo, Walter. 2005. *The Idea of Latin America*. Malden, MA: Blackwell.

Miliani, Domingo. 1965. "Gabriel García Márquez." *Papel Literario de El Nacional* (Caracas), October 31, 1965, 4.

Monsalve, Alfonso. 1968. "La novela, anuncio de grandes transformaciones." *Lecturas dominicales, El Tiempo* (Bogotá), January 14, 4.

Montero Castro, Roberto. 1967/1968. "A propósito de 'Cien años de soledad'." *Papeles. Revista del Ateneo de Caracas* 5 (November-December 1967/January 1968): 134–36.

Moraña, Mabel. 2005. *Ideologies of Hispanism*. Nashville, TN: Vanderbilt University Press.

——. 2006. "Territorialidad y forasterismo: la polémica Arguedas-Cortázar revisitada." In *José María Arguedas: hacia una poética migrante*, ed. Sergio R. Franco, 103–18. Pittsburgh, PA: Instituto Internacional de Literatura Iberoamericana.

Morcillo, Álvaro. 2016. "La dominación filantrópica. La Rockefeller Foundation y las ciencias sociales en español (1938–1973)." In *Max Weber en Iberoamérica: Nuevas interpretaciones, estudios empíricos y recepción*, ed. Álvaro Morcillo Laiz and Eduardo Weisz, 573–605. Mexico City: Fondo de Cultura Económica.

Moreno Blanco, Juan. 2017. Cien años de soledad, *50 años después*. Cali, Colombia: Universidad del Valle.

Moret, Xavier. 2002. *Tiempo de editores: historia de la edición en España, 1939–1975*. Barcelona: Ediciones Destino.

Moretti, Franco. 1996. *The Modern Epic: The World-System from Goethe to García Márquez*. London: Verso.

——(Ed.). 2006. *The Novel*. Princeton, NJ: Princeton University Press.

Morgan, Stephen, and Christopher Winship. 2007. *Counterfactuals and Causal Inference: Methods and Principles for Social Research*. New York, NY: Cambridge University Press.

Mudrovcic, María Eugenia. 1997. *Mundo Nuevo: cultura y guerra fría en la década del 60*. Rosario: B. Viterbo Editora.

Mukerji, Chandra. 2009. *Impossible Engineering: Technology and Territoriality on the Canal du Midi*. Princeton, NJ: Princeton University Press.

Mukherjee, Ankhi. 2010. " 'What Is a Classic?': International Literary Criticism and the Classic Question." *PMLA* 125(4): 1026–42.

Müller, Gesine. 2018. "Re-mapping World Literature from Macondo." In *Re-mapping World Literature: Writing, Book Markets and Epistemologies between Latin America and the Global South*, ed. Gesine Müller, Jorge J. Locane, and Benjamin Loy, 157–74. Berlin: De Gruyter.

Müller, Gesine, and Dunia Gras Miravet (Eds.). 2015a. *América Latina y la literatura mundial: mercado editorial, redes globales y la invención de un continente*. Madrid: Iberoamericana.

——. 2015b. "Introducción." In *América Latina y la literatura mundial: mercado editorial, redes globales y la invención de un continente*, ed. Gesine Müller and Dunia Gras Miravet, 9–20. Madrid: Iberoamericana.

Muñoz, Boris. 2012. "La alergia del Gabo." *Prodavinci*, March 6.

NPR. 2018. "James Patterson Discusses *One Hundred Years of Solitude*." October 23.

Olaciregui, Julio. 2018. "Dos cartas de Ángel Rama que vaticinaron el éxito de Gabo y Cepeda Samudio." *El Espectador* (Bogotá), October 16.

Olivari, Manuel. 1967. "3 novelistas latinoamericanos fueron consagrados en 1967." *La Prensa* (Lima), December 26.

Onetti, Juan Carlos. 1976. "A fondo: Juan Carlos Onetti." *A fondo*, interview with Joaquín Soler Serrano. Madrid: Radio Televisión Española.

Orbegozo, Manuel Jesús. 1967. "Para llegar a la fama, necesitó 'Cien años de soledad'." *El Comercio Gráfico* (Lima), September 9, 14-15.

Ortega, Carlos. 1967. "Gabriel García Márquez. Su clave: la sinceridad." *Dominical, El Comercio* (Lima), September 10, 10-11.

Orthofer, M. A. 2016. *The Complete Review Guide to Contemporary World Fiction*. New York, NY: Columbia University Press.

Osorio Tejeda, Nelson. 1968. "Mosaico de homenaje a García Márquez." *Dominical, El Siglo* (Santiago), March 6, 9.

Oviedo, José Miguel. 1967. "Macondo: territorio mágico y americano." *Magazine Dominical, El Espectador* (Bogotá), October 15, 1, 3.

Pachón Castro, Gloria. 1966. "La literatura latinoamericana es la única que tiene algo nuevo que ofrecer." *El Tiempo* (Bogotá), March 3, 15.

Pachucki, Mark, and Ronald Breiger. 2010. "Cultural Holes: Beyond Relationality in Social Networks and Culture." *Annual Review of Sociology* 36(1): 205-24.

Padgett, John, and Walter Powell (Eds.). 2012. *The Emergence of Organizations and Markets*. Princeton, NJ: Princeton University Press.

Padua, Jorge. 1979. *El analfabetismo en América Latina: un estudio empírico con especial referencia a los casos de Perú, México y Argentina*. Mexico City: Colegio de México.

Palumbo-Liu, David, Bruce Robbins, and Nirvana Tanoukhi (Eds.). 2011. *Immanuel Wallerstein and the Problem of the World: System, Scale, Culture*. Durham, NC: Duke University Press.

Paternostro, Silvana. 2014. *Soledad & compañía: un retrato compartido de Gabriel García Márquez*. New York, NY: Vintage Español.

Patterson, Orlando. 2010. "The Mechanisms of Cultural Reproduction: Explaining the Puzzle of Persistence." In *Handbook of Cultural Sociology*, ed. John R. Hall, Laura Grindstaff, and Ming-Cheng Lo, 140-51. London: Routledge.

Pavlovic, Tatjana. 2011. *The Mobile Nation: España cambia de piel (1954–1964)*. Bristol, UK: Intellect.

Perés, Ramón D. 1969. *Historia universal de la literatura*. Barcelona: Ramón Sopena.

Pernett, Nicolás. 2014. "García Márquez y la historia de Colombia." *El Malpensante* 152(May): 60-67.

Peterson, Karin. 2003. "Discourse and Display: The Modern Eye, Entrepreneurship, and the Cultural Transformation of the Patchwork Quilt." *Sociological Perspectives* 46(4): 461-90.

Peterson, Richard. 1997. *Creating Country Music: Fabricating Authenticity*. Chicago, IL: University of Chicago Press.

Peterson, Richard, and Narasimhan Anand. 2004. "The Production of Culture Perspective." *Annual Review of Sociology* 30(1): 311-34.

Phillips, Damon J. 2013. *Shaping Jazz: Cities, Labels, and the Global Emergence of an Art Form*. Princeton, NJ: Princeton University Press.

Piatier, Jacqueline. 1965. "'La Littérature latino-américaine sera la grande littérature de demain', affirme Roger Caillois." *Le Monde* (Paris), April 10, 12.

Piazza, Luis Guillermo. 1968. *La mafia*. Mexico City: Joaquín Mortiz.

Pinto, Ismael. 1967a. "América, novela con novelistas." *Expreso* (Lima), August 30, 15.

—. 1967b. "Gabriel García Márquez: conversación informal." *Expreso* (Lima), September 13, 14-15.

Polanyi, Karl. 2001. *The Great Transformation: The Political and Economic Origins of Our Time*. Boston, MA: Beacon.

Poniatowska, Elena. 1965. "Mario Vargas Llosa." *La Cultura en México* 117: i–viii.

—. 1973. "Los pescaditos de oro en el mar de Gabriel García Márquez." In *Todo México*, 223-226. Mexico City: Diana.

Porrúa, Francisco. 2014. "Los secretos del primer editor de 'Cien años de soledad'." *BBC News.*

Primera Plana. 1967. "Para tomar impulso. Gabriel García Márquez: *Los funerales de la Mamá Grande.*" 251: 59.

Prior, Nick. 2013. "Bourdieu and the Sociology of Music Consumption: A Critical Assessment of Recent Developments." *Sociology Compass* 7(3): 181–93.

Radway, Janice. 1997. *A Feeling for Books: The Book-of-the-Month Club, Literary Taste, and Middle-Class Desire.* Chapel Hill, NC: University of North Carolina Press.

Ragin, Charles. 2008. *Redesigning Social Inquiry: Fuzzy Sets and Beyond.* Chicago, IL: University of Chicago Press.

Rama, Ángel. 1964a. "García Márquez, gran americano." *Marcha* (February 7): 28, 30.

—. 1964b. "García Márquez: la violencia americana." *Marcha* (April 17): 22–23.

—. 1967. "Introducción a *Cien años de soledad.*" *Marcha* (September 2): 31.

—(Ed.). 1975. *Primeros cuentos de diez maestros latinoamericanos.* Barcelona: Planeta.

—. 1982. *La novela en América Latina: panoramas 1920–1980.* Bogotá: Procultura.

Reed, Isaac. 2011. *Interpretation and Social Knowledge: On the Use of Theory in the Human Sciences.* Chicago, IL: University of Chicago Press.

Restrepo, Alonso Ángel. 1955a. *La hojarasca.* Bogotá: Ediciones S.L.B.

—. 1955b. "Un novelista que quiere seguir escribiendo novelas." *El Colombiano Literario, El Colombiano* (Medellín), June 26, 1.

Reyes, Alfonso. 1997. *Obras completas XI.* Mexico City: Fondo de Cultura Económica.

Robles, Humberto E. 1976. *Testimonio y tendencia mítica en la obra de José de la Cuadra.* Quito: Editorial Casa de la Cultura Ecuatoriana.

Rocco, Alessandro. 2014. *Gabriel García Márquez and the Cinema: Life and Works.* Woodbridge, UK: Tamesis.

Rodden, John. 2002. *George Orwell: The Politics of Literary Reputation.* New Brunswick, NJ: Transaction Publishers.

Rodríguez Carranza, Luz. 2004. "Literary Periodicals of the 1960's: Proposals for Re-Reading." In *Literary Cultures of Latin America: A Comparative History*, ed. Mario J. Valdés and Djelal Kadir, 108–18. Oxford: Oxford University Press.

Rodríguez Martínez, Mario. 1969. "Los *Cien años de Soledad* de Gabriel García Márquez." *Coral* 9: 16–17.

Rodríguez Monegal, Emir. 1965a. "La nueva novela de Latinoamérica." *Life en Español* (March 15): 54–62.

—. 1965b. "New Latin American Writers." *Bulletin of the American Academy of Arts and Sciences* 18(8): 3–8.

—. 1965c. "The New Novelists." *Encounter* (September): 97–109.

—. 1965d. "Un espejo de espejos entrecruzados." *Life en Español* (August 2): 22–26.

—. 1967a. "Diario de Caracas." *Mundo Nuevo* 17 (November): 4–24.

—. 1967b. "Una cosecha incesante." *Mundo Nuevo* 10 (April): 4.

—. 1968. "Novedad y anacronismo de *Cien años de soledad.*" *Revista nacional de cultura* 185: 3–23.

—. 1972. *El Boom de la novela latinoamericana: ensayo.* Caracas: Editorial Tiempo Nuevo.

—. 1984. "The Boom: A Retrospective." *Review: Literature and Arts of the Americas* 17(33): 30–36.

Rodríguez Morató, Arturo, and Álvaro Santana-Acuña (Eds.). 2017. *La nueva sociología de las artes: una perspectiva hispanohablante y global.* Barcelona: Gedisa.

— (Eds.). Forthcoming. *Sociology of the Arts in Action: New Perspectives on Creation, Production, and Reception.* London: Palgrave Macmillan.

Rodríguez-Carranza, Luz. 2004. "Literary Periodicals of the 1960s: Proposals for Re-Reading." In *Literary Cultures of Latin America: A Comparative History. Institutional Modes and Cultural Modalities*, ed. M.J. Valdés and D. Kadir, 108–111. Oxford: Oxford University Press.

Roh, Franz. 1927. "Realismo mágico. Problemas de la pintura europea más reciente." *Revista de Occidente* 48(June): 274-301.

Rosas Lopátegui, Patricia. 2002. *Testimonios sobre Elena Garro*. Mexico City: Ediciones Castillo.

Rossman, Gabriel. 2012. *Climbing the Charts: What Radio Airplay Tells Us about the Diffusion of Innovation*. Princeton, NJ: Princeton University Press.

Rulfo, Juan. 1977. "A fondo: Juan Rulfo." *A fondo*, interview with Joaquín Soler Serrano. Madrid: Radio Televisión Española.

Runciman, Walter Garrison. 1989. *A Treatise on Social Theory*. Cambridge: Cambridge University Press.

Saldívar, Dasso. 2005. *García Márquez: el viaje a la semilla*. Madrid: Ediciones Folio.

Sánchez Prado, Ignacio (Ed.). 2018. *Pierre Bourdieu in Hispanic Literature and Culture*. London: Palgrave Macmillan.

Santana, Mario. 2000. *Foreigners in the Homeland: The Spanish American New Novel in Spain, 1962–1974*. Lewisburg, London, and Cranbury: Bucknell University Press and Associated University Presses.

—. 2009. "De Mallorca a Cuba: Formentor y la globalización de la literatura hispánica." In *1959: de Collioure a Formentor*, ed. Carme Riera and María Payeras, 285-96. Madrid: Visor.

Santana-Acuña, Álvaro. 2014. "How a Literary Work Becomes a Classic: The Case of *One Hundred Years of Solitude*." *American Journal of Cultural Sociology* 2(1): 97-149.

—. 2016a. "The End of the Traditional Art Gallery?" *Books & Ideas*, May 9.

—. 2016b. "Where Does the Value of Art Begin?" *Books & Ideas*, May 2.

—. 2017. "The Personal History Behind *One Hundred Years of Solitude*." *Time*, May 31.

—. 2020. "El primer año de *Cien años de soledad*." In *García Márquez: nuevas lecturas*, ed. Juan Moreno Blanco. Universidad del Magdalena: Santa Marta.

—. Forthcoming. "Aesthetic Labeling and Scale Shifting in Cultural Production and Circulation." *Journal of World Literature*.

—. Forthcoming. "Spain in the Making and Reception of García Márquez's Works." In *The Oxford Handbook of Gabriel García Márquez*, ed. Gene H. Bell-Villada and Ignacio López-Calvo. New York, NY: Oxford University Press.

Santoro, Marco. 2002. "What is a 'Cantautore?' Distinction and Authorship in Italian (Popular) Music." *Poetics* 30(1-2): 111-32.

Sapiro, Gisèle. 1999. *La Guerre des écrivains : 1940–1953*. Paris: Fayard.

—. 2003. "The Literary Field between the State and the Market." *Poetics* 31(5): 441-64.

—. 2016a. "How Do Literary Works Cross Borders (or Not)?" *Journal of World Literature* 1(1): 81-96.

—. 2016b. "The Metamorphosis of Modes of Consecration in the Literary Field: Academies, Literary Prizes, Festivals." *Poetics* 59(December): 5-19.

Sassen, Saskia. 2006. *Territory, Authority, Rights: From Medieval to Global Assemblages*. Princeton, NJ: Princeton University Press.

Sassoon, Donald. 2001. *Mona Lisa: The History of the World's Most Famous Painting*. London: HarperCollins.

Saunders, Frances Stonor. 2000. *The Cultural Cold War: The CIA and the World of Arts and Letters*. New York, NY: New Press.

Schavelzon, Guillermo. 2002. "Los nueve meses de alquiler atrasado." *Reforma* (October 6).

Schiffrin, André. 2000. *The Business of Books: How International Conglomerates Took over Publishing and Changed the Way We Read*. London: Verso.

Schmutz, Vaughn. 2005. "Retrospective Cultural Consecration in Popular Music." *American Behavioral Scientist* 48(11): 1510-23.

Schoo, Ernesto. 1967. "Los viajes de Simbad García Márquez." *Primera Plana* (Buenos Aires), June 20: 52-54.

Schwartz, Lawrence. 1988. *Creating Faulkner's Reputation: The Politics of Modern Literary Criticism*. Knoxville, TN: University of Tennessee Press.

Segala, Amos. 1999. "La Colección Archivos: trayectoria, objetivos, resultados." *América : Cahiers du CRICCAL* 23: 147-58.

Sewell, William. 2005. *Logics of History: Social Theory and Social Transformation*. Chicago, IL: University of Chicago Press.

Sgourev, Stoyan V., and Niek Althuizen. 2017. "Is It a Masterpiece? Social Construction and Objective Constraint in the Evaluation of Excellence." *Social Psychology Quarterly* 80(4): 289-309.

Shakespeare, William. 2016. *The New Oxford Shakespeare: The Complete Works*. Oxford: Oxford University Press.

Shaw, Donald. 2010. "The Critical Reception of García Márquez." In *The Cambridge Companion to Gabriel García Márquez*, ed. Philip Swanson, 25-40. New York, NY: Cambridge University Press.

Sheridan, Guillermo. 2018. *Paseos por la calle de la amargura y otros rumbos mexicanos*. Mexico City: Penguin Random House Grupo Editorial México.

Siebenmann, Gustav. 1979. "Técnica narrativa e êxito literário." *Letras de hoje* 35(March): 7-24.

Silverstein, Michael. 1976. "Shifters, Linguistic Categories, and Cultural Description." In *Meaning in Anthropology*, ed. Keith H. Basso and Henry A. Selby, 11-55. Albuquerque, NM: University of New Mexico Press.

—. 2003. "Indexical Order and the Dialectics of Sociolinguistic Life." *Language & Communication* 23(3-4): 193-229.

Simmel, Georg. 2005. *Rembrandt: An Essay in the Philosophy of Art*. New York, NY: Routledge.

Simón Martínez, Pedro. 1969. *Recopilación de textos sobre Gabriel García Márquez*. Havana, Cuba: Centro de Investigaciones Literarias, Casa de las Américas.

Sims, Robert Lewis. 1992. *The First García Márquez: A Study of His Journalistic Writing from 1948 to 1955*. Lanham, MD: University Press of America.

Siskind, Mariano. 2014. *Cosmopolitan Desires: Global Modernity and World Literature in Latin America*. Evanston, IL: Northwestern University Press.

Sommer, Doris. 1991. *Foundational Fictions: The National Romances of Latin America*. Berkeley, CA: University of California Press.

Sorensen, Diana. 2007. *A Turbulent Decade Remembered: Scenes from the Latin American Sixties*. Stanford, CA: Stanford University Press.

Sosnowski, Saúl (Ed.). 1999. *La cultura de un siglo. América Latina en sus revistas*. Buenos Aires: Alianza Editorial.

Speer, Mary. 2018. "Minzu and the Reception of Gabriel García Márquez." Baltimore, MD: Johns Hopkins University.

Spender, Stephen, and Melvin J. Lasky. 1965. "Rediscovering Latin America: Foreword." *Encounter* (September): 3-4.

Spillman, Lyn. 1999. "Enriching Exchange: Cultural Dimensions of Markets." *American Journal of Economics and Sociology* 58(4): 1047-71.

Stone, Peter H. 1981. "Gabriel García Márquez, The Art of Fiction No. 69." *The Paris Review* 82(Winter): 44-73.

Strandvad, Sara Malou. 2012. "Attached by the Product: A Socio-Material Direction in the Sociology of Art." *Cultural Sociology* 6(2): 163-76.

Suárez, Juana. 2015. "De casas y haciendas azucareras en el gótico tropical: Carne de tu carne y La mansión de Araucaíma." *Cuadernos de cine colombiano* 21: 50-73.

Swanson, Philip (Ed.). 2010. *The Cambridge Companion to Gabriel García Márquez*. New York, NY: Cambridge University Press.

Taylor, Charles. 2004. *Modern Social Imaginaries*. Durham, NC: Duke University Press.

Taylor, Gary. 1989. *Reinventing Shakespeare: A Cultural History, from the Restoration to the Present*. Oxford: Oxford University Press.

Taylor, Gary, and Trish Thomas Henley (Eds.). 2012. *The Oxford Handbook of Thomas Middleton*. Oxford: Oxford University Press.

Thompson, John. 2010. *Merchants of Culture: The Publishing Business in the Twenty-First Century*. Cambridge: Polity.

Thumala Olave, María Angélica. 2018. "Reading Matters: Towards a Cultural Sociology of Reading." *American Journal of Cultural Sociology* 6(3): 417–54.

Tola de Habich, Fernando, and Patricia Grieve (Eds.). 1971. *Los españoles y el boom*. Caracas: Tiempo Nuevo.

Toly, Noah. 2019. *The Gardener's Dirty Hands: Environmental Politics and Christian Ethics*. New York, NY: Oxford University Press.

Tompkins, Jane. 1985. *Sensational Designs: The Cultural Work of American Fiction, 1790–1860*. New York, NY: Oxford University Press.

Toro Martínez, Juan. 1968. "Macondo a secas." *El Nacional* (Caracas), February 1, C-1.

Trollope, Anthony. 1950 [1883]. *An Autobiography*. London: Oxford University Press.

Valdés, María Elena de, and Mario Valdés. 1990. *Approaches to Teaching García Márquez's* One Hundred Years of Solitude. New York, NY: Modern Language Association of America.

Valdéz, Zoé. 2010. "Gabriel García Márquez ¿esbirro o es burro? Por Reinaldo Arenas." *Libertad, Verdad y Vida*. September 14.

Valente, Ignacio. 1969. "García Márquez: *Cien años de soledad*." *Coral* 9: 7–8.

Varela, Nuria. 2014. "García Márquez, el genio al que le perdonaron todo." *La Marea* (Madrid), April 24.

Vargas, Germán. 1967. "Autor de una obra que hará ruido." *Encuentro Liberal* 1 (April 29): 21–22.

Vargas Llosa, Mario. 1969. "*Cien años de soledad*: Amadís de América." *Coral* 9: 18–22.

—. 1971. *García Márquez: historia de un deicidio*. La Paz, Bolivia: Difusión.

—. 1996. *La utopía arcaica: José María Arguedas y las ficciones del indigenismo*. Mexico City: Fondo de Cultura Económica.

Velthuis, Olav. 2005. *Talking Prices: Symbolic Meanings of Prices on the Market for Contemporary Art*. Princeton, NJ: Princeton University Press.

Verboord, Marc. 2009. "The Legitimacy of Book Critics in the Age of the Internet and Omnivorousness: Expert Critics, Internet Critics and Peer Critics in Flanders and the Netherlands." *European Sociological Review* 26(1): 623–37.

—. 2011. "Market Logic and Cultural Consecration in French, German and American Bestseller Lists, 1970–2007." *Poetics* 39(4): 290–315.

Verboord, Marc, and Kees van Rees. 2009. "Literary Education Curriculum and Institutional Contexts: Textbook Content and Teachers' Textbook Usage in Dutch Literary Education, 1968–2000." *Poetics* 37(1): 74–97.

Verdesio, Gustavo. 2003. "An Amnesic Nation: The Erasure of Indigenous Pasts by Uruguayan Expert Knowledges." In *Beyond Imagined Communities: Reading and Writing the Nation in Nineteenth-Century Latin America*, ed. Charles Chasteen and Sara Castro-Klarén, 196–224. Washington and Baltimore: Woodrow Wilson Center Press and Johns Hopkins University Press.

Vilas, Manuel. 2015. "Querido Pedro: llega 'Cien años de soledad'." *Babelia, El País* (Madrid), November 21, 12–13.

Vineberg, Steve. 1982. "Herzog's *Fitzcarraldo*: Eraserhead on the Amazon?" *Stanford Daily*, October 28, 10.

Volkening, Ernesto. 1963. "Gabriel García Márquez o el trópico desembrujado." *Eco: Revista de la Cultura de Occidente* 40 (August): 275–304.

Wagner-Pacifici, Robin. 2010. "The Cultural Sociological Experience of Cultural Objects." In *Handbook of Cultural Sociology*, ed. John Hall, Laura Grindstaff, and Ming-Cheng Lo, 109–17. London: Routledge.

Weber, Max. 2015. *Los fundamentos racionales y sociológicos de la música*. Madrid: Tecnos.

Weber, William. 1986. "The Rise of Classical Repertoire in Nineteenth-Century Orchestral Concerts."
    In *The Orchestra: Origins and Transformations*, ed. Joan Peyser, 361–86. New York, NY: Scribner.

Weiss, J. 2014. *The Lights of Home: A Century of Latin American Writers in Paris*. New York, NY: Taylor &
    Francis.

White, Cynthia, and Harrison White. 1993. *Canvases and Careers: Institutional Change in the French
    Painting World*. Chicago, IL: University of Chicago Press.

Widmann, Andreas Martin. 2009. *Kontrafaktische Geschichtsdarstellung: Untersuchungen an Romanen von
    Günter Grass, Thomas Pynchon, Thomas Brussig, Michael Kleeberg, Philip Roth und Christoph Ransmayr*.
    Heidelberg: Universitätsverlag Winter.

Wishnia, Kenneth J. A. 1999. *Twentieth-Century Ecuadorian Narrative: New Readings in the Context of the
    Americas*. Lewisburg, PA: Bucknell University Press.

Witkin, Robert. 1997. "Constructing a Sociology for an Icon of Aesthetic Modernity: Olympia
    Revisited." *Sociological Theory* 15(2): 101–25.

Young, David, and Keith Hollaman. 1984. *Magical Realist Fiction: An Anthology*. New York, NY:
    Longman.

Zalamea, Jorge. 1967. "Carta abierta de Jorge Zalamea a Álvaro Bejarano." *Occidente* (Cali), September 4.

Zamora, Lois, and Wendy Faris (Eds.). 1995. *Magical Realism: Theory, History, Community*. Durham, NC:
    Duke University Press.

Zapata, Juan Carlos. 2007. *Gabo nació en Caracas no en Aracataca*. Caracas: Alfa.

Zeng, Li-jun. 2009. "Chinese Interpretation of *One Hundred Years of Solitude*." *Journal of Southwest
    University (Social Sciences Edition)* 2.

INDEX

characters, *One Hundred Years of Solitude*

Aureliano (last Buendía): alternative death, 145, 146; death, 2, 143; influence of, 200; pig's tail, 133, 143, 144, 145, 161

Aureliano Buendía, Colonel, 1, *151*; absent from manuscript, 144, 146; alternative birth and death, 146, 149; biography cannot be written, *8*, 12, 104; first appearances, 7, 88, 105; influence of, 238, 240; inspiration for, 314n13; inserting and constructing character of, 145-46; and opening line, 148; Soledad, original wife of, 106; wars and, 146, 320n66

Buendía, family, 2, 128, 135, 143, 145, *151*, 152, 161; first appearance, 105-6; incest and, 144, *151*; original generations, 144; influence of, 192, 200, 223, 234, 236; original story of, 144

discarded characters: César Triste, 133, 144; Evangelina, 106; Natanael, 106; Rebeca de Asís, 146; Soledad, 106

José Arcadio Buendía (son), *151*, 326n4; constructing character, 146; death, 88, 143; first appearance, 88

José Arcadio Buendía (father), 1, 109-10, 147-48, *151*; death, 326n13; influence of, 204, 236, 240; kills Prudencio Aguilar, 143

Remedios the Beauty, 137, *151*; alternatives to her ascent, 146; first appearance, 106; influence of her ascent, 164, 174, 230-31, 240, 245-49, *248*, 326n15; not beautiful, 249; as Rebeca de Asís, 146; as religious character, 146

other characters: Melquíades, 143, 240; Meme, 106; Prudencio Aguilar, 143; Rebeca, 88, 106; wandering Jew, 143

Úrsula Iguarán, *151*; birth of Aureliano and, 148, 149; first appearances, 7, 107; sees dead Prudencio Aguilar, 143; as Soledad, 106

events, *One Hundred Years of Solitude*

banana massacre, 144, 148, *151*; inspiration of, 260

birds, attack, 88, 143

firing squad. *See* opening line

flying carpets, 108, 133; influence of, 186, 247, 249

galleon in jungle, 18, 127, 143, 161

hurricane, 2, 143; wind and, 106, 245

ice, discovery of. *See* opening line

incest. *See* Buendía, family

insomnia plague, *151*; influence of, 238, 239

rain in Macondo, *151*, 271; first appearance, 106; influence of, 222

termites, and red ants, 143, 149

yellow butterflies, influence of, 222, 240, 247, *251*

places, *One Hundred Years of Solitude*

house, 143; first appearances, 78, 105-6; inspiration for, 141-42

Macondo, 119-20, 142-43, 149, *151*, 152, 219, 222, 223; indexicals and, 301; Macondian, 241, 326n22;

collaborators (*continued*)
19–22, 23, 31, 34, 38. *See also* critics; cultural brokers; gatekeepers; *One Hundred Years of Solitude*; publishers; scholars

Collazos, Óscar, 184, 194

Collection d'oeuvre representatives (UNESCO), 30

collections: with promotions, 58; publishers and, 54, 55, 61, 65; writers and, 58. *See also specific collections*

collective representations, classics and, 288–91

Collège de France, 85

Colombia, 43, 59, 65, 74–75, 79, 94, 111, 116, 135, 154, 199, 212, 217, 240; Aracataca, 76; Barranquilla, 78–86; Bogotá, 77–78, 86–89; Cartagena, 78–86; Ciénaga, 258; Cesar Department, 84; La Guajira, 84; Magdalena Department, 84; Magdalena River, 149; Valley of Upar, 84, 107; Zipaquirá, 76. *See also* Caribbean

competition, classics with collaboration, adaptation and, 298–99

Comprimido (periodical), 85, 315n27

conferences, for writers, 26, 98–99, 180

conflict, controversy and: collaboration and, 308n17; Latin American Novel with, 178–87; with literature and changing idea of Latin America, 181–83; local traditions and outside influences with, 308n12; with Macondism, specter of, 186; with New Latin American Novel, normalizing, 183–86; novel without collaborators, 187–92; novel without periodicals, 193–95; novel without publishers, 195–99; with politics and literature, 179–81. *See also* García Márquez, Gabriel

Congreso Cultural in Havana, 28

Congreso de Instituciones Hispánicas, 30

Congress for Freedom of Culture, 193

Congress of Intellectuals, 21, 27

Conte, Rafael, 53, 265; *Narraciones de la España desterrada*, 196

Contemporáneos (periodical), 33

Continental Organization of Book Fairs (Organización continental de los festivales del libro), 65

contracts: subsidiary rights and, 62–63; for writers, 62, 66–67, 68

Cornejo Polar, Antonio, 182

Coronavirus (Covid-19), 239

Cortázar, Julio, 19, 22, 28, 63, 82, 124, 153, 161, 177, 180, 181, 183, 192, 265; *Bestiary*, 43, 60, 259;

censorship and, 54; controversies, 184–86, 192, 274; *Final Exam*, 56; "House Taken Over," 43; Hybrid Generation and, 20, 23, 31, 34, 36, 43, 44; influence of, 36, 37, 39, 60, 68, 69, 97, 125, 259, 264; literary agents and, 61; rejections and, 56. *See also Hopscotch*

cosmopolitanism: Faulkner and, 82; language and, 18–19; Latin Americanism and, 4, 15–19, 20, 23–24, 38, 41–42; Latin American novel and, 38–39; nature and, 17–18; Western literature and, 16

costeño, 77, 81, 94, 154, 167, 258

costumbrista style, 83, 89, 167, 256–57, 276

counterfactuals, 327nn2–3; classics and, 301–2. *See also* art counterfactuals; García Márquez, Gabriel; *One Hundred Years of Solitude*

Couto, Mia: *Sleepwalking Land*, 211

covers: Latin American writers on periodicals', 34, 35; *One Hundred Years of Solitude*, 57, 160–61

Crack, 183, 212

creative process, artists and, 13. *See also* networked creativity

Creole jargon (*jerga criolla*), 19, 50, 71

Creoles, 182–83, 276–77

Crítica (award), 32

critics, 119–20, 213; on censorship, 49; classics and, 175; collaboration of three generations of, 22; film, 87–88; with sales, 175; scholars and, 290; writers and, 22, 23, 36, 37, 154–55, 163–68

critique génétique, 141, 319n56

Croix du Sud, La (collection), 30, 309n39

Cromos (periodical), 33

Crónica (periodical), 33, 85–86, 105

Cuadernos Americanos (periodical), 33

Cuadernos Hispanoamericanos (periodical), 29

Cuba, 29, 47, 59, 95, 179, 266

Cuban Revolution, 29, 54, 309n35; artists and, 179; Mafia Group and, 98; nationalism and, 14; region-spanning literary traditions and, 27; Soviet Union and, 29. *See also* García Márquez, Gabriel

Cuevas, José Luis, 316n51

Cultura en México, La, supplement of *Siempre!* (periodical), 21, 33, 35, 36, 57, 97, 115, 117, 137, 152, 153, 165, 194–95, 217, 270–1, 309n45

cultural brokers, classics and, 288–91; *One Hundred Years of Solitude* and, 5, 174–75, 278–79. *See also* collaborators

cultural making, classics and, 284